Springer Series in Transitional Justice

Series Editor

More information about this series at http://www.springer.com/series/11233

Jasmina Brankovic • Hugo van der Merwe
Editors

Advocating Transitional Justice in Africa

The Role of Civil Society

Springer

Editors
Jasmina Brankovic
University of Cape Town
Centre for the Study of Violence
and Reconciliation
Cape Town, South Africa

Hugo van der Merwe
Centre for the Study of Violence
and Reconciliation
Cape Town, South Africa

Springer Series in Transitional Justice
ISBN 978-3-319-70415-9 ISBN 978-3-319-70417-3 (eBook)
https://doi.org/10.1007/978-3-319-70417-3

Library of Congress Control Number: 2017962102

Printed on acid-free paper

This Springer imprint is published by Springer Nature
The registered company is Springer International Publishing AG
The registered company address is: Gewerbestrasse 11, 6330 Cham, Switzerland

Foreword

The Long Arc of Transitional Justice

This great volume of written work—*Advocating Transitional Justice in Africa: The Role of Civil Society*—does what virtually no other labour of the intellect has done heretofore. Authored by movement activists and thinkers in the fields of human rights and transitional justice, the volume wrestles with the complex place and roles of transitional justice in the project of societal reconstruction in Africa. The authors are steeped in the theory and practice of transitional justice. Many have toiled in the vineyards and the tumult of social transformation in the aftermath of conflict. They thus excavate the hopes and fears of the reformer who seeks a better tomorrow. Even so, the authors do not take an adulatory approach to transitional justice. They agonise over its shortcomings as they seek to edify its great promises.

Since its inception in the 1990s, transitional justice has been a labour of civil society. While international institutions today embrace transitional justice—most principally the United Nations—civil society has been the moving spirit behind its dogma. In Africa, the loudest voices for transitional justice have come from the nongovernmental sector. The "eye of the people"—as civil society is known—became the guardian of transitional justice in Africa. However, as the authors clearly bear out, Africa was not a tabula rasa on which the concept was reinscribed without interrogation. To their credit, the contributors demonstrate through case studies the tortured path that transitional justice has endured in Africa. They point to both conceptual and structural bottlenecks that must be addressed if the framework of transitional justice is to bear fruit on the continent.

The deficits of transitional justice and its application in Africa echo the arguments of the shortcomings of the human rights discourse and the liberal paradigm on which it rests. The writers in the volume explicitly and implicitly realise these shortfalls and point to the need for a dialogic, conceptual and situational canvas on which transitional justice can become a more effective tool for social transformation. They decry the one-size-fits-all blueprint advanced by the West. Instead, they seek a more nuanced and interactive framework informed by local conditions but anchored in particular unarguable universal standards. They all agree that transitional justice is a project of hope and an indispensable tool in the hands of reformers. Nevertheless, they plead for the complexity of the continent and ask for rethinking transitional justice to indigenise the concept.

This volume will serve as a timely and thought-provoking guide for activists, thinkers and policy makers—as well as students of transitional justice—interested in the tension between the universal and the particular in the arduous struggle for liberation. Often, civil society actors in Africa have been accused of consuming the ideas of others, but not producing enough, if any, of their own. This volume makes clear the spuriousness of this claim and firmly plants an African flag in the field of ideas. The arc of transitional justice has been long and uneven. Its effectiveness and success in Africa are the subject of intense debate. I view that debate as a healthy one. The authors here agree and take that debate a notch higher. None of them is a naysayer. However, they are all interested in the project of transitional justice as a key experiment for social recovery.

I recommend this rich volume to all those concerned with the human condition. In these pages, dedicated and introspective social actors who span the diversity of religion, region, culture, gender and national origin unite in affirming transitional justice while at the same time pushing its frontiers. It is a work of enormous vitality and reach. If transitional justice has a future, then I urge those working and thinking in it to embrace the lessons offered herein.

Makau Mutua
SUNY Distinguished Professor
Floyd H. & Hilda L. Hurst Scholar
SUNY Buffalo Law School
State University of New York
Buffalo, NY, USA

Editors' Preface

Transitional Justice as a Field Defined by Practice

Transitional justice is a constantly evolving field of theory and practice. It has been challenged and contested since its influence began to spread through replication and the diffusion of global normative frameworks and mechanisms. One key area of contestation is the relevance of the ideas and tools provided by this field to local activists and advocates pursuing peace and justice agendas in their local communities and countries. This collected volume seeks to engage directly with the questions this raises: How does local civil society pursue transitional justice? How useful do civil society organisations (CSOs) find the avenues for social change that transitional justice processes provide? And to what extent do they influence them?

The question of civil society's role in transitional justice does not simply relate to the relevance of global ideas for local practice. Transitional justice seeks to respond to local needs. Local traction, victim-centredness and community participation are all buzz phrases in the field. It is the practice of transitional justice that will shape our future understanding of the boundaries of the field, its goals, its strategies and its definition.

Whether the field is able to respond to local experiences is however another matter. Generally it remains dominated by North-based scholars, donors, policy makers and transitional justice professionals who have instrumentalised and institutionalised the field in ways that sometimes appear unresponsive to outsider voices. A key challenge remains the absence of these voices from critical debates and particularly the transitional justice literature. While practitioners speak eloquently at transitional justice workshops and conferences, they seldom document their experiences and present their reflections in writing.

The motivation for this book is essentially to address that absence and to highlight the experiences of local practitioners, largely in their own voices. For us as editors, it represents an attempt to bridge the gap between our practitioner colleagues and our academic colleagues and contribute to correcting the imbalance in the academic and policy literature.

We seek to give greater prominence to a practice-based framing of transitional justice's substance and boundaries—its reinvention by local actors grounded in local struggles who seek to mediate between international ideas and agendas on the one hand and local needs, politics and visions of justice and peace on the other. Without this contribution to transitional justice debates, the field will be diminished, as it is constantly threatened by the growth of a bland standardised technical agenda which operates too comfortably in the shadow of persistent global inequalities and more hidden structural injustices.

Transitional justice is a field shaped by civil society. It is an area where academics have found themselves in the midst of policy debates, where activists have become policy advisors and international consultants, and where activists, academics and policy makers have found common ground in developing new ideas and challenging conventional thinking. The boundaries between advocates, activists, scholars and politicians have been blurred through the growth and global acceptance of transitional justice measures as a norm in transitional contexts.

This fluidity has similarly characterised transitional justice ideas and concepts. Yet, as transitional justice has become mainstreamed in international institutions and framed in legal normative prescriptions, it has turned into a somewhat rigid edifice of ideas, with defined problems and prescribed remedies. While some in civil society have sought to concretise certain pillars of transitional justice that serve to define the field, many have broken these down or simply snubbed conventional thinking when addressing their local challenges. These innovative practices need to be addressed in the academic literature, particularly from the perspective of African practitioners.

Civil Society and Transitional Justice in Africa

African civil society has been a prominent player in regional and national transitional justice policy debates. A number of African CSOs have played major roles in shaping their countries' transitional justice mechanisms. The South African Truth and Reconciliation Commission, for example, was designed in large part by civil society through a process of behind-the-scenes policy discussions and big policy conferences (Boraine et al. 2014). Civil society was also central to finalising the legislation that established the commission and then in the implementation of its work (Van der Merwe et al. 1999).

This process of civil society engagement with national transitional justice processes has been replicated in many countries on the continent. In some cases the lack of state capacity meant that CSOs were directly responsible for drafting transitional justice legislation, and in most cases truth commissions and other measures relied particularly on civil society's ability to access victims and marginalised communities. This capacity and local legitimacy—built during conflict or in the midst of ongoing state repression—has given civil society unusual leverage in shaping interventions. At the same time it has moulded particular transitional justice agendas that often put civil society at odds with the state.

Civil society in Africa has also been vocal in relation to the global transitional justice debates. While sometimes caught between the narrowly framed international normative approach and national elite politics, CSOs have managed to articulate a unique approach. They have challenged both international and national policy makers, pushing for transitional justice processes that resonate with local needs and priorities and that speak to broad social concerns regarding peace, democratisation and local conceptions of justice. There are numerous examples of African CSOs that simply jump on the global transitional justice bandwagon or are cowed by the demands of authoritarian regimes. But the voices of civil society in dealing with local community processes, national debates and global arenas provide an encouraging picture of a field characterised by vibrant intellectual debate and innovative interventions.

Highlighting Practitioner Voices

In this book we have sought to offer local practitioners space to reflect on the development and effectiveness of their strategies in promoting transitional justice, to identify the theoretical and contextual influences on their work and to present lessons learnt over two decades of transitional justice interventions on the continent.

Given our years of experience working with practitioners on documenting their experiences and ideas, we realised that this endeavour would be a challenge. While practitioners are more than capable of documenting their experiences, engaging in critical self-reflection and participating actively in theoretical discussions of transitional justice challenges, they do not prioritise writing in their day-to-day work. Our efforts to solicit inputs from our network of colleagues across the continent produced numerous rich inputs, but finding time to revise and edit work within the timeframe of an edited volume meant that many of these inputs could not be included in the book. We remain grateful to those practitioners who participated in the workshops and exchanges, which enriched the reflections and insights that inform the ideas shared in this volume.

Rather than just rely on practitioners' inputs on civil society, we decided to broaden our circle of contributors and invite other researchers who have extensive experience working in collaboration with African CSOs and local academics who have done serious empirical work on these issues. We also sought to address particular gaps that we identified in the collection, such as issues of gender and the role of regional mechanisms. Again, our efforts were only partially successful.

This volume was born out of many years of engagement among a range of CSOs on the African continent, which have collaborated on joint advocacy projects, engaged in knowledge exchange and helped to build mutual capacity to pursue transitional justice initiatives in their local contexts and through regional bodies such as the African Union. Both the editors of this volume, Jasmina Brankovic and Hugo van der Merwe, work with the Centre for the Study of Violence and Reconciliation (CSVR), which has been one of the central partners in these collaborations. The joint initiatives were developed through the African Transitional Justice Research

Network (ATJRN),[1] which brought together key CSOs and African researchers and practitioners to share knowledge and coordinate advocacy efforts.

ATJRN regularly highlighted the need to document local CSO experiences, to facilitate critical reflection and to build local conceptualisations of transitional justice. These engagements led to the establishment of peer review processes among partners (Mncwabe 2011), the establishment of an Institute for African Transitional Justice (convened by the Refugee Law Project at Makerere University), facilitated writing retreats and capacity building among partners to contribute to international advocacy and scholarly platforms (e.g. through the *International Journal of Transitional Justice*, which is managed by CSVR).

A key link between these various forums and this book is a 2010 workshop hosted by CSVR under the auspices of ATJRN: "Advocating Justice: Civil Society and Transitional Justice in Africa". This workshop brought together 18 transitional justice practitioners from across the continent to share their experiences of pursuing transitional justice processes in their respective countries. It produced rich case studies,[2] a workshop report (Brankovic 2010) and a wealth of information that inspired us to explore other channels to make sure that these types of perspectives are more effectively captured and disseminated in academic circles.

Framing an African Approach to Transitional Justice

Transitional justice is fundamentally about both the politics of justice and the cultural conceptions of justice. Writing about the African continent addresses a unique subset of cases that differ from how transitional justice is conceived and pursued in other regions. Africa has been a particularly prominent subject of the field in the last two decades. This is the result of a confluence of factors, such as the political shifts and democratisation following the end of the Cold War, the regional influence of the South African Truth and Reconciliation Commission's reputation, and the prominence of international bodies which have promoted transitional justice through their interventions across the continent. In many of these situations, transitional justice is presented as an externally defined idea. While local actors often see the relevance of the promises made relating to justice, reconciliation and accountability, the practice of transitional justice tends to be presented as the implementation of predesigned templates. This power differential between transitional justice proponents and local "consumers" has become one of the defining features of the African experience of transitional justice.

---

[1] The African Transitional Justice Research Network Steering Committee consisted of representatives from CSVR (South Africa), the Refugee Law Project (Uganda), the Campaign for Good Governance (Sierra Leone), the Center for Democratic Development (Ghana) and the Zimbabwe Lawyers for Human Rights (Zimbabwe).

[2] Centre for the Study of Violence and Reconciliation, "Advocating Justice: Civil Society and Transitional Justice in Africa", http://www.csvr.org.za/publications/latest-publications/2724-advocating-justice-civil-society-and-transitional-justice-in-africa2 (Accessed 26 July 2017).

Civil society has played a key role in reversing this power dynamic, particularly by formulating local transitional justice agendas and partnering with each other to promote more locally responsive approaches, and more recently by working with the African Union on the development of an African Union Transitional Justice Policy. In a similar vein, civil society has worked closely with the African Commission on Human and Peoples' Rights to develop a strategy for engagement with transitional justice. Rather than rejecting transitional justice as yet another externally imposed agenda, African institutions are articulating their own values and norms that draw on African human rights frameworks and reflections on national experiences within the continent.

While there may be some danger of creating a new generic model that presents a regional rather than a global template, this critical psychological and political shift means that transitional justice is seen as something that can be redefined and repurposed for a different agenda. This volume seeks to feed into African transitional justice ownership by providing an up-to-date regional perspective on the field. The chapters speak to the specific local contexts that need to be negotiated by practitioners and provide considerable pause to those who would impose generic frameworks.

The Breadth and Limitations of the Case Studies

Transitional justice in Africa is complex and multifaceted. In response, this volume covers a wide range of regions and initiatives. The contributions have broad geographic scope, including case studies from Southern Africa (Zimbabwe and South Africa), Central Africa (Burundi), East Africa (Kenya and Uganda), North Africa (Libya, Egypt and Tunisia) and West Africa (Liberia and Sierra Leone). They discuss very different forms of conflict, political cultures and historical periods of transition and cover different spurs to transition (negotiated agreement, military victory), stages of political transition (nascent to long past, along with cases of non-transition) and forms of repression and violation (structural injustices, dictatorial regimes, civil war).

Even so, the book has some biases. The chapters focus mainly on nongovernmental organisations (NGOs), paying less attention to community-based organisations, ethnic and religious formations, and popular movements. Some chapters provide a more integrated picture through an analysis of the range of CSO actors involved in collaborative initiatives, and several problematise the role of urban-based professional NGOs. The chapters also focus largely on state-oriented efforts. While many contributors engage with alternative transitional justice initiatives and community-based interventions, the overall orientation is to explore how CSOs navigate their relationship with the state. Given the inadequacy of many state responses, African CSOs have undertaken extensive initiatives themselves to document abuses, memorialise the past, facilitate healing and reconciliation and promote accountability. To address effectively this range of efforts and the complexity of engaging in these roles would require a whole new volume.

The contributions nonetheless analyse and evaluate a broad span of civil society efforts. These include bridging peacebuilding and transitional justice efforts; agenda setting through public consultation processes; popularisation of transitional justice ideas and goals; working with victims and victims' groups to advocate for accountability, truth and reconciliation; monitoring state interventions; and providing assistance to the state in establishing and facilitating truth commissions and other mechanisms. They further include elaborating traditional and community-based measures; highlighting socio-economic inequality and historical injustices; lobbying for the implementation of recommendations that emerge from transitional justice measures; and pursuing international litigation. Civil society is shown to play a wide range of roles in these initiatives, including the provision of expertise, the facilitation of public participation, outreach to victims and affected communities, coalition and network building, and the contribution of mediation, legal, psychosocial and other support, among others.

The chapters underline that civil society evolves over time and in response to changes in global, regional and national contexts. In evaluating transitional justice efforts (in some cases their own), the contributors offer insights into the challenges facing civil society—including within organisations and coalitions themselves—and some suggestions for how to address these challenges. The book begins by framing the case studies in terms of transitional justice and civil society theory and ends by highlighting the centrality of local politics and history to civil society practice on the continent.

Overview of Chapters and Ideas

In the introductory chapter, Jasmina Brankovic examines ways in which civil society theory affects practitioners' approaches to transitional justice in Africa. Brankovic outlines the intersections of mainstream and alternative conceptions of civil society and transitional justice, given their parallel rise in the post-Cold War context. Through a close reading of the case studies, she explores the main tensions that characterise these intersections, namely, the validity of positioning (human rights) NGOs as the most legitimate form of civil society, the significance of associational life based on sectarian ties, the role of "uncivil" collective action and the marginalisation of various local, regional and global dynamics with the centring of the state implied by the state–civil society binary. Brankovic suggests that the practice of transitional justice on the continent is constrained by mainstream conceptions of civil society.

Turning the book's focus to civil society strategies, Andrew Songa analyses the role of the Kenya Transitional Justice Network (KTJN) in shaping Kenya's transitional justice agenda in the context of democratisation. After discussing the dynamics and evolution of Kenyan civil society since independence, Songa zeroes in on KTJN's engagement with the Truth, Justice and Reconciliation Commission, namely, advocating for its establishment, playing both an advisory and a watchdog role during the commission's tenure and then following up on its recommendations. Evaluating KTJN's agenda development and the effectiveness of its strategies, the chapter suggests critical lessons in terms of substantive issues such as ensuring victim participation and promoting gender justice, as well as operational issues such as governance structures and sustainability.

Placing advocacy for a responsive truth commission in a broad frame, James Dhizaala discusses how local civil society in Liberia and the diaspora influenced transitional justice efforts in the wake of the country's 14-year civil war. Dhizaala examines the evolution of civil society during and after the conflict, particularly the role of human rights, faith-based, professional, women's and other diverse organisations in securing Liberia's peace agreement and negotiating seats for civil society representatives in the transitional government. He analyses civil society challenges in designing and implementing the Liberian Truth and Reconciliation Commission and suggests lessons for long-term thinking around transition in postconflict contexts.

Shastry Njeru provides an overview of transitional justice efforts in a very different context—where no political transition has occurred. Njeru discusses the Zimbabwe Human Rights NGO Forum's outreach and sensitisation programme, *Taking Transitional Justice to the People*, and the challenges of implementing it in a constrained political environment. Outlining strategies for holding workshops and trainings on transitional justice in Zimbabwe's highly politicised rural areas, he evaluates the programme's focus on the "pillars" of transitional justice—truth seeking, prosecutions, reparations, institutional reform and memorialisation—and highlights the need for more participatory methods in the design and implementation of outreach programmes, among other lessons learnt.

Continuing with the theme of participation, Zukiswa Puwana and Rita Kesselring's chapter focuses on the advocacy and internal dynamics of the membership-based organisation of apartheid survivors, the Khulumani Support Group. Puwana and Kesselring argue that in response to the sidelining of victims, Khulumani has taken a confrontational approach to addressing the "unfinished business" of apartheid and the South African Truth and Reconciliation Commission in the 20 years since the transition to democracy. The chapter discusses a range of Khulumani strategies, including its development of a national victim database, lawsuit against apartheid-abetting corporations via the United States Alien Tort Statute, collaborations (at times conflictual) with NGOs and academics, and grassroots mobilisation and capacity building. Puwana and Kesselring examine the challenges these strategies have elicited and their impact on survivor solidarity, highlighting the need for early victim participation in transitional justice agenda setting and discussing the compromises involved in choosing legal strategies over political ones.

In her chapter on Burundi, Wendy Lambourne discusses cooperation and contestation among civil society actors—international and local, in the country and in exile—in a postconflict context where control over transitional justice processes has been asserted in different ways by the state (and by the United Nations). Lambourne analyses civil society's strategies of cooperation and resistance, where support for governmental initiatives through a focus on healing, reconciliation and sensitisation regarding the Burundian Truth and Reconciliation Commission is combined with dissent through advocacy for accountability and prosecutions. Her analysis of the work of the Reflection Group on Transitional Justice and the Quaker Peace Network Burundi, two very different groups, indicates how civil society strategies develop in response to shifting opportunities in politically constrained contexts.

Looking at a similarly constraining context, where the state deliberately deploys ineffective transitional justice processes in the absence of political transition, Joanna R. Quinn considers the evolving advocacy of local and international NGOs in Uganda. She notes that civil society has largely moved away from "peace and justice" work, including the customary justice efforts that were the most visible form of transitional justice in the country. In addition to the government's success in shifting civil society and donor attention away from northern Uganda and past violations, Lambourne locates the reason for this move in personnel turnover and lack of institutional memory in organisations, as well as a degree of state co-optation and dearth of innovative approaches within civil society. She argues that communities to a large extent have been left on their own to deal with the events of the past.

Andrew Iliff takes a wider view of engagement between communities and civil society in Africa, examining community-based transitional justice processes that he argues can serve as complements or as alternatives to state-run processes. Iliff notes that community-based initiatives may better reflect the agency of survivors and unravel the complexities of local power dynamics at the root of conflicts. He demonstrates that the urban-based NGOs that largely shape transitional justice on the continent need to engage constructively and thoughtfully with local culture and power dynamics in order to provide effective and responsive interventions. Underlining the density of local authority structures and the turn to ideas of "tradition" and associated canons of practice as central to community-based processes, Iliff draws lessons from the cases of the Acholi Religious Leaders Peace Initiative in Uganda, the Peace Building Network of Zimbabwe and Fambul Tok in Sierra Leone.

Noha Aboueldahab also takes a wide view and shifts the book's focus to North Africa and prosecution efforts linked to the Arab Spring. Discussing diverse civil society actors and the similarities and differences between the contexts of Egypt, Tunisia and Libya, she examines three strategies used before, during and immediately after the political transition in each country: documenting human rights abuses, pursuing litigation despite politicised and weak judiciaries, and emphasising economic crimes, corruption and the connection between civil-political and socio-economic rights abuses. Aboueldahab demonstrates the importance of consistent civil society action and mobilisation in countries where transition appears a distant hope and where regime change may not bring about the political and social transformation it promises.

In the concluding chapter to the volume, Hugo van der Merwe reflects on the position of civil society in African transitional justice debates. He examines the complexity of transitional justice in contexts where colonial exploitation has left a legacy that frames the underlying politics of transition and complicates debates between local and international actors. He draws on the various contributions to the volume to unpack the challenges facing civil society in finding an independent voice that steers between a restrictive global normative discourse and deeply divided national political dynamics, in order to highlight the critical role that African CSOs play in shaping transitional justice locally and also globally.

The case studies in this book illuminate common struggles: the search for peace and security by those most directly impacted by war, the quest to rebuild communities riven by conflict, the demand for the state to take responsibility for its failures and account for its misdeeds, and the struggle for a more just society that deals with inequality and oppression across many social dimensions, including gender. While the contributors offer some lessons they have learnt, drawing out recommendations for transitional justice practice from this complex landscape and painful struggle would seem somewhat trite. What the chapters in fact highlight is the need for constant critical reflection and for innovation. While drawing on international inspiration, and norms and mechanisms that tilt the power balance in critical ways, transitional justice is a field that requires localised solutions. African civil society is an important resource, bringing together as it does a global knowledge base and a localised awareness of resources, needs and priorities.

Cape Town, South Africa

Jasmina Brankovic
Hugo van der Merwe

References

Boraine, A., Levy, J., & Scheffer, R. (Eds.). (1994). *The healing of a nation?* Cape Town: Justice in Transition.

Brankovic, J. (2010). *Advocating justice: Civil society and transitional justice in Africa.* Cape Town: African Transitional Justice Research Network and Centre for the Study of Violence and Reconciliation.

Mncwabe, N. (2010). African transitional justice research network: Critical reflections on a peer learning process. *International Journal of Transitional Justice, 4*(3), 497–508.

Van der Merwe, H., & Schkolne, M. (2017). The role of local civil society in transitional justice. In C. Lawther & L. Moffett (Eds.), *Research handbook on transitional justice*. Edward Elgar: Cheltenham.

Van der Merwe, H., Dewhirst, P., & Hamber, B. (1999). Non-governmental organizations and the truth and reconciliation commission: An impact assessment. *Politikon: South African Journal of Political Studies, 26*(1), 55–79.

Contents

Contributors

Noha Aboueldahab Brookings Doha Center, Doha, Qatar

Jasmina Brankovic University of Cape Town; Centre for the Study of Violence and Reconciliation, Cape Town, South Africa

James Tonny Dhizaala University of Sydney, Sydney, NSW, Australia

Andrew Iliff Harvard Global Health Institute, Cambridge, MA, USA

Rita Kesselring University of Basel, Basel, Switzerland

Wendy Lambourne University of Sydney, Sydney, NSW, Australia

Hugo van der Merwe Centre for the Study of Violence and Reconciliation, Cape Town, South Africa

Shastry Njeru Zimbabwe Human Rights NGO Forum, Harare, Zimbabwe

Zukiswa Puwana Independent, Cape Town, South Africa

Joanna R. Quinn University of Western Ontario, London, ON, Canada

Andrew Songa Kenya Human Rights Commission, Nairobi, Kenya

About the Contributors

Noha Aboueldahab is visiting fellow at the Brookings Doha Center, where she researches transitional justice in the Arab region. Her book, *Transitional Justice and the Prosecution of Political Leaders in the Arab Region: A Comparative Study of Egypt, Libya, Tunisia and Yemen* (Hart 2017), challenges mainstream transitional justice practice and scholarship using original material from almost 50 in-depth interviews she conducted in Egypt, Libya, Tunisia and Yemen between 2011 and 2017. Additionally, she has worked for several United Nations agencies and NGOs in New York, Lebanon and Qatar. She has been interviewed by various media outlets, including Al Jazeera, BBC, Bloomberg, CNN, MSNBC, Sky News, and the *Washington Post.*

James Tonny Dhizaala is a visiting scholar in the Department of Peace and Conflict Studies, University of Sydney, where his research and publications cover the politics of transitional justice in West and East Africa with a focus on Liberia and Uganda. He has lectured for more than 15 years in Australia, the United States, Uganda and Rwanda, and is currently teaching at the University of New South Wales in International Studies. He holds a PhD from the University of Sydney, an MA in Development Studies from the International Institute of Social Studies at Erasmus University Rotterdam and a BA in education from the Islamic University in Uganda.

Andrew Iliff is a programme manager at the Harvard Global Health Institute, where he works on climate change and health security. He has worked on transitional justice initiatives in Rwanda, South Africa and Zimbabwe, most recently with the Centre for Conflict Management and Transformation in Harare as a Yale University Gruber Fellow in Global Justice and Women's Rights. Iliff is a graduate of Harvard College and Yale Law School.

Rita Kesselring is senior lecturer in Social Anthropology at the University of Basel. She worked with the Khulumani Support Group in South Africa for 2 years (intermittently between 2006 and 2013) as part of her research for her MA and PhD theses. She is the author of *Bodies of Truth: Law, Memory, and Emancipation in Post-Apartheid South Africa* (Stanford University Press 2016). Kesselring was a research affiliate at the Department of Social Anthropology, University of Cape Town, and at the Human Rights Institute, University of Connecticut. Her current book project looks at social life in a new mining town in Zambia.

Wendy Lambourne is senior lecturer in the Department of Peace and Conflict Studies at the University of Sydney. Her interdisciplinary research on healing, reconciliation, transitional justice and peacebuilding after genocide and other mass violence has a regional focus on Sub-Saharan Africa and Asia-Pacific. She has published extensively about the results of her field research conducted over the past 20 years in Rwanda, Burundi, Sierra Leone, Cambodia and Timor-Leste. Her current research is concerned with transformative justice, psychosocial peacebuilding and community-based programmes to support torture and trauma survivors from a refugee background living in Australia.

Shastry Njeru (MA) is programme manager for transitional justice and conflict transformation at the Zimbabwe Human Rights NGO Forum, with a focus on the campaign for victim-centred dealing with the past. Njeru is an academic and practitioner with research interests that include dealing with the past, evaluation and post-conflict recovery.

Zukiswa Puwana is a researcher and facilitator based in Cape Town. She holds a BA in Psychology and English from the University of the Western Cape, South Africa, and has worked in the NGO sector for the past 15 years. As a human rights activist, she joined Khulumani Support Group in 2000 as a volunteer and went on to be part of the Provincial Executive Committee as secretary and then treasurer until leaving the organization in 2017.

Andrew Songa is a lawyer and human rights advocate with over 6 years of experience in the areas of legal research, policy formulation and analysis, domestic and international policy advocacy and civic education. His work has centred on the thematic areas of indigenous peoples' rights, forced migration, land rights and transitional justice. He is currently programme manager for transformative justice for the Kenya Human Rights Commission and sits on the board of the Constitution and Reform Education Consortium. Songa is a member of the Steering Committee of the Kenya Transitional Justice Network, the Advisory Committee for the Study of Transitional Justice in Africa currently being undertaken by the African Commission on Human and Peoples' Rights, and the Reference Group assisting the African Commission to draft a General Comment on the Right to Redress for Victims of Torture and Other Ill-Treatment.

Joanna R. Quinn is associate professor of Political Science and director of the Centre for Transitional Justice and Post-Conflict Reconstruction at the University of Western Ontario. Since 1998, Quinn has been engaged in research that considers the role of acknowledgement in overcoming the effects of conflict. She has written widely on the role of acknowledgement in truth commissions and in customary law in Uganda, Haiti, Canada, Fiji and Solomon Islands. She was recently elected to the College of New Scholars, Artists and Scientists of the Royal Society of Canada.

About the Editors

Jasmina Brankovic is a senior researcher with the Centre for the Study of Violence and Reconciliation and the associate editor of the *International Journal of Transitional Justice*. She is a PhD candidate in Political Studies at the University of Cape Town. Brankovic conducts research on comparative transitional justice, civil society and victims' groups, and the intersection of transitional justice and social transformation. She is co-author of *The Global Climate Regime and Transitional Justice* (Routledge 2018).

Hugo van der Merwe is director of research, knowledge and learning at the Centre for the Study of Violence and Reconciliation. Since joining CSVR in 1997, he has developed and managed numerous research advocacy and intervention projects relating to transitional justice, reconciliation and peacebuilding in South Africa and the African continent. Hugo is the co-editor in chief of the *International Journal of Transitional Justice*. His publications include *Assessing the Impact of Transitional Justice* (USIP 2009) and *Truth and Reconciliation in South Africa: Did the TRC Deliver*? (University of Pennsylvania Press 2008). Van der Merwe received his doctorate in conflict analysis and resolution from George Mason University (1999).

Chapter 1
Introduction: Civil Society in African Transitional Justice—Comparing Theory and Practice

Jasmina Brankovic

Introduction

Acknowledging that "civil society 'consultation and participation' have metamorphosed into an article of faith in the practice of transitional justice" (Hovil and Okello 2011: 333), this book examines the role of local civil society in shaping understandings and processes of transitional justice in Africa—a nursery of transitional justice ideas for well over two decades. As editors, we have brought together practitioners and scholars who are either African or have long-standing relationships with African civil society to evaluate the agendas and strategies of local civil society and offer some "lessons learnt" along the way. The chapters present case studies from Southern, Central, East, West and North Africa and a range of moments and types of transition. Among others, these include transitions considered long over, such as in South Africa and Liberia; recent interrupted or "incomplete" transitions, such as in Egypt and Burundi; and situations where political transitions have not occurred but transitional justice processes have been initiated by the state, such as Uganda and Zimbabwe. The case studies focus on transitional justice practice on the continent, providing insight into the motivations and inner workings of major civil society actors in diverse national and regional contexts with different historical and socio-political realities.

This introductory chapter seeks to provide a theoretical context for the case studies, examining the intersections of theory on civil society and transitional justice. Both rose to prominence in the 1980s and 1990s, with the political and normative upheavals that characterised the end of the Cold War, and quickly coalesced into mainstream conceptions aligned with the dominant (neo)liberal paradigm. Mainstream approaches to civil society and transitional justice, described in detail

J. Brankovic (✉)
University of Cape Town; Centre for the Study of Violence and Reconciliation, Cape Town, South Africa
e-mail: jasminabrank@gmail.com

J. Brankovic, H. van der Merwe (eds.), *Advocating Transitional Justice in Africa*, Springer Series in Transitional Justice,
https://doi.org/10.1007/978-3-319-70417-3_1

below, were met with critiques from the start and accompanied by the parallel development of other approaches. These "alternative" approaches broadly sought to describe and respond to realities on the ground in postcolonial states and were positioned as alternatives to the Eurocentrism of mainstream thinking. This chapter examines how civil society theory affects transitional justice practitioners' thinking on and practice of transitional justice. While many variables influence transitional justice in African postcolonial states, the chapter looks specifically at the role of civil society theory. I argue that although most of the case studies are aligned with alternative thinking on transitional justice, and demonstrate the presence and value of alternative conceptions of civil society, they also suggest that the practice of transitional justice in these contexts is constrained by mainstream thinking.

With a focus on Africa, the chapter begins with a brief description of mainstream civil society theory, its critiques and a variety of alternative approaches, acknowledging the multidisciplinarity of the topic. It then outlines the links between civil society theory and mainstream understandings of transitional justice, namely, through democratisation, before describing alternative approaches and examining the literature on civil society and transitional justice. The chapter goes on to provide a close reading of the case studies in this book through the tensions between mainstream and alternative conceptions of civil society, identifying common themes amid the great diversity of the contexts. These tensions concern the nature of the relationship between the state and civil society, the validity of positioning (human rights) nongovernmental organisations (NGOs) as the most legitimate form of civil society and the significance of associational life based on sectarian ties. They also concern the role of "uncivil" collective action, the extent of the divide between private and public, and the possible marginalisation of various local, regional and global dynamics with the centring of the state implied by the state–civil society binary. The chapter closes with reflections on the implications of civil society theory for transitional justice practice in Africa.

Mainstream Civil Society Theory and Critiques

Emerging with Aristotle's descriptions of communities of citizens living within a legitimate political order, the concept of civil society was expanded and lent many of its mainstream characteristics by eighteenth-century Enlightenment thinkers, who also brought in the notion of civil society existing in relation to the state. Locke, for example, viewed the state as an arbiter necessary to address conflict and promote civility among individuals, which in turn needed to be limited so as not to intrude overly on individual freedoms. Montesquieu argued that conflict, particularly that caused by the competitiveness of individuals participating in commercial society, was to be controlled by the rule of law as guaranteed by the state. De Tocqueville linked a rich associational life to the establishment of a democratic state. In the liberal tradition, progress is manifested in the shift from premodern society, in which social relations are bound by kinship and material need, towards "civilised" modern society, in which individuals are guided by rational choice and brought together through voluntary association and commerce under the protective structures of the state. In his critique of liberalism, Hegel introduced the notion that modern society is split between the private and the public, contrasting the private individual in the realm of family (initial sociability and ethics) to the citizen in the realm of civil society (self-interested voluntary association, including through the market) and the state (curbing competition and conflict in civil society to enable universal solidarity), while at the same time reifying the separation between civil society and the state (Hann 1996; Khilnani 2001).

This brief summary already suggests the key elements of the contemporary mainstream approach to civil society. It assumes the stratification of society into the idealised, autonomous and usually vertically aligned realms of family, civil society and state, often with the market as an additional sphere. It preserves the distinction between "modern" and "premodern" forms of association, dismissing those based on kinship, ethnicity and other "primordial" or "traditional" ties as involuntary and irrational. Finally, it emphasises "civility" in civil society, with order, propriety and the use of formal channels and associations trumping disorderly and informal social action (Kasfir 1998). While this understanding of civil society is historically specific to the rise of anti-absolutist liberal capitalism in Europe and attendant theorising on social order and legitimate forms of association, in the late twentieth century it became a "metaphysical truth" in analyses of colonial and postcolonial societies (Kaviraj 2001: 297).

"Civil society" became a catchword in the 1980s and 1990s, amid the economic crises facing states in the global South, the critiques of state-run economic modernisation, and the rollback and decentralisation of the state demanded by international financial institutions providing loans to struggling governments (Shivji 2007). Western donors promoted civil society as crucial both to holding states to account and to providing services that the state previously provided, but presumably less efficiently and responsively (Bukenya and Hickey 2014). Civil society became viewed "as a hitherto missing key to sustained political reform, legitimate states and governments, improved governance, visible state-society and state-economy relationships, and prevention of the kind of political decay that undermined" postcolonial governments in the past (Harbeson 1994: 1–2). As this oft-cited quote on civil society in Africa demonstrates, the discourse on civil society in the 1990s was explicitly linked to the "wave" of democratisation that accompanied the close of the Cold War.

With the crisis of socialism and the global rise of neoliberalism, liberal conceptions were distilled into the mainstream approach to civil society. In Africa, civil society was increasingly promoted as central to democratisation (Diamond 1994), understood to entail both political and economic liberalisation. To counter the totalising tendencies of postcolonial states, civil society is required to be autonomous from the state (Bayart 1986), alternating between adversarial watchdog and informed aide to a newly rationalised, mechanistic state engaged in "good governance", but never seeking to capture state power and even defined as nonpolitical (Putnam 1993). It eschews "uncivil" action, ranging from protest to overtly sectarian demands, in favour of formal channels and processes (Linz and Stepan 1996). It thus embodies a new form of associational life, most effectively represented by the professional NGO (Chazan 1992). Democratisation, and particularly democratic consolidation, is understood to require a civil society that presumably was absent in African countries before their transitions. The mainstream approach thus both seeks to describe civil society and promotes a normative framework for societies in transition.

As applied to Africa, the mainstream approach to civil society has been extensively critiqued since the 1990s. The chief critique is that it is Eurocentric, universalising ideologies emerging from Europe's seventeenth-century transition to capitalism, foregrounding its (neo)liberal emphasis on the "autonomous agentic individual" (Seligman 1992: 5) over other forms of subjectivity and collective action, and promoting a specific form of democracy through development (Mamdani 1995; Shivji 2007). Critics have questioned the separation of society into idealised autonomous realms, particularly in reference to civil society and the state, arguing that this masks the interpenetration of these realms and the pluralistic associational life present in Africa since precolonial times (Osaghae 2005; Comaroff and Comaroff 1999). They note that by sidelining "uncivil" strategies as well as collective action emerging from kinship and ethnic ties, the mainstream concept of civil society does not reflect realities on the ground (Kasfir 1998; Chabal and Daloz 1999). Here, the project of describing civil society is presented as primarily normative and as an imposition of Western frameworks onto postcolonial societies. Linked to critiques of neoliberalism, critiques of the mainstream conception of civil society posit it as at best inapplicable and at worst a prop of neocolonialism.

The mainstream thinking on civil society developed in parallel with a number of alternative approaches. These emerged from questions concerning the degree of interpenetration among the realms of family, civil society, the state and the market, as well as evolving thinking concerning citizenship and collective action in the Cold War and post-Cold War periods. Regarding the relationship of civil society and the state, it must be noted that even liberal thinkers had different views, with Locke, for example, presenting the state as a manifestation of civil society and voluntary association, rather than as a separate sphere. Hegel put forward the notion of the state as a bureaucratic mechanism that holds and enables association in the public sphere, even while acknowledging that the state in this formulation is an idealised "true state" (Kaviraj 2001). Marx critiqued this approach as glossing over the likelihood that elites would use the state machinery to further their own interests, to the extent that the distinction is questionable. Gramsci similarly highlighted the porousness of state and civil society, arguing that the state encompasses both political society, which imposes elite interests through coercion, and civil society, which ensures the hegemony of these interests through persuasion and consent, although elements in civil society can play a counterhegemonic role (Mamdani 1995; Hann 1996).

In the 1960s and 1970s, disaffection with authoritarianism revitalised thinking around civil society in Eastern Europe and Latin America. Drawing on Gramsci, leftists posited social movements as a counter-option to established civil society institutions, such as trade unions and professional associations, viewed as co-opted by the state and as denying the plurality of views and interests in society (Khilnani 2001). Through to the 1990s, particularly throughout the global South, thinking around a more socially responsive civil society ranged from disengagement with the state and a focus on self-rule; to valorisation of pluralism and identity- or issue-based collective action over action through established institutions; to calls for radical democracy with emancipatory politics as a bond among diverse groups, in some cases with inclusivity guaranteed through broad participation (Baker 2002; Mouffe 1993; Dagnino 2007).

While Habermas and other theorists on the left have deployed the concept of civil society as a nursery of new ideas and self-reflexivity in the public sphere, poststructuralist thinkers such as Foucault have problematised the notion of autonomous social realms like civil society and the state while wrestling with what this means for possibilities for resistance and counterhegemonic practice. These questions come to the fore in various discussions of "everyday" politics, or the ways in which marginalised people individually or collectively, "defensively" or "offensively", through necessity or conscious mobilisation, engage in resistance and effect social change (Scott 1985; Bayat 1997; Chatterjee 2001). Often responding to the totalising post-colonial state, these would be considered "uncivil" actions in the mainstream approach. Much of this thinking does not hinge on the distinction between public and private, rather highlighting the interpenetration between the two, and in some cases reflecting feminist theory on how what is perceived as private is public and on the multiplicity of ways and public spaces in which contestations of power occur, including by women (Tripp 1998; Howell 2007). Much of it also does not privilege urban over rural associational life, as does mainstream thinking (Howell 2000).

Critiques of mainstream conceptions of civil society as applied to Africa emerge mainly from these alternative approaches. They underline the plurality and heterogeneity of associational life, the porousness or even lack of distinction between state and civil society, and the blurred line between private and public, while also rejecting the (neo)liberal dichotomy of modernity and tradition for its implication that the former is universal and normal while the latter is residual and pathological (Mamdani 1995). In particular, theorists posit that kinship- and ethnicity-based associational life, along with other forms of sectarian organisation, is an established aspect of civil society on the continent that cannot be dismissed (Ndegwa 1997; Kasfir 1998). Another relevant critique is of the state-centrism of the mainstream conception, given the weak (colonial) roots of the state in Africa, the impact of regional population flows and politics, and the influence of large diasporas on notions of citizenship, along with the interaction of local and global norms (Gallagher 2014; Obadare and Adebanwi 2009). Finally, critics point to the range of "uncivil" collective action occurring on the continent in response to increasing socio-economic inequality and exclusion in the context of economic liberalisation as examples of vibrant civil society (Bond 2014).

Despite the long-standing critiques and the wealth of alternative thinking in civil society theory, the fact is that the mainstream conception of what civil society is and should be remains dominant in practice. In Africa, as elsewhere, international donors, policy makers and experts, along with their counterparts at the domestic level, continue to support the (neo)liberal approach to civil society, most effectively by channelling funding into this global project. Attempts have been made to respond to certain critiques, for example by funding local over international organisations or by fostering citizen participation and state–civil society partnerships, but the professionalised NGO that follows "the rules" remains the most legitimised form of associational life (Bukenya and Hickey 2014). This reality in Africa led Kasfir (1998) to critique mainstream civil society as a normative project with little analytical or descriptive value.

Scholars and practitioners of transitional justice will notice the parallels between the rise, and the critiques, of their field and the mainstream approach to civil society. The following section outlines these parallels, examines how civil society is discussed in relation to transitional justice, and asks how mainstream definitions of civil society came to affect alternative thinking on transitional justice.

Civil Society and Transitional Justice

Like the concept of civil society, transitional justice has roots in antiquity, but emerged as a discrete field in the 1980s and 1990s, in tandem with democratisation in Latin America and Eastern Europe (Elster 2004). The potential of transitional justice, and international justice more broadly, to contribute to democratisation and nation building is what fuelled its speedy evolution into a globally accepted field (Teitel 2003). Like its parent discourse, human rights, transitional justice came to the fore with the crisis of socialism and attempts to articulate new forms of collective action and responsibility, as well as with the rise of neoliberalism, with its focus on individual agency in the context of economic liberalisation and state rationalisation through rapid institutional reform (Arthur 2009; Laplante 2008). The mainstream approach entails a set of legal and quasi-legal state-sponsored mechanisms—short-term and with narrow, "achievable" mandates—designed to ensure accountability for past gross human rights violations, primarily civil–political ones, and to prevent their recurrence by promoting democratic nation building and institutional reform. These "standard practices" (Subotić 2011), born out of transitions from authoritarianism to democracy, are now applied in transitions from conflict to (democratic) peace, in countries that have not undergone regime change, and in long-standing (mainly settler-colonial) democracies.

One of the chief critiques of mainstream transitional justice, particularly in Africa, is that it is a European concept exported as a one-size-fits-all solution to contexts whose political, social and cultural histories make it an ill fit (Okello 2010). The field is seen as overly concerned with retributive responses to violence perpetrated by individuals, sidelining restorative approaches that focus on collective responsibility and repair, which in African contexts may be more culturally relevant. Critics question the "top-down" nature of mainstream transitional justice, which favours state-sponsored mechanisms run by international and local elites and sidelines grassroots or rural participation and local approaches (Shaw and Waldorf 2010; Gready and Robins 2014). They critique its bundling with political and economic liberalisation, noting that it may contribute to instability by deepening social divisions with its focus on accountability, establishing institutions with little local legitimacy, and both ignoring socio-economic inequality and increasing it in the long term (Sriram 2007; Mutua 2009; Kagoro 2012). As with civil society, many of these arguments posit mainstream transitional justice as a form of neocolonialism.

Alternative approaches to transitional justice broaden the parameters of the field. While diverse, they generally aim to be "bottom-up" and holistic, incorporating measures from the global South as well as from other fields, such as memory studies and development. Many eschew the mainstream preoccupation with the state, foregrounding community- and civil society-run mechanisms and local or traditional processes, which often have a more restorative orientation even when they include retributive elements (Fletcher and Weinstein 2002). Emphasising repair, they push for transitional justice to be more victim centred, shifting the focus away from perpetrators and nation building towards victims' demands, everyday needs and participation. Some move the lens from elites to ordinary people affected by past violations, which in transitional contexts often includes shifting the lens from urban to rural areas. A number of these approaches also foreground accountability for past socio-economic injustices, often with the aim of addressing contemporary inequality, including its greater impact on women or marginalised groups (Okello et al. 2012; Ní Aoláin 2012). Some buck the connotations of linear progress and short-term solutions suggested by the term "transitional", arguing for "transformative justice" (Gready and Robins 2014), "distributive justice" (Bergsmo et al. 2010) or "integral justice" (Mani 2014). These alternative approaches are positioned as theoretical responses to evidence on the ground.

A number of transitional justice practitioners in Africa have offered strident critiques of the mainstream approach and attempted to elaborate a more contextually relevant transitional justice in practice (Okello et al. 2012), both in response to local evidence and, perhaps less so, in dialogue with transitional justice theorists. This is exemplified by the pointed name (and content) of the annual Institute for African Transitional Justice, organised in Uganda by the Refugee Law Project and the African Transitional Justice Research Network. Practitioners argue that African civil society shapes transitional justice processes on the continent (Brankovic 2010). Transitional justice theorists largely support this assertion, as it relates to Africa and elsewhere (Crocker 1998; Rangelov and Teitel 2011; Hovil and Okello 2011). Yet, critical analyses of the relationship between civil society and transitional justice are few.

While transitional justice scholars highlight the diversity and plurality of civil society, noting the complex history and ambiguity of the concept and nodding towards forms of associational life such as social movements and sectarian groups, most then focus on the role of formal, professional NGOs, which are posited as "the main civil society role players in transitional justice" (Van der Merwe and Brankovic 2016: 228; Simić and Volčič 2013). The literature offers a number of typologies of NGO engagement with transitional justice, both in relation to the state and to international regimes. For example, David Backer (2003) outlines civil society activities in transitional contexts, such as "data collection and monitoring" and acting as a "parallel authority", and then offers scenarios ranging from "strength and symbiosis" to "hands off the wheel" that describe the relationship between civil society and the state in transitional justice. Aaron Boesenecker and Leslie Vinjamuri (2011) suggest four roles that civil society plays in engaging with international norms in local contexts, namely, as norm makers, norm adaptors, norm facilitators and norm reflectors. Hugo van der Merwe and Jasmina Brankovic (2016) similarly offer a typology of roles that civil society plays in relation to international norms—implementers, opponents, reframers, alternatives and mediators—while also noting that organisations' approaches differ according to the stages of transition, ranging from "active conflict" to "after transitional justice processes". While these works offer insight into NGO strategies and the way that alternative approaches to transitional justice interact with the mainstream one, they do not give an account of associational life in transitional contexts.

Some work has been done on what alternative approaches to transitional justice may mean for civil society. For example, Béatrice Pouligny (2005) argues that the socio-political transformations required in transitions, especially in postconflict contexts, are better effected through the diverse existing forms of associational life, knowledge and resources of the "social base", as opposed to imported notions of legitimate civil society (in the form of "mushrooming" NGOs), transitional processes and state institutions, which promote homogeneity and lack local content. Hovil and Okello (2011) note the reduction of civil society considered legitimate to human rights NGOs that have a facility with global discourses and donor requirements. They also note the disconnect between local NGOs and their "constituency", which in the absence of "accountability mechanisms … that promote self-reflection" leads to NGOs "projecting their own perceptions onto their compatriots" and at times to harmful outcomes (334–335). Such contributions deny the separation of state and civil society, and particularly the notion that they are in opposition, critiquing the valorisation of civil society as always "good", noting that state and civil society representatives often switch from one to the other or play multiple roles, and highlighting the influence of international and regional actors in addition to state actors (Andrieu 2010; Rangelov and Teitel 2011). Clearly, critiques of mainstream understandings of civil society and transitional justice share many elements, not least in drawing on critiques of neoliberalism.

Beyond the focus on NGOs, the interesting thing about how transitional justice scholars and practitioners think about civil society is that even when they articulate a critique of mainstream transitional justice and imply an alternative approach to civil society, they often deploy mainstream definitions of civil society. In an editorial for a special issue on civil society for the leading academic journal on transitional justice, Lucy Hovil and Moses Okello use Helmut Anheier's (2004) definition: "Civil society is the sphere of institutions, organisations and individuals located among the family, the state and the market, in which people associate voluntarily to advance common interests" (Hovil and Okello 2011: 333). In this volume, practitioner Andrew Songa uses Larry Diamond's (1994: 5) definition of civil society as "autonomous from the state, and bound by a legal order or set of shared rules". Also here, scholar James Dhizaala defines civil society as "distinct from the state, the family and the market", borrowing a World Bank (2006: 2) definition. All of these authors' contributions suggest a distinctly un-mainstream thinking on civil society, based on their reflections on the practice of transitional justice on the continent. This begs the question of why they use mainstream definitions.

The next section discusses the extent to which the practices described in this book hold with the mainstream approach, to what extent they differ, and what this suggests about civil society's role in shaping transitional justice on the continent. It does so by examining the contributions to the volume through the main binaries constructed by the mainstream approach and questioned in African contexts: civil society in relation to the state, tradition, religion, the family and the market.

Case Studies of Civil Society and Transitional Justice in Africa

A close reading of the case studies demonstrates the plurality and complexity of associational life on the continent. The chapters indicate that alternative approaches to civil society more accurately describe the realities on the ground than the mainstream approach. This comes through all the more strongly as the normative bias of civil society theory is somewhat bypassed by the book's focus on transitional justice in practice. This section examines the case studies through the main tensions between mainstream and alternative thinking on civil society—outlining common themes despite the significant historical and socio-political differences of the countries under study. Despite being a short overview, it suggests a different way of reading the chapters in the volume.

The interpenetration of state and civil society is evident in the case studies, with the state acting through civil society and civil society pursuing explicitly political aims, including taking state power. Regarding state control, Noha Aboueldahab notes that Libyan state representatives occupied senior positions in civil society organisations before transition. Discussing contemporary Burundi, Wendy Lambourne suggests that a number of organisations, termed *nyakuri*, are understood to be acting politically on behalf of the state, in addition to noting the presence of army and political party representatives in an influential transitional justice group. Andrew Songa mentions retired diplomats and military generals as members of the Concerned Citizens for Peace, a network involved in Kenya's transitional justice efforts. The case studies of the North African countries and Burundi and Uganda discuss the extent of state regulation of civil society, with registration and the threat of closure keeping many groups in line.

With regard to politicised civil society, Shastry Njeru discusses Zimbabwe's National Constitutional Assembly, an umbrella NGO originally aligned with the political opposition that recently became an independent political party in the context of constitutional reform. Aboueldahab notes that in transitional Egypt, several civil society groups announced plans to form political parties, before the return of dictatorship. James Dhizaala argues that the civil society formations which advocated reform in prewar Liberia considered themselves political organisations. They formed the base of the postwar Transitional Justice Working Group, a human rights group that managed to secure seats for civil society representatives in the transitional government by influencing the peace agreement. Andrew Iliff, meanwhile, highlights the porousness between state and civil society at the community level, noting that local state authorities, like other local authorities, can play multiple roles, including as NGO proxies.

These examples mainly refer to situations before or during political transition. While this is due in part to the ongoing nature of these specific transitions, it also appears to fit the mainstream conception that civil society is only legitimate if it is separate from the state in the wake of democratisation (Diamond 1994). Yet, Dhizaala's discussion suggests the continuities in civil society actors and agendas before and after democratisation, particularly as members of civil society continue to hold positions in government institutions and programmes well after transition. A more telling but less obvious example would be post-apartheid South Africa, with Zukiswa Puwana and Rita Kesselring's chapter demonstrating that ordinary citizens in socio-economically marginalised areas assume that community-based organisations are not only politically motivated but also proxies for political parties.

Beyond state–civil society relations, the chapters demonstrate the heterogeneity of civil society and the reductionism of positing (human rights) NGOs as the main civil society and transitional justice actors on the continent (Hovil and Okello 2011). In the North African case studies and in Zimbabwe, South Africa, Uganda and Burundi, trade unions have played a significant role in pressuring states both to democratise and to adopt transitional justice mechanisms. The case studies of Burundi and Tunisia note the role of professional associations, especially lawyers, doctors and educators, in transitional justice advocacy. In the discussions of Uganda, Liberia and Burundi, traditional groups play a role. In the majority of the case studies, and particularly Kenya, Uganda, Zimbabwe, Liberia, Burundi and Egypt, the contributors discuss the prominence of faith-based organisations, citing Catholic, Anglican, Evangelical, Quaker, Muslim and interfaith groups, among others. Iliff and Aboueldahab note the role of charismatic individuals, ranging from human rights lawyers to religious leaders, in spurring collective action. The South African, Liberian and Egyptian cases show the mobilisation of ordinary citizens—who are also survivors, refugees and members of economically marginalised groups—in protest and other "uncivil" actions. This range of associational life is demonstrated largely in passing, given the stated focus of most of the authors on NGOs and their strategies.

In light of the delegitimation of traditional groups in the mainstream approach to civil society, and the critiques of this in the African context (Kasfir 1998), it is important here to discuss groups based on traditional ties. The case studies of Zimbabwe, Uganda and Libya discuss the co-optation of traditional authorities by the state, people's reliance on traditional leaders in the context of state absence and/or repression, and mobilisation of armed resistance to the state based on ethnicity. These and other case studies also, however, show the prevalence of traditional associational life in transitional justice efforts, as well as the links between traditional groups and other facets of civil society and the state. In addition, most references to traditional groups in the chapters are not in relation to traditional justice mechanisms, but rather to organising and advocacy.

Joanna Quinn discusses the participation of Ugandan traditional leaders in the influential Acholi Religious Leaders Peace Initiative, as well as the founding of a victims' group based on Acholi ethnicity and location. She mentions an instance of a traditional group applying for funding from an international donor. Dhizaala notes that the Liberian Truth and Reconciliation Commission collaborated with the Traditional Women Association of Liberia in its outreach work. Njeru discusses traditional leaders' and groups' participation in the Zimbabwe NGO Forum's dialogues on transitional justice, while Iliff notes their role as mobilisers for community-based projects. If, as Iliff demonstrates, understandings and practices of tradition are not static but rather evolving, the mainstream interdict against groups organised around traditional ties appears as an outdated strand of Western Afropessimism. If the concern is that traditional groups are socially divisive, conservative and not part of "good" civil society, this may be put into perspective by the divisions sown by local human rights NGOs through their interactions with the Kenyan and Liberian truth commissions.

Another striking aspect of the case studies is the prominent role played by various faith-based organisations. These are largely considered "good" civil society based on the assumption that they are founded on private faith and the pursuit of a "common good" (apparently unlike traditional associations) (Shankar 2014). Importantly, however, the chapters suggest that faith-based organisations in Kenya, Zimbabwe, South Africa, Burundi and Liberia played a role in peacebuilding efforts, in several cases actively participating in peace negotiations, but had less of a role in transitional justice efforts and their aftermaths. This can be ascribed to divisions regarding whether to privilege peace efforts over accountability, the territorial rifts between the fields of peacebuilding and transitional justice, and possibly concerns over some faith-based groups' political alignment with the state. However, it may be more of a function of dominant human rights NGOs sidelining faith-based organisations in transitional justice, particularly in the implementation phase. Here Njeru's evidence of outreach participants requesting a Church-run truth commission can be contrasted with Lambourne's implication that religious representatives are not civil society in her discussion of the commissioner selection process in Burundi (which may be the implication of her source, the international NGO Impunity Watch).

In line with considerations of what makes "good" civil society is the question of where "uncivil" collective action fits in. Among several examples in the case studies is Dhizaala's description of Liberian women from the Buduburam refugee camp holding a 2-month sit-in by the venue where peace talks were held and using their bodies to block people and supplies from entering the building until a ceasefire was signed. Another example is Puwana and Kesselring's discussion of the apartheid survivors' organisation, Khulumani Support Group, marching on parliament in South Africa to push for adequate reparations. The former action contributed to the signing of the peace accord, and the latter, while not resulting in the reparations programme the survivors demanded, raised awareness of survivors' issues and led to collaboration between Khulumani and a range of other civil society groups.

Both of these actions were run by victims, who, while presumably most affected by transitional justice efforts, play a small role in the case study narratives. The chapters on Kenya, Liberia and Libya discuss NGOs organising victims, but the case studies of Zimbabwe, South Africa, Burundi and also Kenya describe the marginalisation of victims in transitional processes and specifically by NGOs. This is acknowledged as a learning point, for example, with Songa reflecting that the main transitional justice coalition in Kenya could have more effectively advanced gender justice if it had worked not only with mainstream, national NGOs but also with smaller "victim-led" organisations.

This all points to a similar and certainly in some cases interlinked marginalisation of victims' and community-based women's collective action as "uncivil" and as not belonging to "good" civil society, except perhaps as a prop for the more "important" work of NGOs. It may also point to an unspoken sense that this collective action is an expression of private pain in a form that is outside the parameters of commonly accepted forms of expression (Madlingozi 2010; Kesselring 2016). There is little overt discussion of the private in the case studies, except in Puwana and Kesselring's chapter, where they note that Khulumani, which is made up primarily of women, advocates for reparations payments to individual victims (rather than collective compensation) because the "women have learnt through experience that they are the best managers of a household budget" (Chap. 5). This comment provides a glimpse of the blurred line between private and public, and its relationship to "uncivil" civil society, that is largely absent from NGO strategies and analyses of these strategies (Howell 2007). It also points to the centrality of economic concerns, linked to historical and contemporary socio-economic exclusion, to those engaged in "uncivil" action (Robins 2013), which is similarly acknowledged but not discussed in any depth in the chapters.

The final point that should be made about the case studies is that they show that the state-centric view of civil society is too narrow, not simply in the discussions of local organisations' interactions with international norms but also, more importantly, in terms of the multiple sites in which the contestation of power occurs—local, regional and global. In addition to a number of examples above, Iliff's chapter notes the complexity of local dynamics in relation to community and traditional practices outside the state. The case studies of Liberia, Burundi and Libya discuss the influence of civil society in the diaspora on international, regional and domestic state responses to transitional justice efforts. The chapters on Liberia and Zimbabwe mention the influence of—and advocacy aimed at—regional economic communities, and the chapter on Kenya mentions the influence of the African Union. The chapters on Kenya, Liberia, Uganda, Libya, Tunisia and especially Burundi discuss the impact of the United Nations. Puwana and Kesselring describe Khulumani's litigation using the United States Alien Tort Statute against international corporations accused of aiding the security forces under apartheid. Lambourne's contribution mentions organisations being co-opted by "business interests" to undertake activities that indirectly support state actors. The chapters on Kenya, Liberia, Burundi and Egypt note the influence of traditional and social media in raising awareness and prompting collective action at the local and global levels. These and other examples go far beyond the mainstream focus on state–civil society relations, even though most of the chapters' explicit concern is NGOs' efforts with the state.

The next section concludes the chapter with reflections on what the tensions between mainstream and alternative approaches to civil society in the case studies suggest for transitional justice practice, particularly in Africa.

Implications of Civil Society Theory for Transitional Justice Practice in Africa

A close reading of the case studies—and particularly what is written outside the main focus of the chapters—suggests that the nature of African associational life in the context of transitional justice better fits alternative approaches in civil society theory. The chapters show the porousness between state and civil society, a heterogeneous civil society with (human rights) NGOs as but one influential actor, and the significance of associational life based on sectarian ties to effective processes. They show the links between "uncivil" civil society and those most affected by violations and transitional justice efforts, the blurring between private and public in the contestations of power that mark transitions, and the reductionism of the focus on the state required by the state–civil society binary in light of the influence of local, regional and global dynamics. In more ways than outlined above, there is evidence of state, human rights NGO, faith-based, traditional, grassroots, victim, labour, diaspora, international agency and other actors interacting with each other in every constellation, including switching between roles.

This alignment with alternative understandings of civil society seems to make sense, given that most of the contributors support alternative approaches to transitional justice, which aim to be more context specific, holistic, "bottom-up" and sensitive to the ongoing effects of historical injustices (political, social, economic) in the present, foregrounding community-based solutions and victims' demands. Yet, these manifestations of alternative thinking about civil society are peripheral in the case studies. Although it was not a requirement of the call for chapters, the stated focus of the majority of the case studies is NGOs and their activities in relation to the state. Traditional groups, community-based groups and even victims' groups play a minor role in almost all the narratives. Faith-based groups are discussed in relation to peace negotiations, but mostly disappear in the descriptions of transitional justice mechanisms and their aftermaths. While there is direct discussion of international norms, the plurality and complexity of various local, regional and global actors is mentioned only in passing. All of this begs questions similar to the one I asked about why some contributors use mainstream definitions of civil society when their chapters suggest other inclinations.

I argue that the mainstream conception of civil society guides transitional justice practice in the diverse case studies here, and generally across the continent, in subtle ways. This tendency is due in part to the guidance of international donors, agencies and organisations, as discussed by Quinn, Lambourne and Songa. However, practitioners have noted that the influence of international actors can be overstated (Brankovic 2010) and that local civil society may not be "gullible but rather view their international partners as 'useful idiots' to be deployed at whim, whose ideals can be dispensed with after their inevitable departure" (Hovil and Okello 2011: 339). The relationship of local civil society to international partners is characterised by agency as much as dependency and is shaped by too many variables to paint with the same brush. A more likely explanation is norm diffusion and the simple fact of mainstream conceptions being mainstream and thus dominant. Critiques of the mainstream approaches to transitional justice and civil society abound, particularly in theory, but the practice of both remains heavily circumscribed by established ways of doing, even when some elements of practice counter the norm. At the same time, as the number of studies of civil society's role in transitional justice increases, it is possible that these constrained approaches will appear as "best practice" learnt on the ground, thereby reifying the civil society theory biases in transitional justice.

In addition, mainstream thinking describes how civil society is expected to look after democratisation, when the "irrational" elements involved in bringing down the old regime are sidelined so as to prevent their undue and supposedly regressive influence on the newly established democratic state. As liberal democracies, postcolonial states foreground political sovereignty over popular sovereignty and locate legitimate efforts at social change solely in the realms of electoral representation and mainstream civil society. This may be one cause of the challenges NGOs face in following up on transitional justice mechanisms after they close—the marginalisation of "alternative" forms of civil society narrows the scope for contestation and legitimate political action, with NGOs undermining themselves by contributing to this marginalisation. Another challenge is that transitional justice, which gained its legitimacy by contributing to democratisation and nation building, is now applied in contexts far different from the transitions from authoritarianism to democracy that frame its origins. In these contexts, particularly the now increasingly common case of transitional justice processes being used in the absence of political transition or in partial transitions, the mainstream approach to civil society may constrain those parts of civil society that otherwise would contribute to regime change. In this light, NGOs' efforts to position themselves as nonpolitical or "above" politics, as Iliff and Dhizaala describe in their chapters, appear self-defeating, at least in terms of meeting their transitional justice goals, even if not in terms of ensuring their own longevity.

These aspects of the intersections of theory and practice with civil society and transitional justice call for more research. They also suggest the wisdom for practitioners—including for us as the editors of this volume and as practitioners ourselves—of Issa Shivji's reflections that "every practice gives rise to theory and that every action is based on some theoretical or philosophical premise or outlook", but that among NGOs "theory is written off as 'common sense' and therefore not interrogated" (2007: 36). This chapter supports his call "to integrate intellectual and activist discourse" and for NGOs to "fundamentally re-examine their silences and their discourses" in order to "truly play the role of catalysts of change rather than catechists of aid and charity" (46–47).

References

Andrieu, K. (2010). Civilizing peacebuilding: Transitional justice, civil society and the liberal paradigm. *Security Dialogue, 41*(5), 537–558.

Anheier, H. K. (2004). *Civil society: Measurement, evaluation, policy*. London: Earthscan.

Arthur, P. (2009). How 'transitions' reshaped human rights: A conceptual history of transitional justice. *Human Rights Quarterly, 31*(2), 321–367.

Backer, D. (2003). Civil society and transitional justice: Possibilities, patterns and prospects. *Journal of Human Rights, 2*(3), 297–313.

Baker, G. (2002). *Civil society and democratic theory: Alternative voices*. London: Routledge.

Bayart, J.-F. (1986). Civil society in Africa. In P. Chabal (Ed.), *Political domination in Africa*. Cambridge: Cambridge University Press.

Bayat, A. (1997). Un-civil society: The politics of the 'informal people'. *Third World Quarterly, 18*(1), 53–72.

Bergsmo, M., Rodriguez-Garavito, C., Kalmanovitz, P., & Saffon, M. P. (Eds.). (2010). *Distributive justice in transitions*. Oslo: Torkel Opsahl.

Boesenecker, A. P., & Vinjamuri, L. (2011). Lost in translation? Civil society, faith-based organizations and the negotiation of international norms. *International Journal of Transitional Justice, 5*(3), 345–365.

Bond, P. (2014). Africa rising? Afro-optimism and uncivil society in an era of economic volatility. In E. Obadare (Ed.), *The handbook of civil society in Africa* (pp. 233–251). New York: Springer.

Brankovic, J. (2010). *Advocating justice: Civil society and transitional justice in Africa*. Cape Town: African Transitional Justice Research Network and Centre for the Study of Violence and Reconciliation.

Bukenya, B., & Hickey, S. (2014). NGOs, civil society, and development. In E. Obadare (Ed.), *The handbook of civil society in Africa* (pp. 311–335). New York: Springer.

Chabal, P., & Daloz, J.-P. (1999). *Africa works: Disorder as a political instrument*. Oxford: James Currey.

Chatterjee, P. (2001). On civil and political society in post-colonial democracies. In S. Kaviraj & S. Khilnani (Eds.), *Civil society: History and possibilities* (pp. 165–178). Cambridge: Cambridge University Press.

Chazan, N. (1992). Africa's democratic challenge. *World Policy Journal, 9*(2), 279–307.

Comaroff, J. L., & Comaroff, J. (Eds.). (1999). *Civil society and the political imagination in Africa: Critical perspectives*. Chicago, IL: University of Chicago Press.

Crocker, D. A. (1998). Transitional justice and international civil society: Toward a normative framework. *Constellations, 5*(4), 492–517.

Dagnino, E. (2007). Citizenship: A perverse confluence. *Development in Practice, 17*(4/5), 549–556.

Diamond, L. J. (1994). Toward democratic consolidation. *Journal of Democracy, 5*(3), 4–17.

Elster, J. (2004). *Closing the books: Transitional justice in historical perspective*. Cambridge: Cambridge University Press.

Fletcher, L., & Weinstein, H. (2002). Violence and social repair: Rethinking the contribution of justice to reconciliation. *Human Rights Quarterly, 24*(3), 573–639.

Gallagher, J. (2014). 'Good' state, 'bad' state: Loss and longing in postcolonial Zimbabwe. In E. Obadare (Ed.), *The handbook of civil society in Africa* (pp. 61–75). New York: Springer.

Gready, P., & Robins, S. (2014). From transitional to transformative justice: A new agenda for practice. *International Journal of Transitional Justice, 8*(3), 339–361.

Hann, C. (1996). Introduction: Political society and civil anthropology. In C. Hann & E. Dunn (Eds.), *Civil society: Challenging western models* (pp. 1–26). London: Routledge.

Harbeson, J. W. (1994). Civil society and political renaissance in Africa. In J. W. Harbeson, D. Rothchild, & N. Chazan (Eds.), *Civil society and the state in Africa* (pp. 1–29). Boulder, CO: Lynne Rienner.

Hovil, L., & Okello, M. C. (2011). Editorial note. In 'special issue', Civil society, social movements and transitional justice. *International Journal of Transitional Justice, 5*(3), 333–344.

Howell, J. (2000). Making civil society from outside: Challenges for donors. *European Journal of Development Research, 12*(1), 3–32.

Howell, J. (2007). Gender and civil society: Time for cross-border dialogue. *Social Politics, 14*(4), 415–436.

Kagoro, B. (2012). The paradox of alien knowledge, narrative and praxis: Transitional justice and the politics of agenda setting in Africa. In M. C. Okello, C. Dolan, U. Whande, N. Mncwabe, & S. Oola (Eds.), *Where law meets reality: Forging African transitional justice*. Cape Town: Pambazuka Press.

Kasfir, N. (Ed.). (1998). *Civil society and democracy in Africa: Critical perspectives*. London: Frank Cass.

Kaviraj, S. (2001). In search of civil society. In S. Kaviraj & S. Khilnani (Eds.), *Civil society: History and possibilities* (pp. 287–323). Cambridge: Cambridge University Press.

Kesselring, R. (2016). *Bodies of truth: Law, memory, and emancipation in post-apartheid South Africa*. Stanford, CA: Stanford University Press.

Khilnani, S. (2001). The development of civil society. In S. Kaviraj & S. Khilnani (Eds.), *Civil society: History and possibilities* (pp. 11–32). Cambridge: Cambridge University Press.

Laplante, L. J. (2008). Transitional justice and peace building: Diagnosing and addressing the socioeconomic roots of violence through a human rights framework. *International Journal of Transitional Justice, 2*(3), 331–355.

Linz, J. J., & Stepan, A. (1996). Towards consolidated democracy. *Journal of Democracy, 7*(2), 14–33.

Madlingozi, T. (2010). On transitional justice entrepreneurs and the production of victims. *Journal of Human Rights Practice, 2*(2), 208–228.

Mamdani, M. (1995). A critique of the state and civil society paradigm in africanism studies. In M. Mamdani & E. Wamba-dia-Wamba (Eds.), *African studies on social movements and democracy* (pp. 602–616). Dakar: CODESRIA.
Mani, R. (2014). Integral justice for victims. In I. Vanfraechem, A. Pemberton, & F. M. Ndahinda (Eds.), *Justice for victims: Perspectives on rights, transition and reconciliation*. New York: Routledge.
Mouffe, C. (1993). Democratic citizenship and the political community. In C. Mouffe (Ed.), *Dimensions of radical democracy: Pluralism, citizenship, community*. New York: Verso.
Mutua, M. (Ed.). (2009). *Human rights NGOs in East Africa: Political and normative tensions*. Princeton, NJ: University of Pennsylvania Press.
Ndegwa, S. N. (1997). Citizenship and ethnicity: An examination of two transition moments in Kenyan politics. *American Political Science Review, 91*(3), 599–616.
Ní Aoláin, F. (2012). Advancing feminist positioning in the field of transitional justice. *International Journal of Transitional Justice, 6*(2), 205–228.
Obadare, E., & Adebanwi, W. (2009). Transnational resource flow and the paradoxes of belonging: Redirecting the debate on transnationalism, remittances, state and citizenship in Africa. *Review of African Political Economy, 36*(122), 499–517.
Okello, M. C. (2010). Afterword: Elevating transitional local justice or crystallizing global governance? In R. Shaw & L. Waldorf (Eds.), *Localizing transitional justice: Interventions and priorities after mass violence*. Stanford, CA: Stanford University Press.
Okello, M. C., Dolan, C., Whande, U., Mncwabe, N., & Oola, S. (Eds.). (2012). *Where law meets reality: Forging African transitional justice*. Cape Town: Pambazuka Press.
Osaghae, E. E. (2005). Civil society and ethnicity in Africa. *Politeia, 24*(1), 64–84.
Pouligny, B. (2005). Civil society and post-conflict peacebuilding: Ambiguities of international programmes aimed at building 'new' societies. *Security Dialogue, 36*(4), 495–510.
Putnam, R. D. (1993). *Making democracy work: Civic traditions in modern Italy*. Princeton, NJ: Princeton University Press.
Rangelov, I., & Teitel, R. (2011). Global civil society and transitional justice. In M. Albrow & H. Seckinelgin (Eds.), *Global civil society 2011: Globality and the absence of justice*. Basingstoke: Palgrave Macmillan.
Robins, S. (2013). *Families of the missing: A test for contemporary approaches to transitional justice*. London: Routledge.
Scott, J. C. (1985). *Weapons of the weak: Everyday forms of peasant resistance*. New Haven, CT: Yale University Press.
Seligman, A. B. (1992). *The idea of civil society*. New York, NY: Free Press.
Shankar, S. (2014). Civil society and religion. In E. Obadare (Ed.), *The handbook of civil society in Africa* (pp. 25–41). New York: Springer.
Shaw, R., & Waldorf, L. (Eds.). (2010). *Localizing transitional justice: Interventions and priorities after mass violence*. Stanford, CA: Stanford University Press.
Shivji, I. G. (2007). *Silences in NGO discourse: The role and future of NGOs in Africa*. Oxford: Fahamu.
Simić, O., & Volčič, Z. (Eds.). (2013). *Transitional justice and civil society in the Balkans*. New York: Springer.
Sriram, C. L. (2007). Justice as peace? Liberal peacebuilding and strategies of transitional justice. *Global Society, 21*(4), 579–591.
Subotić, J. (2011). The transformation of international transitional justice advocacy. *International Journal of Transitional Justice, 6*(1), 106–125.
Teitel, R. G. (2003). Transitional justice genealogy. *Harvard Human Rights Journal, 16*, 69–94.
Tripp, A. M. (1998). Expanding 'civil society': Women and political space in contemporary Uganda. *Commonwealth and Comparative Politics, 3*(2), 84–107.
Van der Merwe, H., & Brankovic, J. (2016). The role of African civil society in shaping national transitional justice agendas and policies. In S. Williams & H. Woolaver (Eds.), *Civil society and international criminal justice in Africa: Challenges and opportunities*. Juta: Cape Town.
World Bank. (2006). *Civil society and peacebuilding: Potential, limitations and critical factors*. Report No. 36445-GLB.

Chapter 2
Locating Civil Society in Kenya's Transitional Justice Agenda: A Reflection on the Experience of the Kenya Transitional Justice Network with the Truth, Justice and Reconciliation Commission

Andrew Songa

Introduction

This chapter outlines the origins of Kenya's transitional justice agenda and the role of civil society in shaping it, with a focus on Kenya's Truth, Justice and Reconciliation Commission (TJRC) process. It argues that Kenyan civil society played a critical role in the truth, justice and reconciliation process by assuming various roles that include (1) advocacy for the establishment of a truth commission; (2) sensitisation and mobilisation of victim groups to participate in the TJRC; (3) acting as monitors and watchdogs to the process; (4) serving as technical experts advising the TJRC; and (5) advocating for the implementation of the findings and recommendations of the TJRC report.

While there are a variety of coalitions, collaborations and individual initiatives by various civil society organisations (CSOs) with regard to the TJRC process, the chapter focuses on the experiences of the Kenya Transitional Justice Network (KTJN) as a dominant coalition whose interventions traversed all the aforementioned roles. It explores the origins and motivations for the establishment of KTJN, together with the development and implementation of the KTJN agenda, while noting the major decision points for the network that significantly influenced engagement among coalition members and their engagement with state actors. It reflects on lessons learnt thus far. While there is a significant literature on Kenya's transitional justice processes and the impact of civil society on some of these processes, this is an attempt to document the particular experiences of KTJN from my perspective as a representative of the Kenya Human Rights Commission (KHRC) and a member of its leadership since 2012. It relies on records of KTJN's activities, output documents and interviews with key KTJN members and stakeholders, who shall remain anonymous.

A. Songa (✉)
Kenya Human Rights Commission, Nairobi, Kenya
e-mail: songa.andrew59@gmail.com

J. Brankovic, H. van der Merwe (eds.), *Advocating Transitional Justice in Africa*, Springer Series in Transitional Justice,
https://doi.org/10.1007/978-3-319-70417-3_2

A primary conclusion is that civil society in Kenya has played not only a pivotal role in shaping Kenya's transitional justice agenda but also the role of vanguard, seeking to sustain the impetus for implementation of the transitional justice process and accentuating the voices of victims within public debate. Kenya has an expansive transitional justice agenda informed by a motivation to complete Kenya's process of democratisation alongside delivering justice for the victims of the 2007–2008 post-election violence (PEV). The formulation of civil society networks such as KTJN has been a response to the challenge of developing a comprehensive approach to monitoring and actively participating in the implementation process.

In assessing KTJN's experience, a series of key questions emerge with respect to the operations of civil society networks. What governance structures should networks put in place to advance victim-centred and responsive transitional justice processes? How should networks be resourced to ensure that they are sustainable? Finally, how should networks empower victims and contribute to the goal of self-representation in shaping and participating in transitional justice processes?

The chapter begins by providing the historical context of Kenya from the advent of colonialism to the violence witnessed in the aftermath of the 2007 general elections and how this informed the current transitional justice agenda. It then focuses on the actual formulation of the transitional justice agenda as part of a mediated settlement to end the violence. The chapter commences the discussion of civil society's involvement in shaping Kenya's interaction with transitional justice before narrowing in on the specific experience of KTJN and its engagement with the TJRC. The chapter finally reflects on KTJN's approach and highlights its challenges and the lessons learnt so far.

Kenya's Historical Context and the Emergence of a Transitional Justice Agenda

Kenya's venture into transitional justice is informed by a history described as "a catalogue of gross human rights violations, the arrogance of power and the commission of mind boggling economic crimes" (Task Force 2003). The TJRC report divided this history into four epochs: the British colonial era (1895–1963), President Jomo Kenyatta's era (1963–1978), President Daniel Arap Moi's era (1978–2002) and President Mwai Kibaki's era (2002–2008) (TJRC 2013). The colonial era saw numerous military expeditions mounted to deal with what were referred to as "recalcitrant tribes". The results were often massacres, alongside crimes such as theft, rape and destruction of property (TJRC 2013). It was such repression that birthed the Mau freedom struggle in 1952–1955, following the declaration of a state of emergency by the colonial government. This period was characterised by mass detentions and widespread torture that would become the subject of litigation by victims against the British Government some 50 years later (KHRC 2013).

At independence, the Kenyatta and Moi administrations, with a combined tenure of 39 years, appropriated the oppressive tools of the colonial state rather than introducing reforms (Mutua 2001). Prominent features of this time included political assassinations, detentions without trial, torture and introduction of a single-party state. This served to strengthen the resolve of pro-democracy activists and, coupled with international pressure, Kenya reintroduced multiparty democracy in the 1992 general elections. Multiparty elections brought ethnicity-based clashes largely due to politicians stoking ethnic tensions to stay in power. Election-related violence prior to the 2007 general elections was responsible for the displacement of approximately 350,000 persons (UN-OCHA Kenya 2008).

With President Moi constitutionally barred from seeking another term of office, 2002 saw a change of guard and the first electoral win for a united opposition led by Mwai Kibaki under the banner of the National Rainbow Coalition (NARC). President Kibaki initiated numerous reforms, including a radical surgery of the judiciary to purge it of corrupt judges and restore public confidence; the establishment of the Kenya National Commission on Human Rights (KNCHR); the start of several inquiries, including the Taskforce on the Establishment of the Truth, Justice and Reconciliation Commission; and the beginnings of constitutional reform (Mutua 2013).

These initiatives were soon derailed by corruption in the NARC administration (Gathii 2010). In addition, political disagreements and ideological differences on the structure of government within NARC resulted in a highly contested constitutional review process that culminated in a 2005 referendum where the draft constitution proposed by the Kibaki-led faction was defeated in the face of a robust "No" campaign led by the Raila Odinga faction (Musila 2010). NARC disintegrated thereafter and triggered a series of major political realignments that would shape the 2007 general elections.

The 2007 general elections pitted President Kibaki against his hitherto political ally Raila Odinga, who was now at the helm of the Orange Democratic Movement (ODM), a political party born out of an alliance that campaigned against the 2005 draft constitution. The result was an emotive campaign period that led to a close political contest considered a zero-sum game by supporters of each side. President Kibaki was declared the winner by a margin of 231,728 votes (IREC 2008). ODM called on its supporters to engage in mass action to refute the electoral results and declare Odinga the rightful winner. The Party of National Unity (PNU) insisted that any disputes regarding the election results should be handled by the courts. This triggered an unprecedented mass wave of protests and violence in the country, which led to 1,300 fatalities, displacement of 663,921 people and destruction of 78,254 houses (GOK 2012).

The violence consisted of spontaneous attacks in the Rift Valley and Coast regions targeting the Kikuyu and Kisii communities that were perceived as supporters of the PNU. Government facilities were also targeted. Politicians and businessmen enlisted criminal gangs to perpetrate much of the violence. The towns of Naivasha, Nakuru and informal settlements in Nairobi saw Kikuyu gangs target Luos, Luhyas and Kalenjins (deemed supporters of ODM) with a view to evicting them as a form of retaliation for Kalenjin gangs in the North Rift targeting Kikuyus.

The unjustified use of force and serious crimes by the police and other security agents were also identified as prominent features of the violence (CIPEV 2008).

This historical background reveals a catalogue of gross human rights violations and a series of missed opportunities to remedy harms suffered by victims. The failure to break away from our colonial legacy has seen some define the Kenyan state as predatory and illiberal, with its orientation being that of political repression to facilitate economic exploitation (Task Force 2003). A compounded sense of grievance among communities and the non-responsiveness of the state evolved into historical injustices and a culture of impunity within the ruling elite. It is this prevailing environment that led to the unprecedented PEV and a political settlement to end the conflict, which finally compelled the political leadership and the public at large to confront the legacy of political despotism and societal inequity through a transitional justice agenda.

Kenya's Transitional Justice Agenda

Kenya's experience can be characterised as a series of political transitions that did not create sufficient impetus for transitional justice up to the PEV. Various regimes dallied with processes that were of a transitional nature to assuage pressure from civil society and the wider public. Kenya's formal embrace of transitional justice occurred with the 2003 establishment of the Task Force on the Establishment of a Truth, Justice and Reconciliation Commission with a mandate of ascertaining whether the public was in favour of having a truth commission. While the Task Force report recommended the establishment of the TJRC, it was not heeded until the PEV.

The PEV crisis drew the attention of the international community and resulted in the formation of the AU Panel of Eminent African Personalities mandated to shepherd the mediation process (AU Commission 2014). The process, unveiled on January 29, 2008, and chaired by Kofi Annan, would be dubbed the Kenya National Dialogue and Reconciliation (KNDR). The agenda items for KNDR were as follows: (1) Immediate Action to Stop Violence and Restore Fundamental Rights and Liabilities (Agenda 1); (2) Immediate Measures to Address the Humanitarian Crisis, Promote Reconciliation, Healing and Restoration (Agenda 2); (3) How to Overcome the Current Political Crisis (Agenda 3); and (4) Long-term Issues and Solutions (Agenda 4). Through this framework a National Accord was signed on February 28, 2008, and enshrined in law to establish a grand coalition government as a way out of the political crisis (AU Commission 2014). Mwai Kibaki retained the presidency while Raila Odinga took the position of prime minister.

In addition to providing a peaceful settlement to the PEV crisis, the KNDR provided a framework for transitional justice on the basis of its agenda items (Hansen 2013). It saw the establishment of various institutions and mechanisms that would advance truth seeking, holistic justice processes and reparations for victims. It also stated the need for constitutional, legal and institutional reform; tackling poverty and inequity as well as combating regional development imbalances; tackling unemployment, particularly among the youth; consolidating national cohesion and unity; undertaking land reforms; and addressing transparency, accountability and impunity (AU Commission 2014).

The KNDR also resulted in the signing of three agreements on March 4, 2008, that established the implementing institutions to be utilised in this endeavour. One was the Independent Review Commission (IREC), established to assess the electoral infrastructure after the 2007 election results. Another was the Commission of Inquiry into the Post-Election Violence (CIPEV), established as a nonjudicial body to investigate facts and circumstances leading to the PEV, investigate alleged crimes by state security agencies and recommend legal, political or administrative measures that would bring those criminally responsible to account. The third was an agreement on the structure for constitutional review, which included a referendum to enact the new constitution. Finally, the KNDR saw the parties agree to an implementation matrix for long-term issues and solutions.

The KNDR had a number of notable outcomes. First, the grand coalition government resuscitated the constitutional review process. Promulgated on August 27, 2010, the constitution's notable highlights are an expansive bill of rights that recognises economic, social and cultural rights and the introduction of a devolved system government to enhance the public's participation in governance and the articulation of the developmental agenda. The process also consisted of reforms to the judiciary and police, including vetting procedures.

Second, CIPEV recommended the establishment of a Special Tribunal for Kenya for crimes against humanity. CIPEV stated that it would submit a list of names of those most responsible for the PEV to the International Criminal Court (ICC) if the Special Tribunal failed to materialise, which proved prudent as the political class was unable to enact the necessary legislation for the establishment of the tribunal. The ICC's chief prosecutor eventually initiated investigations *proprio motu* on the basis of the CIPEV information, which resulted in charges against William Samoei Ruto and Joshua Arap Sang in Case One and Uhuru Muigai Kenyatta and Francis Muthaura in Case Two. The cases were withdrawn or dropped by 2016, although not before Uhuru Kenyatta and William Ruto utilised their indictments to mobilise their Kikuyu and Kalenjin communities, which were at the epicentre of the PEV, in order to come to power in 2013 as president and deputy president, respectively, and thereby control government policy on the ICC cases (Hansen 2011).

Third, the grand coalition government enacted the Truth, Justice and Reconciliation Act No. 6 of 2008, which established the TJRC and saw its commissioners sworn in on August 3, 2009. The mandate of the TJRC was to inquire into gross human rights violations and historical injustices that occurred in Kenya from December 12, 1963 (independence), to February 28, 2008 (signing of the National Accord). The TJRC issued its final report on May 3, 2013. The implementation of its recommendations remains an ongoing concern, as is discussed below.

The KNDR's process of mediation and its resultant power-sharing agreement significantly influenced the environment for and the scope of Kenya's transitional justice framework and it has been propounded that mediation should be seriously considered as a transitional justice issue, since it establishes the basis for a negotiated sense of justice while also detailing or preempting the manner in which transitional justice is carried out (Musila 2010). The developments within the ambit of criminal accountability and the TJRC process, however, reveal the challenges inherent in relying on a mediation agreement that confers significant powers on the political elite to control the justice process (Hansen 2013). The reality of a reluctant political class in a transitional justice context requires an external element that plays the role of vanguard, namely civil society.

Civil Society's Engagement with Kenya's Transitional Justice Agenda

This chapter identifies with Larry Diamond's definition of civil society "as the realm of organized social life that is voluntary, self-generating, (largely) self-supporting, autonomous from the state and bound by a legal order or set of shared rules" (cited in Bodewes 2013: 4). In addition it recognises civil society to be a heterogeneous space with a polarised nature due to the rules set by the state and the state's tactic of simultaneously incorporating and disengaging with different segments of civil society (Ngunyi 2008).

With regard to transitional justice in particular, civil society has been recognised as playing a critical role by influencing those responsible for shaping, developing and implementing the processes while also being directly involved in implementation (Van der Merwe and Brankovic 2016). It is thus important to appreciate the evolution of civil society's role in Kenya's historical context. During the Kenyatta era, civil society was largely a partner in development with the state, rather than a watchdog. During the Moi era it was an agent of democratisation, with the impetus shifting to restoring political pluralism and putting an end to autocratic rule. During the Kibaki era, its role was institutionalising democracy by advocating for constitutional and institutional reforms, as well as elaborating the notion of transitional justice by calling for the establishment of the TJRC (Lasseko 2009).

As noted above, the KNDR served as the critical facilitator for Kenya's transitional justice framework, and it is well documented that civil society played a major role in shaping the KNDR. The office of the AU Panel summarised the role of civil society in the process as follows:

> Civil society organizations made an immense contribution to the mediation process. Their submissions and meetings with the Panel contextualized the crisis and helped it to formulate appropriate corrective measures. They described the extent of the crisis, the atrocities committed, and the probable outcomes if the negotiations failed. (AU Commission 2014: 30)

Civil society input into the KNDR has also been characterised as effectively utilising a mediation process to advocate for human rights and a transitional justice agenda (Hansen 2013). This input was however provided by a divergent and heterogeneous civil society that applied different approaches in line with their core values and political alignments, as they were not neutral (Kanyinga 2011). The divide in civil society was characterised as between the "conservatives/moderates" or "peace group" and the "progressive/radicals" or "justice group" (Kanyinga 2011; Hansen and Sriram 2015). The peace group reacted to the PEV by advocating for the maintenance of the status quo with respect to election results and placing emphasis on the call for peace—a position that resonated with that of President Kibaki and the PNU. The justice group advocated for truth in exposing electoral malpractices and for accountability of those responsible for the PEV—a position that resonated with that of Raila Odinga and the ODM (Kanyinga 2011).

The conservative/peace advocates would coalesce around Concerned Citizens for Peace (CCP), while the progressive/justice advocates would coalesce around Kenyans for Peace, Truth and Justice (KPTJ). Populated by a strong contingent of religious leaders, retired diplomats and soldiers, CCP's primary objective was to advocate for the discourse of reconciliation when the KNDR was being developed (Bosire and Lynch 2014). KPTJ was populated by organisations from the governance and human rights sector who argued that sustainable peace would only be achieved if it was premised on truth and justice. These perspectives influenced the four agenda items in the KNDR. The peace group would be identified as being at their peak of influence at the time of negotiating the inception of the mediation process through the KNDR (Bosire and Lynch 2014), while the justice group would emerge as the strongest voice in framing the accountability question once the negotiations under KNDR commenced (Musila 2010). The next section focuses on the emergence of the KTJN and its engagement with the TJRC as depictive of one such civil society initiative aimed at being both proactive and reactive to a state-led justice process.

KTJN and Its Engagement with the TJRC

The Origins and Structure of KTJN

The KTJN began as an umbrella body referred to as the Multi-Sectoral Task Force (MSTF), formed in 2008. MTSF's primary focus was the establishment of the TJRC, with its stated mission being to push for a people-centred, effective and credible commission (MSTF 2008a). An appreciation for the true extent of the transitional justice agenda as revealed by the KNDR agreements would see MSTF in 2009 transform into the KTJN, with an expanded mission: "To collaborate towards the realization of transitional justice programmes (components) in Kenya comprising Truth-telling, Criminal Justice, Constitutional Changes, Administrative Changes, Public Capital, Public Land, Gender Justice, Historical Injustices and Victims' Coalition" (KTJN 2009a: 1).

According to KTJN, "truth-telling" entailed focusing on the TJRC and any other judicial processes, public inquiries and historical narrative and documentation processes that resulted in accountability for the gross human rights violations that linked the past to the present. "Criminal justice" would be the avenue for retribution against persons deemed responsible for gross human rights violations, whether in their own capacity or by following "orders from above" and breaking the law with impunity.

"Constitutional change" would be geared towards building consensus on the 2010 constitution as the foundation of an entirely new democratic order, with a people-driven focus. "Administrative change" was essentially institutional reforms to move the society towards a more democratic political system through popular participation in national and local governance, on the widest possible scale. "Public capital" was to focus on addressing corruption as the gross, abusive violation of the public good, resulting in the deterioration of public services, infrastructure and human and economic development of the people and the nation. The "public land" component was to focus on having grabbed public land returned and restored while insisting on a process of land reform in the interest of all the peoples of Kenya and not merely a small inheriting elite.

"Gender justice" was envisaged as ensuring comprehensive redress for gender-based injustices cutting across all the components of transitional justice, while the "historical injustices" component was concerned with capturing the inequities in the distribution and enjoyment of national resources across regions, ethnicity, class, race, gender and generations. Lastly, the "victims' coalition" component was aimed at ensuring that victims of historical injustices are fully supported and strengthened to organise and engage around their issues within the above-mentioned components and processes of transitional justice in Kenya.

KTJN organised itself to consist of general, thematic and working groups. At the general group level, its membership was open to both individuals and organisations, with the only criterion being subscription to the mission and vision of KTJN (KTJN 2009a). These members were organised into the thematic groups of KTJN's focus areas. The working group was designated to be the executive committee responsible for coordinating the network. The 14 organisations in the working group were African Centre for Open Governance (AfriCOG), Centre for the Development of Marginalised Communities (CEDMAC), Centre for Multi-Party Democracy (CMD), Citizens Coalition for Constitutional Change (4Cs), Coalition on Violence Against Women (COVAW), Centre for Rights Education and Awareness (CREAW), Constitution and Reform Education Consortium (CRECO), Federation of Women Lawyers-Kenya (FIDA-K), International Commission of Jurists-Kenya (ICJ-K), International Center for Policy and Conflict (ICPC), Kenya Human Rights Commission (KHRC), Kenya Land Alliance (KLA) and Mazingira Institute and Urgent Action Fund-Africa (UAF-A).

The structure further envisaged various strategic partnerships with state entities that would be tasked with the implementation of the transitional justice agenda and with development partners and international non-governmental organisations (NGOs) that could assist in mobilising resources for KTJN activities. Some of the notable partnerships, which will be discussed below, include the Kenya National Commission on Human Rights (KNCHR), the Office of the High Commissioner for Human Rights (OHCHR) and the German Federal Enterprise for International Cooperation (GiZ).

KTJN was designed to harness the shared purposes typically found in networks formed by NGOs to the benefit of Kenya's transitional justice agenda. These shared purposes include information and learning exchange; coordination of policies, programmes or other activities; obtaining common funding for joint endeavours or the furtherance of the mission; creating new social value; and strengthening members' common identities and interests in the long term (Ashman et al. 2005). The next sections interrogate the extent to which KTJN managed to achieve these objectives, and specifically by engaging with the TJRC process.

How Did the KTJN Agenda Roll Out?

KTJN largely programmed around the implementation matrix contained in the Statement of Principles on Agenda 4 as part of the KNDR agreements. The objective was to harness the opportunity presented by what was essentially a transitional justice policy and programmatic framework that was binding to the grand coalition government. It should be noted that Agenda 4 has been criticised as lacking sufficient coherence as a transitional justice policy due to an emphasis on political reforms and limited guidance on the accountability component (Musila 2009). Nevertheless, KTJN derived the following key issues from the Agenda 4 matrix: constitutional reform (encompassing what the network termed "administrative change" and other institutional reforms), truth-telling through the TJRC process and criminal justice as based on CIPEV's findings and recommendations.

Additionally, the issues in the KTJN framework were informed by previous analyses and documentation (studies, reports, dossiers) carried out by various organisations in the network. Notable examples include an AfriCOG report that interrogated Kenya's past experiences with commissions of inquiry and whether they are useful tools in seeking truth (AfriCOG 2008) and a KHRC report that looked into past state inquiries and compiled a list of individuals to be investigated for gross human rights violations as well as grand corruption and economic crimes (KHRC 2011a). The involvement of a broad cross section of organisations significantly influenced the definition of the transitional justice agenda, including the specific terms used to identify various themes.

The final influence on the KTJN agenda was from external partners and experts who offered insights from experiences in their jurisdictions and on the applicability of international normative frameworks. The International Center for Transitional Justice (ICTJ) provided information on the experiences of countries such as South Africa, Liberia and Sierra Leone, where they had offered technical assistance to truth commissions. The Centre for the Study of Violence and Reconciliation (CSVR) from South Africa and the Office of the High Commissioner on Human Rights (OHCHR) through the Senior Human Rights Advisor based in Nairobi were instrumental in facilitating capacity enhancement forums on transitional justice for KTJN stakeholders. The KTJN agenda was ultimately encapsulated in a toolkit for training and engagement with transitional justice in Kenya that was prepared by some of its members (KHRC et al. 2010).

The component on criminal justice was subject to receding political will amid a polarised political environment. While accountability was identified as a key pillar in the KNDR, the political elite who had been identified as responsible for the PEV were wary of any process that might lead to their indictment (Musila 2009). This resulted in two failed attempts to establish the Special Tribunal in 2009, as the president and prime minister failed to achieve the two-thirds threshold in parliament to pass the required law ("Kenyan MPs Reject Violence Court" 2009).

With regard to the ICC cases, these were terminated amid accusations of non-cooperation against the Kenyan Government by the ICC prosecutor, as well as allegations of interfering with witnesses that led to two ICC warrants of arrest being issued with respect to persons deemed responsible for influencing witnesses (Maliti 2015a). The Kenyan Government repeatedly challenged the admissibility of the ICC cases and engaged in diplomacy aimed at having the cases either deferred or terminated (Hansen 2011). As of September 19, 2016, the ICC had referred Kenya to the Assembly of State Parties to the Rome Statute on account of its non-cooperation (ICC 2016). Throughout all this, KTJN pursued its agenda on criminal justice through interventions characterised as complementary rather than mainstream, as they were undertaken by some KTJN members who were simultaneously members of an independent ICC Working Group established by KPTJ. These organisations were essentially holding the brief for KTJN on this matter and included AfriCOG, COVAW, ICJ-K and KHRC. This was informed by the need to maximise on available resources and to avoid duplication. This chapter cannot offer a detailed account of the initiatives undertaken by these organisations with respect to criminal justice but will rather provide illustrative examples of work done thus far.

KTJN undertook field-based research to ascertain the status of PEV victims and their perspectives on justice (ICJ-K and KHRC 2012), as well as research on prevailing proposals regarding criminal justice in Kenya and other country experiences with a view to prescribing a framework for Kenya's Special Tribunal (KHRC and KPTJ 2013). With the entry of the ICC, organisations such as the KHRC embarked on disseminating information about the court to the public in the face of numerous distortions by the political elites (FIDH and KHRC 2008).

Some KTJN members found themselves taking up the role of diplomacy on international platforms to rebut attempts by the Kenyan Government to have the cases deferred or terminated. The government's request in 2013 to have the ICC cases deferred under Chapter VII of the UN Charter saw AfriCOG, COVAW, ICJ-K and KHRC issue a memorandum to the UN Security Council ("Why the UN Security Should Reject the Application for a Deferral" 2013). KTJN members regularly attended ASP sessions and provided counternarratives to the government's representations on the state of the country and its characterisation of the ICC cases as a threat to peace and security. At the 2015 ASP after the termination of Uhuru Kenyatta's case members circulated a brief outlining what they referred to as a formula for impunity to frustrate the ICC cases (KPTJ 2014).

Finally, various KTJN members came together to bring civil cases at the domestic level aimed at realising the objective of reparations for victims and compelling the state to commence investigations and prosecutions related to the PEV. For example, FIDA-K, KHRC and ICJ-K filed a case along with 25 other petitioners on behalf of internally displaced persons (IDPs) affected by electoral violence in

1992–2008. The case seeks to compel the state to provide reparations in addition to prosecuting those deemed responsible (FIDA-K and others v. A.G. and others, HC Petition 273 of 2011). Another case, filed by COVAW, IMLU, ICJ-K and Physicians for Human Rights (PHR) along with eight other petitioners, focuses on victims of sexual and gender-based violence (SGBV) during the PEV and seeks to compel the state to provide reparations and prosecute these crimes (COVAW and others v. A.G. and others, HC Petition 122 of 2013). Both cases were ongoing at the time of writing.

Institutional reforms targeting the judiciary, police service and land sector were also translated into a complementary agenda, where KTJN deferred to specialised networks such as the National Council on the Administration of Justice (NCAJ), the Police Reforms Working Group (PRWG) and the Land Non-State Actors (LNSA). KTJN members within these networks would revert to KTJN with updates so as to provide a holistic understanding on the status of state compliance with Agenda 4.

On this basis, KTJN's approach to criminal justice and institutional reform largely became one of an information network that harnessed experiences from the interventions of its respective members in different platforms. A significant output from this approach was a KTJN policy brief that assessed Kenya's challenges and options in realising criminal justice and institutional reform in the justice sector, along with truth-seeking processes (KTJN 2013a). It is engaging with the TJRC that crystallised as the focal substantive agenda for KTJN in terms of a programmatic agenda for all its members.

KTJN's Activities with Regard to the TJRC

Advocacy for the Establishment of the TJRC

In its origins as MSTF, the network was at the heart of the legislative process that established the TJRC. MSTF identified critical standards for establishing the TJRC, including in-built mechanisms to shield the TJRC from political manipulation; a clearly defined mandate with links to judicial and other accountability processes; in-built mechanisms to support survivors and provide witness protection in line with international standards; clarity on the provision of amnesty with an explicit undertaking that it would not apply to international crimes; a definitive timeline within which the commission would be required to undertake its work; a clearly outlined structure for the commission, including the qualities expected of prospective commissioners and modalities for its financing and the safeguarding of its independence; and an outline of the implementation phase once the commission completed its work (MSTF 2008a).

MSTF embarked on a robust advocacy campaign for the enactment of TJRC legislation. This entailed convening dialogue forums as stakeholders and with victim groups while also mounting a media campaign to put pressure on the principles of the coalition government. When the Truth Justice and Reconciliation (TJR) Bill was finally tabled, MSTF spearheaded civil society efforts to critique the proposed legislation and recommend amendments. MSTF convened two public dialogues in April 2008 and prepared a memorandum to parliament and a civil society draft of the TJR Bill highlighting its proposed amendments (Omondi 2008). MSTF succeeded in obtaining a raft of amendments to the TJR Bill, the most notable being the insertion of a preamble contextualising the legislation and a narrowing of the application of amnesty provisions (Mue 2008). The TJR Act became operational on March 17, 2009, and the TJRC commissioners were appointed on July 22, 2009.

Friend or Foe? KTJN and the Controversy of the TJRC Chairperson

With the TJRC in place, MSTF transitioned into KTJN and shifted its focus to supporting the operationalisation of the commission and mobilising victim groups and the wider public to engage with the process. KHRC, KLA and FIDA-K undertook a joint monitoring, training, documentation and advocacy project aimed at aiding the TJRC process (KHRC 2011b). The project trained over 800 monitors in July–October 2009, with 100 engaged in January–December 2010 to strengthen the documentation and research element of strategically engaging the emerging transitional justice process under KNDR, such as the TJRC (KHRC 2011b). The monitors were to encourage communities and victim groups to engage with the TJRC and other processes, as well as document the violations they suffered for presentation to the TJRC. CRECO (2012) similarly monitored TJRC hearings across the country.

In addition, KTJN mobilised victims and survivors of gross violations as a movement to engage directly with Kenya's transitional justice processes and shape their outcomes. This was enshrined in the establishment of the National Victims and Survivors Network (NVSN). The idea of NVSN stemmed from a 2008 national convention for survivors of historical injustices convened by MSTF and KNCHR to discuss the prospects for transitional justice under KNDR (MSTF 2008b). A subsequent convention in October 2009 saw NVSN officially established, with a mandate to create a forum for victims to share ideas, information and strategies and to provide collective support for a victim-centred and rights-based TJRC (KTJN 2009b).

While the aforementioned arrangements demonstrated a clear willingness to engage with the TJRC, the commencement of TJRC operations would compel KTJN to reconsider its position while also calling into question the degree of its common purpose, cohesion and decision-making structures. At the inception of the TJRC's work, concerns were raised as to the suitability of its chairperson, Ambassador Bethuel Kiplagat. Ambassador Kiplagat faced allegations pertaining to his previous employment in President Moi's government, which his detractors asserted would present a direct conflict of interest in as far as the commission's mandate was concerned (TJRC 2013).

Amid fears that the controversy would derail the commission, there were immediate calls for the chairperson to resign in the interest of the truth-telling process. This debate proved contentious within KTJN for various reasons. First off, FIDA-K and KNCHR were civil society representatives on the commissioner selection panel

(TJRC 2013). Despite this, there was a strong contingent within KTJN working group that strongly advocated for Ambassador Kiplagat's removal. Working group members such as KHRC, ICPC and ICJ-K began by individually and then collectively under the KTJN banner calling for Ambassador Kiplagat's resignation or, in the alternative, the network's disengagement with the TJRC. This position was far from unanimous, as some members maintained contact with the TJRC and even appeared to intercede on Ambassador Kiplagat's behalf. FIDA-K, for example, was caught in the crossfire within the network when they sought to invite KTJN to a consultation with the TJRC on behalf of the TJRC secretariat, which was extending an olive branch to civil society (personal communications, August 2010). Ambassador Kiplagat refused to step down and caused gridlock in the TJRC's operations which exposed frailties within KTJN.

In what was perceived as a bid to shore up support in the face of mounting hostility from civil society and the public, the TJRC in August 2010 recruited a number of victims to be part of a team of 304 statement takers. Among these victims were members of NVSN who had been trained and referred to the TJRC by some KTJN members earlier in the process. This presented yet another challenge for KTJN, as the TJRC utilised NVSN staff members in press engagements to defend the commission (personal communication, KTJN working group member, August 2010). This tactic created schisms between KTJN and the victim groups that ascribed to it. KTJN was aware that some victim groups in areas such as the Rift Valley were engaging with the TJRC, which by this time had begun its public hearings (KTJN 2010). Additionally, women's groups resolved to continue working with the TJRC, asserting that the public hearings provided them with a platform to address women's marginalisation that they could not pass up (KTJN 2010a).

Acknowledging that insufficient consultations had occurred before members took positions regarding the TJRC, KTJN convened a National Dialogue Forum on the TJRC and Other Options for Justice in Kenya in September 2010 to discuss alternative approaches to justice for victims and to deliberate on how to forge a common path. The forum allowed members to ventilate their concerns, but in the end there was no consensus. The forum instead yielded the following communique:

> While acknowledging the democratic right of some victims to engage with the process, we the Kenya Transitional Justice Network, totally disengage with the TJRC until the credibility crisis has been resolved, we commit ourselves to pursue other options of truth, justice and reparations, including using the newly created constitutional and Agenda 4 organs on historical injustices such as The National Land Commission, the National Human Rights and Equality Commission, Kenya Anti-Corruption and Integrity Commission, and the revamped Judiciary. (Ndivo and Ndunge 2010, Appendix IV)

By the close of 2010, KTJN had divided into two groupings. The first was a core group of "radicals" who felt that the TJRC was a fatally flawed process that could not achieve justice and therefore should not be sanitised through the involvement of civil society and victim groups. This was the position held by most working group members and some victim groups particularly aggrieved by Ambassador Kiplagat's presence, such as the victims of the Wagalla massacre (personal communication, KTJN working group member, March 2015). They pursued a public campaign and a litigation strategy to suspend TJRC activities until Ambassador Kiplagat stepped down. The second was a group of "pragmatists" consisting of victims and organisations that felt that, despite the controversy, it would be essential to engage as the process seemed to be carrying on regardless. They asserted that it was essential to support the victim groups that had decided to engage with the commission and ensure that the substantive public investment did not go to waste. The only remaining point of convergence was that the TJRC process would have to be monitored and so organisations undertook this task as individual entities.

The controversy would have far-reaching ramifications for the TJRC. The vice-chairperson of the commission, Betty Murungi, stepped down on principle. The Ministry of Justice at the height of the crisis considered disbanding the commission ("Kilonzo Tells TJRC Team" 2010). Donors stepped back from supporting the TJRC, which led to considerable strain on the commission's operations (Orengo 2010). The TJRC in its final report singled out KTJN for calling on funders not to support the commission and for KTJN's strategy of engaging the commission in as many legal battles as possible within its broader disengagement and decimation policy (TJRC 2013).

In a bid to resolve the crisis, the TJRC commissioners broke ranks with Ambassador Kiplagat and called for the establishment of a tribunal to investigate the conflict of interest issues. While the tribunal would be established in October 2009, a series of operational and legal challenges meant that its 6-month timeline would lapse without it ever considering the issues it was meant to address. KHRC and ICPC in this period submitted a memorandum to the tribunal calling for Ambassador Kiplagat's ouster (KHRC et al. 2011). The process dragged on for 2 years but had the benefit of getting Ambassador Kiplagat to step aside for that period. This restored public confidence and caused the return of some level of civil society and donor support. The Commission was able again to embark on public hearings around the country. Ambassador Kiplagat however returned to the commission unceremoniously on January 4, 2012, and reopened the controversy.

To safeguard the gains they had made in his absence, the remaining commissioners filed a case at the High Court seeking a prohibition order against Ambassador Kiplagat until the issues surrounding his conflicts of interest were resolved. At this point the TJRC began making overtures to the KTJN "radicals", requesting that they support the legal action and the remainder of the TJRC's operations. KTJN was assuaged by the argument that in Ambassador Kiplagat's absence the TJRC managed to complete most of its work and that, given the immense public investment and that of victims, it would be a shame to allow the process to be derailed at that point. Furthermore, the legal action suggested that there was a sufficient constituency of "progressives" within the commission that was worth engaging.

The litigation attempt did not succeed and Ambassador Kiplagat returned to the commission, albeit with restrictions on his access to information and the development of the commission's final report with regard to the areas deemed to raise a conflict of interest. These areas included political assassinations, massacres and land grabbing. After an almost 3-year lull, the KTJN working group effectively ended its disengagement policy with the TJRC.

KTJN as Technical Experts Advising the TJRC Report Writing Process

By early 2012 it was clear that the TJRC was on course with preparing its final report, albeit with significant challenges on account of its controversial tenure. Having isolated Ambassador Kiplagat from the development of the report to a large extent, the TJRC approached KTJN for technical assistance with the report. KTJN members who had disengaged considered this an opportunity to salvage a flawed process and restore the prospect of recommendations that would be responsive to victims' needs (personal communication, KTJN working group member, March 2015). There were concerns that due to the lack of resources during the crisis, the quality of the statements collected enjoyed limited public confidence (Malombe 2012).

KTJN provided the TJRC with institutional reports and the data associated with them as an aid to populating some of the thematic sections of the report and supplementing the public statements it had gathered, as well as developing position papers on an implementation plan, an implementation mechanism, amnesty and a reparations policy. A stand-out success of this collaboration was the incorporation almost in its entirety of KTJN's proposed reparations policy in the final TJRC report. KTJN's proposal on reparations was spearheaded by ICJ-K, which harnessed institutional experiences in litigating for redress as well as victim perspectives that had been obtained through the NVSN conventions and field-based research (ICJ-K and KHRC 2012; ICTJ 2011).

KTJN as Advocates for the Implementation of the TJRC Report

After seeking two extensions and facing some level of political intrigue with regard to the submission of its report, the TJRC was finally able to present its final report to President Kenyatta. This shifted the focus to findings and recommendations and, more important, the prospects for their implementation, which faced the following challenges: (1) the timelines for publication of the report and tabling it before parliament as required by law were not strictly adhered to and this significantly delayed the implementation process; (2) with the exception of an abridged version that was placed in local newspapers, the actual report was not made widely available as the government printer failed to produce copies as required (a situation that persists to this day); and (3) there was registered dissent from a section of the commissioners with respect to the "Land and Conflict" chapter that had been omitted from the final report. The dissent emerged from the fact that the final draft of the land chapter as approved by all commissioners was subjected to further edits that altered and omitted certain paragraphs before printing (Slye et al. 2013).

To address these unexplained deviations from procedure and law, KTJN immediately embarked on an advocacy campaign for the publication and wide dissemination of the report, in addition to consideration before parliament for implementation to commence. This was done through press statements and direct correspondence with the office of the attorney general, who was responsible for the inordinate delays. This led to the issuance a back-dated gazette notice that officially published the TJRC report. KTJN of its own accord published a simplified version of the report for wide dissemination in the absence of government action (KTJN 2013b).

KTJN also convened a National Convention to sensitise victims and survivors on the findings and recommendations of the report and to afford them an opportunity to develop their perspectives with regard to the responsiveness of the TJRC recommendations to their needs. With KTJN learning from the fallout from its disengagement policy, the implementation phase was purposed to have broad-based consultations from the very beginning. This conference yielded a communique that not only announced victims' aspirations for the implementation of the TJRC report but also informed KTJN's advocacy on the same (KTJN 2013c). The conference established a platform for implementation that emphasised the centrality of victims in the process and holistic reparations (that take due cognisance of tangible and intangible loss) as the required response to victims' needs (Sum 2013).

This was followed up with a series of county-based forums that served to disseminate the findings and recommendations of the TJRC report even further. In addition, KTJN invested in dialogue forums with various policy actors with a role to play in the implementation of the TJRC report. Such dialogues largely centred on the implementation framework in light of amendments to the TJR Act by the National Assembly and options for operationalising reparations within the recommendations. The absence of political will means limited progress has been made, as the report remains within the precincts of parliament awaiting its consideration before an implementation framework can be put in place. KTJN has nevertheless advanced engagements between parliament and victims by facilitating dialogue with various parliamentary organs such as the Justice and Legal Affairs Committee (JLAC) and the Kenya Parliamentary Human Rights Caucus (KEPHRA).

These forums have secured rhetorical commitments from legislators, including the submission of a petition by a legislator on behalf of NVSN ("Parliament to Debate the TJRC Report" 2016) to advance the implementation of the TJRC report. They have also maintained the centrality of the victims' voices in the debate (Kaberia 2016). A significant turning point occurred in March 2015 when the president in his State of the Nation Address urged parliament to consider the TJRC report without further delay and established a fund of 10 billion Kenyan shillings ($9.5 million) over 3 years to encourage measures he described as restorative justice to ameliorate the plight of victims (Maliti 2015b). The president went on to offer a blanket apology for all past wrongs on his behalf and that of his government and all past governments.

While the president's initiative reinvigorated the debate on historical injustices and redress for victims, its ambiguous nature has raised questions on how to reconcile it with the obligations of the TJRC report and in particular the aspect of reparations. KTJN has become the Department of Justice's partner in developing an implementation framework for the president's pledge and the related fund. This partnership has been in the form of a technical committee convened by the department and consisting of representation from various government departments, from KNCHR and from KTJN and NVSN, which were tasked with the mandate of developing regulations to guide the utilisation of the fund. As of August 2017, this collaboration had yielded a draft policy and set of regulations for consideration by the office of the Attorney General.

Reflecting on the KTJN Approach and the Lessons Learnt Thus Far

KTJN's Operations and the Cohesiveness of Its Agenda

An effective network is one that succeeds in achieving its goals, satisfies its members and musters the resources needed to continue its work (Ashman et al. 2005). This must serve as the benchmark for KTJN's future evaluations and purposeful recalibration where necessary. KTJN arguably excelled in providing a forum to shape public debate on the implementation of Agenda 4, influencing the formulation of related policy and developing engagement strategies on the basis of institutional and individual experiences in advancing redress for victims (personal communication, KTJN working group member, March 2015). Despite the numerous challenges encountered in the process, KTJN's work on the TJRC process attests to this.

The challenge lies in the fact that KTJN carved out for itself an ambitious and resource-intensive programme that proved unsustainable. The relegation of various thematic issues such as corruption, land and institutional reform to other networks meant that the nucleus that brought together a broad KTJN membership was lost. This has resulted in a dwindling membership focusing only on truth-telling, criminal justice and reparations. While this has made its interventions sharper and increased the prospects for impact, it has also meant that KTJN is no longer fully accountable to its original mission. In addition, KTJN has had limited opportunities for joint reflection on the extent to which its goals are being achieved, as it had only two reflection meetings in 2013 and 2015, organised by members working on the TJRC process. KTJN's reflection and planning must ascend from being activity oriented and invest more on informing strategy and ascertaining the impact of its interventions.

While at its inception KTJN had ambitions of being a formal institutional network guided by a memorandum of understanding, it remains a network of informal cooperation. KTJN has served as an information network that enables member organisations to learn from each other's approaches to addressing transitional justice issues. It has enabled coordination and joint interventions to avoid duplication while also enhancing utility of resources, and it has accentuated its members' collective influence on policy. Rather than adhering strictly to the executive committee structure proposed at its start, the network has embraced a less rigid structure, inviting various organisations to offer leadership and secretariat duties at various junctures in accordance with their competencies and resources.

At the inception of KTJN, for example, KHRC and ICPC were instrumental in convening dialogue forums, reaching out to victims and developing the objectives of KTJN. Upon reengaging with the TJRC, the Kenya office of ICTJ became an active member of KTJN and provided leadership on interventions regarding reparations and implementation of the TJRC report. This approach, which allows for rotational and opportunistic leadership, has enabled KTJN to be agile and responsive to emerging developments where it would otherwise have been static and encumbered by bureaucracy.

A key challenge presented by this fluid governance structure has been the absence of clearly defined conflict resolution mechanisms. As demonstrated by the dynamics around the TJRC, KTJN has relied largely on conflict avoidance, or employed ad hoc measures such as clear-the-air meetings to resolve disputes. It has been the practice to try and accommodate all perspectives to the extent of undermining cohesiveness by allowing members to act alone or take positions contrary to those of the network. This however should not be construed as constricting opportunities for dissent or autonomous institutional positions; it emphasises the fact that value systems and decisions should reflect the broadest consensus of KTJN's membership if the vision is to be truly realised.

KTJN must work towards a more deliberate governance structure that strikes a balance between guarding against excessive bureaucracy and allowing for inclusive processes in joint decision-making, tracking documentation on the implementation of such decisions and defining clear conflict resolution mechanisms. This can be achieved by revisiting the development of a memorandum of understanding that reflects the vision, values and operational principles of the network. While the notion of rotational leadership and secretariat responsibilities is one that should be embraced, it must be formally ratified rather than assumed, as this will enhance the level of accountability for critical network governance responsibilities such as reflection, refocusing strategy and documentation with a view to ascertaining impact.

KTJN's Engagement with Victims

From the outset, KTJN recognised the centrality of victims in Kenya's transitional justice agenda as being paramount to any prospects for its success. KTJN has sought to promote the involvement of victims in the most expansive way possible: as individual members, through self-initiated victim groups and through the CSOs that have engaged with victims (personal communication, KTJN and NVSN member, March 2015). KTJN nurtured the development of NVSN by investing in dialogue forums as well as enhancing victims' capacities to engage with Kenya's transitional justice agenda, including their membership in KTJN and its advocacy initiatives. Indeed, one of KTJN's strongest achievements has been to evolve NVSN from a pressure group to one that is now considered an active stakeholder in policy formulation processes, for example contributing to the framework of the restorative justice fund.

The principle of open participation has not translated into effective participation in all cases. The decision-making process in the network has not always been inclusive, particularly for victims, as the divisions concerning the TJRC disengagement policy revealed. With annual national conventions being the primary medium for broad-based consultation with victims, victims' input on rapid policy changes tends to be overlooked or presumed. As institutions assume the mantle of leadership on the basis of marshalling resources to move the agenda forward, NVSN tends to find itself marginalised on the basis of not being able to mobilise financial resources. Victim-led initiatives receive minimal support on the basis of being aligned with the programmatic priorities of individual organisations in KTJN that have some activity-based resources.

Facilitating a designated NVSN coordinator, for example, and holding regular meetings that allow victims to reflect on, formulate and communicate positions to the public have been immense challenges. Yet, when this has been achieved, it has had a profound effect on policy actors, as the petitions on the implementation of the TJRC report revealed. Additionally, KTJN has been unable to respond directly to some of the immediate priorities for victims, such as medical and psychosocial support (personal communication, KTJN and NVSN member, March 2015). Despite spearheading the development of NVSN, KTJN has not managed to develop a sustainability strategy for its operations. The end result has been one of victim participation based largely on dependency rather than empowerment (personal communication, KTJN and NVSN member, March 2015).

Strengthening KTJN means strengthening NVSN as an authoritative and credible platform for victims' voices. There must be conscious efforts to enable NVSN extend its outreach, communication and advocacy capacities. This should be done by established member organisations offering mentorship and practical institutional support to the NVSN coordinator, as well as availing funds and fundraising opportunities with donors for NVSN activities. Furthermore, KTJN must within its governance structures accord due recognition to NVSN in leadership and decision-making in a manner that abolishes any notion of linking leadership in the network with financial capabilities. KTJN should also enhance the governance structures of NVSN by encouraging diversity in its leadership, an articulation of key principles and modalities for democratised leadership.

KTJN's Approach to Gender Justice

KTJN sought to approach the issue of gender in Kenya's transitional justice process as both a cross-cutting theme and a specific focus area by including gender-focused organisations within its membership (personal communication, KTJN working group member, April, 2015). The network's executive committee initially included three gender-focused organisations, namely COVAW, CREAW and FIDA-K, with the expectation that they would spearhead the incorporation of a gendered approach. In addition, KHRC, FIDA-K and KLA designed a joint training programme for grassroots activists to foster the documentation of historical and contemporary injustices in a manner reflective of the cross-cutting approach. This initiative was frustrated by KTJN's disengagement policy (KHRC 2011b). By the time of reengagement with the TJRC, only COVAW effectively rejoined KTJN in relation to the implementation of the commission's report.

Despite these challenges, KTJN's late reengagement saw it provide significant technical input on the gender-centred chapters of the TJRC report. More importantly, KTJN's reparations policy draft embraced the cross-cutting and specific theme approach, including broad-based gender equity principles on consultation and participation, while also highlighting the specific needs of women as victims and as beneficiaries of a reparations programme. As noted above, this draft greatly influenced the reparations framework in the TJRC report.

Outside the TJRC process, COVAW, ICJ-K and PHR, a recent member of KTJN, have advanced the cause of reparations for SGBV victims through the constitutional petition referenced above. Their collaboration in this case has accentuated the voices of SGBV survivors in public and policy debates on reparations and expanded the membership of NVSN. Arguably, the focus on mainstream, national gender-focused organisations at the inception of KTJN deprived it of the opportunity to collaborate with smaller but equally impactful and victim-led organisations that would effectively advance the gender justice component.

In the ongoing initiative to advance the implementation of the TJRC report and operationalise the restorative justice fund, KTJN has benefited from the inclusion of organisations such as Grace Agenda Kenya and the Wangu Kanja Foundation, both founded by victims of sexual violence and working with other victims at the community level. There is a need for KTJN not only to continue the expansion of its membership to include other gender-focused organisations but also to reflect on the degree to which it has managed to mainstream gender justice in light of previous challenges with a view to developing more concerted interventions going forward.

Resource Mobilisation and Its Effect on the Scope and Nature of KTJN Activities

KTJN's broad-based agenda presupposed the ability to marshal the necessary resources to match its ambition. Initially, funding was on the basis of the resources that individual organisations could channel towards the common agenda. The potential for KTJN members to fundraise jointly for its agenda is an area that has not been fully explored. A multi-year proposal for KTJN activities in 2012 developed with operational support from PACT Kenya stands as the only such effort (personal communication, KTJN working group member, March 2015). Furthermore, KTJN's fluid governance structure and its TJRC disengagement policy were not assets for joint fundraising.

KTJN has however received support for various stages of its work based on a model of strategic collaborative partnership rather than traditional network donor funding. CSVR, UAF-A and OHCHR were instrumental in supporting the formative stages of KTJN. They informed the formulation of KTJN's agenda through technical support and availed resources for dialogue forums and KTJN publications. GiZ similarly provided instrumental support to KTJN, but only after a cessation of the disengagement policy with the TJRC. KTJN thus received both technical and financial support for developing the reparations policy, publishing simplified versions of the TJRC report and organising dialogue forums to disseminate the findings and recommendations of the TJRC.

It is a recognised trend that governance programmes that support transitional justice, such as GiZ's programme, have reduced in number and stature. Sections of civil society have attributed this trend to diminishing donor interest in transitional justice and a shift towards other themes, such as counterterrorism (LSE Security 2014). In response to this, KTJN members have committed to mainstream the network's activities within their own budgets. This calls for more joint reflection and planning processes that can inform the programming and fundraising efforts of each member. A failure to adopt this approach risks diluting the prospects of consistency and continuity of the network should the organisations not secure enough funds.

Conclusion

Kenya's transitional justice agenda remains an ongoing concern. Criminal accountability is in a state of abeyance courtesy of the termination of the Kenya cases at the ICC and the absence of prosecutions at the national level. The ambitions of institutional reform as well as the implementation of the constitution have not been fully actualised. The TJRC process yielded a report that is yet to be adopted by the legislature, and victims continue to await reparations. Despite all this, significant strides have been made and milestones have been met that call for reflection, particularly the role of civil society in this regard. This chapter has argued that Kenya's transitional justice agenda was derived from the unresolved legacies of colonialism and the clamour for multiparty democracy and constitutional reform which culminated in the PEV. The series of false starts and missed opportunities in this period informed the KNDR, which outlined the transitional justice agenda.

Within this historical context, civil society has evolved in the way it interacts with the state, including as development partners, agents of democracy and advocates for transitional justice. Civil society has played a pivotal role not only in shaping the KNDR and the eventual transitional justice agenda, but also in their implementation and in seeking accountability for the actions of state actors. The political context in Kenya is one of ambivalence and receding political will on transitional justice. Civil society has therefore played the role of vanguard, seeking to sustain the impetus for implementation of the transitional justice agenda and accentuating the voices of victims within public and policy debates.

These experiences have provided insight into the strengths and weaknesses of civil society and in particular their networking component. This chapter has ventured into this conversation through outlining the experience of KTJN thus far as one such civil society network. While it cannot be considered to be a holistic account of KTJN's experience, this chapter hopefully serves as an initial attempt to encourage further introspection on its successes and challenges.

KTJN's experience demonstrates that a loosely defined governance structure can amplify fault lines in the approaches or ideologies of a network's membership, which makes consensus difficult. The experience with KTJN's decision to disengage with the TJRC is particularly instructive. Closely associated with this is the absence of requisite mechanisms to address the power relations within networks and ensure that there is downward accountability. The fallout from the TJRC disengagement policy points to the need for considerable reflection on the internal transparency of networks in terms of sharing information, participation of victims in decision-making and platforms for feedback and lodging of complaints.

Civil society networks must therefore endeavour to establish governance structures that are inclusive, facilitate joint decision-making, enable coordination of activities, include mechanisms for conflict resolution and provide avenues for reflection and course correction. KTJN's current system of rotating leadership and secretariat duties among its members is an appealing model, although it needs to be codified in a memorandum of understanding and ratified by the membership. Regular meetings, consultations, well-defined action plans and opportunities to reflect on impact are key pillars of this approach. Equally essential is empowering victims towards self-representation and self-articulation of needs in transitional justice processes. KTJN's work with NVSN has been highly productive and shrunk the spaces between victims and policy actors, but this requires a more purposeful and sustained form of investment that strengthens its operations and reduces elements of dependency.

Resource mobilisation is another critical factor for networks seeking to influence transitional justice agendas. In KTJN's experience, employing a model of strategic collaborative partnership has been the preferred option. In seeking out relationships that avail funds and some level of technical assistance, networks benefit from insights from external experiences while establishing a donor relationship based on actual buy-in to the vision rather than an abstract interaction with a project cycle. The longevity of transitional justice processes and long-term outcomes however mean that donor fatigue is a common feature. Members of civil society networks must therefore endeavour to mainstream the operations of the network in their operational plans as a way of ensuring its sustainability, rather than relying only on joint funding.

A key challenge for civil society in Kenya has remained the breadth of the country's transitional justice agenda, which was driven by the motivation to complete a stalled process of democratisation. While civil society was instrumental in shaping this agenda, it quickly became apparent that following through by engaging in monitoring and implementation processes was going to be a Herculean task. In KTJN's experience, it is more appropriate to carve out specific areas of intervention and acknowledge that one will operate within a wider galaxy of specialised organisations that can work on the areas not within the scope of your network. The objective should be to achieve synergy with others and work towards the common purpose of holding the state accountable for the agenda as a whole. This approach helps avoid duplication of efforts, maximise utility of resources and reduce the chances of burnout institutionally.

Kenya's transitional justice process is far from over. As advocates, authors and implementers of transitional justice processes, civil society must stay engaged. Networks such as KTJN remain critical to informing the current phase of implementation and ensuring that the processes meet the intended outcomes of justice, national healing and reconciliation. As civil society continues to play the role of vanguard, it must equally subject itself to transparent reflections on its strategies and their impact. As it was with its formulation, the successful implementation of Kenya's transitional justice agenda is to a large extent dependent on a robust and responsive civil society. It is my hope that the reflections within this chapter will serve to advance and strengthen this cause.

References

Admin. (2016, January 19). Parliament to debate the TJRC report after petition from victims is tabled. *Journalists for Justice*. Retrieved from http://www.jfjustice.net/kenya.

African Centre for Open Governance (AfriCOG). (2008). *Postponing the truth: How commissions of inquiry are used to circumvent justice in Kenya.*

African Union Commission. Coordination and Liaison Office of the Panel of Eminent African Personalities. (2014). *Back from the brink: The 2008 mediation process and reforms in Kenya.*

Ashman, D., Charles, C., Cuenca, A. M., Luca, C., Singer, B., & Schmith, M. (2005). *Supporting civil society networks in international development programs* (1st ed.). Washington, DC.

Bodewes, C. (2013). *Civil society in Africa: The role of a Catholic Parish in a Kenyan slum.* Newcastle upon Tyne: Cambridge Scholars Publishing.

Bosire, L. K., & Lynch, G. (2014). Kenya's search for truth and justice: The role of civil society. *International Journal of Transitional Justice, 8*(2), 256–276.

Commission of Inquiry into the Post-Election Violence (CIPEV). (2008). *Report of the commission of inquiry into the post-election violence*. Nairobi: Government Printer.

Constitution and Reform Education Consortium (CRECO). (2012). *The quest for an elusive justice: A report on observation of the truth, justice and reconciliation commission of Kenya (TJRC-K).*

Gathii, J.T. (2010). *Kenya's long anti-corruption agenda—1952–2010: Prospects and challenges of the ethics and anti-corruption commission under the 2010 constitution.* Albany Law School Research Paper No. 35.

Government of Kenya. Ministry of State for Special Programmes. (2012). *Progress on resettlement of internally displaced persons as at 6th January, 2012.*

Hansen, T. O. (2011). Transitional justice in Kenya? An assessment of the accountability process in light of domestic politics and security concerns. *California Western International Law Journal, 42*(1), 1–35.

Hansen, T. O. (2013). Kenya's power-sharing arrangement and its implications for transitional justice. *The International Journal of Human Rights, 17*(2), 307–327.

Hansen, T. O., & Sriram, C. L. (2015). Fighting for justice (and survival): Kenyan civil society accountability strategies and their enemies. *International Journal of Transitional Justice, 9*(3), 407–427.

Independent Review Commission. (2008). *Report of the independent review commission on the general elections held in Kenya on 27 December 2007.* Nairobi: Government Printer.

International Center for Transitional Justice. (2011). *"To live as other Kenyans do": A study of the reparative demands of Kenyan victims of human rights violations*. Nairobi.

International Commission of Jurists-Kenya and Kenya Human Rights Commission. (2012). *Elusive justice: A status report on victims of 2007–2008 post election violence in Kenya.*

International Criminal Court. (2016). *Second decision on Prosecution's application for a finding of non-compliance under Article 87(7) of the Statute.*

International Federation for Human Rights and Kenya Human Rights Commission. (2008). *Kenya and International Criminal Court: Questions and answers.*

Kaberia, J. (2016, February 11). MPs pledge to adopt TJRC report by March, but fear resistance. *Capital News.*

Kanyinga, K. (2011). Stopping a conflagration: The response of Kenyan civil society to the post-2007 election violence. *Politikon, 38*(1), 85–109.

Kenya Human Rights Commission. (2011a). *Lest we forget: The faces of impunity in Kenya.*
Kenya Human Rights Commission. (2011b). *Justice delayed: A status report in historical injustices in Kenya.*
Kenya Human Rights Commission. (2013, June 21). *The Mau Mau settlement: Setting the record straight.* Press release.
Kenya Human Rights Commission and Kenyans for Peace, Truth and Justice. (2013). *Securing justice: Establishing a domestic mechanism for the 2007/8 post-election violence in Kenya.*
Kenya Human Rights Commission, International Center for Policy and Conflict and International Center for Transitional Justice. (2011). *Memoranda to the Tribunal appointed to investigate the conduct of the Chair of the TJRC under the TJRC Act Number 6 of 2008.* Unpublished internal document.
Kenya Human Rights Commission, International Commission of Jurists-Kenya and International Center for Policy and Conflict. (2010). *Transitional justice in Kenya: A toolkit for training and engagement.*
Kenya Transitional Justice Network. (2009a). *Structure and strategy framework for the Kenya transitional justice network.* Unpublished internal document.
Kenya Transitional Justice Network. (2009b). *Report of the 2nd victims' convention held at Kasarani Sports View Hotel from 4th–6th October, 2009.* Unpublished internal document.
Kenya Transitional Justice Network. (2010). *Consultative and briefing meeting on the TJRC crisis held at KHRC on 19th July 2010.* Unpublished internal document.
Kenya Transitional Justice Network. (2013a). *Transitional justice approaches: In the context of the implementation of agenda item number 4.*
Kenya Transitional Justice Network. (2013b). *Summary of the Truth, Justice and Reconciliation Commission report.*
Kenya Transitional Justice Network. (2013c). *In defence of truth and justice: Victim and survivor perspectives on the implementation of the TJRC report.* Unpublished document.
Kenyan MPs reject violence court. (2009, February 12). *BBC News Africa.* Retrieved from http://news.bbc.co.uk/2/hi/africa/7886395.stm
Kenyans for Peace, Truth and Justice. (2014). *Kenya's 7-step formula for impunity.*
Kilonzo tells TJRC team to quit. (2010, April 19). *Daily Nation.* Retrieved from http://www.nation.co.ke/news/Kilonzo-tells-TJRC-team-to-quit/-/1056/902226/-/view/printVersion/-/m8ml2o/-/index.html.
Lasseko, M. (2009). Role of civil society in transitional justice process: The evolving Kenyan experience. In W. Kaguongo & G. M. Musila (Eds.), *Judiciary watch report, vol. VIII, 2009.* Nairobi: The Kenyan Section of the International Commission of Jurists.
LSE Security. (2014). *Civil society dialogue on transitional justice in East Africa and the Balkans: Report on a conference convened by LSE security in transition at the British Institute in East Africa, Nairobi, funded by MacArthur Foundation and the European Research Council.*
Maliti, T. (2015a). *Who are the witnesses in the second Kenya bribery case at the ICC?—Part 1.*
Maliti, T. (2015b). *Kenyan president and chief justice apologize for past injustices.*
Malombe, D. (2012). The politics of truth commissions in Africa: A case study of Kenya. In M. Okello, C. Dolan, U. Whande, N. Mncwabe, L. Onegi, & S. Oola (Eds.), *Where law meets reality: Forging African transitional justice.* Cape Town: Pambazuka Press.
Merwe, H., & Brankovic, J. (2016). The role of African civil society in shaping national transitional justice agendas and policies. In: S. Williams, H. Woolaver, & G. Bradfield (Eds.), *Acta Juridica.* Cape Town: Faculty of Law, University of Cape Town.
MSTF. (2008a). *Multi-sectoral task force on truth, justice and reconciliation commission 11th April 2008.* Unpublished internal document. MSTF.
MSTF. (2008b). *Victims/Survivors convention on transitional justice 16-17th October 2008.* Unpublished internal document.
Mue, N. (2008). *Report on engagement with the parliamentary committee on legal affairs and the administration of justice on the TJRC bill.* Unpublished internal document. MSTF.
Musila, G. M. (2009). Options for transitional justice in Kenya: Autonomy and the challenge of external prescriptions. *International Journal of Transitional Justice, 3*(3), 445–464.

Musila, G.M. (2010). *Learning on the job? The 2007–2008 crisis and role of the African Union in transitional justice in Kenya.*

Mutua, M. (2001). Justice under siege: The rule of law and judicial subservience in Kenya. *Human Rights Quarterly, 23*(1), 96–118.

Mutua, M. (2013). Why Kenya is a nation in embryo. In S. Wakhungu-Githuku (Ed.), *50 years since independence: Where is Kenya?* (pp. 238–245). Nairobi: Footprints Press.

Ndivo, L., & Ndunge, P. (2010). *Report of the national dialogue forum on the truth, justice and reconciliation: A failed promise*? Unpublished internal Kenya Transitional Justice Network document.

Ngunyi, M. (2008). *Consultant's report in civil society in the post-amendment context: Prepared for the royal Norwegian embassy, Nairobi, Kenya.*

Omondi, R.A. (2008). *Multi-sectoral task force on truth, justice and reconciliation process: Review of truth justice and reconciliation bill.* Unpublished internal MSTF document.

Orengo, P. (2010, October 22). TJRC official quits as team goes broke. *Standard Digital.* Retrieved from http://www.standardmedia.co.ke/business/article/2000020812/tjrc-official-quits-as-team-goes-broke.

Slye, R.C., Dinka, B., & Chawatama, G. (2013). *Dissent: Statement by international commissioners.*

Sum, A. (2013, August 29). Human rights abuse victims want truth justice and reconciliation commission report made public. *Standard Digital.* Retrieved from http://www.standardmedia.co.ke/m/?articleID=2000092175&story_title=Human-rights-abuse-victims-want-TJRC-report-madepublic.

Task Force on the Establishment of a Truth, Justice and Reconciliation Commission. (2003). *Report of the task force on the establishment of a truth justice and reconciliation commission.* Nairobi: Government Printer.

Truth Justice and Reconciliation Commission (TJRC). (2013). *Report of the Truth, Justice and Reconciliation Commission.*

UN-OCHA Kenya. (2008). *Frequently asked questions on IDPs* [Fact sheet]. Retrieved from http://reliefweb.int/sites/reliefweb.int/files/resources/D925666D168061D64925753300256FA5-Full_Report.pdf.

Why the UN security should reject the application for a deferral of the Kenyan cases before the international criminal court: A memorandum from Kenyan civil society organizations. (2013).

Chapter 3
Transitional Justice in Liberia: The Interface Between Civil Society Organisations and the Liberian Truth and Reconciliation Commission

James Tonny Dhizaala

Introduction

Fourteen years of civil war left devastating consequences for the Liberian people. During the first Liberian civil war (1989–1997) and the second Liberian civil war (1999–2003) horrific human rights abuses were perpetrated with impunity against civilians by both government forces and rebel groups. These included widespread and systematic rape, assault, mutilation and torture, killing, numerous large-scale massacres, detention without trial, summary executions, extortion, destruction of property, forced labour and large-scale forced conscription and use of child combatants (TRC 2009: 169–195). At the height of the civil war, women fleeing the fighting were raped by government soldiers at checkpoints (Simmons 2003). Other atrocities ranged from the National Patriotic Front of Liberia's (NPFL) slaughter of 500 Mandingos in Lofa County (Ellis 2007: 79) and the Armed Forces of Liberia's (AFL) killing of 600 displaced persons mainly of Gio and Mano ethnicity at St. Peter's Lutheran Church in Monrovia (Pham 2004: 101), to NPFL rebels testing people's ability to speak the Gio or Mano dialects and putting those who failed to death on the spot (Outram 1997: 360). It was a bloody civil war in which by 1990 over 5,000 Liberians had been killed (Howe 1990) and over 500,000 had fled the country (Human Rights Watch 1990: 2). The war resulted in an influx of Liberian refugees to Ivory Coast, Guinea, Ghana, Sierra Leone and Nigeria. By 1995 as many as 700,000 of the 2.5 million Liberians were refugees in other West African states (Lowenkopf 1995: 94). A large number of these refugees made their way to the United States, Canada and various European countries.

J.T. Dhizaala (✉)
University of Sydney, Sydney, NSW, Australia
e-mail: jdhi2457@uni.sydney.edu.au

J. Brankovic, H. van der Merwe (eds.), *Advocating Transitional Justice in Africa*, Springer Series in Transitional Justice,
https://doi.org/10.1007/978-3-319-70417-3_3

After several previous peace negotiations failed to stop the war,[1] the warring parties signed the Comprehensive Peace Agreement (CPA) on August 18, 2003, in Accra, Ghana, brokered by the Economic Community of West African States (ECOWAS) with the support of civil society organisations (CSOs) and the international community. Signed between the government of Liberia and two leading rebel groups, Liberians United for Reconciliation and Democracy (LURD) and the Movement for Democracy in Liberia (MODEL), the CPA marked the beginning of Liberia's transition from war to peace. The transition commenced with the deployment of a United Nations Mission in Liberia (UNMIL) peacekeeping mission to monitor the ceasefire, restore order and create the political space for rebuilding state apparatuses and social fabric ruptured by years of civil war. The Liberian Truth and Reconciliation Commission (LTRC) was established by the National Transitional Legislative Assembly of Liberia (NTLA) of the National Transitional Government of Liberia (NTGL) in 2005. The LTRC is the only transitional justice process provided for by the CPA, despite demands by prominent CSO representatives for criminal prosecutions of alleged perpetrators, especially former warlords.

This chapter first sets the context for the interface between CSOs and the LTRC, discussing the nature of civil society engagement with conflict resolution and peacebuilding during the war, as well as CSO activities during the peace negotiations and in the NTGL and NTLA. It examines the working relationship between CSOs and the LTRC, including the drafting of the law that established the commission, the selection of commissioners, and the launch and operationalisation of the LTRC. It then discusses CSOs' role in the aftermath of the LTRC. The chapter is based on 4 years of research on the LTRC and its contribution to peace and reconciliation. It draws insights from my interviews with civil society representatives,[2] victims, witnesses and alleged perpetrators, and from two LTRC conferences I attended in the United States and Liberia between July 2009 and November 2010.

This chapter defines civil society as "a broad range of organisations, such as community groups, women groups, faith-based organizations, registered charitable organizations, independent media, professional associations, think tanks, independent educational organizations and social movements" (World Bank 2006: 2), operating in the public sphere and freely engaging to advance their interests, distinct from the state, the family and the market. The chapter argues that Liberia had a vibrant civil society before the civil war, through which citizens worked for change. When war broke out, CSOs became actively involved in finding a peaceful resolution by organising conflict resolution workshops and peace conferences, lobbying warring parties and carrying out demonstrations to galvanise local support so as to

[1] See United States Institute of Peace (2003), "Peace Agreements: Liberia", http://www.usip.org/publications/peace-agreements-liberia (Accessed 4 May 2016).

[2] UNMIL Human Rights Section, Catholic Relief Services (CRS), International Center for Transitional Justice (ICTJ), Lutheran Church Massacre Survivors Association (LUMASA), Association of Evangelicals of Liberia (AEL), West Africa Network for Peacebuilding (WANEP), Women in Peacebuilding Network (WIPNET), OXFAM-Liberia, Advocates for Human Rights, Union of Liberian Organisations in the United Kingdom (ULO-UK), European Federation of Liberian Associations (EFLA) and Union of Liberian Associations in USA (ULAA).

mount pressure on government and rebel groups to reach a peace agreement. After the CPA, CSOs took on a central role in running the NTGL and legislative assembly. Their involvement in the direct running of government resulted in a mixed bag of the good, the bad and the ugly. Although civil society's image was tarnished due to corruption in government, the chapter argues that its role in drafting and passing the LTRC Act and in vetting the LTRC commissioners was indispensable. While some outspoken CSOs were critical of the LTRC commissioners' managerial, procedural and structural arrangements, and even distanced themselves from implementing the LTRC's mandate during its lifetime, the responsibility of implementing the LTRC final report's recommendations has become mainly the responsibility of CSOs. The lack of a formal structure for CSOs' engagement with the transitional process and the LTRC's ad hoc relationship with CSOs resulted in the LTRC underutilising CSOs' capacities and networks. Nevertheless the engagement between CSOs and the LTRC resulted in new agendas for both CSOs and government.

Liberian Civil Society Before and During the Civil War

In Liberia and for this chapter there are four categories of CSOs: the politically oriented, which are involved in advocacy, monitoring and lobbying government for policy change and in informing and mobilising the general citizenry for action; the faith based, which are involved in providing relief and humanitarian assistance, development and empowerment from a religious perspective; non-faith based, which are involved in delivering relief and humanitarian assistance, development and empowerment without a religious orientation; and those in the diaspora, which are a mixture of the categories based in Liberia.

Before the outbreak of civil war, well-established Liberian politically oriented CSOs, such as the Progressive Alliance of Liberia and the Movement for Justice in Africa, advocated for rapid political reform, calling for the adoption of socialism, an activist pan-Africanist foreign policy and a response to injustice and poverty. During this time CSOs demanded political reforms, accountability and transparency in government, and their character was mainly political (Lund 2006: 3). The remnants of these organisations organised themselves into the Transitional Justice Working Group (TJWG), which was involved in the peace negotiations, and hence some of its members worked their way into the NTGL and NTLA. There were also faith-based and non-faith-based CSOs, such as Samaritan's Purse (SP), Serving in Mission (SIM), Eternal Love Winning Africa (ELWA), Orphan Relief and Rescue (ORR) and Catholic Relief Services (CRS), which were involved in the provision of healthcare, education and agricultural services and in building and managing schools and hospitals.

While these CSOs had various strengths, they had no experience in dealing with massive human rights abuses. Following the start of the civil war in 1989 many of the CSOs' activities were influenced by international non-governmental organisations (NGOs) and international agencies, which offered financial support and training in conflict resolution, peacebuilding, coping with humanitarian emergencies, trauma counselling and other services. Formed in response to the humanitarian catastrophe created by the war, CSOs flourished, including a broad spectrum of faith-based organisations, NGOs, women's organisations and professional associations.

Some CSOs, such as the Catholic Justice and Peace Commission (JPC) and the Center for Law and Human Rights Education (CLHRE), documented atrocities and human rights abuses carried out by ever-multiplying warring factions during the civil war (Pham 2006: 82). Women's organisations, such as the Liberian Women's Initiative (LWI), which was born out of the civil war, documented the systematic use of rape of women and girls as a weapon of war and the massive recruitment of child soldiers. Through its media releases, LWI raised awareness in the international community about the suffering of women and children inflicted by all warring parties during the civil war.

In the absence of efficient state structures, a number of CSOs partnered with international NGOs to provide relief and humanitarian services to the people of Liberia (Atuobi 2010: 2). They also assisted with disarmament and mediating with warring parties. Susukuu[3] and the Special Emergency Life Food (SELF) programme, for example, provided humanitarian relief to war-affected populations. In addition, Susukuu was instrumental during the state's first disarmament programme, encouraging thousands of combatants to surrender their arms in return for assistance packages. An estimated 15,000 combatants gave up their arms under Susukuu's school-for-guns programme, which also increased school enrolment rates (Toure 2002: 10).

Some CSOs, particularly the Liberian Inter-Faith Mediation Committee (IMC) and the Liberia Leadership Forum, engaged in conflict resolution and peacebuilding initiatives. Through their relationships with donors, these CSOs acquired conflict resolution and peacebuilding skills which gave them the ability to undertake activities such as psychosocial care, retraining of ex-combatants, awareness raising, trust building between warring parties, lobbying for them to reach peace agreements and organising community reconciliation events. According to a religious leader working with the Association of Evangelicals of Liberia (AEL) I interviewed, CSOs worked to bring about peace in the country long before the establishment of the LTRC:

> As a church organization and as a pastor, it is our job to see that peace returns to our country and that our people are reconciled. Even before the TRC, we went to refugee camps where Liberians were in Guinea, Ivory Coast, advocating for peace. We held workshops there, where we analysed the causes for the conflict and got people to look at the historical roots of the war and get them to see the need for peace. We also held radio programs focusing on peace and reconciliation and these helped a lot in making people aware of the need for peace building and reconciliation in our torn country. (Quoted in Dhizaala 2013: 90)

In fact, CSOs were at the forefront of all Liberian peace negotiations aimed at finding a lasting solution to the civil war. Starting in 1990, the IMC was actively

[3] Susukuu was an offshoot of the Movement for Justice in Africa, one of the oldest CSOs in Liberia, which was entrusted with a socio-economic advisory role to government since the 1970s.

involved in the search for peace.[4] It spearheaded the first effort towards a negotiated settlement by holding a consultative meeting in June 1990 between the parties to the conflict, namely representatives of the Doe regime, the NPFL and the AFL in Freetown (Dunn 1998). To garner local public support for this peace initiative, the IMC organised two massive "peace marches" through Monrovia on June 14 and 26, 1990. It also organised "stay-at-home protests" in March 1995 and February 1996 against "rewarding" warlords with positions in government (Pham 2006: 82). In addition, the IMC initiated a campaign to encourage disarmament in the country.

In 2002, IMC and the Liberia Leadership Forum called for and organised peace talks between the government and LURD and MODEL at a peace conference in Ghana (Hayner 2007: 7), moderated by Abdulsalami Abubakar, an ECOWAS representative and the former president of Nigeria. During the peace talks, stakes were high because the warring parties were locked in a military stalemate. Local CSOs and regional and international organisations increased pressure on them to end the civil war. The Special Court for Sierra Leone's indictment against Charles Taylor on June 4, 2003, forced him to step down from power, which opened the way for the CPA to be signed later in the year (Hayner 2007; Neill and Ward 2005).[5]

Another factor in the peace negotiations was Women of Liberia Mass Action for Peace's campaign, which started in early April 2003 in Monrovia. These Christian and Muslim women joined together to protest the deteriorating security situation in the country. In their effort to see that peace returned to Liberia, they sent several women representatives from Monrovia to Accra to mobilise Liberian women residing in the Buduburam refugee camp to continue their anti-war protest while the peace talks were going on. In solidarity was the West Africa Network for Peacebuilding (WANEP); the women made ribbons stating, "Peace for Liberia now", and pinned them on delegates at the peace talks to symbolise the urgent need for peace. They mounted a 2-month vigil in front of the building where the peace negotiations were held, presented several position statements to the delegates, scheduled meetings with delegates and mediators and threatened to strip off their clothes in protest against delays. The women urged delegates to reach a ceasefire. They blocked the entrance and exit of the conference hall and sent a letter to the chief mediator telling him that they were not allowing delegates to leave the hall and no food would enter the hall until the ceasefire was signed (Schirch and Sewak 2005: 9–10). This brought the women's demand for a ceasefire and signing of a peace agreement to the attention of the delegates.

[4] The IMC is an amalgamation of the Liberian Council of Churches (LCC) and the National Muslim Council of Liberia (NMCL). The negotiations included the Banjul and Standing Mediation Committee (SMC) (1990), the Yamoussoukro Accord (1991), the Cotonou Agreement (1993), the Akosombo Peace Talks (1994) and the Abuja Accord (1995).

[5] Taylor handed power to Vice President Moses Blah a week later, on August 11, 2002. At the invitation of the president of Nigeria, Taylor left Liberia for Calabar, Nigeria, with a rather ominous promise, "I leave you with these parting words: God willing, I will come back" (Jarrett Murphy 2003).

Civil Society's Engagement in the Peace Negotiations and the Transitional Government

After Charles Taylor was removed from the picture, he tried to short-circuit the possibility of holding him and his cronies accountable for the atrocities committed (Hayner 2007: 18). Taylor influenced the Liberian legislature to pass an amnesty law just days before he left office.[6] International observers to the peace negotiations insisted that amnesty for serious crimes was not allowed under international law. Politically oriented CSOs in TJWG and the Association of Female Lawyers of Liberia (AFELL), whose members served as delegates, and others lobbied the parties on the perimeter of the formal meetings, kept an eye on the discussion of amnesty and sent messages to the chairman of the peace negotiations insisting that any amnesty provision should exclude crimes against humanity, war crimes and other serious abuses such as rape. While international and local CSO representatives pushed for a war crimes tribunal in Liberia, similar to the Special Court for Sierra Leone, the peace negotiations were in a stalemate. Negotiators realised that granting amnesty to rebels might encourage wars in the future but that any threat of prosecution would make it difficult to end the war, as the faction leaders vowed to continue fighting.

Several factors influenced the negotiations concerning an amnesty clause in the CPA: that all previous peace efforts excluded amnesty provisions; that national courts were dilapidated from the war; and that in neighbouring Sierra Leone the peace agreement granted a blanket amnesty. The warring parties thus had little to worry about as regards prosecutions and felt it was not necessary to insist on legal immunity, instead bargaining for political power in the transitional government. They refused to sign a ceasefire agreement until they received some guarantee of their role in the interim government. General Abubakar, the mediator, argued that some atrocities were so severe that they could simply never be amnestied and had to be brought to justice (Hayner 2007: 15). He suggested, however, that the decision on establishing a war crimes tribunal should wait until a new government was elected.

As a result, instead of having a war crimes tribunal and cutting short any discussion of amnesty, a truth commission was proposed, and it was fairly quickly accepted (Hayner 2007: 8). According to Conmany Wesseh, who actively participated in the CPA negotiations, the "warring parties agreed to the truth commission concept because they wanted to prevent the establishment of a war crimes tribunal" (quoted in Pajibo 2007: 290). During the peace talks, the Cable News Network (CNN) provided live coverage from Monrovia of the rebels' indiscriminate shelling of the city and of gangs and militias committing violence in the streets. With the warring parties' delegates using the CNN coverage as a bargaining chip, the other delegates felt

[6] Act to Grant Immunity from Both Civil and Criminal Proceedings against All Persons within the Jurisdiction of Republic of Liberia from Acts or Crimes Committed during the Civil War from December 1989 to August 2003, passed on August 7, 2003.

the pressure to give in to their demands for positions in the transitional government. One CSO participant in the negotiations recalls how "one or two rockets would be sent into Monrovia, and people in Monrovia would be telling us 'you have to give them anything they want, to get it to stop.' … Once they felt they were getting what they wanted, the fighting would simmer down. Sometimes I thought they were blackmailing us" (Hayner 2007: 14). I think it was fair enough for the CSO representatives to agree to postpone the discussion of human rights accountability to the future because at that time the immediate need was to reach a ceasefire that would stop the killing in Liberia. Thus when the warring parties agreed to a ceasefire on June 17, 2003, and shortly thereafter to the CPA, it was a big achievement and a relief for the CSO participants and other delegates and observers.

CSO representatives, who were former employees of organisations, adopted a new approach in the CPA from the previous vague lines of separation between civil society and civilian political groups that cast themselves as non-partisan advocates. This time they sought not only to be included in the Accra peace negotiations but also for a formal role in the transitional government being negotiated. The argument was that with most of Liberia's political class tainted by complicity in the war or worse, leaders from civil society needed to step in and participate directly in governance (Pham 2004). CSOs' participation in the peace negotiations resulted in a four-way power-sharing arrangement that distributed positions in the NTGL cabinet, the NTLA and the civil service among representatives of civil society, the National Patriotic Party (NPP) that emerged from NPFL, and the LURD and MODEL rebels.

Civil society and special interest groups were allocated 7 of the 76 seats in the NTLA.[7] The position of vice chair of the executive body of the NTGL went to Wesley Momo Johnson, a representative of civil society. In the NTGL cabinet, CSO representatives headed six ministries.[8] CSO representatives were also entrusted with managing 16 government agencies,[9] and some of Liberia's publicly owned corporations and autonomous government agencies and commissions.[10]

---

[7] The NTLA was composed of 76 members distributed as follows: (a) the three warring factions with 12 representatives from MODEL, 12 representatives from LURD and 12 representatives from the former government of Liberia; (b) one seat for each of the 18 registered political parties that participated in the peace negotiations; (c) one seat each for the 15 political subdivisions, or counties, of the country; and (d) seven seats for civil society and interest groups. For further details, see Article 14 of the Comprehensive Peace Agreement.

[8] National security, education, gender and development, information, rural development, and youth and sports.

[9] The Bureau of Immigration and Naturalization, the Bureau of General Auditing, the Bureau of State Enterprises, the Center for National Documents and Records, the Civil Service Agency, the John F. Kennedy Memorial Medical Center, the Independent National Human Rights Commission, the Liberia National Police Force, the Truth and Reconciliation Commission, the National Bureau of Investigation, the National Fire Services, the National Food Assistance Agency, the Contracts and Monopoly Commission, the National Elections Commission and the Governance Reform Commission.

[10] The Agriculture Industrial Training Board, the Liberia Domestic Airport Authority, the Liberia Mining Corporation, Liberia National Lotteries, the Liberia Rubber Development Unit, the Liberia National Oil Company, the Monrovia Transit Authority, the National Housing and Savings Bank, the National Housing Authority and the National Insurance Corporation.

The formal participation of representatives of civil society in government brought a new dimension to state–society relations. Civil society representatives' involvement in the transitional government can be regarded as recognition of their invaluable contribution to the peace process. One may also view their participation as a first direct step to promoting democracy in government, as CSOs were for a long time advocates of transparency, accountability, anti-corruption initiatives and fair elections. Now was the time to put actions to words.

However, the NTGL and the NTLA faced endemic corruption ranging from gross financial and administrative malpractice to misappropriation of government money, awarding of contracts for service provision and equipment, and unauthorised payment of medical bills. Several heads of corporations were charged with economic sabotage and fraud, including siphoning off government money and stealing thousands of dollars (Human Rights Watch 2005: 33). According to *The Perspective* (2004), most of the legislative debates were centred on their financial benefits, including purchases of luxury vehicles and retirement packages. Because of the corruption in government, the image of the leadership, including CSOs representatives, was tainted. The corruption undermined these representatives' integrity and capacity to advocate for transparency and accountability, and left many Liberians questioning the motives of CSO leaders serving in the legislative or executive branch of government.

By taking positions in the NTGL and the NTLA, civil society representatives went beyond their traditional roles of advocates, educators and watchdogs. One might argue that they should not have participated in government because this contradicted civil society's role as an independent monitor, a role that is most effectively performed from outside government. Since they occupied only seven seats in the NTLA, one might also argue that their influence in the government was minimal. Even if not all CSO representatives were implicated in the corruption, since they served in a government that failed to deliver basic services, their credibility as being "above" politics and as impartial monitors of government was questioned. This ghost came back later to haunt CSO representatives as LTRC commissioners. Nevertheless, the role of CSO representatives in the NTGL and the NTLA was important in preventing the warlords from completely dominating the government. Their level of influence can be measured by their ability to successfully ensure the enactment of a comprehensive LTRC Act.

Civil Society and the Liberian Truth and Reconciliation Commission

The LTRC Act envisioned the commission as a forum to address issues of impunity, give victims and perpetrators of human rights violations the opportunity to share their experiences, and provide a clear picture of the past so as to facilitate genuine healing and reconciliation (United States Institute of Peace 2003: 11). This vision of the LTRC did not totally arise as a result of grassroots and collective civil society demands because during the initial peace negotiations the Liberian general public and the CSOs' major concern was reaching a ceasefire. The idea of the LTRC as the only transitional justice process was a product of the compromise reached by the delegates to the CPA negotiations. While CSOs advocated for a transitional justice process similar to that in Sierra Leone, where the Truth and Reconciliation Commission and the Special Court for Sierra Leone operated concurrently, the warring parties wanted amnesty and international observers wanted a form of criminal accountability. So the dynamics and ideas that informed the CPA agreement were primarily based on international debates and perspectives on transitional justice, especially with regard to truth commissions.

Since the South African Truth and Reconciliation Commission (SATRC) was regarded as a first step to reconciling South Africans after apartheid, many African countries transitioning from war to peace wished to emulate the South African example of balancing powerful opposing interests. South Africa's ambassador to Senegal, Rantobeng William Mokou, attributes the SATRC's success to Nelson Mandela's determination to bring about reconciliation, observing, "I think much has been achieved by the [SA]TRC judging by the fact that other countries want to emulate the way in which we dealt with our problems in South Africa".[11] Coupled with the Sierra Leone Truth and Reconciliation Commission having just submitted its final report, the delegates to the CPA thought it fitting to recommend a truth commission for Liberia.

The LTRC bill was enacted into law almost 2 years after the NTGL and the NTLA were instituted. Although the NTLA was dominated by former warlords and remnants of Charles Taylor's government (United States Institute of Peace 2003: 16), the Act establishing the LTRC was comprehensive, aligning with Jane Alexander's core objectives for truth commissions, which include compiling a comprehensive record of human rights violations; providing a suitable platform for victims to share their suffering and experiences; providing official acknowledgement and condemnation of violations; identifying root causes and the institutions responsible for violations; and making recommendations for further measures related to prevention of violations, accountability, justice, reparations, institutional reform and promoting respect for human rights (Alexander 2003: 32). The credit for this goes to both the CSO representatives in the NTGL and CSO activities outside the legislature. The Act was a result of CSOs' wide consultations, participation, debates and negotiations with various interest groups at the national and international levels.

The CSO representatives in the NTLA were concerned about the significance and relevance of the LTRC in contributing to unity, peace and reconciliation, and in line with this requirement was the general public agitation for accountability for war crimes. The Forum for the Establishment of a War Crimes Court in Liberia (FEWCCIL) submitted a petition to the Liberian parliament to establish a war crimes court in Liberia. The petition caught the attention of the media and a public

---

[11] "South Africa's reconciliation sets example in Africa", Panapress, August 18, 2001, www.panapress.com/South-Africa-s-reconciliation-sets-example-in-Africa--12-55008 (Accessed 12 September 2016).

debate ensued (Amnesty International 2008). Since Charles Taylor was on trial in The Hague, CSOs wanted other former warlords to face similar retributive justice. They also wanted to ensure that victims would get some form of reparations. They raised these concerns in legislature debates during the drafting of the LTRC bill, and pressed for an enabling mandate that would hold perpetrators accountable for human rights abuses.

Meanwhile, CSOs outside government campaigned and lobbied government officials to draft an enabling LTRC legislation to address various concerns. They sent a petition to legislators demanding specific concerns to be covered by the LTRC mandate. LWI, for example, focused on the plight of women and children during the war by drawing attention to atrocities such as rape, and criticised the mass recruitment of child soldiers by the warring factions. LWI succeeded in placing women's and children's issues on the LTRC's agenda. Local CSOs, international NGOs and members of the Liberian diaspora also campaigned for the LTRC bill to open the way for criminal prosecutions, reparations and exposure of past abuses committed against Liberians. These CSO strategies undermined efforts by former warlords in the NTGL to argue against a strong LTRC, at the time in support of the CSOs' demand for a comprehensive mandate.

Seeing that government officials were struggling with how to draft an innovative and broad mandate to address all gross human rights violations, violations of international humanitarian law and economic crimes, the Center for Democratic Empowerment (CEDE) coordinated and provided some funding for activities leading up to the production of the LTRC draft bill. With additional United Nations Development Programme funding for an initial workshop, CSOs constituted a technical committee composed of a coalition of 20 local CSO representatives named TJWG[12] and international experts on truth commissions in Africa that took on the responsibility of producing a draft of the LTRC Act (Pajibo 2010: 3). As a strategy to ensure a robust truth commission, this draft was subjected to a peer review process and shared for comment with additional experts who had participated in truth commissions in other countries, especially South Africa and Sierra Leone.[13]

In September 2004, when the draft LTRC Act was presented to government, the NTGL expressed serious reservations about provisions relating to the inclusion of non-Liberians as LTRC commissioners, arguing that they would lack in-depth understanding of the historical events under investigation. To reach a compromise,

---

[12] TJWG member organisations included the Center for Democratic Empowerment, Foundation for Human Rights and Democracy, Association of Female Lawyers in Liberia, Catholic Justice and Peace Commission, Center for Democratic Empowerment, Flomo Theater, Humanist Watch Liberia, Liberia Democracy Institute, National Human Rights Center of Liberia, Pentecostal Church of God Action for Development and Peace, Movement for Democracy and Human Rights, Forum for African Women Educationalists, Liberia Democracy Watch, Fore-Runners of Children Universal Rights for Survival Growth and Development, West Africa Peacebuilding Network, Foundation for International Dignity and True Witness.

[13] The International Center for Transitional Justice and Yasmin Sooka, a former commissioner of the SATRC and Sierra Leone TRC, made comments on the draft that led to amendments being made.

CSO representatives, the UNMIL human rights section, the Liberian Ministry of Justice and the executive entered into negotiations and agreed that all commissioners should be Liberians. Knowing very well that there were no Liberians with experience in implementing truth commission, the drafters of the LTRC bill included a clause to capacitate future commissioners with skills, knowledge and exposure through the inclusion of an International Technical Advisory Committee (ITAC) of three people,[14] who would work directly with the commissioners to fulfil the LTRC mandate.

In preparation for the launch of the LTRC Act, and since according to TJWG "people don't know what the issues are … they don't know what a truth and reconciliation commission is" (Amnesty International 2004: 21), TJWG undertook an extensive campaign to raise public awareness and to obtain the views of the general population on the LTRC. During a 3-month preparatory period prior to the launch of the LTRC, members of TJWG carried out several awareness-raising workshops in different Liberian counties, educating the population about the role of LTRC. They also conducted outreach activities throughout the country, ranging from distributing door-to-door pamphlets with information on the commission and its working methods to holding media briefings with radio, television and newspaper outlets to explain the functions and powers of the LTRC.

Members of TJWG engaged the public through live national radio and television broadcasts discussing the draft of the LTRC Act and receiving feedback. They published the draft in leading daily newspapers and conducted community outreach on the content of the bill across the country. After 3 months of public outreach and consultation, on February 7, 2005, the NTGL forwarded the draft of the LTRC Act to the NTLA as an "urgent passage" issue. CSOs worked tirelessly to ensure that the LTRC Act was comprehensive, covering a range of harms, from discussing discrimination against indigenous Liberians by Americo-Liberians to identifying causes of the Liberian civil war, apportioning responsibility for human rights abuses, identifying victims and victim groups, and rebuilding and reconciling the country. No wonder, then, that when a vote was called to pass the bill, former warlords and their party members sought to block the law because it could lead to them being held accountable. Nevertheless, on May 12, 2005, the NTLA passed the LTRC Act after a tie vote, which was broken by the speaker of the assembly.

After the LTRC Act was passed, CSOs sought to identify the right people to serve as LTRC commissioners. The LTRC Act stipulated that the commission would have nine commissioners, all Liberian nationals, including at least four women. The credit for the gender balance in the Act goes to women's groups that were active in peacebuilding and the peace negotiations, particularly LWI. Since in a prolonged civil war individuals may have several roles at one time, including victim, perpetrator, witness and bystander, finding commissioners whose hands were not "soaked with blood" was very challenging. The drafters of the LTRC Act, especially the CSOs, had this in mind when they included Article V, Section 8, which provided for

[14] The individuals were to be of international distinction and reputation, with two individuals nominated by ECOWAS and one by the United Nations High Commissioner for Human Rights.

a selection panel for commissioners made up of individuals of integrity, repute and good standing in public life. Article V, Section 11, stipulated that the commissioners must have credibility, high integrity and honour; not be known or perceived as human rights violators or members of groups involved in human rights violations; and not have a prior conviction for a crime.

In the commissioner selection process, three CSO representatives were part of the independent vetting panel, along with an ECOWAS representative who headed the panel, two representatives from political parties and one representative from UNMIL. Largely in response to civil society pressure (Allen et al. 2010: 15),[15] the nomination and selection process was transparent and open to public input. The commissioners were a balanced representation of Liberian society, perceived as impartial, and of diverse political, religious, professional and regional backgrounds.[16] Since almost all were previously involved in civil society activities (Aaron et al. 2008: 159–164),[17] CSOs assumed that they would work collaboratively with civil society to fulfil the LTRC's mandate.

While the commissioners had experience with CSO activities, none of them had prior knowledge of managing an institution of the LTRC's nature. In preparing them for the task ahead, TJWG collaborated with international organisations to provide short trainings on the history and origins of truth commissions (including their functions, objectives and importance), best practice, approaches and experiences of other truth commissions, and human rights and humanitarian law. The commissioners also received training in investigating human rights violations, technical issues in conducting public and in-camera hearings, ensuring psychosocial care and support for victims and others coming before the LTRC, conflict prevention and resolution and providing reparations (LTRC 2009: 39). UNMIL offered training on investigatory procedures, case management and international human rights and humanitarian law (United Nations 2009: 7).

Before the real work of the LTRC started, TJWG, in conjunction with international experts, trained over 300 commission staff members, including statement takers, investigators, psychosocial support providers and county coordinators. It

[15] In early 2004, Gyude Bryant, chairman of the NTGL, appointed 9 commissioners prior to the passage of the LTRC Act, but since this appointment process lacked transparency, civil society and UN actors called successfully for the process to be aborted and pushed for a more participatory selection process once the LTRC bill was enacted by the legislature.

[16] Article V, Section 11, of the LTRC Act provides the basic framework by which to vet commissioners, but the selection committee, which is mandated in Sections 8 and 9 of the same article, developed more (Aaron et al. 2008).

[17] The commissioners were Cllr. Jerome J. Verdier, the chairperson and a human rights lawyer and civil society activist; Dede A. Dolopei, co-chairperson and an administrator, manager, social worker and peace activist; Oumu K. Syllah, a registered nurse, HIV/AIDS counsellor and social worker; John H.T. Stewart, Jr., a journalist, human rights advocate and activist; Massa A. Washington, a journalist, peace advocate and diaspora Liberian representative; Cllr. Pearl Brown Bull, a lawyer, peacebuilding activist, women's and human rights advocate and politician; Shielkh Ka Kafum ba Konneh, a Muslim authority and conflict resolution and peacebuilding activist; Gerald B. Coleman, an electrical engineer, project manager and spiritual elder; and Bishop Arthur F. Kulah, a Methodist pastor, educator, administrator and author.

assisted with the establishment of LTRC offices in Liberia's 15 counties (LTRC 2008: 29–30). The LTRC contracted Benetech to coordinate specialised staff training in data entry, coding and categorising human rights violations and victims' names and locations.[18] In preparation for the official launch of the LTRC's hearings and statement taking, a sensitisation and awareness-raising outreach campaign was conducted by Julie Endee, a Liberian communications expert, peace advocate, campaigner for the rights of women and children and cultural ambassador. In these outreach programmes community mobilisers from CSOs resident in counties of Liberia underwent training in communications and social mobilisation (LTRC 2008). The CSO mobilisers utilised these skills in educating the populace about the LTRC mandate and encouraged citizens to participate by giving statements and testimony. They also facilitated the distribution of 15,000 copies of the LTRC's informational question-and-answer brochure, distributed copies of the 1986 constitution to schools and communities for civic education, and conducted sensitisation and awareness-raising workshops about the LTRC process (TRC 2009: 64–65).

After all the preparations were made and the commissioners were ready, the LTRC was launched on January 20, 2006, at a public ceremony presided over by President Ellen Johnson-Sirleaf. The cracks soon started to show, and they were quickly identified by the major CSOs. Instead of helping the commissioners overcome weaknesses, CSOs opted to place the LTRC under scrutiny, criticising it on the grounds of weak managerial, structural and procedural arrangements and raising doubts as to how the LTRC would deliver on its ambitious mandate. For example, CSOs questioned the LTRC's efficacy for hiring few technical staff and not having a comprehensive work plan and budget before officially launching operations (Allen et al. 2010: 15). They asked why it did not have an in-house legal team to make sophisticated legal evaluations, such as those required for determining whether specific acts amount to violations of international human rights law (Amnesty International 2008). Arguably, the major CSOs' non-cooperation and reluctance to find solutions to the commissioners' challenges is one of the reasons why the LTRC sidelined strong and vocal CSOs like IMC, WANEP, the Women in Peacebuilding Network (WIPNET) and the Association of Evangelicals of Liberia (AEL), and instead opted to collaborate with little known CSOs, such as the Liberian National Girl Guides Association, Boys Scouts of Liberia, the Artists Association of Liberia, Liberian Crusaders for Peace, the Roller Skaters Association of Liberia, the Women on the Move Association and the Traditional Women Association. Mainstream human rights and women's organisations, like LWI, which was the vanguard of the peace talks and advocacy in Liberia, were also sidelined after the launch of the LTRC.

Despite outreach work before the launch, the commission's outreach programme was not efficient in educating and sensitising the population on the mandate of the LTRC. While I was doing research in Liberia, many civil society respondents expressed frustration about the commission's methods. I also discovered that most

[18] Benetech Human Rights Data Analysis Group is a California-based organisation contracted for 3 years to help in establishing analytical objectives, collecting data and designing and implementing an information management system.

Liberians had unrealistic expectations of the LTRC. A case in point is that victims expected the LTRC to compensate them for their suffering. Some Liberians expected the LTRC to hold former warlords accountable for the crimes perpetrated during the civil war through a local court of law or an international court as in Sierra Leone. A June 2007 survey showed that while 80% of the adult population in Liberia was aware of the LTRC, less than half were aware of its powers to recommend amnesties, prosecutions and reparations (Koscis 2007). A good outreach programme would have made most Liberians aware of the LTRC's mandate, processes, structure, role and limitations, so that they would have realistic expectations, which would have boosted public confidence and participation in statement giving and hearings. CSOs failed to maximally utilise their existing community outreach structures for the benefit of LTRC activities. A good working relationship with community-based organisations, NGOs and church groupings would have tremendously assisted in building a more functional relationship with Liberians in rural areas, permitting the LTRC not only to work with them but also to interact with them during hearings and statement taking. As observed in a UNMIL report, statement takers could not reach certain remote areas where serious human rights violations are known to have occurred (UNMIL 2008: 24).

When LTRC commissioners were accused of lacking integrity, with one commissioner identified as an Americo-Liberian sympathiser and another accused of having participated in human rights abuses during the civil war (Allen et al. 2010: 15), the chairperson was said to lack the leadership traits needed to head a commission of that nature and fellow commissioners began to undermine his leadership (Steinberg 2009: 135–144). Coupled with the LTRC's lack of a strategy and financial plan, the developments regarding commissioners further disillusioned major CSOs, including TJWG. When the LTRC was hit with financial hardship, most CSOs just stood by and watched. Instead of trying to come to some form of rescue by fundraising, CSOs decided to revert to the traditional role of watchdog, assessing and evaluating the commission's work. The LTRC became increasingly reluctant to involve CSOs in its processes. A case in point is that the LTRC did not place its statement-taking processes within faith- and community-based organisation structures, more often using statement-takers working for a salary, not volunteers. If the LTRC had solicited civil society participation and community involvement in recruiting and using volunteers, the statement-taking exercise would not have halted when the LTRC hit financial difficulties.

Another example is failures in the commission's psychosocial support. Even if the LTRC initially devised an ambitious plan for psychosocial support to victims, perpetrators, family members, commissioners and staff (Amnesty International 2008: 23), the psychosocial unit was scaled down as a result of the commission's inability to raise money to cover its entire budget and the LTRC could not provide such services throughout the country. Without psychosocial support, some statement-givers chose not to come forward, which hampered the ability of the LTRC to come up with the full truth. During the war and continuing during the time of the LTRC, international NGOs, such as Save the Children, Médecins du Monde, the Center for Victims of Torture and the Lutheran World Federation/World Service, trained many counsellors in providing group trauma counselling, mediating in personal disputes and community conflicts and offering other trauma-healing and psychosocial support, particularly in remote regions (Abramowitz 2016: 214–280). The LTRC, however, did not use these organisations' psychosocial services during the hearings and statement taking. A respondent working with a psychosocial support CSO decried to me the failure of CSOs to offer their services and the LTRC's failure to seek assistance:

> Our organisation's conflict mediation program brings together people in the community and creates a safe environment where people can understand the perspectives for others. Victim-perpetrator encounter is the most threatening type of situation. It is only safe if properly facilitated. The TRC's hearing sessions were not a safe environment for some victims, especially rape victims to openly tell their stories. It was too confronting for victims to stand in public or even in private sessions and narrate their ordeal to strangers who would do nothing to help them recover from traumatic experience, but only to listen to their stories. Ours is a voluntary interaction, a safe environment of closeness. (Quoted in Dhizaala 2013: 272)

Despite the problems in their relationship with the LTRC, CSOs welcomed the commission's draft report when it was released on June 30, 2009. The commission recommended reparations and rehabilitation of victims and perpetrators in need of specialised psychosocial and other rehabilitation services; legal, institutional and other reforms; conditional amnesty; and continuing investigations and inquiries into particular matters. CSOs were the first to embrace the report and congratulate the commissioners on work well done. Some CSOs, such as CEDE, JPC, FEWCCIL and the National Human Rights Council of Liberia, welcomed the report because it listed well-known perpetrators and recommended their prosecution in a domestic or international court. The report contrasted with the popular Liberian dogma of "let bygones be bygones", especially by former warlords, and instead pushed for justice to prevail over impunity by not turning a blind eye to the rapes, sexual slavery, torture and inhumane deaths that characterised Liberia's civil war.

LTRC Final Report Sets a New Agenda for Civil Society Engagement

The LTRC report and its recommendations have attracted mixed reactions. While on the one hand ordinary Liberian citizens are happy that the report lists those who bear the greatest responsibility for the human rights abuses perpetrated before and during the civil war and are determined to see its implementation, on the other hand alleged perpetrators and warlords, a number of whom have joined the executive, legislature and judiciary, have reservations about the report and want it withdrawn. Former leaders of warring factions, under a group calling itself Signatories to the Accra Comprehensive Peace Accord, who are now government officials, held a press conference a week after the LTRC report's release. They dismissed the entire report and accused LTRC Chair Jerome Verdier of treason for trying to overthrow Johnson-Sirleaf's government (Weah 2012: 1).

Commenting on these developments, Kanio Gbala, head of the NGO Civic Initiative and a member of TJWG, noted:

> There are many factors to consolidating peace. One is impunity and ensuring rule of law is in place. … When it comes to the names on the list [for prosecutions or sanctions] it is public knowledge what these people did. We do not need to pass a blanket judgment [on them]. … Some people want to incite division but we must see these recommendations as a tool to move to the next step. People must recognize even if prosecutions are considered, it will take years to put in place. … We have to go beyond the prosecutions to look at all the recommendations, such as involving communities in reconciliation, institutional reform, guarding the country's collective memory of the war. We should use these recommendations as a platform for dialogue and discussion to remember this country's history so we can move on. (IRIN 2009)

Joe Pemagbi, head of the Liberia Programme of the Open Society Institute, which supported the TRC, was not hesitant to note that "there are some recommendations that people consider to be controversial, but that is for Liberians to determine. … We have supported the work of the commission [TRC] and would now like to follow up on the recommendations" (IRIN 2009).

The LTRC report provided a foundation for the government and CSOs to build on, although CSOs disagreed with some of the LTRC's recommendations. For example, they critiqued its suggestion that the government grant amnesty to Joseph Blahyi, a.k.a. General Butt Naked,[19] who admitted responsibility for the deaths of some 20,000 people. This recommendation is regarded as inconsistent by human rights organisations, such as the FEWCCIL, on the grounds that amnesty for a self-confessed perpetrator is against international humanitarian law. Some recommendations were also successfully challenged both through the media and in court, such as the LTRC's recommendation for public sanction of 49 individuals (including Richelieu Archie Williams, who petitioned the court) who committed certain criminal offenses to be barred for 30 years from holding public office (TRC 2009: 361).

Nonetheless, CSOs are now building on what the LTRC process started with bottom-up peace and reconciliation efforts. A CSO chairperson observed how the organisation's activities and programmes link to the work of the LTRC:

> We now face the reality of the day. The TRC is phasing out, so what next? Whether the process went on rightly or there were gaps or no gaps, we have come to the crucial point in our history. The TRC is winding up. Whatever recommendation that comes out of that commission determines our fate as a nation. So we as civil society organisation we think that it is no longer time to continue pressing that you did good, you have done this correct or you are wrong. Who is right and who is wrong is not important right now. What is important is how we claim that space that the TRC has created. (Dhizaala 2013: 272)

The space created by the LTRC process includes the political space of open public discussion of the nature of human rights atrocities, victims and perpetrators, reparations to individuals and communities, memorialisation of the dead, and individual and community reconciliation.

---

[19] Due to his predilection to fight the enemy naked in the belief that this would protect him.

Since the release of the commission's report, additional truth-telling and reconciliation initiatives have been initiated in response to issues arising from the LTRC process, with a focus on restorative measures. The LTRC called for the establishment of a traditional dispute resolution mechanism called the National Palava Hut Forum as a complementary tool for justice and national reconciliation at the local level that would require all factions to appear before it (LTRC 2008). The traditional palava hut process used prior to the Liberian civil war is a restorative dispute resolution mechanism convened by elders to settle community matters such as extramarital affairs, divorces, land disputes, debt and occasionally theft and murder. It sought confession of the wrongful act, apology for the harm committed and forgiveness from the victim, followed by cleansing rituals and restitution (Pajibo 2007: 18–19).

CSOs such as TJWG, AFELL, the Women NGOs Secretariat of Liberia (WONGOSOL), the Liberian Massacre and Survivors' Association (LIMASA) and the Liberian Council of Churches (LCC) reviewed the LTRC's final report and started to conduct advocacy at national government level for implementation of LTRC recommendations. The Lutheran Church Massacre Survivors Association (LUMASA) reviewed the report, and in early 2010 petitioned the legislature to include reparations on its agenda for that year (Allen et al. 2010: 30). The Lutheran Church, in collaboration with the Christian Health Association of Liberia (CHAL), which in 1991 initiated a trauma healing and reconciliation programme, also has been doing trauma healing and reconciliation activities via the training of pastors, lay leaders and health workers. Since the LTRC report, it has adapted its programme to address relations between victims and perpetrators of civil war violence. And several "crusades" have been staged to preach forgiveness and peace. The bishop-elect of the Lutheran Church emphasised how his first preoccupation would be genuine reconciliation among all Lutheran members in the country (Castelli 2013).

Diaspora CSOs are building on the LTRC's reconciliation efforts to heal victims of the civil war who fled Liberia. In another example of collective restorative measures, LWI has organised victim support roundtables for women to facilitate healing through storytelling. In the roundtables Liberian war victims in the United States meet to share their experiences. Similarly, the Coalition for Justice (CJL), a US-based coalition of five Liberian CSOs, sees reconciliation as a product of justice and views the LTRC report as worthwhile to implement as a means to justice. In an open letter to President Johnson-Sirleaf, CJL argued that to ensure sustained peace and a strong foundation for national unity, justice for the victims of the Liberian civil war must be provided.[20]

The LTRC report passed through the legislature, which established a major follow-up body, the Independent National Commission on Human Rights (INCHR), based on its recommendations. Under the banner of the National Human Rights Action Plan (NHRAP), INCHR seeks to guarantee civil, political, social, economic and cultural rights, with a specific focus on the issues of women, children and persons with disabilities, and to provide for the implementation of the country's

[20] "An open letter to President Sirleaf", Newstime Africa, December 18, 2012, http://www.newstimeafrica.com/archives/30190 (Accessed 15 November 2016).

regional and international human rights obligations and of the recommendations made during the universal periodic review.

In 2013, the government announced an Agenda for Transformation (AfT), a development plan, which prioritises the development of the justice sector and addresses cross-cutting issues impacting on human rights and vulnerable groups. In Chap. 8 of the AfT, the government outlines strategies for strengthening reconciliation of various segments of Liberian society and commits to investing in institutions that help manage cleavages and resolve conflicts in a peaceful manner (e.g., the Palava Hut Forum) and to addressing issues raised by the LTRC (Republic of Liberia 2016: 38).

Also in 2013, the government adopted a Strategic Roadmap for National Healing, Peacebuilding and Reconciliation in Liberia (2013–2030) designed to foster coherence among institutions, systems, mechanisms and human resources that support reconciliation. The roadmap is framed in 12 thematic components[21] and contextualised in the three strategies of accounting for the past, managing the present and planning for the future. President Johnson-Sirleaf (2013) emphasised that the road map is "a multi-dimensional process of overcoming social, political, and religious cleavages; mending and transforming relationships; healing the physical and psychological wounds from the civil war, as well as confronting and addressing historical wrongs including the structural root causes of and potential areas of conflicts in our country". The road map has provided grounds for future intervention by CSOs and other actors.

Conclusion

This chapter has argued that before the outbreak of the civil war in Liberia, CSOs were active in their traditional roles as advocacy and watchdog groups, in addition to directly providing social and health services. When the civil war started, CSOs had to take on the additional responsibility of providing humanitarian assistance and finding a peaceful resolution to the conflict. Liberian CSOs were involved in the peace negotiations through dialogue, as emissaries, as organisers of peace conferences and by lobbying warring parties to negotiate for the end of the conflict. Because of their successful involvement in the peace process, representatives of many of these CSOs were then involved in the NTGL and NTLA, taking on leadership and managerial roles in ministries, state corporations and government agencies—a move that both dented civil society's image because of corruption issues in the transitional government and boosted its involvement in the drafting of the LTRC Act and the vetting of LTRC commissioners. In the process of implementing the

[21] The road map marks the following as key components of the country's national reconciliation programme: the *palava* hut process of addressing past wrongs; memorialisation, reparation, diaspora and reconciliation; political dialogue; conflict prevention and mediation; women's recovery and empowerment; children and youth recovery and empowerment; psychosocial recovery and empowerment of persons with disabilities; inclusive people's history and collective identity; transformative education system; and constitutional law reforms.

LTRC's mandate, CSOs were critical of the weak managerial, structural and procedural arrangements made by the commissioners, which caused outspoken CSOs to be sidelined by the commission. Nevertheless, after the LTRC final report was released, CSOs integrated many of its recommendations into their activities.

The most consistent issue identified by CSOs that participated in Liberia's transitional justice process is the lack of a formal structure for their engagement. The text of the CPA did not designate which specific CSO or individual should assume which role in the NTGL and NTLA; as a result the process of engagement was the scene of rather inappropriate rows as civil society leaders, who presented themselves as non-political, non-governmental and representative, contended with one another for positions in government. With CSO leaders having entered the political fray, the ability of CSOs to remain credibly "above" politics and act as neutral monitors of the implementation of the CPA was questionable.

One lesson learnt through the Liberian civil society experience is that a truth commission with a short lifespan (2 years in this case) can only achieve limited goals. Since the LTRC did not replace CSOs' traditional role but instead complemented it, CSOs were able to take over from the commission by building on its ambitious initiatives for conflict resolution, peacebuilding and reconciliation and integrating them into their agendas. While the LTRC sought CSO participation with the aim of accessing civil society networks for broader outreach to fulfil its mandate, such engagement was uneven and sometimes viewed as less important. The difficulties for CSOs in engaging with the LTRC resulted from poor coordination and the LTRC's ad hoc relationship with CSOs, resulting in the commission's failure to take advantage of CSOs' capacities and networks. The commission would have had more of an impact had CSOs worked collaboratively with the LTRC by volunteering their human resources, finances and networks where necessary. With the closing of the LTRC come new challenges and opportunities. Liberian CSOs are bracing themselves for the challenges, and embracing the new opportunities.

CSOs' engagement with the LTRC resulted in a new agenda for civil society after the release of the commission's final report. Many CSOs took the LTRC's recommendations on board in their programmes. For example, CSOs are now conducting memorialisation activities to commemorate victims of the civil war, advocating for the establishment of a special criminal court for Liberia and distributing cash and cows as a form of reparation. It can be argued that CSOs' engagement with the LTRC also resulted in a new agenda for the government of Liberia, which has adopted a set of commissions and strategic policies to address some of the LTRC's recommendations.

References

Aaron, S., Toe, S., & Weah, A. (2008). *Impunity under attack: The evolution and imperative of the Liberian truth commission*. Silver Spring, MD: Image Group Press.

Abramowitz, S. (2016). *Searching for normal in the wake of the Liberian war*. Philadelphia, PA: University of Pennsylvania Press.

Alexander, J. (2003). *A scoping study of transitional justice and poverty reduction*. Final report for the UK Department for International Development.

Allen, P., Weah, A., & Goodfriend, L. (2010). *Beyond the truth and reconciliation commission: Transitional justice options in Liberia*. New York: International Center for Transitional Justice.
Amnesty International. (2004). *Liberia: One year after Accra—Immense human rights challenges remain*. AI Index AFR 34/012/2004.
Amnesty International. (2008). *Liberia: Towards the final phase of the Truth and Reconciliation Commission*. AI Index AFR 34/002/2008.
Atuobi, S. (2010). *State-civil society interface in Liberia's post-conflict peacebuilding*. KAIPTC Occasional Paper No. 30.
Castelli, L. (2013). Liberia's reconciliation: The current state of affairs. *Journal of Religion, Conflict, and Peace, 5*(1).
Dhizaala, J. (2013). *The Liberian Truth and Reconciliation Commission: Contribution to peace and reconciliation*. Doctoral dissertation, University of Sydney.
Dunn, E. (1998). Liberia's internal responses to ECOMOG's interventionist efforts. In K. Magyar & C. Morgan (Eds.), *Peacekeeping in Africa: ECOMOG in Liberia*. London: Macmillan and St. Martin's Press.
Ellis, S. (2007). *The mask of anarchy: The destruction of Liberia and the religious dimension of an African civil war* (2nd ed.). New York: New York University Press.
Hayner, P. (2007). *Negotiating peace in Liberia: Preserving the possibility for justice*. New York: Centre for Humanitarian Dialogue and International Center for Transitional Justice.
Howe, M. (1990). Liberian exiles struggle to survive. *The New York Times*.
Human Rights Watch. (1990). *Liberia: A human rights disaster violations of the laws of war by all parties to the conflict*.
Human Rights Watch. (2005). *Liberia at a crossroads: Human rights challenges for the new government*.
Jarrett M. (2003, August). *Liberia's Taylor goes into exile*. CBSNEWS.
Koscis, S. (2007). *Survey finds Liberians aware of truth commission, but not its powers*. Washington, DC: BBC World Service Trust.
Lowenkopf, M. (1995). Liberia: Putting the state back together. In W. Zartman (Ed.), *Collapsed states: The disintegration of restoration of legitimate authority* (pp. 19–108). Boulder, CO: Lynne Rienner Publishers.
Lund, M. (2006). The changing policy context for civil society building. In *Building civil society in post-conflict environment: From the micro to the macro*. Woodrow Wilson International Centre for Scholars Occasional Paper Series, Issue 1.
Neill, O., & Ward, L. (2005). *Building peace on fragile foundations: The Liberian challenge*. KAIPTC Paper 6.
Outram, Q. (1997). "It's terminal either way": An analysis of armed conflict, 1989–1996. *Review of African Political Economy, 73*, 355–271.
Pajibo, E. (2007). Civil society and transitional justice in Liberia: A practitioner's reflection from the field. *International Journal of Transitional Justice, 1*(2), 287–296.
Pajibo, E. (2010). *Advocating justice: Civil society and transitional justice in Africa: Liberia case study*. Paper presented at African Transitional Justice Research Network Workshop. Johannesburg, South Africa.
Pham, P. (2004). *Liberia: Portrait of a failed state*. New York: Reed Press.
Pham, P. (2006). Liberia and Sierra Leone: A study of comparative human rights approaches by civil society actors. *Interdisciplinary Journal of Human Rights Law, 1*(1).
Republic of Liberia. (2016). *Agenda for transformation, steps towards Liberian Rising 2030, Monrovia, Liberia*.
Schirch, L., & Sewak, M. (2005). *The role of women in peacebuilding: The role of civil society in prevention of armed conflict, an integrated program of research*. Retrieved March 12, 2016, from http://www.gppac.net/resources.
Simmons, A. (2003). Rape a weapon in liberian war. *Los Angeles Times*.
Steinberg, J. (2009). Briefing Liberia's experiment with transitional justice. *African Affairs, 109*(434), 135–144.

The Perspective. (2004). *Briefing notes on government's huge spending and practice of national neglect*. Retrieved March 8, 2016, from http://www.theperspective.org/2004/june/briefing-notes.html.

Toure, A. (2002). *The role of civil society in national reconciliation and peacebuilding in Liberia*. International Peace Academy.

Truth and Reconciliation Commission of Liberia. (2008). *Preliminary findings and determinations*.

Truth and Reconciliation Commission of Liberia. (2009). *The Truth and Reconciliation Commission of Liberia consolidated final report (Vol. II)*.

United Nations. (2009). Annual report of the United Nations High Commissioner for Human Rights and Reports of the Office of the High Commissioner and Secretary General: Analytical study on human rights and transitional justice. General Assembly, Human Rights Council, Twelfth session, Agenda item 2, A/HRC/12/18.

United Nations Mission in Liberia. (2008). *Report on the human rights situation in Liberia, May–October 2007*. Human Rights and Protection Section.

United States Institute of Peace. (2003). *Peace agreements: Liberia peace agreement digital collection*. Retrieved April 10, 2016, from http://www.usip.org/publications/peace-agreements-liberia.

Weah, A. (2012). Hopes and uncertainties: Liberia's journey to end impunity. *International Journal for Transitional Justice, 6*(2), 331–343.

World Bank. (2006). *Civil society and peacebuilding potential, limitations and critical factors* (Report No. 36445-GLB).

Chapter 4
Taking Transitional Justice to the People: Challenges for Civil Society in Zimbabwe

Shastry Njeru

Introduction

This chapter contributes to the discussion on the role of civil society in transitional justice in Africa through a review of the Zimbabwe Human Rights NGO Forum's *Taking Transitional Justice to the People* outreach programme, which ran from 2009 to 2011.[1] This programme was designed to prepare citizens for an envisaged transitional justice process that was to take place in Zimbabwe following years of human rights violations. Zimbabwe had experienced multiple episodes of political violence resulting in systematic violations of human rights, which a euphoric Zimbabwean society least expected at the time of independence.

I would like to thank my colleagues at the Zimbabwe Human Rights NGO Forum who were involved in the initial planning and implementation of the *Taking Transitional Justice to the People* outreach programme. The immensity of their work motivated this piece. These were courageous people, including Brian Penduka (programmes coordinator), the late Eileen Sawyer (advisor to the director), Abel Chikomo (executive director) and Dzikamai Bere (initial researcher for the transitional justice programme). I also want to thank Michelle Matsvaire (legal projects officer) for reading through the chapter and gleaning out mistakes.

[1] The Forum is a coalition of 21 human rights NGOs in Zimbabwe that, while having their own objectives, are concerned with the level and nature of human rights abuses in the country perpetrated mainly, though not exclusively, by state agents and their ancillaries. It came into existence at the time of the food riots in 1998. Over the years the Forum has litigated on behalf of victims in local and regional courts, registering various successes. The Forum introduced and lobbied successfully for transitional justice at a time when many civil society organisations in Zimbabwe hesitated. The constitution that was framed and agreed on in 2013 now provides for transitional justice in Section 252.

S. Njeru (✉)
Zimbabwe Human Rights NGO Forum, Harare, Zimbabwe
e-mail: shastry@hrforum.co.zw

J. Brankovic, H. van der Merwe (eds.), *Advocating Transitional Justice in Africa*, Springer Series in Transitional Justice,
https://doi.org/10.1007/978-3-319-70417-3_4

Ironically, the postcolonial state in Zimbabwe continued with the "broad structural and human rights abuses that were a constitutive part of colonial rule" (Eppel and Raftopoulos 2008: 2). The history of Zimbabwe is characterised by three major periods of human rights abuses: the war of liberation (1965–1979), the disturbances in Matabeleland and the Midlands (1980–1988) and the era of violence since 2000 (Eppel 2003). The human rights abuses of the colonial period were a result of the "struggles between the violent structural exclusions of settler colonial ideology and practice, and the often intolerant assertions for unity by a nationalist movement" (Eppel and Raftopoulos 2008: 2–3). The postcolonial administration was brutal and militaristic and violated human rights. The state also amnestied perpetrators of rights violations.

Connected to the foregoing, the Zimbabwean Government did not attend to issues of justice and accountability or how they can be freely aired and discussed. These challenges were reinforced by a combination of state repression and citizen fear that pervaded "the realities and consciousness of the general population, as well as those who endeavoured to further justice and accountability agenda" (Forum 2006: 2).

Until the 1990s, the accountability agenda was on the backburner for most in civil society (Forum 2006). When discussed, it remained in the circles of a few human rights activists and lawyers, to the exclusion of victims. The Forum confirms the existence of this weakness: "The debate around transitional justice options in Zimbabwean civil society is embryonic and remains largely confined to a small grouping of non-governmental organisations" (7). Most human rights non-governmental organisations (NGOs) focused their attention only on monitoring and documenting violations and, where possible, seeking relief for victims through the courts and other local remedial mechanisms. Even with these embryonic developments, it is particularly important to note that civil society in Zimbabwe was not very vocal on or active in stamping out the state's malpractices and holding it accountable. As such, there was systematic failure by civil society to take legal action for violations committed by the state against its people. This weakness was addressed by the "widespread discourses during the constitutional debates of the late 1990s, where justice and accountability concerns were raised though in relation to constitutional reforms of the year 2000, but not in relation to retrospective notions of liability" (7).

Civil society in Zimbabwe was wrongly viewed as a force for democratising the authoritarian state. It was "eulogized as the ultimate medical compound, capable of curing (all) ills" (Stewart 1997: 16). This glorious description did not fit the bill in terms of confronting sensitive issues like dealing with the past. In fact, civil society was not only "vulnerable" (van de Walle 2002: 76) but also "weak and dependent" (Mandaza 1994: 269). Civic groups, generally urban-based NGOs, were unlikely to take risks or to be innovative and challenge the status quo (Edwards 1998). Restricted mainly to urban centres, civil society existed among the indigenous "petty bourgeois element and … [was] factionalised along urban and rural spaces, and in some cases mirroring the state which they sought to confront" (Moyo 1993: 4). It was observed that most civil society organisations in Zimbabwe did "not encourage an interest in matters beyond their own immediate concerns". Instead, they sought to "typically equate their own narrow aims with those of the public realm" and thus to "manipulate the [environment] for their own selfish purposes" (4). This explains the thin civil society participation in transitional justice issues before and during the outreach period, and how the ruling party, the Zimbabwe African National Union–Patriotic Front (ZANU-PF), was able to claim to be "the sole legitimate representative of the people" (7).

Following the formation of the opposition party Movement for Democratic Change (MDC) in 1999 and the subsequent litany of violations and repression towards opposition parties by the government, there was a massive growth in interest in accountability for human rights abuses, institutional reform and reparations for victims. Discussions during the subsequent drafting of a new constitution raised these important concerns onto a pedestal. For instance, the National Constitutional Assembly (NCA)[2] campaigned for a truth commission tasked with "investigations of past violations to 'provide remedies for people injured by such abuses', to 'promote reconciliation in order to avoid conflict in the future', and to 'prevent conflict in the future by engaging in mediation and dispute settlement'" (NCA 2002a, b: 60). The MDC had similar recommendations under its policy rubric of constitutionalism, truth and justice (MDC 2003).

At this juncture, it was becoming clearer that meaningful civil society engagement and support was a critical precondition for the effective implementation of transitional justice options. This was one of the lessons of the constitutional reforms that occurred from 1999 to 2000: despite state limitations, participation of the people could enable them to make informed decisions and choices. This experience informed the design of the Forum's outreach efforts. The Forum sought to motivate the people's involvement and ownership of the transitional justice process, to heighten their stake to determine, participate in and benefit from the future transitional justice project. To create this citizen buy-in and trust, the Forum insisted on a victim-centred strategy that would cater for the needs of victims in a meaningful way. It recognised that, for maximum results, the process had to be extensive in consultation with victims and the broader community (Lesizwe 2004).

This chapter critically reviews the Zimbabwean context and its effects on transitional justice from the viewpoint of a civil society initiative. The chapter starts by reviewing Zimbabwe's history and transitional justice context. It discusses attempts to deal with the past in the country before presenting an overview of the Forum's outreach programme and the methods it used. The final part of the chapter reviews the options for transitional justice in Zimbabwe as reflected in participants' discussions during the outreach. It concludes that no matter how difficult it can be to push for transitional justice in a nontransitional context, such a process is necessary to finding closure and lasting peace. The chapter benefits from the author's close relationship with the project and the Forum, where the author implemented and observed the unfolding of the transitional justice initiatives in Zimbabwe.[3]

---

[2] The NCA was an NGO founded in 1997 by Zimbabwean individuals and civic organisations, among which were trade unions, opposition parties, student groups, women's groups, representatives of the informal sector, and church groups. The NCA was inspired by the popular uprising of the 1990s and came to see the constitution as an ideal umbrella cause in pursuing an array of political, social and economic causes.

[3] The perspectives advanced in this chapter are entirely those of the author, not of the Forum.

Context

Zimbabwe has a highly defined profile of violence predating colonialism (CCSF 2014). Lloyd Sachikonye (2011) chronicles this litany of violence in *When a State Turns on Its Citizens*. He notes that violence was experienced from the onset of the British colonial occupation in 1893 through to the First and Second Chimurenga Wars and the post-independence Gukurahundi atrocities of 1983, and that it steadily increased in rural areas from 2000, particularly during elections. It is argued that the 2000, 2002, 2005 and 2008 political violence was a result of the highly charged and contested nature of elections in Zimbabwe (CCSF 2014). The violent land reforms from 2000 and Operation Murambatsvina in 2005 (ostensibly to clear cities of informal settlements and businesses) are also cases of political violence (Forum 2001).

Many assert, however, that the "2008 pre-runoff election violence is arguably one of the brutish episodes of Zimbabwe's electoral violence" (Forum 2001: 1). This period witnessed killings, displacement, arson, abductions, rape, torture and beatings, and the most vulnerable groups were women and children (CSVR 2009). These various violent experiences were inadequately addressed by transitional mechanisms such as the Lancaster House Conference of 1979, the 1987 Unity Accord between ZANU and the Zimbabwe African People's Union (ZAPU) and even the Global Political Agreement of 2008 entered into by ZANU-PF and the two MDC formations (MDC-Tsvangirai and MDC-Mutambara) (Masunungure 2009).

Arguably, these mechanisms have been used to placate the "disenchanted and not necessarily providing healing and justice to the people worst hit by violence", and more so, these processes have been monopolised by the "political actors who occupy the echelons of power" (CCSF 2014: 2). There was no involvement of the masses. Political actors made no deliberate reference to extending attempts to deal with the past to the people who have suffered. This resulted in approaches meant just to "close the books", without any form of accountability for past wrongs and with impunity as the major tool.

The Policy of Reconciliation declared by then Prime Minister of Zimbabwe Robert Mugabe in 1980 is a case in point:

> If yesterday I fought as an enemy, today you have become a friend and ally with the same national interest, loyalty, rights and duties as myself. If yesterday you hated me, today you cannot avoid the love that binds you to me and me to you. Is it not folly, therefore, that in these circumstances anybody should seek to revive the wounds and grievances of the past? The wrongs of the past must now stand forgiven and forgotten. If ever we look to the past, let us do so for the lesson the past has taught us, namely that oppression and racism are inequities that must never again find scope in our political and social system. ("Democracy, a Way" 1980)

The "saintly" pronouncements above were quickly discounted by the actions of ZANU-PF and Mr. Mugabe in particular. Since ZANU-PF captured state power in 1980, the party has maintained hegemony over Zimbabwe through violent means. Joshua Nkomo writes about ZANU-PF's determination to eliminate other political parties as early as November 1980, noting that "speakers, including several ZANU ministers, insulted ZAPU … and said all minority parties should be 'crushed'" (Nkomo 2001: 189). These vitriolic charges from ZANU-PF resulted in years of infamous Gukurahundi pogroms in Matabeleland and the Midlands, in which many were killed. President Mugabe's description of the Gukurahundi as a "moment of madness" (Doran 2015) years after his "reconciliation" speech confirms ZANU-PF's lack of desire for accountability and justice for the wronged in Zimbabwe.

The political contestations in post-independence Zimbabwe bear testimony to how uncompromising ZANU-PF became. Muscular methods of contesting for power were its principle, from primitive stone-throwing and beating with sticks to state-organised and sophisticated violence orchestrated by the ruling party taking advantage of its levers of power (Sachikonye 2011: 17). ZANU-PF wanted to retain power by hook and by crook. This included intimidation, violence, property destruction and post-election retribution to those who dared to campaign or be elected on a ticket other than ZANU-PF. After such violence, President Mugabe would find ways of pardoning those responsible, confirming impunity and that those who kill for the president will not be punished.

However, blanket amnesties were increasingly being delegitimised internationally as a result of the growth of an international human rights culture. This change led to the setting up of courts such as the International Criminal Tribunals for the former Yugoslavia and Rwanda and the International Criminal Court (Ramsbotham et al. 2005), as the quest for accountability began to grow worldwide. In addition, holistic approaches including alternative dispute resolution mechanisms gained credibility as appropriate forms of intervention in diverse conflict and postconflict contexts. While this shift long failed to get traction in Zimbabwe—with any civil society organisation that considered accountability projects viewed as an agent of regime change and an enemy of the state—the situation changed after 2008.

The year 2008 witnessed a political and economic crisis that led to massive violence. The violence was a result of ZANU-PF losing its majority in parliament to MDC in that year's elections. In response ZANU-PF staged an operation to hold on to power through intimidation and violence against the opposition. It is alleged that soldiers, police and intelligence operatives committed the bulk of these acts of violence (Makhowa 2013). The escalation forced opposition leader Morgan Tsvangirai to announce his withdrawal from the 2008 presidential elections, citing unprecedented levels of state-orchestrated violence against rural areas believed to be MDC strongholds (Smith-Höhn 2009a, b). Nevertheless, the elections went ahead, resulting in a resounding 86% victory for President Mugabe. This electoral victory for ZANU-PF was aided by the manipulation of the results by the institution responsible for administering elections (Smith-Höhn 2009a, b). The results were dismissed as a sham by practically all observer groups (Makhowa 2013), and the impasse that followed necessitated a power-sharing arrangement in Zimbabwe.

As a forerunner to the Global Political Agreement, on July 21, 2008, ZANU-PF and the MDC formations signed a memorandum of understanding (MOU), committing their parties to "creating a genuine, viable, permanent, and sustainable solution to the Zimbabwe situation" (Zimbabwe Memorandum of Understanding 2008: 1) through a Government of National Unity (GNU). This required cessation of violence, the disbanding of militia groups, paramilitary camps and illegal roadblocks, and the normalisation of the political environment, among other key factors. However, the months following the MOU helped to consolidate mistrust among the political parties. MDC in particular felt it was undermined, not consulted and often ignored by ZANU-PF on important issues.

On September 15, 2008, the parties signed a power-sharing agreement brokered by then South African President Thabo Mbeki under the mandate of the Southern African Development Community (Eppel and Raftopoulos 2008). The implementation of the Global Political Agreement (GPA) was tenuous as a result of the struggles for the state between ZANU-PF and the MDC formations, which resembled a "zero-sum game, a peace treaty rather than a genuine transitional arrangement" (RAU 2009: 1). The sense was that "access to the state was the sine qua non for employment, patronage and future employment" (Eppel and Raftopoulos 2008: 10). The GPA ended up worsening the ideological and political tensions between the "distributive" and combative ZANU-PF on the one hand and the "democratisation" MDC and the rest of civil society on the other (RAU 2009). However, the agreement "did establish a basis for moving the political situation forward", even if it was silent "in the area of Transitional Justice" (Forum 2010: 2).

The Forum took advantage of the growing momentum for dealing with the past even among political actors. It did not see transitional justice efforts as a novel exercise in Zimbabwe, but just as a way of scaling up the "struggle for justice and accountability" (1). Therefore, it assumed that its *Taking Transitional Justice to the People* outreach programme would easily strike a chord with the people, and that ZANU-PF and the MDC formations would accept it as providing the "ripe moment" for dealing with the Zimbabwean situation, including its past. The Forum notes that ZANU-PF "never demonstrated a willingness to address issues of accountability for human rights violations—principally, it is suggested, because it was (and remains) one of the primary perpetrators" (Forum 2006: 9). The MDC formations also did not really assist, as they "neither sought to make this issue a deal breaker in the negotiations, nor had the political muscle to enforce such an inclusion" (2). But to the credit of the GPA, it managed to "give consideration to the setting up of a mechanism to properly advise on what measures might be necessary and practicable to achieve national healing, cohesion and unity in respect of victims of pre and post-independence political conflicts" (GPA 2009: 7), which the Forum exploited. Technically, this opened a window of opportunity for starting processes of peace-building and dealing with the past. This included the constitutional reform process and the establishment of the Organ for National Healing, Reconciliation and Integration (ONHRI).

The period witnessed legislative and legal reforms that "opened up new spaces for democratization and reforms in the political structure of the country" (GPA 2009: 4). However, some of these strides in the political arena were not translated into political and economic stability. The Zimbabwe Institute (2012) argues that the GPA managed to stabilise the economy but did not transform it. The government is believed to have failed to develop innovative policies to deal with economic challenges, to build consensus on key economic challenges and processes, which were to include reindustrialisation and an agricultural revival policy, as well as to deal with corruption, transparency and accountability in the utilisation of resources (4).

To summarise, on paper the GPA provided such amenable terms and conditions that it looked promising for a good operating and political environment, but in practice it also sowed tension and confusion. Despite this, the Forum embraced some of the opportunities and began its outreach campaign to "create awareness amongst ordinary Zimbabweans on what transitional justice is all about" (Forum 2009: 3).

Dealing with the Past: Which Past, Whose Past and Why?

Already in 2003, the Forum began to turn the slow wheels of transitional justice advocacy in Zimbabwe, which would gather speed only after 2008. The Forum began by organising a symposium in Johannesburg (Forum 2003) and subsequently a workshop in Harare 5 years later (Forum 2008a, b) to discuss options for justice and redress for human rights abuses in Zimbabwe. Seventy civil society organisations and individuals from Zimbabwe and the region with an interest in transitional justice participated. Many academics and practitioners with experience of South Africa's transitional justice process were present, particularly at the Johannesburg symposium. However, reflecting the dominance of urban NGOs in Zimbabwean civil society and debates on transitional justice, the Forum neglected to invite victims and survivors to either meeting. This approach may have been influenced by the nascence of the concept of transitional justice in Zimbabwe and the decision to involve regional practitioners and theorists at this brainstorming stage.

Participants in the meetings noted a decline in citizens' faith in the legal system to address the "ever-increasing violations" against Zimbabwe's citizens, and in political will to address them. Impunity had become an epidemic. There were calls from civil society to develop its "own positions on how to redress the abuses, using both domestic and international legal and institutional mechanisms". In the broadest of terms, the symposium and workshop participants agreed to "explore how best to achieve justice in the broadest possible sense for the many victims of the past and present human rights abuses in Zimbabwe" (Forum 2010: 9). It is this concentration on civil and political rights violations that became one of the weaknesses of the *Taking Transitional Justice to the People* outreach programme. Social and economic rights were severely marginalised.

Participants agreed on the following principles that they thought would drive an effective and legitimate transitional justice process in Zimbabwe:

- Victim centred
- Comprehensive, inclusive, consultative participation for all stakeholders, particularly victims

- Establishment of the truth
- Justice, compensation and reparations
- Acknowledgement
- National healing and reconciliation
- Non-repetition (never again)
- Gender sensitive
- No to blanket amnesty
- Transparency and accountability
- Nation building and reintegration (Forum 2010: 2)

The two meetings convinced the Forum that violence was repeatedly visited upon Zimbabweans because the voices of victims were ignored or suppressed by the state. Few had the audacity to talk about past violence openly. In light of the legacy of human rights abuses in the pre- and post-independence eras, the Forum recognised the potential for transitional justice to bring closure to the violent past. This forced the Forum to acknowledge the absence of victims in its activities and led its members to reach out to the people and talk about options for dealing with the past. This move was also a way of broadening the legitimacy of transitional justice discourse in Zimbabwe, and to gain buy-in from those affected by state-sponsored violence. It is important to note that at this time, there were no fully developed and coordinated voices of victims; nevertheless, their input was received through those individuals who heard about the outreach and participated. Victims' voices became organised a few years after the outreach programme.

The moral philosophy of the Forum in this work was founded on what it termed "non-negotiable minimum demands for a transitional justice process" (NTJWG 2015: 3). Most of these demands were shaped by the experience of the Forum leadership, international norms and contributions from the rest of civil society that had mandated the Forum to lead the process in Zimbabwe. Victims were not consulted. The non-negotiable demands released through a press statement by the Forum included:

- No amnesty for crimes against humanity, torture, rape and other sexual offences, and economic crimes such as corruption
- No extinguishing of civil claims against the perpetrators or the state
- Comprehensive reparations for victims of human rights violations
- No guarantee of job security for those found responsible for gross human rights violations and corruption
- A credible and independent truth-seeking inquiry into conflicts of the past which holds perpetrators to account and which provides victims the opportunity to tell their stories with a view to promoting national healing
- Independent monitoring and reform of operations and structures of the police, army, paramilitary, security coordination, administration of justice, food distribution and other organs of state involved in the implementation of the transition
- Development of interim or transitional rules to guarantee the rule of law and upholding of all basic rights during the transition, including the right to

engage in political activities. These rules must be enforceable. They must be encapsulated in amendments to the constitution or an interim constitution. Such rules must remain in place until free and fair elections are held and until a final Constitution, endorsed by the people, is in place
- Gender equity in official bodies and for transitional justice initiatives to pay particular attention to marginalised communities in Zimbabwe (Forum 2008a, b: 1)

The Forum's demands paid no attention to endogenous or traditional mechanisms in Zimbabwe, similar to the *gacaca* courts in Rwanda or *mato oput* among the Acholis of Uganda. This may be because of the Forum's alignment with dominant international approaches to transitional justice, which have reservations regarding the effectiveness of traditional mechanisms. The other reason may be newness of this Western model to the Zimbabwean culture and the lack of sound comparative research in Zimbabwe on the efficacy of the approaches in the context. The Forum would not try to experiment with a diversified raft of traditional practices at that moment.

The Forum realised that in order to reach the majority of victims of organised violence and torture in Zimbabwe, it would need to extend its activities to rural areas. Rural communities have limited access to justice and resources to pursue remedies against perpetrators. In addition, the Forum wanted to strengthen its victim-centred approach and create opportunities for victims to speak about options for dealing with the past that suit their diverse experiences in space and time. The victims the Forum reached out to include about 7000 cases represented by its lawyers. These included cases of women raped on political grounds, relatives of victims of politically motivated murder, farmers whose land was appropriated unlawfully and many others who were tortured, humiliated and disappeared.

One of the expectations of *Taking Transitional Justice to the People* was the development of a shared national narrative on Zimbabwe's past. The Forum observed that this proved difficult, mainly because the Zimbabwean conflicts were "generational", with "each level leaving different footprints, causing different interpretation" among citizens (Forum 2012: 10). For example, the Forum posits that, besides the liberation struggle in the 1970s, conflict episodes in Zimbabwe did not appear to have a categorical "national" scope in terms of intensity, meaning and interpretation. This affected the development of "collective reckoning on the legacies of human rights abuses" (4). In this conundrum, the question became which, and whose, past had to be addressed?

The Forum's pragmatic response was that all the past that was practically possible to address needed to be looked into (Forum 2012). There was no big or small past, an Ndebele past or Shona past, colonial or postcolonial past:

> Victims of all past human-rights abuses have the right to redress and to be consulted about the nature of the mechanisms that will be established to address their needs. The mechanisms that are established must be victim centred, and must be capable of addressing the needs of the victims in a meaningful way. Prior to the establishment of these mechanisms, there must be an extensive process of consultation with the victims' broader community about the mechanisms and the broader community about the sorts of persons who should be made responsible for operating them. (Lesizwe 2004: 8)

The effectiveness of the process was to be determined by the availability of evidence, the nature of the violations, the availability of the victims to be acknowledged and compensated and the resources. The Forum discouraged a process that dwelt on historical myths, anecdotes or one-sided self-victimising or glorifying narratives, which carried the potential to divide the nation and result in a failure to address critical injustices. This meant responding to negative legends such as that Ndebele warriors raided the Shona for their wives, children and cattle before the arrival of the white settlers. Partisan narratives at community level often dwelt on such narratives, rather than substantive issues of policy. To avert the Balkanisation of Zimbabwean narratives along petty historical and material lines shaped by tribal experiences, the Forum's *Taking Transitional Justice to the People* was focused on discernible and chronological periods: "the pre-colonial, colonial/liberation struggle period, post-independence up to 1990 and the post 2000 up to 2008" (Forum 2012: 4). To this end, the Forum emphasised the importance of immortalising evidential memory (memory that can be traced to concrete evidence) as a secret of redemption (Bevernage 2010) and non-recurrence as the basis for "a comprehensive transitional justice process in Zimbabwe" (Forum 2012: 4).

The periods identified by the Forum had clear patterns of state-sponsored human rights violations across the country. At the same time the Forum noted that the violations in precolonial times were due to state formation in the eighteenth-century Southern Africa. These had to be set aside in the quest for justice in modern Zimbabwe,[4] but the abuses post-Second World War could not be ignored, thanks to the massive developments in humanitarian and international human rights law applicable to Zimbabwe now. The participants, however, agreed that violations that occurred before the Second World War would be important for memorialisation. In addition to the liberation war, the period just after independence and the post-2000 period were highlighted as critical for postconflict review. While the Forum would not prescribe the important periods or where to start, as this must be the people's prerogative, it understood that "choosing where one starts the narratives of conflict constitutes an ideological statement" (Lerma 2011: 122). The Forum focused on explaining the transitional justice options (pillars) available for participants, and the consequences and practicality of each option.

Despite these efforts by the Forum in the communities, there were doubts among the leading civil society organisations at the time whether Zimbabwe was ready for transitional justice. They spent more time debating whether the country was on the path to transition than worrying about transitional justice (Crisis 2013). This doubt fell

[4]The lack of sound documentation of the excesses of state formation in Southern Africa led to the need to be pragmatic about transitional justice in Zimbabwe. It was agreed that an effective process should rely on sound evidence, not just conjectures. However, this should not downplay the role of early settlers in the violent expropriation of African land. The focus on the post-Second World War period was made easier by the development of international law and human rights jurisprudence. Besides, the land issue was settled in Zimbabwe, albeit in a violent way, during the land reform programmes from 2000.

happily into the arms of the state, which went all the way to show that there were no political changes necessary, let alone transitions to be experienced in the short run.

The Outreach Programme

The Forum carried out *Taking Transitional Justice to the People* in order to fulfil its broad goal of creating awareness among ordinary people on what transitional justice is all about. This outreach had the specific objectives of training participants on:

- The nature and history of transitional justice
- The aims and objectives of transitional justice mechanisms
- The options and challenges of transitional justice within the Zimbabwean context (Forum 2009: 3)

To achieve these objectives, the Forum started by deploying its staff to 51 constituencies in the provinces and districts where significant levels of human rights violations had been documented before and after 2008. The Forum had initially identified 84 electoral constituencies for outreach, but ended up working in 51 communities due to a combination of resource constraints, inhibitive political tensions in some areas and threats to the outreach teams in others (Table 4.1). The choice of the target constituencies for outreach was based on the Zimbabwe Political Crisis Map.[5] The lead facilitators for the meetings were mainly lawyers from the Forum's legal unit and the Forum's researchers, who were assisted by an academic with a background in the social sciences. At the beginning of the outreach, the Forum deployed a minimum of four facilitators for every meeting. In the final phase of the outreach, two facilitators, who had become the core of the programme, were responsible for the meetings.

Three broad approaches defined this outreach work: training, consultation and citizen involvement in transitional justice work and processes. The Forum's vision was to create awareness of transitional justice among rural and urban people, and to establish a cadre of activists who would become the critical drivers of the transitional justice process in Zimbabwe and shape the discussion going forward. Although the consultation approach was not thoroughly developed, the programme gave participants the opportunity to review their challenges and discuss their options for redress.

The planning for the outreach programme required a thorough understanding of the areas most affected by political violence, including the local political dynamics and resources. This necessitated a good environmental analysis to determine the levels of threat and the capacity for turning threats into violence by local vigilantes. The Forum staff that facilitated the outreach was prepared for the task beforehand, and even for their withdrawal in the event of a viable threat. They had mobile

[5] Zimbabwe Political Crisis Map was created by Ushahidi to identify violence hotspots during the 2008 political crisis in Zimbabwe.

Table 4.1 Outreach areas by province[a]

Harare	Mashonaland East	Mashonaland Central	Mashonaland West	Manicaland	Midlands	Masvingo	Matabeleland North	Matabeleland South
Epworth	Goromonzi South	Bindura	Chegutu	Buhera Central	Chirumhanzi	Chiredzi South	Binga North	Bulilima
Mbare		Mt. Darwin South	Chinhoyi	Chipinge Central	Gokwe-Kana		Lupane East	
Zengeza West		Muzarabani	Hurungwe	Makoni Central	Mberngwa East		Nkayi	
		Shamva North	Kariba	Mutasa Central	Mberengwa West		Umguza	
		Shamva South	Makonde	Mutasa North	Shurugwi			
			Manyame	Nyanga South	Zvishavane			
			Mhondoro Mubaira					
			Sanyati					
			Zvimba West					

Source: Forum (2010: 124)

[a]Seven out of the 51 constituencies where meetings were held were rural. Most of the violations in Zimbabwe happen in rural areas, which statistically are believed to be the stronghold for the ruling ZANU-PF. It is alleged that ZANU-PF and the state are the major perpetrators of human rights violations

phones, off-road vehicles and legal backing, should anything happen. The participants, however, had none of this support. They simply braved the situation. After contributing their views, experiences and fears, they would go back to their villages or communities, where they were "welcomed" by local gatekeepers, militia and party stalwarts who might threaten them for participating. This was the structural weakness of the outreach from the outset, for which the designers of the programme had made few plans.

The outreach was conducted as a result of brave hearts. It was a daredevil adventure since the government had not announced a public policy directed at preparing the people for such an exercise. This increased the vulnerability of the project to political activism on the ground. In addition, there was no political pressure from the opposition MDC formations for accountability at the government level to create the necessary momentum or political legitimacy for the work. Because the policy foundations for the exercise were shaky, this presented opportunities for government predation on the programme and idea. Some government and local partisan agencies started to describe the programme as mischief bent on causing despondency among citizens. The uncritical and apostolic partisan supporter challenged the motive of *Taking Transitional Justice to the People*. To some it was a regime change programme by another name, and to others it was an exercise in opening old wounds (Rusere 2016). Thus, the programme attracted negative attention from the government and other critics. It became haunted, the most "monitored" action during the GPA era (Jesuit-Zimbabwe 2012). The consequences of this monitoring were only noticed years later when the then executive director of the Forum was arrested for operating an illegal and "unregistered" institution in 2012. This manoeuvre was clearly meant to stop the programme, and it threatened the Forum to its existential core.

In February 2009 the Forum took its first trip to the communities for the outreach programme. This, and the many others that followed, was like voyages of discovery: exciting and yet full of foreboding. By June 2010, 51 constituencies had been visited and successful meetings had been held with community members as planned. A total of 2,357 people attended these meetings, 43% women and 57% men (Forum 2010: 124). The majority of participants, ranging in age from 21 to 70 (Forum 2009: 10), expressed their desire for institutionalising transitional justice in order to deal comprehensively with the past in Zimbabwe. The Forum used local coordinators seconded by its member organisations to invite all its participants. There was no discrimination on participation. All people, whether from ZANU-PF or other political parties, including government officials, were free to participate.

During the outreach the Forum staff discussed various versions of transitional justice that had begun to do the rounds in the media and how different groups were advocating for varying modi operandi. For instance, the staff noted that the state's focus was on forgiveness, while the NCA's focus was on institutional reform and setting up a truth, justice, reconciliation and conflict-prevention commission (NCA 2001). The Forum also noted the National Association of Non-Governmental

Organisations' (NANGO) advocacy for truth seeking, prosecutions, reparations and institutional reform as mechanisms of transitional justice. Other viewpoints they discussed were the private media demanding trials and indictments of political elites by the ICC (Muvingi 2011). The practicality of each approach was considered and it was left to the people to choose the best option for their context.

None of the programme facilitators had formal or practical training in transitional justice. In addition, none had training in peacebuilding or postconflict transformation. But all had experience in human rights work. At the core of the Forum's message was the call for the "pillars" of transitional justice—prosecutions, truth telling, reparations and institutional reform as necessities to "combating impunity and advance reconciliation" (Bosire 2006: 3). This approach meant that the outreach programme narrowed the transitional justice concept to legalistic formalities, which made the idea difficult to support for perpetrators and their supporters, while at the same time creating high expectations for justice among victims. In relation to both these groups, the Forum had no ready answers. The Forum also followed the tendency of most NGOs in Zimbabwe in only discussing the possibility of state-run processes with the participants, without considering alternatives or civil society-run processes.

In addition, the Forum staff had not understood transitional justice in a "transformative" sense (Gready et al. 2010), but from a legalistic point of view. As such, discussion of the social machinery of oppression or structural violence and its relationship to everyday violence was conspicuously absent from most programme meetings. This changed from 2011 going forward, as the Forum started to underscore the structural, fundamental problems that abet conflicts in the first place, such as gender issues and tradition. The Forum also took into account the role of illicit minerals such as diamonds, arguing that there is a connection between the military and mining industry complex and past human rights violations.

It also began to emphasise the transitional justice in the everyday life and the importance of restorative justice over retributive justice in its programming at the community level. This was a response to the fast developments in the transitional justice field, with the ascendency of traditional and everyday mechanisms in restoring relations after conflict (Huyse 2008: 1–21), and to practical lessons in dealing with egregious acts in the African context.

With *Taking Transitional Justice to the People*, the concept of transitional justice was introduced for virtually the first time to ordinary citizens of Zimbabwe. The most difficult challenge was to condense or even translate the concept, as "transitional justice" was basically an alien term, with no local equivalents. Even academics struggled with applying the concept to everyday-life challenges. Participants in the outreach programme wanted transitional justice in the everyday life and for Forum staff to use appropriate language, not imported academic constructions. However, the staff used the term in its pure technical sense and defined it using the United Nations parlance. This may explain why in a post-outreach survey the Forum conducted in 2011, 82% of respondents from the communities where the outreach was conducted professed ignorance of the transitional justice concept (Forum 2011).

Obstacles to Participation

The *Taking Transitional Justice to the People* project began just a few months after the tempestuous elections and violent presidential run-off in 2008. The Forum reports that 10,456 citizens were victims of human rights violations during the election and immediate post-election period, of whom 107 died (Forum 2008a, b: 49). Initiating an outreach programme for the people, many shell-shocked and living among neighbours who were perpetrators, was a difficult proposition. Most of the people in the communities targeted by the outreach programme had been traumatised by what they went through either as community members or directly as individuals. In Chipinge, in Manicaland Province, a group of participants "approached the facilitators in confidence and reported that they were unable to participate freely for fear of the war veterans and militias who had threatened unspecified action" (Forum 2010: 16).

ZANU-PF political leaders and activists prevented active participation in many parts of the country. In all such cases they did not consult the people before making their interventions. In Zvimba West, local ZANU-PF officials, who accused some participants of speaking ill of the military during the outreach meetings, threatened unspecified action, and a retired major in the company of ZANU-PF members threatened other participants with disappearance and loss of their livelihoods. In Mberengwa West, two prominent ZANU-PF members, the chairperson and a councillor, stopped preparations for a meeting, claiming that "the subject of transitional justice and national healing was forbidden" and ZANU-PF was the only instrument that could relax that censure (16). In the view of the councillor, the transitional justice meetings were politically sensitive and could not be allowed to go on as they ruffled feathers. The experience was similar in Mberengwa South and North.

In Chipinge, ZANU-PF activists turned the tables against the Forum staff and accused them of organising a political meeting. Fortunately the meeting was allowed to proceed, but participants were not allowed to contribute because the "people of Chipinge had nothing to say" (16). The few who tried to contribute were disrupted by the activists chanting slogans. Similar tactics were encountered in Mount Darwin, where the police had to step in to protect participants from ZANU-PF activists (a rare case at the time).

In some cases ZANU-PF activists refused to attend meetings for reasons such as that the MDC had just announced that it would not work with ZANU-PF in government, as was the case during a meeting held in Mbare, Harare. In Mhondoro-Mubaira, ZANU-PF ordered traditional leaders not to participate during discussions. The police also played a significant role in curtailing participation, for example in

Bindura, Shurugwi and Beitbridge, by coming up with reasons to stop, disrupt or postpone the meetings. For instance, the police chief in Bindura stopped a meeting stating that the organisers had not received clearance from the Ministry of Justice (17), although there is no law compelling organisers of meetings to be cleared by the Ministry of Justice. In Shurugwi and Chirumhanzu in Midlands Province police postponed meetings stating that there were conflicts in the GNU regarding the constitution-making process. Even a case of water shortage in Beitbridge was used to stop a meeting. However, there were many cases where participation was exceptionally smooth and people exercised their liberties to air their concerns and demands for dealing with the past.

Options for Transitional Justice that Emerged from the Outreach

Since 2003, civil society, the political opposition and the labour movement, particularly the Zimbabwe Congress of Trade Unions (ZCTU), have argued that a transitional justice process is needed in Zimbabwe. At the community level, citizens, particularly victims, called for both justice and to be heard (Forum 2010). However, despite these foundational aspirations in a segment of Zimbabwean society, the Forum understood that ZANU-PF controlled the state, including the monopoly on violence. It retained control of the Ministry of Justice, the Central Intelligence Organisation and the army, and the president had absolute power to appoint the chief of police, which gave him control over the Joint Operational Command, or the National Security Council under the auspices of the GPA (Forum 2006). These loomed as foreboding institutions, reminding Zimbabwean society of the limits to their desire for accountability and democratisation. In addition, the Zimbabwean bureaucracy was militarised and military chiefs were deployed to the highest positions in parastatals, with a vested interest in maintaining the status quo of impunity (Eppel and Raftopoulos 2008). Thus, the Forum recognised that transitional justice was not going to be an easy process. Nonetheless, the outreach programme elicited a number of ideas regarding what ordinary citizens needed from such a process.

Truth Seeking

Truth seeking was one of the pillars of transitional justice highlighted by the Forum facilitators during the outreach meetings. Following on the previous mandate given by civil society during the 2003 Johannesburg symposium, the Forum emphasised during its workshops the setting up of a Truth and Justice Commission to handle this aspect of dealing with the past in Zimbabwe. The Forum argued that, through the work of the commission, the facts of past events would be established, thereby giving voice to victims and their relatives. In addition, the commission would be able to establish an official record of causes of the conflict and provide recommendations for institutional reforms to prevent future violations. The Forum also emphasised that the findings of the Commission could "be used as a body of evidence for the purposes of reparations, for vetting public institutions of identified perpetrators or criminal justice investigations at a later, less politically risky, time". The official recognition of the truth, and acceptance of a new "shared" truth about the past, could contribute to the process of healing and reconciliation (Domingo 2012: 4).

The participants in the outreach programme corroborated and highlighted the establishment of a truth recovery processes. Additionally, many people interviewed in the Forum's follow-up survey wanted a Church-run truth commission (Forum 2011: 19). However, it was generally noted that for the truth commissions to be effective, it would need to be "independent from political interferences, impartial and adequately resourced" (Forum 2010: 119). This would be achievable through wide consultations in the appointment of the commissioners. In addition, participants expressed a preference for a truth recovery process that would allow victims to speak freely about their experiences and concerns, particularly experiences of violence committed at night, without any witnesses present, and that would enable the identification of perpetrators.

Prosecutions

Most of the facilitators in the earlier stages of the outreach programme were lawyers, and they found it easy to highlight the retributive aspect of transitional justice. The lawyers were drawn from the Forum's litigation unit and had vast experience in court actions, but little or no experience in alternative justice methods. In the meetings, prosecution was argued as the best way of achieving justice for victims, and to some extent imposed on the participants. The Forum saw retributive justice as able "to give victims and their families a means of justice and catharsis, to officially confirm the facts and to end impunity and deter potential future perpetrators". It further argued that if "trials are perceived as legitimate, they can also signal the commitment and ability of a government to uphold the rule of law, due process and human rights" (Domingo 2012: 4). While criminal prosecutions were at the core of the Forum's messaging, other forms of justice were discussed, such as the nonpunitive forms that included acknowledgement, proper history records, archiving, community reparations, reburials and commemorations.

The Forum and participants recognised that there were immediate challenges that needed to be addressed before justice could be done. First, there was no democratic transition in Zimbabwe, and ZANU-PF would not allow a process that would expose it. Second, the MDC was not powerful enough in the GNU to cause the international community to push for the arrest and prosecution of Zimbabwean political leaders complicit in violence. More so, there were real fears that ZANU-PF would issue a blanket amnesty to perpetrators, as is its age-old practice. Nonetheless, participants called for perpetrators to be prosecuted before matters of reconciliation were considered. They suggested that prosecution would deter perpetrators from continued acts of violence and that this would stop the culture of violence. In addition, participants thought that it would be justice for the victims when "perpetrators are brought to the book and are punished for their offences" (Forum 2010: 24), thus making "everyone accountable for the atrocities committed" (31).

Reparations

Reparations found resonance with the traditional practice in Zimbabwe, which says that the solution to an avenging spirit is to appease it (*Mushonga wengozi kuiripa*). Many Zimbabweans have lost so much during the difficult times, including property and their livelihoods, as well as relatives and friends. Most of the Zimbabweans interviewed in the Forum's follow-up survey said that they would not find satisfaction in the incarceration of the perpetrator only, but also needed some form of restitution. Some asked who would be arrested in the case of the perpetrator being dead or unknown at the time of trails or reparations. In light of historical injustices, some respondents argued for reparations that emphasised compensation, with the state expected to take full responsibility (Forum 2011: 19). Respondents also challenged the state to compensate victims and their families for their losses during land reforms.

Participants in the outreach programme agreed that material and nonmaterial reparations were needed, including reburial of the dead, acknowledgement by the state for the political violence, individual compensation where possible and collective reparations where wrongs were meted out to groups. However, participants also recognised that the state would likely plead that it faced resource constraints and call for prioritisation of national issues. Most participants noted that public acknowledgement by the state would cost nothing and that the state should give this form of reparations, although not in the manner of President Mugabe who acknowledged past violations by saying that Gukurahundi was a "moment of madness" (Coltart 2016: 58).

Institutional Reform

The Forum approached institutional reform from the perspective that, in Zimbabwe, perpetrators had not been charged for their actions because of the protection they received from the state. During the outreach meetings, the Forum staff argued for the establishment of guarantees that serious human rights and international law violations committed in the past would not be repeated. To achieve this, the staff argued that it was of primary importance to reform institutions that have committed violations or failed to prevent them. In light of the impunity enjoyed by perpetrators of serious violations of human rights, and the repetition of crimes, successful reform of the country's justice and security sectors was considered crucial.

The participants responded to these suggestions by identifying institutions and agencies of the state that urgently needed to be reformed. Traditional leadership, because it is not only what many people understand most but also the first line of contact with the national authority for most local people, was identified as needing urgent reform. Seventy per cent of Zimbabwean citizens live under a traditional authority in the rural areas. The traditional leadership takes care of the community's spiritual, social and sometimes economic matters, mediating on issues of deaths, births, land, water, rain and local resources like access to trees for construction and energy.

The government has been accused of capturing traditional authorities for use in controlling and manipulating the electoral choices of citizens (Matyszak 2010). To this end, participants and traditional leaders attending the meetings argued for strengthening the traditional authorities and securing them against political influence (Forum 2010: 42), so that they are able to deal with the everyday issues of transitional justice. The main line of argument from the participants was that the traditional leadership is proximate to the people's daily challenges, including poverty. Its weakened authority has meant that the leadership is unable to deal meaningfully with "urgent matters like starvation or political violence" and any other "crisis in the times of conflict" (42).

Another problem that participants wanted addressed was the politicisation of the traditional authorities. There were claims that the institution was patently partisan, and this exposed the leadership to political manipulation by the government and politicians. Participants wanted a revaluation of local conflict management resources embodied in traditional authorities and practices, as these have practicality, resilience and legitimacy. The transformation of traditional authorities was suggested in Mashonaland West to include rebranding of the institution from being a subject of ridicule as "part of the terrorist group" that "facilitate[s] torture of people of divergent views" to being honourable custodians of values, customs and culture (Forum 2010: 45). To this end, the Forum advocated for reforms to traditional mechanisms that can effectively complement conventional judicial systems, as they have real potential for promoting justice, reconciliation and a culture of democracy, as well as offering ways of restoring a sense of accountability.

Security was another important sector that was extensively discussed as needing reform. The ambit of the security sector included the military, police, intelligence and prisons, as well as non-state structures such as the war veterans and youth militias of the 1980s and 2000s. These are institutions that the ZANU-PF component of the GPA controlled, resulting in "subtle military rule". The security sector was conceived of as a "willing and effective midwife of ZANU PF political ambitions" (Musavengana 2011: 30). All participants had challenges with the security sector and its lack of professionalism and partisan inclinations. For instance, participants alleged that the Central Intelligence Organisation had abrogated its duty to detect national threats in becoming the president's private guard, and thus a major perpetrator of gross human rights violations. It has been established that the Central Intelligence Organisation's tactics include "abductions and use of torture to extract information from political opponents, human rights defenders and ordinary citizens" (32). As such, participants do not view this body as complementary to a democratic society.

The security sector has also encroached on public institutions. Concerns about the "Zanufication of the public service, traditional leadership structures, youth training centers, and militarization of the public institutions" (34) are widespread. This was manifested through the deployment of "retired military, police and intelligence personnel to key public institutions including the electoral commission, strategic grain reserve, judiciary, and prison services, and parastatals". While there is nothing wrong with retired security personnel taking up positions in these institutions on a competitive basis, this particular deployment of ex-service men "to public institutions was an active pursuit of partisan agenda of retaining ZANU PF hegemony" (34). The pronouncements and actions tailored to advance a political agenda by these serving and ex-service men reinforced some of the partisan allegations levelled against them.[6]

The National Youth Service programme, meanwhile, was converted into an anti-MDC indoctrination programme and a pro-ZANU-PF support group. Particularly in 2002 and 2008, Youth Service training centres became torture camps, where members and supporters of opposition parties were tortured and raped. Indoctrinated youth and war veterans became the vanguard for the violent land dispossession campaign. This is confirmed by a former youth militia member, who noted, "We are ZANU PF's 'B' team. The army is the 'A' team and we do things the government does not want the 'A' team to do" (Solidarity Peace Trust 2003:54).

Against calls by both the MDC formations and Thabo Mbeki to have security sector reforms instituted, high-ranking officials in President Mugabe's government have remained resolute that there will be no such reforms. Defence Minister Emmerson Mnangagwa, for example, told senior military personnel that there would be no reforms as long as he remained in government (International Crisis Group 2013). These manoeuvres caused anxiety among the impartial participants in the outreach programme. In Matabeleland, there were concerns on the unbecoming behaviour of some security personnel. Participants made remarks like, "The police and CIO have become law unto themselves. Whatever they want to do to whoever, they do without fear [*Indel'ampholisa lama CIO enza ngayo angani bahlala kwelabo ilizwe hatshi kuleli esikilo. Benza santando benganakile lutho*]" (Forum 2010: 58). One participant in Mashonaland West noted, "If I was in power, I would replace all the security forces with a totally new force" (82). Participants argued that vetting or disbanding the elements of the current security sector and building a new, professional stock were central to transitional justice in Zimbabwe.

[6] In 2009, General Constantine Chiwenga, commander of Zimbabwe Defence Forces, said that he would have difficulties in saluting Mr. Morgan Tsvangirai because he lacked liberation war credentials. See http://messagefromafrica.com/2009/02/22/i-will-have-difficulties-saluting-tsvangirai-constantine-chiwenga (Accessed 14 December 2017).

Memorialisation

The outreach programme spent very little time on memorialisation. Although memorialisation is understood as a symbolic form of reparations, the outreach meetings did not dwell much on it. Most of the people who attended the meetings were victims who met their perpetrators on a daily basis and wanted to be materially compensated for injuries suffered. In addition, the people tended to memorialise their dead using quotidian traditional and spiritual strategies. Thus, the issue took a back seat.

The orientation of the Forum facilitators also possibly led to this lack of emphasis on memorialisation. The staff placed more emphasis on prosecutions and institutional reform. In addition to their professional orientation, part of the reason for this may be the intimidation and judicial harassment of human rights defenders and other civil society activists at the time, which constrained the space for memorialisation and truth telling. In fact, the government actively stifled any attempts at memory building. For example, in Matabeleland North, an opposition member of parliament and co-chairperson of the ONHRI was arrested for organising a memorial ceremony for the Gukurahundi atrocities.

It is the National Transitional Justice Working Group, a platform developed and coordinated by the Forum in 2013, which was to take up the issue of memorialisation (NTJWG 2015). During the outreach programme, the Forum focused on issues that they saw as directly affecting the people, including material reparations, acknowledgement, justice, truth, accountability and institutional reform (Forum 2011).

Conclusion

The Zimbabwe Human Rights NGO Forum managed to conclude an outreach programme that would become the exemplar in the transitional justice discourse in Zimbabwe. From this programme, the Forum learnt about doing sensitive outreach in difficult environments. It also learnt that civil society organisations need to approach communities with an open mind, rather than with templates for what they want people to know and accept. In *Taking Transitional Justice to the People*, participants, even when they were meeting the concept of transitional justice for the first time, ascribed their own meanings to it depending on their individual and collective experiences. To them, transitional justice could not be "one shoe fits all".

For transitional justice, timing is important. This is what the Forum understood, thanks to the outreach. The programme revealed that in contexts that are not postconflict *stricto sensu*, introducing programmes to deal with the past is not easy, but it is also not an impossibility. For participants, the past had to be dealt with now, despite the structural and political challenges and the technical and social constraints that needed to be overcome, such as penetrating "besieged" and threatened communities or talking about past violations in a context where the perpetrator government still controls citizens' behaviour through its absolute monopoly over violence.

Programmes of this nature require thorough planning and preparation in advance to be effective; it cannot be just a hunch. You cannot learn on the job, so to speak. Zimbabwean civil society, including the Forum, has learnt from its age-old weakness of excluding beneficiaries at the conceptualisation and design stages of its programmes and how this negatively affects the quality of the outcome. The top-down model used in the design and implementation of the Forum's outreach programme left many issues unclear, only to be addressed during implementation, including as essential a problem as how to translate the term "transitional justice".

The Forum also recognised that regional stereotyping is a challenge in Zimbabwe that needs to be overcome if collective approaches to dealing with the past are to be achieved. Even though the Forum benefited from its broad membership to access certain areas during its outreach, some organisations in the Mashonaland region still find it difficult to break into the Matabeleland region and take a lead in unravelling the past. Regional NGOs do not always allow easy passage or freely assist national NGOs. It's a turf issue. This is not healthy for reckoning with the past in Zimbabwe.

However, to limit the constraints noted above, the Forum found that communal storytelling and bottom-up processes are powerful tools in the recovery process. The involvement of local people in collecting and documenting local truth is in itself a mechanism for communal healing and reconciliation. Through this process structural issues are reviewed, and, combined with storytelling and local history as well as "top-down" truth recovery (through the work of the National Peace and Reconciliation Commission), the complete picture of what transpired is drawn. This is because communities desire inclusion in matters that affect them. Thus, communal involvement provides a voice to victims and marginalised communities. The result is that previously untold stories are heard and recorded. This serves to "underline the validity of different experiences between and within communities, and emphasise the importance of individual and grassroots experiences, thus providing an alternative to dominant 'macro' narratives" (McEvoy 2006: 10). By offering spaces for reflection, community-based work also offers the "possibilities of healing when there are internal communal divisions. Such deliberations could in turn feed into a broader societal process of truth recovery, whether or not there was a formal, state-sponsored mechanism" (10). This point needs to be highlighted by implementers of transitional justice projects.

In its current form, transitional justice in Zimbabwe will not easily address the concerns raised during *Taking Transitional Justice to the People*. There is too much residual violence resulting from the unresolved cases of past violence on the ground to allow communities and individuals to express themselves. Those in power are too frightened to let the people participate openly in dealing with the past. Civil society is constrained, weak and divided. These tensions militate against a national project, such as transitional justice or dealing with the past. Yet the Forum, with the bigger picture of a healed and accountable society in sight, will continue with its work. There are no obstacles too big and power too fearful to stop the Forum's current commitment to dealing with the past in Zimbabwe.

References

Bevernage, B. (2010). Writing the past out of the present: History and the politics of time in transitional justice. *History Workshop Journal, 69*, 111–131

Bosire, L. (2006). *Overpromised, undelivered: Transitional justice in Sub-Sahara Africa*. New York: International Center for Transitional Justice.

Centre for the Study of Violence and Reconciliation. (2009). *Subliminal terror? Human rights violations and torture in Zimbabwe during 2008*.

Church and Civil Society Forum (2014). *Traditional Mechanisms for Transitional Justice*. www.ccsf.org.zw/sites/default/files/publications/TraditionalMechanismscopy.pdf

Coltart, D. (2016). *The struggle continues: 50 years of Tyranny in Zimbabwe*. Harare: Weaver Press.

Crisis in Zimbabwe Coalition. (2013). *Transition barometer* (5th ed.).

Domingo, P. (2012). *Dealing with legacies of violence: Transitional justice and governance transitions*. ODI Background Note.

Doran, S. (2015, May 18). Mugabe's complicity in Gukurahundi. *The NewsDay*. Retrieved from

Edwards, M. (1998). *Nailing the jelly to the wall: NGOs, civil society and international development*. London: Edwards Associates.

Eppel, S. (2003). *A brief history of violations of human rights in Zimbabwe since to present*. New York: International Centre for Transitional Justice.

Eppel, S., & Raftopoulos, B. (2008). *Political crisis, mediation and the prospects for transitional justice in Zimbabwe*. Report for the Developing a Transformation Agenda for Zimbabwe.

Forum (2003). Political Violence Report. The Forum, April 2003, Harare. Retreived http://archive.niza.nl/docs/200305261608238172.pdf

GPA. (2009). Global Political Agreement, September 2009.

Gready, P., Boesten, J., Crawford, G., & Wilding, P. (2010). *Transformative justice—A concept note*. Retrieved from http://www.wun.ac.uk/files/transformative_justice_-_concept_note_web_version.pdf

Huyse, L. (2008). Introduction: Tradition-based approaches in peacemaking, transitional justice and reconciliation policies. In *Traditional justice and reconciliation after violent conflict: Learning from African experiences*. International Institute for Democracy and Electoral Assistance.

International Crisis Group. (2013). *Zimbabwe: Election scenarios*. Africa Report, 202, 6 May. Retrieved from http://www.refworld.org/pdfid/518916c84.pdf

Jesuit-Zimbabwe. (2012). *Communication, prepared for Jesuit-Zimbabwe*. Retrieved from http://www.jesuitszimbabwe.co.zw/index.php/what-we-do/media

Lerma, J. C. (2011). Recognizing conflict and escaping violence: Contemporary Colombian migration. *International Journal of Business, Humanities and Technology, 1*(1).

Lesizwe, T. (2004). Civil society and justice in Zimbabwe. In *Summary of the proceedings of a symposium held in Johannesburg*, August 11–13, 2003.

Makhowa, G. (2013). Examining Zimbabwe's global political agreement. *Southern African Peace and Security Studies, 2*(1).

Mandaza, I. (1994). The state and democracy in Southern Africa: Towards a conceptual framework. In E. E. Osaghae (Ed.), *Between state and civil Society in Africa: Perspectives on development* (pp. 249–271). Dakar: CODESRIA.

Masunungure, E. (2009). *Zimbabwe's agonizing but irreversable political transition*. Paper presented at the European Conference on African Studies, Respacing Africa, June 4–7, 2009.
Matyszak, D. A. (2010). *Formal structures of power in rural Zimbabwe*. Prepared for Research & Advocacy Unit. Retrieved from http://www.swradioafrica.com/Documents/FormalStructuresofPowerinRuralZimbabwe.pdf
McEvoy, K. (2006). *Making peace with the past: Options for truth recovery regarding the conflict in and about Northern Ireland.* Belfast: Healing Through Remembering.
Movement for Democratic Change. (2003). *From crisis to democratic human-centred development: Values, goals and policies of the Movement for Democratic Change*.
Moyo, J. N. (1993). Civil society in Zimbabwe, *Zambezia, 6*. Retrieved from http://pdfproc.lib.msu.edu/?file=/DMC/AfricanJournals/pdfs/JournaloftheUniversityofZimbabwe/vol20n1/juz020001002.pdf
Musavengana, T. (2011). *Security sector: No transition without transformation*. Retrieved from http://www.osisa.org/sites/default/files/sup_files/SecuritysectoinZimbabweTakawiraMusavengana.pdf
Muvingi, S. (2011). Transitional justice and pre-transition in Zimbabwe. *Conflict Trends, 1*.
National Constitutional Assembly. (2001). *Proposed draft constitution of Zimbabwe*.
National Constitutional Assembly. (2002a). *Proposed draft constitution of Zimbabwe*.
National Constitutional Assembly. (2002b). *Proposed draft constitution of Zimbabwe*.
Nkomo, J. (2001). *The story of my life*. London: Methuen Publishing.
NTJWG. (2015). *Guiding principles for transitional justice policy and practice in Zimbabwe*.
Ramsbotham, O., Woodhouse, T., & Hugh, M. (2005). *Contemporary conflict resolution: The prevention, management and transformation of deadly conflicts* (2nd ed.). Cambridge: Malden.
Reseach and Advocacy Unit. (2009). *Transitional Justice in Zimbabwe: A pilot survey of the views of activists and victims*.
Rusere, P. (2016, October 16). Spiking regime change agenda. *The Patriot*. Retrieved from http://www.thepatriot.co.zw/top-news/spiking-regime-change-agenda/
Sachikonye, L. (2011). *When a state turns on its citizens*. Harare: Weaver Press.
Smith-Höhn, J. (2009a). *Unpacking the Zimbabwe crisis: A situation report*. Retrieved from https://www.issafrica.org/publications/situation-reports
Smith-Höhn, J. (2009b). *Unpacking the Zimbabwean crisis: A situation report*. Institute for Security Studies. Retrieved from https://www.issafrica.org/uploads/MADAGASCAR15OCT09.PDF
Solidarity Peace Trust. (2003). *National youth service training—"Shaping youths in a truly Zimbabwean manner". An overview of youth militia training and activities in Zimbabwe, October 2000—August 2003*. Prepared for the Solidarity Peace Trust, 5 September, 2003. Retrieved from http://www.solidaritypeacetrust.org/download/report-files/youth_militia.pdf
Stewart, S. (1997). Happy ever after in the marketplace: Non-government organisations and uncivil society. *Review of African Political Economy, 24*(71), 11–34.
Van de Walle, N. (2002). Africa's range of regimes. *Journal of Democracy, 13*(2), 66–80.
Zimbabwe Human Rights NGO Forum. (2001). *Politically motivated violence in Zimbabwe 2000–2001*.
Zimbabwe Human Rights NGO Forum. (2006). *Exploring transitional justice options in contemporary Zimbabwe*.
Zimbabwe Human Rights NGO Forum. (2008a). Press Release: Minimum demands adopted by participants at the transitional justice workshop "Options for Zimbabwe" held at the Holiday Inn, Harare 9–10 September 2008. Retrieved from http://www.hrforumzim.org/press-releases/minimum-demands-adopted-by-participants-at-the-transitional-justice-workshop-"option-for-zimbabwe-held-at-the-holiday-inn-harare-on-9-—10-september-2008/
Zimbabwe Human Rights NGO Forum. (2008b). *Annual report*.
Zimbabwe Human Rights NGO Forum. (2009). *Taking transitional justice to the people: Outreach report* (Vol. 1).
Zimbabwe Human Rights NGO Forum. (2010). *Taking transitional justice to the people: Outreach report* (Vol. 2).

Zimbabwe Human Rights NGO Forum. (2011). *Transitional justice national survey: A report on the people's recommendations and perceptions*, July.

Zimbabwe Human Rights NGO Forum. (2012). *'How far back should we go?' An analysis of the preferred periodical options for transitional justice in Zimbabwe* (p. 1). Transitional Justice in Zimbabwe Special Paper, June 2012.

Zimbabwe Memorandum of Understanding (2008). Memorandum of Understanding Between ZANU PF and Two Movement for Democratic Change Formations, 21July 2008. Retrieved from http://archive.kubatana.net/docs/demgg/mou_080721.pdf

Chapter 5
Persistent Injuries, the Law and Politics: The South African Victims' Support Group Khulumani and Its Struggle for Redress

Zukiswa Puwana and Rita Kesselring

Introduction

South Africa is often cited as a prime example of a successful transitional justice process. Whether the narrative of its success is true or not is, of course, debatable. However, this contribution argues that, from the perspective of victims of apartheid-era abuses, South Africa still grapples with an unfinished transitional justice project and its consequences on society as a whole and on victims in particular. Although South Africa has implemented various measures to repair and redress the past, reconcile different groups and ensure that a system like apartheid will never occur again, there has not been a major shift in victims' socio-economic standing in South African society. Twenty years after the first hearings of the Truth and Reconciliation Commission (TRC), the main pillar of the transitional justice process in South Africa, it is high time to critically look back and judge the institution's impact on victims' lives. Precisely because the Commission enjoys such an exemplary reputation and replication across the globe, it must be given special scrutiny. From a victims' perspective, is it justified that the South African case has acquired such a celebrated status globally?

The aim of this chapter is twofold: firstly, to review the TRC's success for victims by looking at its aftermath and, secondly, to examine victims' role in working towards a more victim-centred discussion on how transitional justice measures should be rolled out. In the first part of this chapter, we review the transition phase—from

Z. Puwana
Independent, Cape Town, South Africa
e-mail: khaliphaz@yahoo.com

R. Kesselring (✉)
University of Basel, Basel, Switzerland
e-mail: rita.kesselring@unibas.ch

J. Brankovic, H. van der Merwe (eds.), *Advocating Transitional Justice in Africa*, Springer Series in Transitional Justice,
https://doi.org/10.1007/978-3-319-70417-3_5

apartheid-era South Africa to a country with a democratically elected government—and the TRC by asking whether victims figured as a priority or rather as a side story. We argue for the latter. Despite—or precisely because of—its negligence of the victims' question, the Commission had a strong effect on victims' lives and position in South African society in its aftermath.

The effect the TRC has had on victims is the topic of the second part of this chapter. Victims' groups have challenged the shortcomings of the government's follow-up of the TRC's recommendations, as a result of which victims have received some attention from the state and the South African public. The strategies used have come with their own challenges, though, and have not been without repercussions. In sum, we show that the Commission—*through its effects*—occupies an ambivalent role in the lives of the majority of apartheid victims. In the conclusion, we therefore suggest several avenues for making transitional justice processes more successful for those who suffer the most after a transition from an unjust regime.

We critically examine some of the processes that followed from the TRC's work by focusing on one among many civil society actors engaged with transitional justice issues in South Africa since the mid-1990s: Khulumani Support Group, and specifically the Western Cape branch of Khulumani (Khulumani WC). Khulumani is a national victims' group which has been involved in transitional justice matters since the inception of the TRC in 1996. In the past 20 years, it has grown into a 105,000-member-strong advocacy and support group. In the course of its lifetime, it has come to cover a wide range of key concerns, including recognition of and redress for all apartheid victims, scrutiny of business' role in the perpetration of human rights violations under apartheid, public access to information coming out of civil and criminal cases of prosecuting perpetrators, involvement of victims in processes of pardon and indemnity of perpetrators and, underlying all these activities, empowerment of victims socially, politically and economically. In its activities, Khulumani has used a combination of political and legal approaches within South Africa and beyond.

We write from two vantage points. Firstly, judging the success of an institution such as the TRC is easier when some time has passed since its lifespan. Secondly, both authors hold intimate knowledge of Khulumani WC. Zukiswa Puwana was with the group for 16 years starting as a volunteer and ending as an elected member of the provincial Executive Committee. Rita Kesselring conducted anthropological, long-term research on Khulumani for 20 months between 2006 and 2013. Our reflections on the effect of the transitional justice process in South Africa on victims and on the workings of Khulumani WC in this chapter are based on many hours of working with the group, attending meetings and participating in its activities.

Amnesty Provision amid Intensified Violence

The situation apartheid victims find themselves in today was considerably shaped by how the transition from an apartheid state to a democratically elected government came about. In the years following the release of Nelson Mandela and the unbanning of the liberation movements in 1990, South Africa experienced the bloodiest period in the history of apartheid. Intense, fragile and frequently interrupted negotiations among the leaders of various political organisations went ahead while thousands of people lost their lives.

In May 1990, the first meeting between the governing National Party and the most prominent liberation movement, the African National Congress (ANC), took place in Cape Town. The parties agreed to indemnity from prosecution for returning ANC exiles and to the release of some political prisoners. Later in the year, the ANC agreed to a suspension of the armed struggle. A National Peace Accord paved the way for formal negotiations and the Interim Constitution was ratified in November 1993.

During the negotiations, a central question was what, after the elections, would happen to the losing party. Should there be a blanket amnesty for all atrocities committed or should the perpetrators of political crimes be put on trial? It was very late in the negotiations that the parties settled on an amnesty process. In 1993, the leadership of the ANC largely accepted that there would be no trials for apartheid-era crimes and that there might be some investigation into its own wrongdoing (cf. Bell and Ntsebeza 2003; Doxader 2003; Van Zyl Slabbert 2000), while the National Party and the apartheid security forces compromised on their idea of a blanket amnesty. At the time, questions of forgiveness and reconciliation were not seen as important.

The legal obligation to establish a state institution empowered to grant conditional amnesty to perpetrators was enshrined in the Interim Constitution. Victims' rights were much more vaguely described.

> These [divisions of the past] can now be addressed on the basis that there is a need for understanding but not for vengeance, a need for reparation but not for retaliation, a need for ubuntu but not for victimisation. (Postamble, Interim Constitution of the Republic of South Africa Act, No. 200 of 1993)

The country prepared for the first democratic elections, which took place in April 1994 and brought the ANC to power. Shortly thereafter, the first postapartheid minister of justice, Dullah Omar, opened a lengthy consultative process as to what an inquiry into past political crimes would look like, and he proposed a truth commission. Civil society organisations, individuals, religious groups and international advisors were prominently involved. These constituencies filed proposals and recommendations, participated in a series of workshops and presented their submissions at hearings.[1] Among other things, they advocated for a victim-centred approach, for instance through funds for nongovernmental organisations (NGOs) to provide assistance to victims, such as counselling and socio-economic empowerment.[2] Not everyone in the ANC was happy with an inquiry into the party's own

[1] For the various submissions made by organisations and individuals, see http://truth.wwl.wits.ac.za/coll_home.php.

[2] See, for instance, Proposal for the Establishment of the Commission for Truth and Reconciliation in South Africa prepared by the Trauma Centre for Victims of Violence and Torture (June 30, 1994). Retrieved from http://truth.wwl.wits.ac.za/doc_page.php?did=1016&li=cat.

abuses. Victims, on the other hand, are on record as calling for a much tougher course of action and prosecutions of perpetrators (Boraine 1995).

In short, the main concerns in the early 1990s were surely not victims or processes of reconciliation but putting an end to violence. As the following section demonstrates, the main transitional justice issue was amnesty and not reparations, and the main theme was (the treatment of suspected) perpetrators and not victims.

Victims' Rights: A Side Story in the Transitional Years

The Promotion of National Unity and Reconciliation Act of 1995 led to the establishment of the TRC, which consisted of three committees: the Committee on Human Rights Violations, the Amnesty Committee and the Reparation and Rehabilitation Committee. The Act gave power to the Amnesty Committee to grant amnesty to those who made full disclosure of their crimes in cases where political motivation and proportionality between the act and the political objective pursued were proven. Perpetrators were not required to express any remorse for their actions. Importantly, if amnesty was refused, the Commission stated that the applicant could face criminal or civil prosecutions in the future.[3]

The Act not only concretised amnesty provisions but also teased out victims' rights. The "need for reparations" cited in the Interim Constitution was given expression in the Act, which defines reparations as "any form of compensation, ex gratia payment, restitution, rehabilitation or recognition" (Section 1 (xiv)). The reparation measures were to be sourced from a soon-to-be-established "President's Fund" (Section 42). The only—and excluding—qualification for reparations was that the recipient had to be a victim of a gross violation of human rights as defined in Section 1 of the Act and "as found by the Commission" (TRC 1998, vol. 5: 176).[4]

The Reparation and Rehabilitation Committee worked for 15 months starting in April 1996. Thousands of citizens came to give statements in town halls, hospitals and churches all around the country, thus reopening wounds to inform the public about the atrocities they experienced. It received statements from 21,290 persons of

[3] The amnesty provision in the TRC Act was challenged in South Africa's highest court, the Constitutional Court. In its decision in *Azanian People's Organization (AZAPO) and Others v. the President of the Republic of South Africa and Others*, the Constitutional Court ruled that the granting of amnesty was constitutional, and at the same time asserted that perpetrators who failed to satisfy the amnesty requirements could face civil and criminal charges.

[4] In terms of Section 1 of the Act, victims are (a) persons who, individually or together with one or more persons, suffered harm in the form of physical or mental injury, emotional suffering, pecuniary loss or a substantial impairment of human rights (1) as a result of a gross violation of human rights, or (2) as a result of an act associated with a political objective for which amnesty has been granted; (b) persons who, individually or together with one or more persons, suffered harm in the form of physical or mental injury, emotional suffering, pecuniary loss or a substantial impairment of human rights, as a result of such person intervening to assist persons contemplated in paragraph (a) who were in distress or to prevent victimisation of such persons; and (c) such relatives or dependents of victims as may be prescribed.

whom "more than 19,050 persons were found to be victims of a gross violation of human rights" (TRC 2003, vol. 7: 1). In addition, 2,975 persons were identified as victims during the amnesty process.[5]

Most of the persons who gave statements did so in place of a family member who was murdered or had disappeared (Ross 2002). They told what they knew to a statement-taker in a formalised process (Wilson 2000). Victims received a letter which acknowledged their statement, some were visited by an investigator and, at some stage, they were informed whether they qualified for reparations. In this process, there was little psychosocial support provided.

Victims had to wait for the president to make a decision regarding reparations for another 5 years, though, because it took the Amnesty Committee until 2003 to table their findings and recommendations with regard to amnesty.[6] Survivors and victims could challenge the amnesty applications publicly and often did so, but they were disadvantaged by inconsistent notification about relevant cases, the court-like nature of the hearings and often the poor quality of their legal representation (Chapman and Van der Merwe 2008c: 11; Sarkin-Hughes 2004: 199ff).

In our opinion, the TRC was charged with a monumental task: to retell, to understand and to classify the South African past and, wherever possible, to contribute to the country's future by facilitating closure through reconciliation. Scholars working on the TRC largely agree that the Commission did not fulfil these formidable expectations. From its very inception, the TRC was accompanied by critical scholarship and received many recommendations from NGOs and other concerned bodies from both abroad and South Africa (cf. Fullard and Rousseau 2008). Not only in transitional justice scholarship but also in South African society itself the TRC came to have a decisive role in shaping what proceeded from it (despite the multiplicity of voices within the TRC, see Fullard and Rousseau 2008).

After the TRC

Among victims, the TRC had different effects. It distinguished between those falling into its category of victim and those failing to meet the requirements. It further distinguished between those who gave statements and those who chose not to,[7] or who missed the opportunity to do so. It thereby distinguished between those who

[5] The list of victims as identified by the TRC (2003, vol. 7:936–976) can be accessed on Khulumani's home page: http://khulumani.net/khulumani/documents/file/35-trc-report-volume-7-victims-list.html.

[6] The Amnesty Committee held its last public hearing in December 2000 and finished its work at its official dissolution by President Mbeki on May 13, 2001. It held more than 250 public hearings, and received between 7,115 and 7,127 amnesty applications. This number was deflated by the granting of indemnity, immunity or presidential pardon to many thousands of prisoners during the negotiation process (Sarkin-Hughes 2004:194ff).

[7] See Ross (2003:172) and (2002:163) for a list of reasons why people decided not to give a statement.

were entitled to financial redress and those who were not. Only a few victims of apartheid were able to fully claim "victim" status (Khulumani Support Group 2016).

As a result, there was this "list" that is a closed list of the persons who had qualified for victim status. The list most likely does not include thousands of persons who would qualify for such. As Mahmood Mamdani notes,

> The result was a list of individuals, with no reference to groups. But if the violence of apartheid targeted groups more than specific individuals, it would not be surprising if most victims of apartheid turned out to be unidentified individuals. This, in turn, would be an argument for giving reparations to communities rather than individuals. (Mamdani 2002: 40)

The "list" suggests not only that victimhood can be assessed and redressed individually but also that there is a set number of victims. Everyone who is not on the list has ever since not benefited from any reparations. Certainly, the Commission's intention was the opposite. It attempted—discursively (although not legally)—to integrate everyone's suffering and pain into a shared understanding of victimhood (Wilson 2000: 80). To do that, it used a representative—individualised—victimhood which was meant to speak to and for everyone.

The aspect of the TRC's mandate which was possibly most consequential for victims' lives up to today was that it could not make binding recommendations for provisions of reparations and redress. This, however, is the case with most truth commissions. The state poorly followed the recommendations of the TRC. One major negligence has been the almost non-existent follow-up on prosecuting perpetrators who were not granted amnesty. In terms of the recommendations that concerned victims directly, the Reparation and Rehabilitation Committee recommended Individual Reparation Grants of R20,000 a year for a period of 6 years. Instead, the then President Thabo Mbeki decided on a one-time payment of R30,000 per victim or surviving family. The announcement was made in 2003, thus 7 years after victims gave their statements to the Committee. The government's delay in paying out individual reparations and the lack of any clear idea of how to roll out the recommended community reparations (see below) have become the major issues of contestation for victims—and despair.

It was only in 2005 that the South African Government established a TRC Unit in the Department of Justice that was supposed to take forward the recommendation of community reparations. Its precise mandate and organisation have remained unclear up to today. The TRC Unit was established to develop and implement programmes for communities which are particularly ridden by the legacy of apartheid-era violence. These programmes should be financed from the President's Fund. The President's Fund is another major pending TRC-related issue. Many states including Switzerland and Germany contributed to it. Since its establishment in the mid-1990s, it has accumulated more than R1 billion (USD70 million) (Gontsana 2016).

In May 2011, the Department of Justice gazetted draft regulations for assistance to victims in respect of basic and higher education and in relation to medical benefits for victims and their dependents, and invited responses. The regulations indicated that only victims identified and listed by the TRC were eligible. Civil society groups harshly criticised the "closed list" approach and demanded that the process be stopped until "meaningful consultation are carried out with victims and interested parties".[8]

In sum, victims came to judge the TRC by the state's poor follow-up of the Commission's recommendations. Measured against the expectations raised by the TRC process, the state has failed on all accounts to properly deliver on them.

Reflecting on the many strong civil society initiatives demanding to take the "unfinished business" of the TRC further, Chapman and Van der Merwe (2008a) write:

> In some respects, the TRC seems to have made more of an impact on civil society in South Africa [than the government]. Many organizations in civil society have taken on various transitional justice tasks relating to expanding and deepening the work of the TRC. Some of these initiatives are clearly more suited for civil society actors, but others have been developed to fill the gap left by government. Continued efforts are also aimed at lobbying government to fulfill its own transitional justice obligations. (Chapman and Van der Merwe 2008b: 282)

They suggest that the TRC prompted various initiatives which draw on the shortcomings of its work. And, indeed, the lack of follow-up and the exclusion of most victims from the TRC process were obvious failures for Khulumani to draw on in their demands. However, victims and other civil society actors first had to establish the societal ground for such criticism which was not self-evident to the ordinary not directly affected South African or to the international community.

A clear sign that apartheid victimhood indeed was an issue a decade or longer after the first democratic elections was the exponential increase in persons who joined Khulumani as members.

Khulumani Support Group

Launched in 1995, Khulumani has grown into a national structure of provincial, regional and local area committees which all work under one umbrella organisation, Khulumani Support Group. It is in its form the only membership organisation of apartheid-era victims in South Africa.[9] At the time of writing, Khulumani had

[8] Press Statement of the South African Coalition for Transitional Justice, June 2011: http://www.csvr.org.za/index.php/media-articles/news-and-events/56-latest-news/2498-press-statement-the-state-must-honour-its-reparations-obligations-to-all-victims-victims-reject-the-dojs-closed-list-approach-.html. The statement of the South African Coalition for Transitional Justice can be accessed on https://www.ictj.org/sites/default/files/SACTJ-South-Africa-Reparations-Submission-2011-English.pdf.

[9] The Centre for the Study of Violence and Reconciliation ran a Truth Recovery Project in which it constructed a South African Disappearances Database. It is not a membership-based database but addresses similar issues as Khulumani. In South Africa, there are also many military veteran and ex-combatant associations. Khulumani and these associations have different target groups, but there are surely overlaps in members. Government recently created a Department of Military Veterans, and in 2011, parliament passed the Military Veterans' Act which empowers the Department to assist military veterans.

around 105,000 members. Between 2009 and 2012 alone, about 20,000 people applied for membership—a number equivalent to the entire TRC list of victims. Only about 10% of Khulumani's members were officially recognised as "victims" by the TRC and granted reparations (Madlingozi 2007a: 120).

Members are individuals who survived some form of violence inflicted by the apartheid security forces, its collaborators or the liberation movements, such as torture, detention without trial and severe ill treatment of various sorts, including sexual assault, abuse or harassment, banning and banishment orders, deliberate withholding of medical attention, food and water, destruction of homes, and mutilation of body parts. Members are also those whose family members were abducted, disappeared or killed by the apartheid regime.

Each and every member has an entry in Khulumani's national database. To become a member, applicants have to present their identification document and a copy of a death certificate if the victim status is linked to a death in the family. A data collector fills in a Needs Assessment Form with the prospective member. The form is structured in four parts: the applicant's personal details, "urgent needs" today, violation which the applicant experienced directly or indirectly and "reparation", that is, the support the applicant has received to mitigate the impact of the violation on his or her family, as well as whether the applicant was declared a victim by the TRC.

The nine provincial branches—and the regional branches within them—each have their own history. The Gauteng Province branch started as a self-help group in 1995 during the time of the TRC hearings (Wilson 2000, 2001), whose meetings were hosted by the Centre for the Study of Violence and Reconciliation. Given that the national office in Johannesburg is also the provincial office of Gauteng, the province is best equipped in terms of finances and staff. Within Gauteng Province, the East Rand branch has been a particularly active one, and, more recently, the Sebokeng branch has emerged as a strong and vocal group. KwaZulu-Natal Province has had a well-funded Khulumani office in Durban for many years. Its staff undertook regular and frequent field trips to various parts of the province and thus acquired thousands of new members. The province started its own database already in 1998. Some provinces, such as Northern Cape and Mpumalanga, only recently opened a formal office space, unburdening founding members who had been administering the work from their own homes.

Khulumani Western Cape, which is the focus of the remainder of this chapter, has always been seen as an exceptional branch in many ways (cf. Backer 2005, 2010; Colvin 2004a, b, 2006). Before it launched as Khulumani WC in September 2000, the group was called Ex-Political Prisoners and Torture Survivors and its meetings were hosted by the Trauma Centre. In the late 1990s, the Trauma Centre offered individual counselling and monthly group counselling. The group took on a life on its own and joined Khulumani (Colvin 2004a).

The Western Cape branch has its office in Salt River, Cape Town. It has a Provincial Executive Committee made up of representatives from several local areas and from towns outside Cape Town, including Worcester and Paarl. It is supported by a youth coordinator, an office assistant and a fieldworker. Khulumani WC has used its proximity to parliament extensively to stage marches and hand over memoranda during sessions. As a way not only to work through painful experiences but also to make its concerns public and more accessible, Khulumani WC, at the initiative of the Human Rights Media Centre, Cape Town, whose director Shirley Gunn is, a Khulumani board member herself, has undertaken several memory projects. These include *Breaking the Silence: A Luta Continua*, a traveling exhibition (cf. Gunn 2007; Gunn and Krwala 2008), and two documentary films, *We Never Give Up I* and *II*, produced by Cahal McLaughlin (2002, 2012).

Research and collaborations have always been important for Khulumani WC.[10] They have helped to mobilise solidarity and contributed to critical reflection within the group and among its leaders. In a few cases, Khulumani WC was able to capitalise on scholarly interest by being directly involved in the design and implementation of research projects, but often scholars conduct short-term research, come with their preformulated ideas of what they will hear when engaging with victims and thus rather profit from the keenness of Khulumani WC to participate in international knowledge production.

The organisation who most strongly spoke out against this way of sharing knowledge and insights has been the Human Rights Media Centre, with which Khulumani WC has collaborated on different projects over many years. The rights- and subject-centred approach that the Centre deploys in its work has sensitised and empowered members in engaging with researchers and forming partnerships.

The unequal power dynamics in research and knowledge production have remained a dilemma, though, because refusing to cooperate means less publicity and positive exchange. The executive structure of Khulumani WC has made a successful effort in negotiating with incoming researchers for their own benefit before allowing them to speak to its members.

In Pursuit of Justice and Redress

The South African TRC became an exemplary case across the world. One could argue that international and regional actors had to uphold the success story to render it a model for other conflict-prone regions and countries. Many TRC commissioners became (albeit critical) advocates for the set-up of truth commissions around the world. As a result, on the international policy level, there was little criticism of the institution as a whole, or of the process as it unravelled in the South African case in particular. South Africa was arranging itself with an incomplete transition, the

[10] Many of these collaborations are with South African NGO or research and policy institutions such as the Centre for the Study of Violence and Reconciliation (Hamber 2006, 2009; Hamber and Wilson 2002; Sonis and Van der Merwe 2004; Gobodo-Madikizela and Van der Merwe 2007; Van der Merwe and Chapman 2008; Makhalemele 2004). Tshepo Madlingozi, Khulumani's national advocacy coordinator, has also published papers on transitional justice, drawing on his experiences within the organisation (Madlingozi 2007a, b, 2010).

consequences of which are only coming to the fore 20 years later. Today, notions of persistent racism and a general structural legacy of apartheid across milieus and classes are alive as never before. It seems as if the past is catching up, specifically among a young generation of students (Hefferman and Nieftagodien 2016).

For victims, this incompleteness of the transition, the upholding and even entrenchment of structural inequality, is nothing new. Khulumani's demands have always been that the state review its compromised dealing with the past, and deliver on the integration of everybody into a new South Africa. While these demands were successfully kept out of the public domain for nearly a decade, not least because South Africans were busy rebuilding their own lives, they dramatically came to the fore in 2002 when apartheid victims filed suit against multinational companies who allegedly aided and abetted the security branches of the apartheid regime.

The decision to file suit against companies came out of a long process of international collaboration and lobbying for debt release or relief by the millennium (cf. Kesselring 2012) in which Khulumani played a key role. While this so-called apartheid litigation was directed at businesses which did not disclose their role in the perpetration of human rights violations under apartheid rule, for victims, it was primarily about waking up their own government when the political avenue to provide a more inclusive redress scheme seemed to be of no avail. The apartheid litigation was filed under the Alien Tort Statute, which gives non-US citizens the right to sue in US Federal Courts over violations of international law. The demand to address experiences of injustice and the role of multinational corporations in them were backed by national and international NGOs and individuals. For the global human rights movement, the case was about the applicability of the Alien Tort Stature to pursue corporate liability.

South Africans and individuals and organisations around the world wrote letters in support of the applicants. For instance, former Archbishop Desmond Tutu, in his capacity as former chairperson of the TRC, emphasised that the apartheid litigation was in line with what the TRC had found:

> The obtaining of compensation for victims of apartheid, to supplement the very modest amount per victim to be rewarded as reparation under the TRC process, could promote reconciliation, by addressing the needs of those apartheid victims dissatisfied with the small monetary value of TRC reparations.[11]

In the course of the suit's 14 years in courts, the South African Government has changed its position at least twice (cf. Kesselring 2012). Initially, the South African Cabinet assured that government neither supported nor opposed legal action in this matter. On the occasion of the tabling of the two final volumes of the TRC Report to the National Houses of Parliament and the Nation on April 15, 2003, however, President Mbeki strongly condemned the legal actions:

> We consider it completely unacceptable that matters that are central to the future of our country should be adjudicated in foreign courts which bear no responsibility for the well-being of

[11] Brief of Amici Curiae Commissioners and Committee Members of South Africa's Truth and Reconciliation Commission in Support of Appellants, August 30, 2005, p. 10, fn. 10.

> our country and the observance of the perspective contained in our constitution of the promotion of national reconciliation.

Then South African Minister of Trade and Industry Alec Erwin addressed Parliament by saying, "We are opposed to and indeed contemptuous of attempts to use unsound extra-territorial legal precepts in the USA to seek personal financial gain in South Africa".[12] He condemned "the abuse to use the law of another land to undermine our sovereign right to settle our past and build our future as we see fit", and reproached the plaintiffs for "break[ing] that indefinable collectivist identity that was the origin of our strength" and for "exploit[ing] our history". The late Kader Asmal, then minister of education, argued that South Africa "does not need the help of ambulance chasers and contingency fee operators, whether in Switzerland, the Netherlands, or the United States of America".

Even though the government later softened its stance, plaintiffs were labelled unpatriotic and treacherous at the time. As a possibly unintended consequence of the filing of the lawsuits, the relation between victims, international and regional solidarity groups, and the South African state was put to a test. Or, more to the point, for victims, the stance of its government in relation to past atrocities and its redress beyond the TRC crystallised with the help of the apartheid litigation. The litigation had serious repercussions on the possibility of a dialogue between the South African Government and victims seeking redress (for more details on the apartheid litigation, see Kesselring 2016a).

While victims have experienced strong support from TRC commissioners, politicians and South African NGOs and interest groups, it was not strong enough to change a discourse of the ungrateful victim calling on an international body (the US courts) to fiddle with domestic affairs.

Khulumani also helped compile several court cases on pardons, the prosecution policy and negotiations with government around collective reparations beyond the victims on the TRC list. It forms part of the South African Coalition of Transitional Justice, an umbrella organisation standing in for the rights of victims and holding government accountable to its obligations.[13]

A more recent example of how a legal case can spur a political discussion is the ongoing trial against four apartheid-era policemen accused in a case of disappearance and murder. Twenty-three-year-old anti-apartheid activist Nokuthula Simelane was abducted and tortured by the security branch in 1983 and her remains were never found. More than three decades later, in February 2016, the National Prosecuting Authority (NPA) finally charged the four policemen of murder and kidnapping. Importantly, this is one of the few cases the NPA took up from a list of about 300 the TRC recommended for follow-up in 2002—and only because the

[12] Debate on the Truth and Reconciliation Commission Report: Speech by Minister of Trade and Industry, Alec Erwin, 15 April 2003. Retrieved from http://millenniums-entwicklungsziele.de/documents/Reactionstrc.pdf.

[13] For more information on the court cases and the coalition, see https://www.ictj.org/our-work/regions-and-countries/south-africa and http://www.saha.org.za/news/2011/June/sactj_submission_on_trc_reparations_regulations.htm.

Simelane family launched a High Court case. The public support in reaction to the announcement to finally prosecute Simelane's killers is indicative of what is at stake here. Why has it taken the NPA so long, and why have so few perpetrators denied amnesty by the TRC—and others who did not even apply for it—been brought to trial?

Khulumani knows of numerous cases like this, with families trying to find the means and support to bring them to court or public attention. As much as such cases are about the prosecution of perpetrators, for Khulumani members they are also—and primarily—a source of information to learn the whereabouts of their loved ones. By denying justice to society, the NPA denies justice to thousands of individuals to find closure.

The Internal Repercussions of Going to Court

The litigation had strong repercussions within Khulumani WC. For one, as we witnessed in many meetings but also in daily encounters with members, it raised hopes for quick payments. Most Khulumani members did not give statements to the TRC and thus did not qualify for reparations. The litigation offered a crucial remedy to this shortcoming. In this sense, victims put their hopes in the legal process to finally give them what every victim deserves. However, apart from a meagre settlement sum from General Motors (see Kesselring 2012), which was too little to even start thinking of distributing it among members, no money came out of 14 years of judicial process. Luckily, Khulumani has been represented by lawyers who work on a contingency basis.

The fact that money might be paid out put the solidary among members at risk on multiple occasions, however. Many times, individual members accused an executive committee member that he or she "ate the money", that is, used his or her position and access to the lawyers and misappropriated what was meant for the communities. Such accusations could easily turn critical for the safety of the accused and needed a lot of attention, with the executive committee calling for a special meeting to rectify the misinformation.

Another factor connected to the possible payout of redress money was the question of who would benefit and in which way. The papers filed in court did not elaborate on this. Never was there a possible damages lump sum mentioned, and it was therefore up to victims to think through what would happen in case of an out-of-court settlement or a decision by the court.

Many spoke out for individual payments, largely, they said, because they have become suspicious of community funding projects as so often rolled out by political parties or municipalities in South Africa. In their experience, payments at the community level mean that a ward councillor and his or her friends benefit, and that the majority is left out. Especially women have learnt through experience that they are the best managers of a household budget. Members also debated among themselves whether the gravity and the kind of injury should be reflected in the amount of money a person would receive. Finally, it should be noted that, as happened years earlier when victims who gave statements to the TRC were anticipating the reparation payment, several members (who were automatically plaintiffs and thus potential beneficiaries) started projects, such as converting a shack into a brick house, which they hoped to pay off with the money coming from the litigation.

Lawyers, most of all the South African advisor to the litigation, Charles Abrahams, were always cautious not to raise hopes among Khulumani members, but they also often found themselves in the role of motivating members to not give up their hopes, a concern they shared with us repeatedly.

In other words, while the apartheid litigation is formulated around legal accountability, the political campaigns around the litigation have been much broader and far reaching. On the positive side, the apartheid litigation managed to bring victims' concerns, which were previously sidelined and dismissed by the government, into the public realm. At the very least, the international litigation helped to generate the conditions for a more critical (local and international) public of government's role in transitional justice processes.

Khulumani WC Among Many Civil Society Actors

In the landscape of South African civil society organisations concerned with the legacy of apartheid-era crimes, Khulumani is, apart from military veterans' groups, the only group that is not only membership based but also has victims as members (see above). Apart from numerous initiatives which it started on its own, as a result of its unique status as a victim and membership-based organisation, Khulumani WC has often been asked to join coalitions, participate in marches, sign statements and join discussions, among other kinds of activities initiated by other organisations. Examples are the Centre for the Study of Violence and Reconciliation, the Institute of Justice and Reconciliation and the Human Rights Media Centre. While such a network of partner organisations has been vital to maintaining a public discussion of victimhood and redress, the specificity of these partnerships and of Khulumani has presented challenges.

Given Khulumani's unique organisational structure, participating in equal partnerships with other organisations is not easy. Khulumani WC (unlike the national office in Johannesburg) does not have formally trained staff. It is also not an NGO with, for instance, a research agenda. Rather, it is there to serve its members to the best of its abilities, with access to very little funding, and equipped primarily with its own experiences of victimhood. Translating victimhood into a public and political discourse is difficult for victims who have to deal with the aftereffects of violent experiences on a daily basis. As a result, professional, research NGOs are potentially better positioned to speak authoritatively. While Khulumani WC has by and large profited from collaborations with other NGOs, they have also ended up being talked about *on their behalf* (e.g. Méndez 2016).

As a consequence, in meetings and press conferences, Khulumani members often become a sort of "show case", the immediate voice which needs analysis by NGOs, with the media and scholars presenting the "bigger picture". Such situations produce a hierarchy between the "knowledgeable" and the "directly affected". Ultimately, the NGOs generate a discourse which, for many victims, is out of reach and difficult to connect with their own experiences.

Khulumani WC has tried to professionalise the flow of information, the media's access to its members and the information it produces. There are two main challenges which have contributed to the limited success of such endeavours. Firstly, there are very few members who are prepared and equipped to speak out publicly or to a professional audience. Only a handful of members, we suggest, most of them executive committee members, have successfully managed to distance themselves from their own, immediate experience of victimhood enough to feel comfortable speaking out about it, and to relate their thoughts and demands to an audience which does not share their experiences.

Secondly, over the past two decades, it has been challenging to receive funding for Khulumani WC to professionalise. Particularly in the past few years, the global funding landscape has shifted to a scheme which funds projects instead of running costs, NGOs instead of self-support groups and large and stable organisations instead of fragile groups which cannot absorb a large budget. Khulumani WC does not fit into this rigid funding scheme; its concerns are sometimes difficult to communicate to donors (such as are they a political or a self-support group, and are they representing victims or run by victims). The only donor which gave consistent funding until early 2017 for the office rent in Salt River and a fieldworker is the Fund for Development and Partnership in Africa (FEPA), a small organisation based in Switzerland.

Finally, Khulumani WC suffers from the general global understanding that South Africa has successfully come to terms with its past and the focus should be on looking forward rather than looking back.

Khulumani WC in the Communities

Just as relationships with other organisations are key to any possible success but not always easy, similarly Khulumani WC's standing in the communities where its members come from has two sides to it. For instance, Khulumani WC is a non-partisan organisation which does not exclude anyone from becoming a member if he or she qualifies as such. In this, it is exceptional. Many groups differentiate themselves along political party lines. As a result, Khulumani WC is often misread as a critic of government and of the ruling ANC, or accused of only being open to some community members but not others. Generally, however, community members from marginalised areas like the townships of Langa, Gugulethu, Philippi and Khayelitsha are happy to finally meet a group which is genuinely not interested in party politics and takes up the everyday concerns of ordinary women and men.

The fact that Khulumani WC directly engages with communities through its fieldworker also causes rifts within communities. For example, Khulumani is often misread as only representing the victims of one specific incident during the apartheid era, and thus accused of leaving out the majority of victims. While this is not the case, the fieldworker can only do so much in so many communities and necessarily some benefit more than others. This accusation is one of the reasons why the general meetings are held in a "neutral" space in Salt River, a suburb away from where members live.

But even within the communities, not everyone agrees with Khulumani WC's argument that the state has not satisfyingly dealt with the past and that the past matters still today. Many want to move forward, and are tired of neighbours persistently pointing to the past to explain their condition today.

For its members and others, Khulumani WC oftentimes takes on tasks which are typically government's responsibility. For instance, executive committee members and the fieldworker tirelessly advise members on how to access social grants and where they can get medical treatment.

The main challenge for Khulumani WC in terms of its relations with communities is that it primarily operates within the city of Cape Town and tends to neglect the rural areas in Western Cape Province. This is a problem for many organisations in South Africa. Unless there is funding for regular outreach in rural areas or several offices spread across an area, this bias towards the urban will not change.

In recent years, Khulumani WC, like Khulumani as a whole, has been trying to expand its reach beyond apartheid victimhood by including groups victimised by migration, xenophobic violence and unfair labour conditions, among other factors. However, faced with countless needs from apartheid victims, such an expansion has been a practical challenge. The national office has rolled out a number of programmes,[14] but Khulumani WC has struggled to initiate programmes which explicitly address vulnerable groups in general apart from targeted contributions in projects initiated by other partners in the region.

Overcoming Victimhood

Transitional justice is a buzzword stipulating all sorts of things in different places across the globe. In South Africa, more than 20 years after the successful abolition of the apartheid system, many South Africans for a number of reasons do not want to engage with the past anymore. To them, Khulumani is an awkward reminder of

[14] See Khulumani's website: www.khulumani.net.

something that people would rather do away with.[15] The problem is that the damage apartheid caused is far from being redressed or healed. It is not only Khulumani members who know this but also emerging social movements that are protesting an education system in pieces, poor or non-existent service delivery, and a corrupt and self-interested government, to name but a few issues.[16]

What all these movements have in common is the realisation that the transition to democracy has not brought what was hoped for, that the state has failed on its promises and that the past does indeed still shape the way things are today. Apartheid victims are the embodiment of this emerging consciousness, which is increasingly translated into open criticism of the current state of affairs and which can be broadly summarised under the umbrella term *transitional justice*, that is, how to become a more just society.

Against this background, Khulumani has often been misunderstood as being preoccupied with the past—looking back instead of looking forward. This is a gross misunderstanding of victims' demands. Acknowledging and redressing past experiences enable a society to make a positive contribution to the future. The South African state has failed to realise this, and the international community has largely fallen for its line of a successful transition.

Conclusion and Lessons Learnt

Victims' demands are, next to their embodied memories of harm and hopes for justice, centrally shaped by the TRC. What is more, only the existence of the TRC made certain processes in its aftermath possible. On the one hand, the TRC shaped government policies with regard to apartheid-era crimes and the prosecution of perpetrators; on the other hand, its mandate and limitations provided justification and legitimacy to challenges to those policies. The TRC is thus a central point of reference for all actors involved. Furthermore, the articulation of victims' social concerns in courts has resulted in renewed attention to their demands in South African society.

While the TRC fell far short of a victim-centred approach and did not meet victims' expectations, it gave victims more prominence than they had before. It gave relevance to their experiences. One important conclusion that can be drawn from the South African case in terms of transitional justice is that a truth commission does raise awareness of victims' plight and needs. As short-lived as it is, this public consciousness can be used to build upon. As we tried to show above, however, there is

[15] Here, we mainly refer to a general sense among Khulumani WC's members. However, such perception and experience are also backed up by, for instance, data from the Reconciliation Barometer Project (http://www.ijr.org.za/political-analysis-SARB.php).

[16] See, for instance, findings from research at the Social Change Research Unit, University of Johannesburg (Alexander et al. 2015).

a very different side to this coin: the fact that the TRC dealt so prominently with victims also meant that the general public, and the international community, was more or less satisfied and thought victims' lives were to improve as a result. One could even argue that the TRC, a governmental institution born out of a political negotiation, stole the show and diverted attention from victims' concerns. As we showed above, victims ever since the TRC have struggled to explain why the past is not resolved.

In what follows, we propose five lessons learnt through the South African transitional justice process which we believe, if considered early on in a transitional set-up in other contexts, can make the transition process more just for victims. Firstly, the South African case shows that the course for reparations and redress in a (post) transition country is set early. In South Africa, ever since the list of victims was publicised in the final report of the TRC (2003, vol. 7), there was little chance for Khulumani and others to successfully lobby for a reopening of the TRC process to those who were left out. This means that victims' groups need to campaign for an inclusive notion of victimhood early in the negotiation process.

Secondly, the victims' question needs to be part of peace negotiations. As we showed, reparations and redress were not a topic in South Africa in the early 1990s, but rather amnesty and indemnity. One could read it as the powerful being preoccupied with saving their skin first and foremost. In this process, victims are too easily forgotten. If the victims' question is not on the negotiation table, it is hard to get it back in once the transitional years unfold. In the case of South Africa, victims' concerns were not a priority and, later, victims never fully managed to bring their plight to government's *enduring* attention. To achieve this, it seems that relationships to those in office are crucial. As in any context, to have an impact, an issue must grab a person's attention and emotion—preferably a person who is in a decision-making position.

Thirdly, we argue that victims' groups need to have a modest—and locally anchored—professional structure in order to be heard in media and in the public in ways that bring political and social acknowledgement. As a victims' and membership-based organisation, Khulumani WC did not have an easy standing in a post-apartheid landscape where many well-educated freedom fighters founded their own NGOs or accepted offers of a government post. While this might be particular to the South African situation, in any transitional or postconflict situation the fate of victims is quickly decided *for* victims instead of *by* them (e.g. Méndez 2016). It is important that victims' groups develop strong organisational skills which allow them to raise funding for their programmes and enter into partnerships with sympathetic civil society formations, within the country and beyond, on an equal standing. Khulumani WC, in comparison to the other provincial branches of Khulumani but also more generally, has been relatively successful in raising funds, running its own programmes and entering into direct and equal relationships with partner organisations and communities.

Fourthly, taking legal recourse against the state or other entities such as companies is a double-edged sword. We showed that the "apartheid litigation" in the United States came as a last resort to victims after political avenues to gain attention and recognition proved very difficult. Going to court creates attention, in the public, in government ministries and internationally (and possibly some reparations), but it also creates confusion, expectations and hierarchies among victims. This is, of course, not the plaintiffs' fault but is rather due to the logic of the law (cf. Kesselring 2016b). Plaintiffs need strong bonds among themselves to not be corrupted by the legal process and the complex political processes that follow from it.

Fifthly, we strongly propose that the recommendations of a truth commission should be binding for the state. The South African case shows that the Commission had moderately radical suggestions as to how to redress the past. It was, however, up to the president and the various ministries to choose and implement from a list of recommendations—something they hardly did. Making recommendations binding would ensure that the transition is followed through.[17] As a result of legally binding recommendations, civil society actors would have much more power to put pressure on their government. Certainly, this suggestion needs to be applied in conjunction with our points above, particularly that the Commission's reach be as inclusive as possible.

In 2003, the year when the TRC's report was finally tabled to parliament, S'fiso Ngesi took a critical look at how the TRC had been used by the political system:

> Many politicians are indifferent to the plight of those who have been left behind. The victims who were temporarily acknowledged by the system have been let down. They have been forgotten. [...] There is a difference between political peace and reconciliation. In South Africa, we have used the TRC process to achieve a temporary political peace. I use the word 'temporary' because the peace is fragile. Its future depends on how the state deals with victims and those who are unable to share in the fruits of the new South Africa. (Ngesi 2003: 311)

The TRC was a deal, a pact between the new and the old state, and victims somehow played along. Up to today, this "peace", as fragile as it indeed is, has not been broken. Victims have been patient, they have struggled to get by and many have already passed on without recognition or the assurance that their grandchildren will grow up in a better South Africa. Outright resistance to the current state of affairs and against the government will most probably not come from victims, for they are too old, too broken but also too faithful to the project of liberation. Resistance, however, is growing in other corners of society, including among students, township residents and workers. Khulumani members by and large share their concerns and will join in. They know that the past needs to be addressed openly in order to imagine a future for all.

---

[17] A truth commission's recommendations are rarely binding. Exceptions are the recommendations of Guatemala's Historical Clarification Commission and El Salvador's Commission on the Truth. Both commissions operated on the basis of peace accords, which were binding on the government.

References

Alexander, P., Runciman, C., & Maruping, B. (2015). *South African police service data on crowd incidents: A preliminary analysis*. South African research chair in social change, social change research unit, University of Johannesburg.

Backer, D. (2005). Evaluating transitional justice in South Africa from a victim's perspective. *Journal of the International Institute, 12*(2), 443–456.

Backer, D. (2010). Watching a bargain unravel? A panel study of victims' attitudes about transitional justice in Cape Town, South Africa. *International Journal of Transitional Justice, 4*(3), 443–456.

Bell, T., & Ntsebeza, D. B. (2003). *Unfinished business: South Africa, apartheid and truth*. London: Verso.

Boraine, A. (1995). Introduction. In A. Boraine & J. Levy (Eds.), *The healing of a nation?* (pp. xiii–xxiv). Cape Town: Justice in Transition.

Chapman, A. R., & Van der Merwe, H. (Eds.). (2008a). *Truth and reconciliation in South Africa: Did the TRC deliver?* Philadelphia, PA: University of Pennsylvania Press.

Chapman, A. R., & Van der Merwe, H. (2008b). Reflections on the South African experience. In A. Chapman & H. van der Merwe (Eds.), *Truth and reconciliation in South Africa: Did the TRC deliver?* (pp. 280–300). Philadelphia, PA: University of Pennsylvania Press.

Chapman, A. R., & Van der Merwe, H. (2008c). Introduction: Assessing the South African transitional justice model. In A. Chapman & H. van der Merwe (Eds.), *Truth and reconciliation in South Africa: Did the TRC deliver?* (pp. 1–22). Philadelphia, PA: University of Pennsylvania Press.

Colvin, C. (2004a). *Performing the signs of injury: Critical perspectives on traumatic storytelling after apartheid*. Doctoral dissertation, University of Virginia.

Colvin, C. (2004b). Ambivalent narrations: Pursuing the political through traumatic storytelling. *PoLAR: Political and Legal Anthropology Review, 27*(1), 72–89.

Colvin, C. (2006). Shifting geographies of suffering and recovery: Traumatic storytelling after apartheid. In T. Luedke & H. West (Eds.), *Borders and healers: Brokering therapeutic resources in Southeast Africa* (pp. 167–169). Bloomington, IN: Indiana University Press.

Doxader, E. (2003). Easy to forget or never (again) hard to remember? History, memory and the "publicity" of amnesty. In C. Villa-Vicencio & E. Doxtader (Eds.), *The provocations of amnesty: Memory, justice and impunity* (pp. 121–155). Cape Town: David Philip Publishers.

Fullard, M., & Rousseau, N. (2008). Uncertain borders: The TRC and the (un)making of public myths. *Kronos, 34*(1).

Gobodo-Madikizela, P., & Van der Merwe, C. N. (2007). *Narrating our healing: Perspectives on working through trauma*. Cambridge: Cambridge Scholars.

Gontsana, M.-A. (2016, July). Apartheid compensation process flawed, says Khulumani. Allocation of R1 billion President's Fund money questioned. *Ground-Up*. Retrieved from http://www.groundup.org.za/article/apartheid-compensation-process-flawed-says-khulumani/.

Gunn, S. (2007). *If trees could speak: The Trojan Horse story*. Cape Town: Human Rights Media Centre.

Gunn, S., & Krwala, S. (Eds.). (2008). *Knocking on … Mothers and daughters in struggle in South Africa*. Johannesburg: Centre for the Study of Violence and Reconciliation and Human Rights Media Centre.

Hamber, B. (2006). Narrowing the micro and macro: A psychological perspective on reparations in societies in transition. In P. De Greiff (Ed.), *The handbook of reparations* (pp. 560–588). Oxford: Oxford University Press.

Hamber, B. (2009). *Transforming societies after political violence: Truth, reconciliation, and mental health*. New York: Springer.

Hamber, B., & Wilson, R. A. (2002). Symbolic closure through memory, reparation and revenge in post-conflict societies. *Journal of Human Rights, 1*(1), 35–53.

Hefferman, A., & Nieftagodien, N. (Eds.). (2016). *Students must rise: Youth struggle in South Africa before and beyond Soweto '76*. Johannesburg: University of Witwatersrand Press.

Kesselring, R. (2012). Corporate apartheid-era human rights violations before US courts: Political and legal controversies around victimhood in today's South Africa. *Stichproben: Vienna Journal of African Studies, Human Rights in Africa, 23*, 77–105.
Kesselring, R. (2016a). *Bodies of truth: Law, memory and emancipation in post-apartheid South Africa*. Stanford, CA: Stanford University Press.
Kesselring, R. (2016b). An injury to one is an injury to all? Class actions in South African courts and their social effects on plaintiffs. *PoLAR, 39*(2), 74–88.
Khulumani Support Group. (2016, April). *Khulumani Support Group commemorates the twentieth anniversary of the first TRC victim hearing in East London on 15 April with an open letter to all former TRC commissioners and staff.* Statement issued by the National Contact Centre of Khulumani Support Group. Retrieved from http://khulumani.net/khulumani/statements/item/1219-khulumani-support-group-commemorates-the-twentieth-anniversary-of-the-first-trc-victim-hearing-in-east-london-on-15-april-with-an-open-letter-to-all-former-trc-commisioners-and-staff.html
Madlingozi, T. (2007a). Good victim, bad victim: Apartheid's beneficiaries, victims, and the struggle for social justice. In K. Van Marle (Ed.), *Law, memory, and the legacy of apartheid: Ten years after AZAPO v. President of South Africa* (pp. 107–126). Pretoria: Pretoria University Law Press.
Madlingozi, T. (2007b). Post-apartheid social movements and the quest for the elusive "new" South Africa. *Journal of Law and Society, 34*(1), 77–98.
Madlingozi, T. (2010). On transitional justice entrepreneurs and the production of victims. *Journal of Human Rights Practice, 2*(2), 208–228.
Makhalemele, O. (2004). *Southern Africa reconciliation project: Khulumani case study*. Johannesburg: Centre for the Study of Violence and Reconciliation.
Mamdani, M. (2002). Amnesty or impunity? A preliminary critique of the report of the Truth and Reconciliation Commission of South Africa. *Diacritics Ethics, 32*(3/4), 33–59.
McLaughlin, C. (2002). *We never give up*. Cape Town: Human Rights Media Centre.
McLaughlin, C. (2012). *We never give up II*. Cape Town: Human Rights Media Centre.
Méndez, J. E. (2016). Victims as protagonists in transitional justice. *International Journal of Transitional Justice, 10*(1), 1–5.
Ngesi S'fiso, D. B. (2003). The presidential pardons and the media: Healing a wound with salt. In C. Villa-Vicencio & E. Doxtader (Eds.), *The provocations of amnesty: Memory, justice and impunity* (pp. 294–308). Cape Town: David Philip Publishers.
Ross, F. C. (2002). *Bearing witness: Women and the truth and reconciliation commission*. London: Pluto Press.
Ross, F. C. (2003). Using rights to measure wrongs: A case study of method and moral in the work of the South African Truth and Reconciliation Commission. In R. A. Wilson & J. P. Mitchell (Eds.), *Human rights in global perspective: Anthropological studies of rights, claims and entitlements* (pp. 163–182). London: Routledge.
Sarkin-Hughes, J. (2004). *Carrots and sticks: The TRC and the South African amnesty process*. Antwerp: Intersentia.
Sonis, J., & Van der Merwe, H. (2004). *Survivor perspectives on the South African TRC*. Johannesburg: Centre for the Study of Violence and Reconciliation.
Truth and Reconciliation Commission. (1998). *Truth and Reconciliation Commission final report* (Vol. 1–5). Cape Town: Juta.
Truth and Reconciliation Commission. (2003). *Truth and Reconciliation Commission final report* (Vol. 6–7). Cape Town: Juta.
Van der Merwe, H., & Chapman, A. R. (2008). Did the TRC deliver? In A. Chapman & H. van der Merwe (Eds.), *Truth and reconciliation in South Africa: Did the TRC deliver?* (pp. 241–279). Philadelphia, PA: University of Pennsylvania Press.
Van Zyl Slabbert, F. (2000). Truth without reconciliation, reconciliation without truth. In W. James & L. Van den Vijver (Eds.), *After the TRC: Reflections on truth and reconciliation in South Africa* (pp. 64–73). Cape Town: David Philip Publishers.
Wilson, R. A. (2000). Reconciliation and revenge in post-apartheid South Africa: Rethinking legal pluralism and human rights. *Current Anthropology, 41*(1), 75–98.
Wilson, R. A. (2001). *The politics of truth and reconciliation in South Africa: Legitimizing the post-apartheid state*. Cambridge: Cambridge University Press.

Chapter 6
Cooperation and Conflict: Civil Society Resistance and Engagement with Transitional Justice in Burundi

Wendy Lambourne

Introduction

The Central African country of Burundi has experienced cycles of political and interethnic violence and mass atrocities starting soon after gaining independence from Belgium in 1962. Contestations and contradictions abound in attempting to account for this turbulent past organised primarily around conflict between the Tutsi minority and the Hutu majority, but also around internal and cross-cutting divisions within the political elite (Lemarchand 1996; Watt 2016). Accusations of genocide have been made in both directions, focusing on the crisis of 1972 and subsequent massacres targeting each ethnic group in turn. According to Lemarchand, the use of the term genocide in relation to Burundi has been "designed to discredit rather than to illuminate" (Lemarchand 1996: xxvi). It is within this atmosphere of mutual distrust and violence that civil society began to emerge as a significant force in Burundian politics in the early 1990s.

This chapter is concerned with the role of civil society in efforts to deal with the past which have been pursued since the signing of the Arusha Peace and Reconciliation Agreement in 2000 and the subsequent creation of a power-sharing government in Burundi. In relation to transitional justice, the Arusha Agreement called for the establishment of a Truth and Reconciliation Commission (*Commission*

This research was supported in part by funding from the Faculty of Arts and Social Sciences at the University of Sydney. I am indebted to Trauma Healing and Reconciliation Services (THARS) and its executive director, Dr. David Niyonzima, for hosting my research visits to Burundi over the past 4 years, and to Raphael Manirakiza, a former civil society activist who left Burundi in mid-2013, for the translation of key documents and helping to fill some of the gaps in my knowledge and understanding of the Burundian political context and the role of civil society. I take full responsibility for any mistakes or misinformation I may have unwittingly reproduced in this chapter.

W. Lambourne (✉)
University of Sydney, Sydney, NSW, Australia
e-mail: wendy.lambourne@sydney.edu.au

J. Brankovic, H. van der Merwe (eds.), *Advocating Transitional Justice in Africa*, Springer Series in Transitional Justice,
https://doi.org/10.1007/978-3-319-70417-3_6

pour la Vérité et la Réconciliation, or CVR) as well as an international judicial commission of inquiry which was intended to lead to the creation of an international tribunal to deal with the crimes of the past. Interim negotiations for a special tribunal foundered, however, and the Burundian Government delayed implementation of legislation for the creation of the CVR. In May 2014, the legislation was finally passed and promulgated by the president, but before the CVR could become operational violence again broke out in Burundi following the president's announcement in April 2015 that he would stand for a third term, which was seen by many as against the provisions of the constitution and the Arusha Agreement. The CVR finally commenced operations in March 2016, in the face of continuing political instability and violence, disappearances, extrajudicial killings and massive refugee flows, which have divided civil society and affected their ability to participate in the CVR (Impunity Watch 2016).

Drawing on field research conducted in Burundi between 2012 and 2016,[1] this chapter considers examples of cooperation and contestation, empowerment and resistance, among civil society actors and in their relationship with the United Nations (UN), the Burundian Government and the transitional justice process. The challenges faced by local civil society organisations (CSOs) and networks as they pursue different strategies in relation to transitional justice in Burundi reveal tensions between diverse agendas and priorities, as well as overlap and mutual support.

The chapter discusses initiatives from local CSOs Centre for the Warning and Prevention of Conflict (*Centre d'Alerte et Prévention de Conflits*, or CENAP) and the Reflection Group on Transitional Justice (*Groupe de Réflexion sur la Justice Transitionnelle*, or GRJT), which CENAP helped to create, as well as the Quaker Peace Network (QPN) Burundi and its member organisations, which are supporting trauma healing and reconciliation in local communities and have proposed a Burundian model of transitional justice. The chapter also includes reference to civil society participation in the Forum of Community Facilitators in Transitional Justice (*Forum National des Relais Communautaire en Justice de Transition*, or FONAREC/JT), established by the UN Transitional Justice Unit in Burundi, and more recently the convening of a new platform of international and local CSOs by the president of the CVR.

In order to provide a context for the analysis of civil society engagement with transitional justice in Burundi, the chapter starts with a brief account of the violent conflict and the emergence of CSOs. The chapter examines sites of resistance and trends in cooperation and conflict evident in civil society initiatives and attempts to influence the transitional justice process. It concludes with some observations about how the current crisis is turning existing differences in civil society perspectives into signifi-

[1] Sources included participant observation, interviews and meetings during 8 separate visits to Burundi between May 2012 and August 2016, and 1 visit to Rwanda in August 2016, with a number of different representatives or members of government, the United Nations, funding bodies and local and international NGOs, including CENAP, FORSC, Impunity Watch, Global Rights, GiZ, THARS, QPN Burundi, MiPAREC, AMEPCI, *La Benevolencija Grands Lacs*, AFSC, *RCN Justice & Democratie*, members of FONAREC, GRJT and the UN Transitional Justice Unit. Individual interviewees and informants are not directly named in the interests of confidentiality and security.

cant divisions based on politics and ethnicity, with CSOs seemingly split between those (mostly Hutu) remaining in the country who support the CVR and those (mostly Tutsi) who are in exile and alienated from the transitional justice process.[2]

Cycles of Political and Ethnic Violence

The kingdom of Burundi in the Great Lakes region of central Africa was colonised and administered first by Germany from 1890 and then by Belgium after the end of the First World War until Burundi became independent in 1962. As in neighbouring Rwanda, the colonial power had deepened pre-existing differences between the three ethnic groups, the majority Hutu who were farmers (approximately 85% of the population), cattle-owning Tutsi (14%) and original pygmy inhabitants, the Twa (1%), setting the stage for ethnic politics to emerge in the postcolonial period. But unlike Rwanda, post-independence Burundi, after a brief period of shared rule, became dominated by Tutsi-led governments. The country was beset by a series of political assassinations and coups d'état starting with the crisis of 1965, followed and preceded by massacres and revenge killings as the population became further divided on both ethnic and political grounds. The year 1972 is especially remembered by the Hutu population for a genocide committed by the Tutsi government, when approximately 200,000 Hutu were killed and 300,000 fled as refugees, mostly to neighbouring Tanzania. In 1988 a localised Hutu revolt was crushed by the Tutsi army with further mass killings which were not investigated. A culture of impunity had been created, along with collective trauma and fear of the other ethnic group affecting the whole population.

As part of a post-Cold War move to multiethnic, multiparty politics in Burundi, the first Hutu president took office in July 1993, but he was assassinated in October. Approximately 50,000 Tutsis were killed in a revenge massacre, and 700,000 Hutus fled in fear of reprisal killings. The ensuing civil war resulted in further refugee flows, internally displaced persons (IDPs), many wounded and more than 300,000 deaths. The war was officially ended with the signing of the Arusha Agreement on August 28, 2000, and the UN provided a peacekeeping mission which supervised the election of a power-sharing government in 2005. However, the fighting continued until December 2008 when the last of the rebel groups, the Party for the Liberation of the Hutu People–National Liberation Forces (*Parti pour la Libération du Peuple Hutu–Forces Nationales de Libération*, or Palipehutu-FNL), finally agreed to disarm, but only after assurances that they would not be arrested and prosecuted (Vandeginste 2012). Other transitional justice issues that were discussed during the final peace negotiations included the release of combatants and prisoners of war, integration of

[2] Note that this conclusion reflects the perspective of those in exile and the diaspora, including both Hutu and Tutsi, who are openly opposed to the third term of the current president. Civil society leaders remaining in Burundi who are supporting the CVR process do not necessarily see themselves as taking a political position, but rather as supporting peace, reconciliation and healing for their fellow Burundians. Personal interviews, Bujumbura, Kigali and Sydney, July–August 2016.

former combatants into the security forces and the rebels' preference for a "Truth, Forgiveness and Reconciliation Commission" (Vandeginste 2012: 3). Eventually the CVR was created, but prosecutions have not been pursued, despite advocacy from civil society, support from the political opposition and strong pressure from the UN.

Defining and Understanding Civil Society in Burundi

Civil society may be defined as "social organisations occupying the space between the household and the state that enable people to coordinate their management of resources and activities" (Layton 2006: 3). Civil society may be defined as non-profit, voluntary, non-political organisations, but may also include corporations, religious organisations, media groups and political parties. In Burundi we can see how these different categories of civil society groupings have developed over time to become particularly strong in terms of religious institutions and media groups, as well as voluntary non-profit organisations which may be linked in partnership with major international NGOs. Political party affiliation came to define Burundian social relations more than ethnic groups in the post-civil war period, and at least until April 2015 was providing a significant form of civil society organisation in local communities.

Civil society can be seen as playing two major roles: (1) complementing the capacity of states in delivering essential services to citizens, particularly in cases where states have become weak due to poor governance structures, and (2) providing oversight to ensure governmental accountability (Centre for Conflict Resolution 2005). In Burundi, both kinds of CSOs existed prior to the end of the civil war and in the post-Arusha period (Omara and Ackson 2010). For example, the first CSOs, Ligue ITEKA and SONERA, were human rights NGOs formed by academics in Burundi in the early 1990s which played a significant role in the second category, investigating human rights violations and speaking out against torture and corruption. In subsequent decades a large number of CSOs in the first category emerged, including NGOs dealing with a wide variety of issues from women's and youth associations to religious organisations and those working on women's and children's rights, development, health, education, HIV/AIDS and poverty eradication (Omara and Ackson 2010). The human rights NGO Association for the Protection of Human Rights and Detained Persons (APRODH) was established in 2001 with a focus on the rights of prisoners and victims of torture. Faith-based charity organisations have provided humanitarian assistance to orphans and others affected by the war, and a number of Quaker organisations emerged following the end of the war focusing on peacebuilding, reconciliation and development, including Ministry for Peace and Reconciliation under the Cross (MiPAREC), Trauma Healing and Reconciliation Services (THARS) and several NGOs focusing specifically on children and women in need (Watt 2016).[3] Many of these NGOs, including APRODH

[3] Many of these human rights, peace and development NGOs, while based in the capital city of Bujumbura, also have a strong presence and connection with communities in rural areas, including especially the second biggest province of Gitega.

and THARS, were started by victims and focus on the rights (second category) or needs (first category) of victims of torture, sexual violence, child abuse or other violence suffered during the civil war and since the war officially ended.

The emergence of a vibrant civil society in Burundi was assisted by the involvement of external actors in the various peace processes. New opposition groups and members of civil society, including especially religious leaders, were invited by the Burundian Government to observe the Arusha peace talks in 2000. According to Quaker leaders in Burundi, they were encouraged by the approach of the mediator, former South African President and elder statesman, Nelson Mandela, who allowed some of the civil society observers to speak in the official plenary. Although they were able to "lobby the political parties and to insert some issues on the agenda" (Manirakiza 2016: 56), other civil society members disagreed with this assessment and expressed their frustration at not being invited as full participants in the process.[4]

Burundian civil society members subsequently became more empowered to participate in the governance of their country through the principles set out in the Arusha Agreement and enshrined in the constitution of 2003 in relation to the development of a multiparty political system (Omara and Ackson 2010). For example, Burundian civil society actors played a key role in the Global Platform for the Prevention of Armed Conflict (GPPAC) campaign which resulted in the creation of the United Nations Peacebuilding Commission (UNPBC).[5] The UNPBC started operations in Burundi in 2006, with civil society playing an active role in its work on poverty reduction and peacebuilding priorities for the country. In this way, an international CSO, GPPAC, facilitated the already active local Burundian civil society actors in acquiring a voice on the international stage and in influencing national policy outcomes.

As explained by Uvin, "Burundians became angry" as a result of the civil war and the experience of ordinary Burundians that "nobody in power gave a damn about the needs of the poor" (Uvin 2009: 76). Rural Burundians revealed a similar lack of trust in the government to provide any sense of the rule of law or services for the community, which has been reflected in the increasing assertiveness of civil society in the capital city of Bujumbura and criticism of the government also observed by Uvin (2009).

One of the most important changes in civil society following the end of the civil war was the growth in independent media, which provided alternative voices and means of communicating information outside of the normal channels of government-controlled media and communications, creating a more informed citizenry (Uvin 2009; Omara and Ackson 2010). Trade unions also developed, and Burundian NGOs proliferated and strengthened in opposition as well as support of the government, creating an apparently pluralist civil society.[6]

[4] Interviews conducted in Bujumbura in August 2016.

[5] Personal interview, Kigali, August 2016.

[6] Examples of the increasing influence of CSOs at the time included the release from prison of several opposition and CSO leaders, and the allowing of CSOs which had been suspended to recommence operations.

Civil society in Burundi has thus from its origins played both roles identified earlier in this chapter, in supporting the delivery of services by the government, such as faith-based peace or charity organisations, and providing a critical voice through the media, trade unions and human rights NGOs. The relationship between these two groups in civil society has fluctuated over time depending on the political context.

For example, following the 2005 elections which installed as president Pierre Nkurunziza, the leader of the newly formed political party of former rebels, the National Council for the Defence of Democracy–Forces for the Defence of Democracy (*Conseil National pour la Défense de Démocratie–Forces pour la Défense de Démocratie*, or CNDD-FDD), several events served to unite the different CSOs and strengthened them in working together against the government.[7] The first of these events was the massacre of more than 30 civilians alleged to be supporters of the opposition rebel group Palipehutu-FNL in Muyinga Province in 2006 (Human Rights Watch 2008), followed in 2007 by the "illegal sale" of the presidential jet by the president.

In 2009, the extrajudicial killing of leading anti-corruption activist Ernest Manirumva, who was vice president of the CSO Anti-corruption and Economic Malpractice Observatory (*Observatoire de Lutte contre la Corruption et les Malversations Economiques*, or OLUCOME), had a profound impact on Burundian civil society activists, who mounted a campaign calling for justice through the CSO umbrella organisation, Forum for the Strengthening of Civil Society (*Forum pour le Reinforcement de la Société Civile*, or FORSC). The government issued an ordinance banning the activities of FORSC, and other CSO members and journalists who publicly denounced Manirumva's killing and the failings of judicial inquiries into the case were subjected to threats and intimidation.[8] When the trial verdict was finally announced in 2012 a group of 13 Burundian and 7 international NGOs issued a joint statement condemning the trial for failing to investigate senior figures in the Burundian security and police services (Human Rights Watch 2012). In addition to Ligue ITEKA, FORSC and OLUCOME, the Burundian civil society signatories included prominent human rights NGO APRODH and the Forum of Burundian Journalists (*Union Burundaise des Journalistes*, or UBJ).

The Burundian Government responded by creating "dummy" or front NGOs (*nyakuri*) to support its policies and activities, which had the effect of creating, or appearing to create, divisions in civil society where otherwise none might have existed.[9] For example, some (mostly Hutu) religious organisations which supported the

[7] This was in contrast to the initial position of a number of CSOs and opposition political parties which had determined to give the new CNDD-FDD government a chance and not actively oppose it.

[8] http://reliefweb.int/report/burundi/burundi-reverse-ban-civil-society-group (Accessed 10 December 2016).

[9] The civil society leaders and organisations discussed in this chapter should be distinguished from those which have been created by the government as "front" NGOs, ostensibly to counterbalance the perceived opposition bias of existing CSOs. They include PISC-Burundi (the platform for Burundian civil society) and CAPES+ (the collective of associations of people infected and affected by HIV/AIDS), which have praised the Burundian Government's banning of other CSOs since April 2015 as well as the expulsion of the UN High Commissioner for Human Rights, and

ruling party were co-opted through business interests and travelled the country supporting activities such as a choir associated with the first lady (*Komezagusenga*, or "keep praying") and a soccer team (Alleluya FC) led by the president.[10] At the same time, competition for funding, poor resource sustainability and lack of trust reduced cooperation and coordination between local Burundian CSOs (Omara and Ackson 2010), and perceptions of ethnic bias in the member organisations of FORSC limited its potential effectiveness as a coordinating body for Burundian civil society.

In the few years leading up to the political crisis that began in April 2015, the relationship between CSOs and the government had been steadily improving and freedom of speech and the media was lauded as a positive development.[11] This occurred despite setbacks such as the new media law introduced in June 2013 which limited the protection of journalistic sources and banned reporting on stories related to national defence, security, public safety or the economy (IMS 2015). The role of Burundian civil society in holding to account an oppressive government was becoming less significant and there was some curtailment in civil society activity. However, the previous flourishing of civil society took an even sharper downturn in late April 2015 when the government forcibly shut down the independent media outlets and began imprisoning and targeting for assassination civil society leaders opposed to the third term of President Nkurunziza. Journalists who worked for private radio stations, along with the leaders of FORSC and Ligue ITEKA, fled into exile, mostly to neighbouring Rwanda, where their resistance has continued through online reporting and activism. The founder and president of APRODH, Pierre Claver Mbonimpa, survived an assassination attempt and was medically evacuated to Belgium where he remains in exile while continuing to campaign for human rights.[12] Those civil society leaders who remained openly operating in the country during the political crisis, mostly Hutu, were seen by some of those in exile, mostly Tutsi, as *nyakuri*, whether or not they actively support the ruling party.[13] Civil society was thus becoming more divided along both political and ethnic lines as a result of the crisis.[14]

It was in this oppressive and violent environment and threatened return to the ethnic "politics of the past" that the government declared the commencement of the operations of the CVR. As will be argued in this chapter, the timing of this move can

denounced the politicisation of civil society groups such as APRODH and FORSC. http://www.iwacu-burundi.org/englishnews/pisc-burundi-and-capes-praise-government-ban-on-other-civil-society-organisations/ (Accessed 10 December 2016).

[10] Interviews conducted in Sydney and Bujumbura, July–August 2016.

[11] Meetings with CSO leaders in Bujumbura in 2012 and 2013, and interviews conducted in 2014.

[12] In 2016, Mbunimpa was the recipient of the Alison des Forges Award for Extraordinary Activism. https://www.hrw.org/news/2016/09/01/pierre-claver-mbonimpa-burundi (Accessed 10 December 2016).

[13] Interviews conducted in Bujumbura and Kigali, August 2016.

[14] While this perception of increasing division was reported by some civil society leaders in exile in Kigali, it was not reported by all, and it was not the view expressed by civil society leaders remaining in Burundi who were more likely to express solidarity with those in exile. My preliminary analysis suggested that the division was not between Hutu and Tutsi, or between those who supported and those who opposed the ruling party, but between those who were united across ethnic lines in working for peace whether inside the country or in exile, and those who were more actively opposing the president's third term and perceived the struggle in more political and ethnic terms.

be seen as a deliberate attempt to limit the participation and impact of civil society in relation to the CVR and maximise control by the ruling elite over its functioning and outcomes.

The Road to Transitional Justice in Burundi, Paved with Mixed Intentions

The establishment of the CVR in Burundi followed a protracted period of government prevarication, UN pressure and civil society lobbying from the signing of the Arusha Agreement. While Arusha set up the terms for transitional justice in Burundi, negotiations between the UN and the government resulted in a watering down of the original commitment to an international judicial commission of inquiry and a possible international criminal tribunal, to just the proposed national truth commission (Vandeginste 2012). An interim agreement to establish a special chamber within the Burundian court system was replaced by a proposal for a special tribunal, but this was later shelved as well, as was the negotiation of a mixed international and domestic truth commission, so that the CVR became a purely domestic institution (ICTJ 2011; Taylor 2013b).

Legislation for the establishment of the CVR was first adopted in December 2004, but it was not implemented. Further progress was delayed until the government agreed to national consultations on transitional justice following the recommendation of a report arising from a May 2004 UN assessment mission, published in March 2005 and known as the Kalomoh report after the assistant secretary-general for political affairs, Tuliameni Kalomoh, who led the mission (Vandeginste 2009). The national consultations in Burundi arose because of the insistence of the UN, and the terms of the process were set out in an agreement signed eventually in November 2007 between the Burundian Government, civil society and the UN (ICTJ 2011).[15] Consistent with the UN's subsequently published guiding principles, these terms included assurances that the consultations would be independent, balanced and inclusive of women and different categories of victims (UNDPA 2010; ICTJ 2011).

However, the consultations, which were carried out in 2009, did not give respondents the opportunity to express their preference on the type of transitional justice mechanism, but instead asked about specific aspects of each of the four key pillars of transitional justice as defined by the UN, namely a truth and reconciliation commission in order to seek the truth and a special tribunal to achieve prosecutions, along with reparations and institutional reform (Government of Burundi 2010). The consultations also asked about the period of inquiry to be covered by transitional justice, and about what Burundians thought would assist in building reconciliation and a sustainable peace. Other than these two more open questions, it is clear that the UN was able to impose not only its predefined four pillars but also the types of transitional justice mechanisms available to Burundians, thereby severely constrain-

[15] The consultations were funded by the UN Peacebuilding Fund.

ing the potential impact of civil society on the design of the transitional justice process (Manirakiza 2016: 42).

The results of the national consultations released in 2010 were interpreted as revealing majority support for the establishment of a truth and reconciliation commission with a mixed national and international composition and a mandate to investigate the full range of crimes from independence in 1962 until the end of the civil war in 2008, as well as provision for reparations (Boloquy et al. 2013; Government of Burundi 2010).[16] However, the public preference for a mixed truth commission was not pursued. After the 2010 elections, the Burundian Government established a technical committee to elaborate the law for the creation of the CVR and present it to parliament. The committee, which was composed of seven members appointed by the government, on October 18, 2011, released its report, known as the Kavakure report after the head of the committee, Minister Laurent Kavakure. Kavakure was then special adviser to the president after having served previously as ambassador to Belgium and foreign affairs minister. His key role on the technical committee suggests that the report's recommendations for the planned CVR would not be independent of government power and interests. On the other hand, as one of my informants explained, it seems that civil society through the GRJT did have some influence on the drafting of the Kavakure report, as discussed later in this chapter.[17]

In August 2011, the American Friends Service Committee (a US-based Quaker NGO) organised a conference on "Transitional Justice Mechanisms: Lessons Learned from Truth and Reconciliation Commissions" in Bujumbura which was attended by 41 members of international and local civil society, government representatives, the UN and diplomats from embassies in Burundi, as well as 14 foreign participants from South Africa, Sierra Leone, Liberia, Democratic Republic of Congo, Kenya, Uganda, the USA and Spain, including several who had served as commissioners in various truth commissions. The participants included Burundian members of the technical committee which had a few months previously produced the Kavakure report on the creation of the CVR. The conference was thus a significant opportunity for Burundian civil society to share knowledge and ideas about other truth commissions and the potential for the CVR planned in Burundi.

One of the observations was that in Africa, economic, social and cultural rights are a critical issue in addition to the civil and political rights violations which are normally the main focus of truth commissions (AFSC Burundi 2011: 14). A concern was also expressed about the potential impact on already existing successful community-based peace and reconciliation initiatives, such as the local Peace

[16] Some CSOs have subsequently called for the CVR to stop its work and to recommence when the mandate can be expanded to cover human rights violations committed in association with the political crisis commencing in April 2015. In November 2016 the UN Human Rights Council set up an independent commission of inquiry to investigate human rights violations in Burundi since April 2015, which is mandated to engage with Burundian authorities and other stakeholders, including civil society, refugees, UN agencies and regional bodies. The International Criminal Court (ICC) meanwhile is continuing its preliminary examination of alleged crimes against humanity committed in Burundi since April 2015. Atrocities Watch Africa, *Burundi Watch Update* 14–20 November & 21–27 November 2016, http://www.atrocitieswatch.org.

[17] Interview conducted in Bujumbura, August 2016.

Committees supported by MiPAREC, once the CVR was established (AFSC Burundi 2011: 15). The report of the conference listed 26 recommendations in relation to the creation and organisation of the CVR, strategies to promote participation and protection of witnesses and victims, and the ideal law for the establishment of the CVR (AFSC Burundi 2011: 5–7). As with the results of the national consultations, most of these recommendations, including those about transparency and civil society participation, were not implemented in the eventual creation of the CVR.

President Nkurunziza announced that the CVR would be launched by the 50th anniversary of independence on July 1, 2012 (Vandeginste 2012: 2), and several draft versions of a law with guiding principles for the proposed CVR were presented to parliament by the technical committee. The UN and international and local civil society actively opposed the draft law on various grounds, including that it failed to comply with international standards and best practices for truth commissions, and that it did not reflect the wishes of the population as expressed in the national consultations (Impunity Watch 2013). The third draft of the law, which was presented to parliament in December 2012, showed that civil society lobbying had made no impact, and furthermore included "a number of revisions to the original version of the draft law that mark[ed] a clear regression in the protection of the rights of victims in Burundi" (Impunity Watch 2013: 3). It included amendments that provided for pardon in exchange for confessions (conditional amnesty), and gave the Burundian Government the sole authority to nominate and select the commissioners instead of opening the process to public participation (Boloquy et al. 2013). This development was disturbing for local civil society members of the GRJT who were "neutral professionals or opposed to the ruling party".[18] But it was not surprising given that the government included a number of former rebel leaders who could be accused of genocide, war crimes and crimes against humanity through the CVR, and who thus had a vested interest in maximising their control of the commission (Boloquy et al. 2013). In the end there was an open nomination process, but the selection of commissioners from those nominated was made by the government in a non-transparent process.

By contrast, 53% of respondents in the national consultations rejected political involvement in the appointment of the commissioners, fuelled by mistrust of their political leaders, and 77% preferred to see a hybrid commission comprising both foreign and Burundian commissioners as a means to counter political influence and potential corruption (Boloquy et al. 2013). Approximately 88% of respondents indicated that civil society should be involved in selecting the commissioners, while an overwhelming majority (93%) of respondents believed that the commissioners should include members of civil society, compared with 73% who thought they should include representatives from the government (Government of Burundi 2010). Under the guise of state sovereignty, the Burundian Government indicated that it would exclude international commissioners and declined to allow an international presence during the nomination process (Impunity Watch 2013). Concern was expressed by both local and international NGOs about the implications of the lack of international involvement in the CVR for witness protection, especially in the

[18] Interview with local civil society member of the GRJT, August 2016.

context of government intimidation and extrajudicial killings.[19] The draft legislation was also seen as inadequate in terms of accounting for gender sensitivity and witness protection more generally (Impunity Watch 2013). These and other changes in the draft law signalled the government's intention to retain political control over the mandate and functioning of the CVR, going against most of the advice of the UN and preferences of civil society and the general population.

In July 2013 when I was in Burundi, expectations were high among local civil society that the parliament would pass the third draft of the legislation in its current sitting.[20] However, it took until May 2014 before the law was finally passed and promulgated by the president,[21] and almost another 2 years before the CVR finally commenced operations in March 2016, after the results of a much-criticised nomination process for the commissioners were announced in December 2014. Some Burundian local civil society representatives did not stand because of their objections to the process, while others nominated in the hope that if they were selected they could make a positive difference to the work of the commission.[22] Of the 11 selected commissioners, 6 were religious leaders, 2 were representatives of the ruling party, 2 were representatives of opposition political parties[23] and 1 was a senator and member of the minority Batwa ethnic group—all religious or political party representatives, and no representatives of civil society, who might be considered more neutral, professional or likely to criticise the ruling party (Impunity Watch 2014).[24] Four were women, as required by the legislation, six were Hutu and four were Tutsi. The commissioners were chosen by the government from a group of 33 preselected candidates from a total of 725 nominations (Rwanda News Agency 2014).

The ruling party has thus continued to assert its control over the transitional justice process, delaying the creation of the CVR until a time when there is no freedom of speech or security for those who give testimony or criticise the government (FORSC 2016). The UN, meanwhile, maintained a mandate in its political missions to support transitional justice through the Transitional Justice Unit (TJU) of the UN Office in Burundi (BNUB) which replaced the UN Integrated Office in Burundi (BINUB) and ran from January 2011 until the end of 2014.[25] Impotent to affect the

---

[19] Meetings with local and international civil society representatives, July 2013, June 2014 and August 2016.

[20] Meetings with local civil society members of the GRJT, July 2013.

[21] For an analysis of how the Burundian Government was appearing to comply with international obligations in relation to transitional justice while failing to genuinely commit to their implementation, see Taylor (2013b).

[22] Interviews conducted in Bujumbura, June 2014.

[23] Allegedly *nyakuri* and not genuine opposition parties. Interviews conducted in Bujumbura and Sydney, July–August 2016.

[24] Meetings with local civil society members in Bujumbura, August 2016, and in Sydney since the establishment of the CVR in early 2016, considering the political nature of the appointment of commissioners and confirming the perception that none of those appointed genuinely represented civil society. This perception represented the perspective that religious leaders had been co-opted to a partisan political agenda.

[25] UN Security Council resolution 2137 of 13 February 2014, which extended the mandate of BNUB to the end of 2014, included the following in relation to transitional justice: 15. *Calls upon* the Government of Burundi to work with international partners and BNUB for the establishment

Burundian Government's policies and facing the threat of expulsion from the country, the TJU turned its attention to supporting civil society engagement in transitional justice in addition to its existing project on witness protection preparing for the eventual creation of the CVR.[26] However, despite significant investment, the TJU's efforts were not effective in targeting the needs of civil society.

Civil society representatives interviewed in Burundi in 2012 and 2013 revealed disappointment with the UN's approach. They reported a lack of support for transitional justice-related programmes in local communities from the BNUB/TJU because of constraints in the type of funding available. They also expressed surprise about the TJU's approach to creating the Forum of Community Facilitators in Transitional Justice (*Forum National des Relais Communautaire en Justice de Transition*, or FONAREC/JT) independently of existing civil society groups working on transitional justice. FONAREC/JT, which was created with the aim of training community facilitators at all levels of Burundian society throughout the country as a form of popular participation in transitional justice, was later abandoned as its shortcomings were recognised by the UN itself (Lambourne 2014).[27]

FONAREC/JT was a flawed process in a number of ways, including its failure to build on the existing capacity, experience and involvement of CSOs in transitional justice, and its focus on transmitting knowledge about the key pillars of transitional justice as defined by the UN rather than on an authentic engagement in understanding local civil society perspectives and priorities (Lambourne 2014; FONAREC/JT 2012). While it had the potential to be successful in providing a first level of outreach in terms of transparency by informing and sensitising the population about the proposed CVR, it did not appear to be designed to fulfil the second and third levels of outreach in terms of gathering civil society feedback on the implementation of the CVR or input to the design of the CVR or other aspects of transitional justice (Lambourne 2012). A member of the GRJT told me that in his observation the civil society members selected to be community facilitators in FONAREC/JT were not necessarily interested in transitional justice, unlike the members of the GRJT who were not invited.[28] This resulted in a lack of sustainability for the project, which the UN had intended would become locally owned and run, as the volunteer community facilitators who had been elected would not carry out their functions without continuing support from the TJU. BNUB and the TJU had a finite life, however, and so did FONAREC/JT, it seems, ending even before it was fully implemented.[29]

---

of transitional justice mechanisms, including a credible and consensual Truth and Reconciliation Commission to help foster an effective reconciliation of all Burundians and durable peace in Burundi, in accordance with the results of the work of the Technical Committee, the 2009 national consultations, Security Council Resolution 1606 (UNSC 2005) as well as the Arusha Agreement of August 28, 2000.

[26] Note that in October 2016 the UN High Commissioner for Human Rights, whose mandate included transitional justice, was expelled by the Burundian Government.

[27] Interview with the Head of the TJU, Robert Kotchani, in Bujumbura, June 2014.

[28] See also Lambourne (2014) for an account of the election process and interviews with some of the FONAREC/JT community facilitators.

[29] Interviews conducted in Bujumubura and Gitega, Burundi, July 2013, June 2014 and December 2014.

Civil Society Cooperation and Resistance and Transitional Justice in Burundi

Local civil society actors in Burundi, with support from international NGOs, have played two primary roles in relation to transitional justice reflecting the categories outlined by the Centre for Conflict Resolution (2005) and mentioned earlier in this chapter: apparent support for the government through their focus on healing and reconciliation and sensitisation about the CVR, and resistance to the government position on transitional justice with their focus on accountability and prosecutions. Some civil society activities and organisations, such as the QPN Burundi, might not be so easily categorised, as they seek to hold the government to account and offer alternative models of transitional justice while at the same time pursuing objectives consistent with the government position.

These differences were apparent in the work of the above-mentioned GRJT, but have become more significant in the wake of the April 2015 political and security crisis and the narrowing of any opportunity for resistance within Burundi. Divisions along political and ethnic lines are emerging between CSOs operating in the first category or straddling both categories which have remained active in Burundi, and those clearly within the second category whose leaders are mostly now in hiding or in exile.[30] The strength and potential impact of CSO resistance thus appear to have been undermined by the breaking down of civil society cooperation across the two categories in line with the need to be seen as supporting or opposing the ruling party.

Two significant NGO initiatives will be discussed in detail in order to further explore the dynamics of cooperation and resistance within local civil society actors in Burundi, and how they have been impacted post-April 2015: CENAP and the GRJT, as well as QPN Burundi and its model for transitional justice.

CENAP and the GRJT

The GRJT was formed in 2008 as the result of a recommendation put forward by a National Forum convened by local Burundian NGO CENAP as the culmination of its research, supported by Interpeace, an independent international peacebuilding organisation based in Geneva, on perceptions of Burundians about the obstacles to peace. A working group on transitional justice was created as a result of the National Forum which led to the GRJT being formed. CENAP convened monthly meetings of the GRJT during 2009 in order to continue the research and reflection based on the responses and solutions suggested by civil society. At some stage, it seems that the primary leadership role in the GRJT was taken over by Global Rights, an international NGO headed locally by well-known Burundian civil society leader

[30] Interviews conducted with civil society leaders in Bujumbura and Kigali, August 2016.

Louis Marie Nindorera, brother of Eugène who was the founding president of Ligue ITEKA.[31] The mission of the GRJT was to enable information exchange and strengthening of civil society involvement in the transitional justice process in Burundi, which culminated in at least two significant public statements, as detailed below, and a number of individual NGO initiatives.[32]

The GRJT issued a report in December 2011 commenting on the Kavakure report and making six recommendations in relation to the draft law for the establishment of the CVR concerning the procedure for the nomination of commissioners; composition of the CVR and role of the proposed International Consultative Council that would set up the CVR; gender and children's rights; protection of victims and witnesses; the mandate of the CVR and crimes covered; and the establishment of a Special Tribunal (GRJT 2011). Along with the UN and local civil society groups, its members made submissions to the government regarding subsequent versions of the draft law.[33] These comments included criticisms that it failed to comply with international standards and did not reflect the findings of the national consultations. For example, a memorandum issued by the GRJT on June 23, 2014, signed by representatives of 15 NGOs, including the umbrella organisation FORSC, noted,

> At several times, with a collaborative spirit and in order to be able to clearly respect the rights of victims in transitional justice, the GRJT member organizations produced and presented recommendations to improve the draft of that law [to set up the CVR]. The GRJT member organizations realised unfortunately that most of those recommendations were not taken into account. They take note of the fact but do not give up.

The memorandum called for increased transparency in the process for selection of commissioners, noting the lack of provisions for an "equitable constitution" of the membership of the CVR and questioning how the commission could be "representative and inclusive" (GRJT 2014). It also encouraged members of civil society and especially faith-based organisations to nominate themselves to be commissioners, and cautioned those selected "to consider the whole consequences and responsibilities of being part of a commission whose composition will not be deemed competent, neutral and independent and that may not be powerful enough to respect the voice of victims and to achieve the goal of having the truth". The memorandum warned against perceptions of an unbalanced and politically partisan commission that would undermine its independence and efficiency and the "trust, collaboration and future support" of CSOs, including members of the GRJT, victims and witnesses and international partners of the government. It concluded by calling for accountability and punishment of the perpetrators of human rights crimes "in order to generate trust, the enthusiastic participation and support of the victims, [and] those who witnessed horrible crimes in the past" so they would "feel safe and comfortable to collaborate with

[31] The original founding of the GRJT is remembered differently by a number of local civil society members who told me that it was run by Impunity Watch and/or Global Rights and started by Louis Marie Nindorera.

[32] It is possible that additional group statements were issued, but they are not on public record.

[33] See Boloquy et al. (2013) and Taylor (2013b) for an analysis of the draft law and the potential for the proposed TRC to meet the needs of the local population.

the CVR". This appears to have been an unusual achievement of compromise, given the conflicting views of members on the issue of prosecutions, that was agreed between the signatories after considerable discussion and negotiation under pressure to respond quickly to the government call for nominations for commissioners which opened on June 5 and was due to close on June 27, 2014.[34]

The GRJT's advocacy in response to the successive drafts of the CVR law was affected by a lack of consensus on some issues, and in particular significant contestation over attitudes towards prosecutions.[35] Apparently one group composed mainly of the faith-based members of the GRJT was calling for pardon and forgiveness, or truth telling for healing purposes, while the other group of NGOs was looking towards prosecution of perpetrators and was adamant about not forgiving them before they were held to account before the courts.[36] While the former were primarily concerned with addressing the needs of victims, the latter were focused more on advocating for the rights of victims. The government, by contrast, had one clear view against prosecutions which it was conveying to the population as a form of "instruction about the need for national reconciliation".[37] The effectiveness of the GRJT as a site of resistance to state power was thus limited by the differences between civil society members of the group because of their strong but divergent individual expressions of resistance.

However, in 2011 the group managed to harmonise its various views to come up with one voice in order to contribute to the Kavakure commission, and in 2014 they were able to collaborate in a powerful call for accountability and greater transparency in the CVR. Although they had limited impact on the selection of CVR commissioners and the structure of the CVR, the GRJT did have some influence on the scope of the commission's mandate and had a meeting with the CVR commissioners.[38]

Despite the limited number of group actions, GRJT members individually have initiated programmes or activities inspired by their association with the original CENAP initiative and membership of the GRJT. For example, local NGO Association for Memory and Protection of Humanity against International Crimes (AMEPCI), working closely with local victims' associations, has expressed its resistance by organising annual commemorations and ad hoc events presenting victim and witness testimony, and by endeavouring to maintain memorials despite the lack of

[34] Interview with civil society members of the GRJT in June 2014; original memorandum in French on file with the author. According to another civil society member of the GRJT interviewed in August 2016, the memorandum was sent out by Ligue ITEKA before it was agreed by the group.

[35] When conducting my field research in Burundi I was unable to find records of the group's members, meetings or activities, other than a limited number of memoranda issued in the past few years, so I have relied primarily on interviews with members of the group for this analysis.

[36] Interviews with civil society members of GRJT conducted in Bujumbura in 2012 and August 2016.

[37] Interview with civil society leader conducted in Bujumbura in 2012.

[38] Interview with civil society leader in Bujumbura, August 2016.

support for memorialisation or documentation by the government.[39] Such commemoration activities were recommended by the original working group on transitional justice created following the 2008 National Forum organised by CENAP and Interpeace. The working group also noted the divergent perspectives of Burundians on how to deal with the past in terms of the contested relationships between truth and national reconciliation, amnesty and prosecutions, which were subsequently reflected in the emergence of two groups of NGOs in the GRJT representing these divergent perspectives.

It appears that the GRJT was relatively informal, that it did not meet regularly but rather on an ad hoc basis and that it was otherwise not very active publicly despite substantive discussions and debates about transitional justice issues within the group.[40] The composition of the GRJT was broad and went beyond traditional NGOs to include representatives of the army, Catholic Church and political parties, as well as a presidential adviser. At one stage the meetings were attended by diplomats from the various embassies in Bujumbura, including from Switzerland and Belgium, and by representatives from the US Department of State and US Agency for International Development, but their attendance had dropped off in recent years.[41] One local civil society leader suggested that the members of the GRJT were not sufficiently close to the communities, but instead were speaking as individuals from their own personal perspectives.[42] He also expressed frustration that the informal nature of the group meant there was no accountability for its impact or performance, and that members were unwilling to take the initiative to further transitional justice activities independent of the UN or government. This view accorded with that of another local civil society leader who commented on the negative impact of competition between NGOs on their ability and willingness to cooperate through the GRJT as well as more generally in response to government policies and practices.

The GRJT ceased to meet and appeared to be no longer active in questioning the operations of the CVR after the selection of the commissioners in December 2014 and the onset of political violence in April 2015, although there were still postings on the e-group and its key members continued to operate, either in Burundi or in exile.[43] CENAP, THARS and other former members of the GRJT who were still in the country became active on the committee that was formed by the new civil society platform established in July 2016 to support the activities of the CVR.[44]

[39] On at least one occasion, the general secretary and spokesperson of AMEPCI, Aloys Batungwanayo, led a campaign objecting to the Burundian Government bulldozing mass gravesites to make way for a road.

[40] Interview with civil society member of the GRJT, Bujumbura, 2012.

[41] Interview with civil society member of the GRJT, Bujumbura, 2012.

[42] Interview with civil society member of the GRJT, Bujumbura, 2012.

[43] Interviews with civil society members of the GRJT in Bujumbura in August 2016.

[44] Interviews with civil society leaders in Bujumbura in August 2016; copy of letter dated July 22, 2016, on file with the author, from the president of the CVR, Jean Louis Nahimana, inviting civil society representatives to a workshop to set up the civil society platform. The initiative to involve civil society in the CVR was supported by the American Friends Service Committee comprising local staff based in Bujumbura.

The leaders of other GRJT member organisations, such as FORSC and APRODH, had gone into exile and were no longer operating in Burundi when the CVR was established in March 2016. This reflects a move from differences of opinion in the group to a significant division into two groups post-April 2015, and the alleged domination of the new civil society platform to support the CVR by the front NGOs created by the ruling party, PISC-Burundi and CAPES+ (FORSC 2016).[45]

Quaker Peace Network Burundi: Daring to Propose a Burundian Model of Transitional Justice

QPN Burundi comprises local Quaker-based CSOs working on trauma healing, reconciliation, peacebuilding and development. These include THARS, MiPAREC and Healing and Rebuilding Our Communities (HROC), which have all been involved in various ways in supporting transitional justice in Burundi, including through membership of the GRJT. THARS has been particularly active, with a programme of trauma healing and reconciliation workshops and initiatives designed to assist in preparing Burundians psychologically for the CVR (Lambourne and Niyonzima 2016). THARS also has plans for psychosocial accompaniment for the CVR hearings and has conducted research on the level of trauma in the population and attitudes of Burundians towards various aspects of transitional justice, including the CVR.[46]

In mid-2013, I facilitated a workshop about transitional justice initiated by THARS and QPN Burundi which was attended by 20 QPN civil society leaders.[47] The workshop enabled the participants to learn about how transitional justice is defined and implemented by international scholars and practitioners, and to explore their own ideas about the core concepts of transitional justice including truth, justice and reconciliation. As a result, QPN Burundi developed its own local model of transitional justice which it launched publicly a year later in June 2014 at a media conference attended by a significant representation of civil society leaders in Bujumbura, a representative from the BNUB TJU and a Quaker member of parliament.

The QPN Burundi Model of Transitional Justice proposed an alternative, culturally adapted version of the UN's five key pillars of transitional justice: accountability, truth daring, positive relations, leadership development and community empowerment (QPN Burundi 2014). Of note was the focus on accountability rather

[45] Interviews with civil society leaders in Bujumbura and Kigali, August 2016.

[46] THARS and GIZ ZFD, "Study of the Needs in Psychosocial Accompaniment for Victims during the Process of Transitional Justice and particularly during the phase of preparation and implementation of the Truth and Reconciliation Commission in Burundi", Phase 1, study done in the provinces of Ngozi, Kayanza, Gitega and Makamba, April 2012 (official English translation from the original report released in French).

[47] The 3-day workshop "Transitional Justice: Theory and Practice" was organised by QPN Burundi in conjunction with THARS and conducted by Dr. Wendy Lambourne, Centre for Peace and Conflict Studies, University of Sydney. It was held at the THARS Training Centre in Gitega, Burundi, on July 9–11, 2013.

than prosecutions, a broader concept which does not exclude the possibility of prosecutions in the longer term, but allows for other forms of accountability which might be less threatening to the ruling elite in the short term. The model suggested that accountability could comprise the "clarification of the actions by the presumed perpetrators themselves" and a focus on moral or symbolic reparations in recognition of the inability of perpetrators to provide appropriate monetary compensation. The QPN Burundi model defined accountability as "a commitment by the perpetrators, or presumed perpetrators … to recognize and to reveal to the victims and the community their involvement in the crimes committed in order to create a peaceful environment favourable for forgiveness and reconciliation".[48]

With regard to truth, the QPN Burundi model emphasised the need for Burundians to recognise that "the historical truth differs from one social group to another or from an individual to another". It encouraged the setting up of a framework and culture to support all Burundians to tell the truth and share their past experiences in order to facilitate justice, healing, forgiveness, reconciliation, reintegration, sustainable peace and political, social and economic development.

Unlike the UN model, the QPN Burundi model did not include reparations as a key pillar, in recognition of the extreme poverty which made it unlikely that meaningful reparations could be forthcoming. Instead, it included as a pillar the idea of "positive relations" through the "establishment of an environment that enables exchange where everyone feels considered and valued, brings something positive for national peacebuilding". In place of institutional reform, the QPN Burundi model suggested the need to focus on "leadership development", understood as "the encouragement and the guidance of a visionary who has the skills and confidence to mentor others in order to respond to the needs of the community". The values of a good leader were defined as including a readiness to serve, sense of responsibility, flexibility, accessibility, humility and accountability.

Finally, the QPN Burundi model replaced national consultations as a key pillar with "community empowerment", understood as "the capacity building of a community to be able to express itself, be responsible and defend and advocate for its interests". It advocates for community empowerment at the social level, including education and activities to support healing, dialogue, memorialisation and peacebuilding; at the economic level, including microloans, social solidarity, professional training and responsible management of the environment; and at the political level, including civic and citizenship education, holding leaders accountable, participation in decision-making and valuing the democratic rights of every Burundian.

The public launch of the QPN Burundi model created some controversy and much lively debate among civil society actors and representatives of the government and UN because of its apparent downplaying of the call for an end to impunity emphasised by the UN and other civil society members of the GRJT. Religious lead-

[48] It is this aspect of the model which has led to misleading perceptions that the Quaker NGOs must therefore be aligned politically with the ruling party, and, since April 2015, that their support of the CVR is driven by their Hutu ethnicity. Interviews conducted in Bujumbura in 2014 and 2016, and Kigali and Sydney in 2016.

ers who were calling for forgiveness and reconciliation had already been labelled by human rights and transitional justice actors as being aligned with the government and a culture of impunity.[49] As a result, the UN responded with scepticism about the motivations of any faith-based actors, including QPN Burundi, and assumed that calls for reconciliation must mean lack of accountability. Meetings of QPN civil society leaders with the UN TJU failed to make any impression on the UN's attitude to transitional justice priorities in Burundi, despite assurances that they were not trying to replace the UN model, but rather to propose a complementary model that could be more effective in the cultural, socio-economic and political context of Burundi.

Following the onset of the political crisis in April 2015, the QPN Burundi member organisations became more significant players in transitional justice, as FORSC and many of its members fled Burundi into exile. But QPN Burundi itself became less active. Plans for working groups implementing different aspects of the QPN Burundi model of transitional justice were not followed through, although individual organisations have implemented projects relating to its five key pillars and especially the fifth pillar on community empowerment. THARS has continued to run healing and dialogue workshops which incorporate opportunities for personal accountability, while MiPAREC has focused on its network of peace committees in local rural communities. HROC, meanwhile, initiated a programme of workshops in Bujumbura focusing on civic and citizenship education as well as healing and community rebuilding, and a new focus on leadership development. So, to some extent, the QPN Burundi model has been implemented as envisioned though programmes of local Quaker organisations, but at the time of writing, a more coordinated implementation had not eventuated.

Conclusion

The UN Secretary-General declared in his 2004 report on the *Rule of Law and Transitional Justice in Conflict and Post-conflict Societies* that "the most successful transitional justice experiences owe a large part of their success to the quantity and quality of public and victim consultation carried out" (Annan 2004, para. 16). Scholars and practitioners before and since have expressed concern about the exclusion of civil society views and the lack of focus on victims in the top-down nationally and internationally driven transitional justice industry (Crocker 2000; Lundy and McGovern 2008; Lambourne 2012). As discussed above, despite the UN's adoption of national consultations as the fifth pillar of transitional justice, the implementation of this measure by the Government of Burundi was limited both in its execution and its follow-up in terms of the range of options provided for public comment and the extent to which the opinions gathered were ignored rather than

[49] By contrast, QPN Burundi and Quaker NGO leaders were generally perceived as politically neutral and have worked either independently or cooperatively under the banner of the GRJT.

helping to shape the approach taken to transitional justice, including the construction of the CVR.

It has been a significant challenge for civil society in Burundi to have a meaningful say in the proposed CVR, despite the national consultations and UN presence with its expanded support for civil society, and the formation and efforts of the GRJT. With the Burundian Government strongly asserting control over the design and implementation of the CVR, civil society has remained actively engaged, even since the onset of political violence in April 2015, including those in exile who are continuing to campaign in relation to the CVR. At the time of writing this chapter, a new civil society platform was being set up to engage civil society in supporting the CVR's activities and the implementation of its mandate. It was too soon to assess the impact of the initiative, but a large number of NGOs participated in the first workshop, and early indications were that a core group of civil society leaders who had participated in the GRJT, including from CENAP and THARS, were taking on leadership roles.[50] At the same time, however, allegations that the new platform is dominated by *nyakuri* do not bode well for its ability to play a critical role in the effective functioning of the CVR to ascertain the full truth of the past violence and human rights abuses (FORSC 2016).

Local civil society actors have questioned their lack of influence over the transitional justice process, despite evidence that in other areas civil society had been successful in influencing government policy in the past, especially when it engaged in media campaigns.[51] Vandeginste maintains that "societal pressure from below has not been very significant", at least in terms of its impact on government decision-making in relation to transitional justice, despite the creation of the GRJT (Vandeginste 2009: 8).[52] In addition to the national consultations, several international and local civil society initiatives have reported on research revealing further insights into the needs, expectations and priorities of victims and others in the Burundian population (Boloquy et al. 2013; Taylor 2013a). As with the national consultations, the government appears to have ignored these efforts by civil society individually and through the GRJT to participate in the design and implementation of transitional justice processes in Burundi—except for those religious organisations[53] which appeared to be aligned with the government position on amnesties and reconciliation.

The examples discussed in this chapter provide evidence of a proactive and inventive local civil society exhibiting cooperation, activism and resistance in relation to transitional justice in Burundi, especially through the creation of the GRJT and the work of QPN Burundi member organisations. At the same time, they reveal contestation and division between different groups of NGOs which has been more

[50] Interviews with civil society leaders from CENAP and THARS, Bujumbura, August 2016.

[51] Interview with representative of local civil society media organisation, Bujumbura, July 2013.

[52] According to Pacifique Manirakiza (2016: 56–57), civil society in Burundi had a minimal impact on transitional justice policies because it was not sufficiently proactive and strategic in its mobilisation.

[53] Mostly new evangelical Protestant churches. The Roman Catholic Church has openly expressed its opposition to the President's third term.

or less evident at different stages of the civil war and its aftermath. One group of NGOs was more directly involved in the defence of human rights, media freedom and fight against corruption, and therefore more closely identified with opposition politics and civil society resistance. This group directly challenged the government by advocating for prosecutions as part of transitional justice. Since the political crisis and violent crackdown against those seen as opposed to the ruling party began in April 2015, many of the civil society leaders in this group were threatened and fled the country into exile and were thus no longer in a position to be directly involved in the transitional justice process and the CVR in particular.

By contrast, another group of CSOs has been proactive in supporting peacebuilding and development through self-help groups, trauma healing and reconciliation in local communities, as well as sensitisation of the population in preparation for the CVR. While these latter activities may not directly challenge the government on issues of policy and practice, they arguably create sites of resistance to official transitional justice mechanisms and priorities by focusing on alternative, informal approaches to support justice and reconciliation. This was especially the case with the potential for implementation of the QPN Burundi model of transitional justice, but since the onset of the political crisis these NGOs, although they remained working in Burundi, focused on individual programmes rather than working in a coordinated way to implement the model. NGOs in this group did, however, become actively involved in the new civil society platform set up to support the CVR. The concern here is that more of these NGOs, which were perceived as either neutral or supportive of the ruling party, may appear to be co-opted by the government and lose their sense of independence and ability to resist.

The most significant sites of coordinated civil society activism and resistance in Burundi have stemmed from coalescence in crisis, both during the civil war and more recently in supporting the April 2015 nonviolent protests against the president's third term, which were nevertheless violently crushed by the president's forces. The conflict evolved, however, such that differences became divisions across both political party and, increasingly, ethnic lines, as the two groups of NGOs involved in the GRJT found themselves separated geographically as well as ideologically. As in its efforts to control the transitional justice process, the UN, meanwhile, has remained largely impotent in the wings, calling for dialogue and peaceful negotiations, and unable or unwilling to intervene and challenge the sovereign power of the Burundian Government nor support civil society resistance. The UN is, however, through the International Criminal Court and the Human Rights Council, attempting to put some pressure on the ruling party through investigations of alleged human rights violations committed in Burundi since April 2015. The climate has therefore not been conducive to the effective operation of the CVR, and remains so at the time of writing, with continuing intimidation of the political opposition, no freedom of speech, political control of information, limited resources and a local civil society that has become divided, if not silenced (Impunity Watch 2016).[54]

[54] http://www.rfi.fr/emission/20160511-filip-reyntjens-burundi-universite-anvers-genocide-1972-ethnicite (Accessed 19 June 2016); interviews conducted in Bujumubra and rural areas of Burundi in June and December 2014, April 2015 and August 2016.

References

American Friends Service Committee. (2011). *Transitional justice mechanisms: Lessons learned from truth and reconciliation commissions*. Bujumbura: AFSC Burundi.

Annan, K. (2004). *Report of the Secretary-General on the Rule of Law and Transitional Justice in Conflict and Post-conflict Societies*. UN Doc. S/2004/616.

Boloquy, M., Mawad, S., & Taylor, D. (2013). Victim perspectives on the independence of the TRC. *Victimes á la UNE, 2*, Impunity Watch, February 2013.

Crocker, D. (2000). Truth commissions, transitional justice, and civil society. In R. I. Rotberg & D. Thompson (Eds.), *Truth v. justice: The morality of truth commissions* (pp. 109–114). Princeton, NJ: Princeton University Press.

FONAREC/JT. (2012). *Le guide du relais communautaire en justice de dransition*. Bujumbura, United Nations, September 2012. Translated from the French and Kirundi.

FORSC. (2016). *Au-delà d'une mission, la CVR a une responsabilité historique et doit s'abstenir d'initier la recherche de la vérité à sens unique*.

Government of Burundi & United Nations. (2010, April 20). *Rapport des Consultations Nationales sur la mise en place des Mécanismes de Justice de Transition au Burundi*.

Groupe de Réflexion sur la Justice Transitionnelle. (2011). *Observations du GRJT sur le Rapport du Comité Technique Chargé de la Préparation de la Mise en Place des Mécanismes de Justice Transitionnelle au Burundi*. Retrieved December 7, 2011, from http://www.impunitywatch.org/docs/GRJT_Rapport_Dec2011-Burundi.pdf

Groupe de Réflexion sur la Justice Transitionnelle. (2014). *Le parlement el gouvernement Burundais à la croisée des chemins*.

Human Rights Watch. (2008). *Burundi: Muyinga massacre convictions a victory*.

Human Rights Watch. (2012). *Burundi: Verdict in activist's killing fails to deliver justice*. .

Impunity Watch. (2013, January). Burundi's Draft Law on the Proposed TRC. Policy Brief.

Impunity Watch. (2014). Sincerity of Burundi's commitment to TJ under scrutiny as TRC commissioners sworn in; four-year TRC mandate officially begins. Policy Brief.

Impunity Watch. (2016). Burundi's TRC officially launched: But will victims participate? Policy Brief.

International Center for Transitional Justice. (2011). *The transitional justice process in Burundi*. In French.

International Media Support. (2015). *Radio silence: Burundi's media during the 2015 election crisis*.

Lambourne, W. (2012). Outreach, inreach and civil society participation in transitional justice. In N. Palmer, P. Clark, & D. Granville (Eds.), *Critical perspectives in transitional justice* (pp. 235–261). Antwerp: Intersentia.

Lambourne, W. (2014). What are the pillars of transitional justice? The United Nations and the justice cascade in Burundi. *Macquarie Law Journal, 13*, 41–60.

Lambourne, W., & Niyonzima, D. (2016). Breaking cycles of trauma and violence: Psychosocial approaches to healing and reconciliation in Burundi. In P. Gobodo-Madikizela (Ed.), *Breaking intergenerational cycles of repetition: A global dialogue on historical trauma and memory* (pp. 291–307). Opladen: Barbara Budrich.

Layton, R. (2006). *Order and anarchy: Civil society, social disorder and war*. Cambridge: Cambridge University Press.

Lemarchand, R. (1996). *Burundi: Ethnic conflict and genocide*. Cambridge: Woodrow Wilson Center Press and Cambridge University Press.

Lundy, P., & McGovern, M. (2008). The role of community in participatory transitional justice. In K. McEvoy & L. McGregor (Eds.), *Transitional justice from below* (pp. 99–120). Oxford: Hart Publishing.

Manirakiza, P. (2016). The politics of transitional justice in Burundi. In T. Murithi (Ed.), *The politics of transitional justice in the Great Lakes region of Africa* (pp. 25–62). Johannesburg: Jacana Media.

Omara, A. & Ackson, T. (2010). *Civil society and good governance in Burundi: Promoting inclusiveness and people participation in the East African Community*. A report of the fact-finding mission to Burundi. Kampala: Fountain Publishers.

Quaker Peace Network Burundi. (2014). *QPN Burundi transitional justice model.*

Taylor, D. (2013a). Truth under the avocado trees: Local needs and Burundi's TRC: Whither the truth? *Journal of Eastern African Studies, 7*(3), 450–470.

Taylor, D. (2013b). We have no influence: International discourse and the instrumentalisation of transitional justice in burundi. *Stability: International Journal of Security and Development, 2*(3), 1–10.

United Nations. Department of Political Affairs. (2010). *Guidance note of the secretary-general: United Nations approach to transitional justice.* DPA/UNSG/2010-00904.

United Nations Security Council. (2005, June). Security Council Resolution 1606, UN SCOR, 5207th Meeting. UN Doc. S/RES/1606.

Uvin, P. (2009). *Life after violence: A people's story of Burundi.* London: Zed Books.

Vandeginste, S. (2009). Transitional justice for Burundi: A long and winding road. In K. Ambos, J. Large, & M. Wierda (Eds.), *Building a future on peace and justice* (pp. 393–422). New York: Springer.

Vandeginste, S. (2012). Burundi's Truth and Reconciliation Commission: How to shed light on the past while standing in the dark shadow of politics? *International Journal of Transitional Justice, 6*(2), 355–365.

Watt, N. (2016). *Burundi: Biography of a small African country* (2nd ed.). London: Hurst & Co.

Chapter 7
Madly Off in All Directions: Civil Society and the Use of Customary Justice as Transitional Justice in Uganda

Joanna R. Quinn

Introduction

Transitional justice has typically relied on a handful of mechanisms, including trials, truth commissions and reparation programmes, in seeking justice after conflict. In many societies, however, these mechanisms have less salience and value than do customary practices of justice (Quinn 2009b: 47–49; Quinn 2015a: 242; Allen 2006: 145; Waldorf 2006: 1; Opiyo interview 2012). In Uganda, communities in the greater west, south and central regions have simply not engaged with the typical transitional justice mechanisms (Quinn 2010; Quinn 2015b: 225). Civil society in Uganda, largely in the form of nongovernmental organisations (NGOs), but also religious organisations like the Acholi Religious Leaders Peace Initiative (ARLPI) at the height of the conflict in northern Uganda, for example, has taken on at least some of the burden of helping communities in dealing with a complicated and still-difficult past. As is discussed below, the wide range of transitional justice mechanisms available to Ugandans has, for a variety of reasons, been out of reach. Some Ugandans wanted access to retributive, court-based justice, which is now available only for the highest ranking perpetrators in the form of the International Criminal Division of the High Court. Others wanted a truth-seeking process, which has been denied. Some put stock in the amnesty that was made available. And others attempted to avail themselves of reparations. But all of this has been ad hoc. No systematic transitional justice approach has been implemented. The national Transitional Justice Policy, which had been talked about for several years with civil society, remained un-implemented at the time of writing, as discussed below. Instead, civil

Research for this project was carried out with assistance from the Social Sciences and Humanities Research Council, with research assistance from Tamara Hinan and Tammy Lambert.

J.R. Quinn (✉)
University of Western Ontario, London, ON, Canada
e-mail: jquinn2@uwo.ca

J. Brankovic, H. van der Merwe (eds.), *Advocating Transitional Justice in Africa*, Springer Series in Transitional Justice,
https://doi.org/10.1007/978-3-319-70417-3_7

society at the community level turned to customary justice, a community-based system of practices that is well known to the people who use it. In Uganda, customary justice has taken the place of "foreign" practices like trials and truth commissions in pursuing similar objectives as mechanisms more often used elsewhere.

At the height of the conflict in northern Uganda, the use of customary justice[1] was very much on the agenda, both for the government and for civil society.[2] Numerous efforts were underway to promote its codification, integrate its operations into transitional justice systems, and develop broader recognition for its contribution. Yet today, in large part due to a series of directives from the president's office, the attention of Ugandan civil society has shifted to a series of other activities, leaving the debate and the preparations that had been generated in a kind of limbo. The people who were once at the forefront of the customary justice campaign—that is, those who were the leaders in *transitional* justice efforts in the country—have, in many cases, been reassigned or have moved on of their own accord to other work. Shifts in priorities and modes of engagement by both the international donor community and the Government of Uganda (GOU) have led to civil society diverting their attention to other goals.

This chapter considers the role and activities of NGOs in Uganda that are, and were formerly, working within the domestic framework, and working to satisfy the demands of the government so that they will be permitted to carry out their work, or risk being shut down. It examines their work against the backdrop of international precedent, which suggests how and when transitional justice efforts should be mounted, and tends to predict modes of success. It also considers just how transitional justice demands in Uganda have been met through the use of customary practices of justice and acknowledgement, in the absence of a coherent governmental transitional justice strategy.

Although other civil society actors, including community-based organisations (CBOs), have worked in this sector, this chapter focuses primarily on NGOs and international nongovernmental organisations (INGOs), since their work is (a) at the national level, and (b) the GOU has put in place new controls to severely restrict and limit NGO activities. The chapter explores the changing circumstances in which transitional justice is being contemplated, including a shift in the focus of civil society away from northern Uganda, and a change in the personnel who oversee such projects at those civil society organisations. It further considers the breakdown in communication between these groups and the international donor community, and the role of donor influence on these agendas, which continue to be manipulated by the Ugandan Government.

As part of a larger, ongoing study, I have been engaged since 2004 in an examination and analysis of the use of customary practices of justice and acknowledgement

[1] I use the term "customary justice", recognizing that the practices in use have changed over time. The commonly used term in Uganda is "traditional justice".

[2] These mechanisms are used across Uganda, but the northern Uganda conflict opened up a space to be able to talk about their use. The agreements signed at Juba, between the Lord's Resistance Army and the Government of Uganda, somewhat codified them (Quinn 2009a).

in Uganda. I am specifically interested in the role that these processes play in a society's acknowledgement of past crimes and abuses, as part of a larger programme of transitional justice and social rebuilding. I am further concerned with how they are able to succeed where other "western" approaches, like the truth commission, have failed (Quinn 2010). In total, I conducted 29 interviews in May and June 2012 with representatives of the NGO and INGO community in Uganda. Some of the data that supports the arguments made in this chapter is further corroborated by interviews I conducted with members of other stakeholder groups, including conflict-affected women, government officials and religious leaders, between 2004 and 2015 as part of that broader study, and a couple of interviews from 2016.

Together, these data provide a comprehensive picture of the situation surrounding the use of customary justice and how it has changed over time. I was interested to see whether and how the organisations see customary justice as having any utility in the overall justice process, following the conflicts that have been experienced in Uganda since independence. I specifically targeted those groups that had been working on ideas of "peace and justice" or "reconciliation", as transitional justice is often called there. And in many cases, I purposely went back to talk to NGO and INGO staffers whom I had interviewed in previous rounds of research. What I found was that, although the organisations themselves remained, two major changes were apparent. First, many of the people I knew were no longer in those roles, either because they had begun working on other issues within the same organisation or because they had moved on to different organisations. Second, the organisations themselves were no longer focused on the possibility of incorporating customary justice into a broader system of justice, and customary justice work had been all but abandoned.

The picture that emerges, then, conveys a sense of what has been happening in the discussion and implementation of transitional justice broadly and customary justice specifically in Uganda. The chapter clearly articulates a particular perspective from among the members of civil society with whom I spoke, although I recognise that these views might not be universal. But the complex history of conflict in Uganda must be taken into account in order to understand the contours and nuances of the debate I outline in the chapter.

Background

Since the time of independence in 1962, Uganda has been wracked by conflict. Under both Idi Amin and Milton Obote, many thousands of Ugandans were wounded and killed. It is estimated that between 300,000 (Briggs 1998: 23) and 500,000 (Museveni 1997: 41) Ugandans were killed during the time of Idi Amin, from 1971 to 1979, largely in central Uganda. Under the rule of Obote, between 1980 and 1985, approximately 300,000 (*Uganda* 1998: 53; Ofcansky 1996: 55) to 500,000 (Nadduli interview 2004) were killed, again mostly in central Uganda and in Luweero District in particular.

The current president, Yoweri Museveni, and the National Resistance Army (now National Resistance Movement, or NRM) seized power by means of military force in 1986. As with his predecessors, Museveni met with considerable opposition from many of the 56 different ethnocultural groups throughout the country. Since coming to power, Museveni has faced more than 27 armed insurgencies,[3] including the most famous in the modern era: the Lord's Resistance Army (LRA) under the leadership of the now-infamous Joseph Kony. The LRA waged a conflict against the GOU in northern Uganda from roughly 1986 to 2008, displacing more than 1.8 million people, abducting children for use as child soldiers and carrying out vicious campaigns of brutality throughout much of the region.

These multiple conflicts have devastated the country. Especially in the north, although also in Luweero Triangle and elsewhere, people continue to suffer the effects of conflict. The physical scars are easy to see: women in Luweero Triangle have been ostracised from their communities because of gynaecological fistulae; former abductees in northern Uganda have only scar tissue where once there were noses and lips; and hospitals and schools are in a state of disrepair. Yet the emotional and social costs, though harder to spot at first glance, remain, too. These "scars" are more difficult to fix.

The State of Ugandan Transitional Justice

Official Mechanisms

An erratic mix of transitional justice instruments has been utilised in Uganda to deal with the millions of violations committed there (Quinn 2009b). In 1971, to appease the international community, Idi Amin appointed a truth commission to deal with disappearances he, himself, had ordered (Carver 1990). In 1986, Museveni appointed another truth commission to consider the abuses committed between 1962 and 1986 (Quinn 2010). Subsequently, the GOU promulgated an Amnesty Act, under which 22,107 ex-combatants received amnesty by July 2008 (Draku interview 2008).[4]

The International Criminal Court (ICC) began an investigation into the crimes perpetrated by Kony and other senior LRA members in 2004 (Quinn 2008). The Ugandan Government established a War Crimes Division, now the International

[3] These include rebellions by the Action Restore Peace, Allied Democratic Forces, Apac, Citizen Army for Multiparty Politics, Force Obote Back, Former Uganda National Army, Holy Spirit Movement, the Lord's Army, Lord's Resistance Army, National Federal Army, National Union for the Liberation of Uganda, Ninth October Movement, People's Redemption Army, Uganda Christian Democratic Army, Uganda Federal Democratic Front, Uganda Freedom Movement, Ugandan National Democratic Army, Uganda National Federal Army, Ugandan National Liberation Front, Ugandan National Rescue Fronts I and II, Ugandan People's Army, Ugandan People's Democratic Army, Uganda Salvation Army and the West Nile Bank Front (Hovil and Lomo 2004: 4; 2005: 6).

[4] This is the latest publicly available data at the time of writing.

Criminal Division, of the High Court to thwart further ICC action, despite the fact that Museveni himself referred the situation in northern Uganda to the ICC's Office of the Prosecutor, ostensibly in exchange for his own immunity, since the Ugandan Government, through the military, reportedly also carried out crimes against humanity and war crimes during the conflict in northern Uganda.[5] Reparations have largely not been paid, despite a government resolution passed in 2014 and another draft policy prepared by the Northern Uganda Social Action Fund (NUSAF). The GOU claims that national development plans like NUSAF and the Peace Recovery and Development Plan (PRDP) II are sufficient, despite their lack of focus on individual harms.[6] Aside from this, the government has empowered national courts and customary courts to hear evidence in both human rights cases and reparations claims.

Uganda is widely known for using a range of international and domestic transitional justice mechanisms, despite the lack of any kind of transition. Yet most of these mechanisms have lain dormant after being implemented, or have been unwilling or unable to provide any form of "justice" to the victims and survivors of the many conflicts that have taken place throughout the country. These processes have all been initiated by the government, which remains in control of the various transitional justice processes, and not by civil society.

Customary Justice

Across the country, Ugandans understand customary justice to be a useful means of resolving conflicts. Even High Court justices, if they have land disputes to resolve, resort to customary justice practices (Tabaro interview 2008). Such practices were of particular utility to the people of northern Uganda during the LRA conflict, when state institutions were unavailable to them. There has been considerable discussion about whether and how these practices could be codified and used more broadly as a means of getting past the atrocities committed in the LRA conflict. As I have written elsewhere, the practices have suffered from a number of changes in Ugandan society, including that the institutions that implement them have clearly changed over time and the utility of traditional practices has come into question; the presence and scope of protracted civil conflict have changed the way people are able to deal with conflict; the stratification of Uganda's many different ethnocultural groups has shaped where and how these mechanisms are used; and a community's

[5] Museveni officially referred the situation to the ICC in December 2003. It has been commonly assumed that Museveni approached the Court first. Information has surfaced that the chief prosecutor actually approached Museveni to ask him to refer the situation. There is a great deal of debate about what this discrepancy means (Waddell and Clark 2008: 43).

[6] A total of 14,000 individual claimants, through the Acholi War Debt Claimants Association, won a court-ordered settlement for their 2006 case, although the funds have been slow to come and there were allegations of fraud and fund mismanagement at the time of writing. A number of similar advocacy groups have sprung up among victims to push for compensation from the GOU.

homogeneity often governs whether or not, and whose, "traditions" are used in a given community (Quinn 2015b).

At the time of independence in 1962, customary practices were made illegal and the outgoing British decided upon a harmonised legal system modelled on the British system (British Colonial Office 1961). The many kingdoms and traditional cultural institutions that existed across the country were banned by President Obote in 1967. Yet the institutions and practices persisted (Briggs 1998: 23). Traditional cultural institutions are today recognised under Article 246 of the 1995 Constitution (Republic of Uganda 1995). Customary practices are now legally provided for under legislation, including Article 129 of the Constitution, which provides for the operation of Local Council Courts[7] at the sub-county, parish and village levels (Uganda: Constitution, Government & Legislation), and the Children Statute of 1996, which grants these courts the authority to mandate any number of remedies, such as reconciliation, compensation, restitution and apology (Republic of Uganda 1996).

The GOU included these practices in the 2008 Agreement on Accountability and Reconciliation and the subsequent Annexure, which emerged out of the Juba Peace Talks (Quinn 2008; Gashirabake interview 2008; Ogoola interview 2008).[8] Although these mechanisms fit broadly within very different approaches to justice, whether retributive or restorative, and fulfil different roles within their respective societies, from cleansing and welcoming estranged persons back home to prosecution and punishment, they draw upon commonly observed customary practices and ideas in the administration of justice in modern times.

These institutions are still widely used throughout the country by many of the 56 ethnocultural groups (Quinn 2009a). The Karamojong use the *akiriket* councils of elders to adjudicate disputes according to custom (Novelli 1999: 169–172, 333–340) through cultural teaching and ritual cleansing ceremonies (Lokeris interview 2004). The Acholi continue to use a complex system of ceremonies in adjudicating everything from petty theft to murder (Harlacher et al. 2006). Throughout the conflict between the LRA and GOU and after, at least two ceremonies were adapted to welcome child soldiers home after they were decommissioned: *mato oput* ("drinking the bitter herb") and *nyono tong gweno* (a welcoming ceremony in which an egg is stepped on over an *opobo* twig) (Finnström 2003: 297–299). These ceremonies are similar to those used by the Langi, called *kayo cuk*, the Iteso, called *ailuc*, and the Madi, called *tonu ci koka* (GOU and LRA 2008: Art.21.1). In the northwest of the country, the Lugbara use a system of elder mediation in family, clan and interclan conflict (Ndrua 1988: 42–56). In 1985, an intertribal reconciliation ceremony, *gomo tong* ("bending the spear"), was held to signify that "from that time there

[7] The LC Courts were formerly known as Resistance Council Courts and "were first introduced in Luweero in 1983 during the struggle for liberation. In 1987 they were legally recognized throughout the country" (Waliggo 2003: 7).

[8] Although these agreements were signed, at the time of writing the final agreement had not been signed for more than 8 years, and both parties had walked away from the talks. When the Working Group's Chairman, Justice Ogoola, retired, much of the "attention fizzled out in the donor community for the work" (Otobi interview 2012).

would be no war or fighting between Acholi and Madi, Kakwa, Lugbara or Alur of West Nile" (Finnström 2003: 299). A similar ceremony, *amelokwit*, took place between the Iteso and the Karamojong in 2004 (Iteso focus group 2006).

In some areas, these practices are no longer used regularly. Customary practices are, in fact, used far less widely in the "greater south" and among Ugandans of Bantu origin (Quinn 2015b). From time to time, however, the Baganda use the customary *kitewuliza*, a juridical process with a strong element of reconciliation, to bring about justice (Waliggo 2005: 1). Among the Bafumbira, land disputes, in particular, are settled through customary practices, with Local Council officials adjudicating (Tabaro interview 2008). The Annexure to the Agreement on Accountability and Reconciliation also lists mechanisms used by the Ankole, called *okurakaba* (GOU and LRA 2008: Art.21.1), although I have uncovered only weak anecdotal evidence of their continued use (Katatumba interview 2008).

People from nearly every ethnocultural group in Uganda have reported to me that "everyone respects these traditions" (Confidential interview 2004) and that reconciliation continues to be an "essential and final part of [the] peaceful settlement of conflict" (Waliggo 2005: 9). At the same time, many young, educated Ugandans who live in the city told me that they have never participated in such ceremonies (Northern Uganda focus group 2006). Still, a common respect for these symbols, ceremonies, institutions and their meanings remains throughout Uganda, even in those areas where such practices are no longer carried out. This has been controversial, and opinions have changed throughout the conflict. Adam Branch (2014), for example, reported that these mechanisms have been distorted and in practice amount to what he calls "ethnojustice".

Civil Society Efforts

The GOU has been reluctant to support formal transitional justice mechanisms in any real way. Although it has initiated a number of processes and institutions, it has largely failed to support them, and has, in fact, backed away from many of them after putting them in place, as it did with the ICC (Quinn 2009b). It is likely that the GOU fears that senior officials will be implicated through legitimate transitional justice processes, and for this reason has simply opted not to act on this front. A draft Transitional Justice Policy that was first promised in 2008 and then made public in 2013 was a specious attempt by the GOU to mollify the ICC, international donors and national NGOs, which worked hard to draft the document for policymakers. NGOs have noted that

> at official levels, steps to implement transitional justice have become highly bureaucratic; opportunities for civil society participation in Transitional Justice Working Group[9] meetings

[9] The Transitional Justice Working Group, a consortium of government, civil society actors and international donors.

and initiatives have greatly diminished, and the space for engagement has become more constricted. (Otim and Kihika 2015: 4)

Notwithstanding earlier promises to the contrary, civil society has been excluded, for the most part, from involvement in and engagement with the transitional justice policy. Civil society actors, including the INGOs International Center for Transitional Justice and *Avocats Sans Frontières* and the Uganda-based African Youth Initiative Network, have complained that "civil society representatives were only invited at the end of the process to attend the validation meeting and to submit comments on the third draft of the transitional justice policy" (Otim and Kihika 2015: fn. 29; ASF 2013: 18).

As a result, CBOs and NGOs tended to focus on the development of customary justice as a means of settling the accounts of the conflict. To be sure, during the conflicts and subsequent occupations by victorious rebel groups, including Museveni's NRM, when there was no rule of law and little protection or justice to be had through any formal mechanisms, the population relied on customary justice to deal with their problems. As noted above, while this reliance has largely disappeared in the south of Uganda, it has continued on a wide scale throughout the greater north, where the LRA conflict was widespread. People have relayed to me how they trust and rely on these practices, which makes customary justice one of the only viable transitional justice responses in modern Uganda. As such, customary practices of justice are a useful lens through which to consider civil society's role in the promotion and implementation of transitional justice in that country.

Civil society in Uganda, as elsewhere in Africa, has many different layers and a rich constellation of actors taking part at each level. The sector is led mainly by national, Uganda-based NGOs and INGOs, many of whom are bolstered by international donors that have pushed for transitional justice initiatives. Faith-based organisations, including the dominant faith groups (the Roman Catholic Church and the Church of Uganda), as well as interfaith groups like the Inter-Religious Council and smaller regional organisations like ARLPI, have played what might be called a supporting role. The same can be said of CBOs, which do not play a role on the national stage but which work with NGOs and INGOs and are often the ones to implement various initiatives. The transitional justice strategy, ad hoc as it is to date, has reluctantly been agreed to by the GOU, which has tended to acquiesce to the demands of civil society and the donor community in implementing any transitional justice initiatives, and then walked away from them almost completely, thereby ensuring that they will not work.

The head of the National NGO Board, a state regulatory agency, defined civil society groups as follows:

A community-based organization (CBO) is supposed to be a very small, small organization doing something for the welfare of the community—even a foreigner cannot be involved; CBOs should operate only at the sub-county level. A non-governmental organization is anything that operates beyond the sub-county level, from the county level upwards. This helps foreigners know their line of working. Civil society and NGOs are always looked as the same, yet civil society is much broader; a country is split into the government sector and private sector, and anything else is civil society—anyone else with a common interest is

> civil society. Civil society is much broader. Some people refer to 'civil society' and they mean 'NGO'. (Okello interview 2015)

NGOs, CBOs, voluntary development organisations, faith-based organisations and trade unions are represented at the national level by the Uganda National Nongovernmental (NGO) Forum, which also offers affiliate membership to such groups "registered in or outside the countries [sic]" (Uganda National NGO Forum 2003). Until 2016, all of these groups were governed by the Non-Governmental Organisations Registration Act, Cap. 113. That Act was repealed and replaced with a new Non-Governmental Organisations Act, which decrees that NGOs must "not engage in any act which is prejudicial to the security and laws of Uganda" (Republic of Uganda 2016: Art. 44(d)). It is important to note that different standards apply, under the Act, to national NGOs than to foreign NGOs, as discussed below. The head of the NGO Board rationalised this, saying "this helps foreigners know their line of working" (Okello interview 2015).

The GOU monitors and constrains all NGO activities. The acting secretary of the NGO Board explained that this tight regulation is necessary for three reasons:

> First, under the security component: NGOs, if not clearly regulated, can be used as agents for terrorists.[10] You need to know if they are giving them money. Second, under the public interest component: Government agencies are given the responsibility for looking after the best interests of the public. If someone says they will do something, is it being done on the ground, or is it only a 'briefcase NGO'? Third, under accountability: The government helps NGOs become accountable to the public. (Okello interview 2015)

As such, the GOU has extraordinary regulatory power over NGOs: "The Minister may, subject to this Act, give to the [National NGO Board] written directions of a general or specific nature relating to its functions to which it shall be bound to comply" (Republic of Uganda 2006: Art. 2(12)). NGOs are often ordered to close if they do not comply. Since these organisations must renew their registration with the GOU annually, most are very concerned about adhering to the GOU's stated priorities. NGOs talk openly about their concerns regarding censure from the NGO Board. One interviewee noted, "The Government requires NGOs to register each year and checks carefully what they are working on. He has been threatening churches and talks to them about things that don't mean anything so they won't insist on important things" (Confidential interview 2012a). In one example, the NGO Board banned 38 Ugandan NGOs in mid-2012 when they were accused of "undermining the national culture by promoting homosexuality" (Smith 2012). In another example, an international donor consultant recounted a particular research project she had been involved with, working with both an NGO and an INGO, wherein the groups "got into trouble with Government for looking into and supporting opposition political parties" (Confidential interview 2012b).

In this way, the GOU attempts to keep a tight grip on NGO activities, even as it outwardly claims that "it is essential for the concept of civil society that their actions are not planned or dictated by the Government" (Republic of Uganda 2010: 4).

[10] The GOU uses the language around "terrorism" as a justification to crack down on NGOs.

In reality, "aid priorities in this country are always political decisions", said one international donor employee, "Political analysis is missing! The Government wants to demonstrate to the world that they are in charge" (Confidential interview 2013).

Changing Circumstances

Where, before, clusters of NGOs and INGOs, donors and donor agencies were actively pushing for a policy of reconciliation and the clear use of customary justice, which was agreed to by the GOU (Republic of Uganda 2007: Art. 3.1.; Republic of Uganda and LRA 2008: Arts. 19–22), by 2012 NGOs were very clear that the use of customary practices and a more general policy of "reconciliation [had] fallen out of fashion" (Nalwoga interview 2012). This has continued.

For example, the Peace, Recovery and Development Plan for Northern Uganda (2007–2010) at least nodded to the need for customary justice and acknowledgement, in specifying the need to "ensure that formal and non-formal accountability and justice mechanisms are in place" (Republic of Uganda 2007: 97). A debate about and preparations for the potential expanded use, broader recognition and codification of customary practices was underway in earnest. The then-current Peace, Recovery and Development Plan for Northern Uganda, Phase 2 (2012–2015) (PRDP II), in contrast, conflated customary and formal mechanisms with dispute resolution and focused on only semi-related questions, including sexual and gender-based violence (Republic of Uganda 2011: 35). The successor to the World Bank-mandated Poverty Eradication Action Plan, which at least talked about the need for social rebuilding and justice in northern Uganda (Ministry of Finance 2004a), was the National Development Plan (Republic of Uganda 2010: 4), which does not mention the conflict in northern Uganda explicitly, nor lay out any kind of reconciliation or justice strategy.[11]

Failure to Implement Official Mechanisms

It is commonly understood throughout the country that questions of justice in Uganda have shifted to "holding the Government and the LRA to account—but only the LRA, really", as one NGO national coordinator told me (Omona interview 2012). This accountability centres on the International Criminal Division of the High Court. The GOU's priorities do not really extend beyond that kind of formal

[11] The National Development Plan does mention the tumultuous period from 1971 to 1979, when Uganda was governed by Idi Amin, although it does not list the insurgencies faced by Museveni since he came to power in 1986, nor the period from 1980 to 1985 when Obote returned to power. It further lists stability and peace as one of its 6 "vision" points without any further elaboration.

justice, presumably because it is concerned with satisfying the requirements of the ICC's Pre-Trial Chamber in relation to the charges against Kony and other top LRA commanders.

The one exception is a small project piloted by the Justice Law and Order Sector (JLOS) in 2012, under the Ministry of Justice, through the Uganda Law Reform Commission.[12] "The Uganda Law Reform Commission was given responsibility to study customary mechanisms, to see whether customary justice can be used, what mechanisms are in place, structures on the ground, and so on" (Adongo interview 2012). Its report was delayed by many months and was not publicly available at the time of writing. JLOS staffers told me, however, that "justice is a process and it's taking its time. The focus has been on formal justice because that was the first step. So now, the next step is to look at informal justice" (Zarifis interview 2012). None of this had been effectively conveyed to any of the groups that used to work on customary justice.

Many of the NGOs and INGOs that formerly carried out research and programming in the area of customary justice are no longer working on this question, although a handful, like the Refugee Law Project, continue the work (Tumuwesigye interview 2012). One NGO representative noted, "For a Ugandan to come out that I am doing research on a cultural aspect, it is now not the right thing to do" (Otobi interview 2012). Yet the people to whom I spoke, all of whom were familiar with the intricacies of the customary justice question, saw inherent value in the customary practices, and often mused that they wished the practices were back on the table. One interviewee said, "Maybe if we had taken the time to deal with issues of reconciliation using the traditional ways, issues of land and domestic violence wouldn't be so big" (Apunyo interview 2012). Another noted, "It's not too late for traditional mechanisms, but this needs to be part of the whole justice framework" (Omona interview 2012). This was substantiated over and over again by my interviewees, who told me that "even formal justice institutions in Uganda are acknowledging that formal justice does not entirely address justice needs" (Ejoyi interview 2012).

Many feel that customary justice has both proper authority and legitimacy: "At a local level, traditional justice has more legitimacy. People relate to it much more strongly" (Opiyo interview 2012). As one international consultant reported to me, "These mechanisms are being used" (Okille interview 2012). As for how frequently, an NGO staffer told me that "people still rely on these traditional things a lot. If you go in the village, you still find it. It is something that has been in our culture for decades and centuries, and cannot go away" (Opobo interview 2012).

[12] "JLOS is a sector-wide approach adopted by Government bringing together institutions with closely linked mandates of administering justice and maintaining law and order and human rights, into developing a common vision, policy framework, unified on objectives and plan over the medium term. It focuses on a holistic approach to improving access to and administration of justice through the sector wide approach to planning, budgeting, programme implementation, monitoring and evaluation". See https://www.jlos.go.ug:442/index.php/about-jlos/our-history.

Shifting Focus and Direction

Another striking change, mentioned by most of the NGOs with which I spoke, is that Museveni has pushed all of the NGOs and INGOs away from their work in northern Uganda and towards the region of Karamoja, in the northeast of the country. As the acting secretary of the NGO Board justified it, the rationale for the GOU to "register, coordinate and monitor NGO activities" is to "provide for the regulation of these freedoms" (Okello interview 2015). He made no secret of the fact that he believed government could and should be in the business of deciding what NGOs are able to do, and forcing them to go in the particular direction the GOU chooses.

Many NGOs told me that they were no longer working in northern Uganda because of a government directive. For example, I was told that "after the Kony war in 2007, the focus moved to Karamoja" (Mugumya interview 2012). The PRDP II explains that the "situation has evolved considerably since [2005–2007] as almost all displaced people have resettled, and the priorities in the North have shifted away from humanitarian support to peace building and development" (Republic of Uganda 2011: 5). The Office of the Prime Minister has declared that "following the resolution of the conflict that faced the region there is renewed impetus for growth" (Office of the Prime Minister, "Northern Uganda"). And the GOU has indicated that the activities once carried out in northern Uganda, including "initiatives [to] promote peaceful resolution of conflicts; undertake peace education and other peace activities in the communities", are now to focus on Karamoja (Republic of Uganda 2010: 366–367). Museveni's wife, Janet Museveni, was appointed minister of state for Karamoja affairs in 2009, and in 2011 she was appointed minister for Karamoja affairs, a move many saw as "rais[ing] the prospect of the Karamoja region's social problems getting attention that goes beyond political tokenism" (Wakabi 2009). One interviewee noted, "Janet's appointment brought the issue to light. For the first time, someone can articulate that to Museveni" (Confidential interview 2013).[13]

Museveni's "push" towards Karamoja has been met with confusion and scepticism from civil society. "MPs are changing the goal posts every day", reported one faith-based NGO worker, who continued, "Government is derailing attention away from other things" (Nalwoga interview 2012). I heard from many people at both NGOs and INGOs that "in 2009, government aid went to Karamoja. But I'm not sure it has rested there" (Otobi interview 2012). The government's stated focus on Karamoja has created an environment in which NGOs feel unable to focus on any other region of the country, despite what they think still remains to be done in northern Uganda. Most Ugandan NGO representatives I spoke with feel that they may only carry out activities explicitly sanctioned by the government, even if their funding comes from other sources.

[13] It is worth noting that opinion on Janet Museveni's involvement is divided. Some contended that "she was not going to change anything after all", or alleged that the Museveni family is engaged in a land grab that will give them access to oil and mineral rights to resources just being discovered in the region. Popular sentiment, though, ultimately gauges her appointment as a back-room deal to enable her eventual succession (Kanyana 2012; Nalugo 2012).

One INGO consultant, who is herself from northern Uganda, wondered whether the Karamoja move was "a broader strategy by the government to deflect attention somehow" (Confidential interview 2012b). The GOU has a complicated history in northern Uganda, owing to the 30-year LRA conflict and the activities of the Uganda People's Defence Force there. The GOU allowed the conflict to go on, unstopped, for years and only reluctantly stepped up its response in the early 2000s. Many of the people to whom I spoke indicated that they felt that the GOU had no desire to rebuild northern Uganda following the conflict, since it viewed northerners as having been supporters of former President Obote, against whom Museveni fought in the 1980s to secure the presidency. Northern Ugandans and a growing number of people across the rest of the country, therefore, suspect malicious neglect of northern Uganda after the LRA conflict to be at the root of Museveni's decision to shift attention to Karamoja. "The Government had a lot to do with pushing international donors away from emergency work in northern Uganda", said one interviewee. "Where international NGOs have come in is that we haven't done a good job in saying those areas still need a lot of work, in getting evidence, in advocacy" (Muculezi interview 2012). The GOU policy has effectively forced NGOs and INGOs to focus on Karamoja at the expense of northern Uganda and even a number of INGOs I interviewed felt obliged to follow this directive, or face having their programmes suspended too.

Other interviewees were quick to point out that "interest is measured regarding the presence of international NGOs. Maybe there are no international NGOs left in Karamoja" (Otobi interview 2012). Others still reported that "international donors are still in the north" (Othieno interview 2012). It is true that the stated focus of the PRDP II is on both northern Uganda *and* Karamoja, although everyone to whom I spoke indicated that they had been shunted away from northern Uganda and towards Karamoja.

Personnel Turnover

This shift has caused a revamping of the kinds of programming that NGOs are able to offer, and significant rearranging of the personnel who are now in place to advise on and carry out such programmes. Of the 29 people I interviewed in the "peace and justice" sector of the NGO and INGO space in Uganda, 21 were new to their jobs within the past year or so. And many of those were people I knew in the past when they served in other capacities. These interviewees were well aware of the implications of the shift that had taken place (Tumuwesigye interview 2012; Ocan interview 2012).

One casualty of this shift is that institutional memory of customary practices built up under old personnel has not been passed along to the people now occupying their positions. Yet, interviewees seemed puzzled by the shift: "There used to be a whole dialogue about national reconciliation. I don't know where that went" (Confidential interview 2012b). I could find no evidence that organisations were doing anything to counter this loss, such as knowledge management, evaluation, and exit interviews. In many cases, the problem was compounded by a lack of personal knowledge about customary practices. Interviewees noted that while the "peace and justice" sector was once staffed with people from northern Uganda, the newcomers are mostly from the west and south of Uganda. Many reported that "people from the west [and south] don't know their [own] culture", let alone the Acholi culture (Ocan interview 2012), or that "if you're not in conflict yourself, then you don't know what the traditions mean" (Nalwoga interview 2012). Others explained the lack of institutional memory this way: "Nationals working on files bring their own exposure and experiences and knowledge of context, and must try to explain that to their managers to show them the importance" (Barigye interview 2012). Still others admitted that they and their staff simply do not understand the conflict in northern Uganda, and so these kinds of matters do not seem important to them (Kizza-Aliba interview 2012).

In any case, the agenda relating to reconciliation and customary practices of justice and acknowledgement is not what it once was.

Communication Breakdown

Another factor in the shift away from customary practices is the disconnect between the people and institutions working in the "peace and justice" sector regarding what is being discussed and the priorities being articulated.

As always, part of the difficulty is that the GOU does not speak with one voice. The Minister of Finance has spoken openly about the problem, proposing that "collaborative efforts between the different parts of Government should be continuously encouraged and promoted" (Ministry of Finance 2004b: 6). Instead, documents spelling out national priorities, as noted above, conflict with one another. The PRDP II signals something quite different from the National Development Plan, both of which are different from the former NUSAF and NUSAF II. Both plans are seen by nearly everyone I spoke with as a cop-out by the government on the important post-conflict justice questions that remain unanswered. As the then coordinator of the Civil Society Organization for Peace in Northern Uganda commented, "The PRDP itself is a problem. It is highly politicised, and has lost its meaning for people" (Omona interview 2012). Some contend that "the realisation of these plans is lacking" (Odong interview 2012). Nearly all agree that "law and order and the conventional justice system has taken over. And the government is moving in that direction in the PRDP, too" (Nalwoga interview 2012).

Outside of these policy documents, the work has largely been left to JLOS. "It is supposed to be going through those channels. The government is trying to limit NGO voices. [International donors and donor organisations] are called to meet with the Prime Minister, who tells them not to do X or Y" (Confidential interview 2012b). JLOS, in turn, takes items to Cabinet for approval. "Cabinet is easy to convince", reported one international technical advisor for JLOS, "The challenge is with

Parliament" (Zarifis interview 2012). Others noted a serious difference of opinion between JLOS and the Minister of Internal Affairs, and between JLOS and the Uganda Law Reform Commission—an agency that ostensibly reports to the JLOS as well (Odong interview 2012).

Another fundamental issue is the failure of JLOS to adequately articulate its goals to the NGO and INGO community, or to take in any of the feedback it regularly gets from that community (Adongo interview 2012). Unlike in other countries where government is unresponsive, in Uganda NGOs are reluctant to work autonomously or to find other channels, although certainly CBOs did so during the height of the LRA conflict, by utilising customary justice. Today, the alternative forms of mobilisation going on are in other, related sectors, such as vocational training for war-affected and formerly abducted youth. Yet people in northern Uganda still feel like their "justice" needs have not been met. JLOS is talking about different priorities to different agencies and sending mixed signals to civil society actors. The significant delay in the publication of the Uganda Law Reform Commission's report, and the subsequent delay in a workshop to disseminate the findings to the NGO community, has not helped (Zarifis interview 2012), nor has the government's failure to articulate and legislate a national transitional justice policy. The NGO and INGO representatives to whom I spoke expressed frustration with the current state of affairs.

In part because of the GOU's abdication of its responsibility in the "peace and justice" sector, civil society has stepped in to fill the gap. Many NGOs play an important role in the GOU's strategy, and are recognised as "development partners" and "main actors" in the PRDP (Republic of Uganda 2007: iii). In many ways this is the GOU paying lip service to NGOs' contribution, since NGOs are only able to do as much as their NGO Board permits allow. This makes for a Catch-22, wherein the GOU says that NGOs are the main actors but then refuses to allow them to act. Nonetheless, the Humanitarian Policy Group notes that the number of specialised NGOs is likely to increase in "response to complex ethical and operational dilemmas" such as the decades of conflict and insecurity in northern Uganda (Macrae et al. 2002: 12). To some extent, that has been the case in Uganda. Several people expressed to me that NGOs do fill a critical gap, in some ways: "NGOs have replaced the vacuum in northern Uganda" (Ejoyi interview 2012).

Donor Influence

There is a question regarding the extent of the GOU's control. As the GOU itself notes, "The Government has to rely on external financing for much of the budget expenditures" (Republic of Uganda 2010: 4). A local newspaper reported that "donors fund[ed] 25 per cent of Uganda's 2012/13 budget by $4.5b (Shs11.2 trillion)" (Monitor Team 2012). These donors have begun to cooperate, and to coordinate their efforts. In early 2006, a Group of Seven Plus One states banded together to support the idea of "peace" in Uganda both morally and financially.[14] A constellation of international governments have put in place a joint agency called the Donor Governance Facility, made up of Denmark, Sweden, Norway, the United Kingdom, Austria, Ireland, the Netherlands and the European Union, which coordinates those countries' funding allocations and sets joint priorities. The facility now funds the JLOS and the Uganda Human Rights Commission, among other GOU agencies in Uganda, for example (Barigye interview 2012). Another group, made up of Ireland, Norway, Sweden and Denmark, supplies "earmarked budget support" to the PRDP II (Republic of Uganda 2011: 2).

Yet, one faith-based NGO staffer echoed what I heard from a few: "The government puts a lot of pressure on donor agencies" (Confidential interview 2012b). Within the NGO community, there is some sense that the government exerts a modicum of control over donors' priorities: "If the government says Karamoja needs X, there's no way donors can't" (Omona interview 2012). As long as this funding is in the direction of the initiatives supported by Museveni's government, the funding does not appear to be problematic: "The government has its consortium. Within that framework, government is managing to herd groups in their direction" (Zedriga interview 2012). And indeed, a senior policymaker in the Ministry of Justice and Constitutional Affairs, when asked whether things have shifted over the past couple of years, asked, "What has changed? Now we are the ones who are in control, not like that time" (Gashirabake interview 2012).

But funding from donors is required if any of the GOU's programming is to go ahead. The PRDP spells out three distinct funding modalities for the work it has planned:

1. PRDP budget grant: GoU provides PRDP grant funding through the budget [36% of which is provided by donors] ….
2. On-budget special projects: Some donors provide support through on-budget "special projects" which are managed by the government (e.g. NUSAF II, funded by the World Bank and DFID, and KALIP and ALREP, which are funded by the EU).
3. Off-budget funding: The third modality is off-budget funding, where donors and other development partners implement projects without the involvement of government, either directly or through NGOs and CSOs (Republic of Uganda 2011: 2).

Little wonder, then, that the GOU seeks to manage NGO activity to some extent, and to regulate the activities in which civil society groups like NGOs are able to participate. The GOU has no control of NGOs if their funding is "off-budget" and flows directly from donors to civil society, effectively by-passing the GOU.

In fact, contrary to most interviewees' perceptions, the GOU must abide by the wishes of international donors if it wants to maintain or increase the funding it receives: "Donors play a pronounced advisory role when the budget is being

[14] The Group of Seven Plus One was composed of Belgium, Germany, Ireland, the Netherlands, Norway, Sweden, the United Kingdom and Canada. See Government of Canada, (n.d.).

formulated, and critics have questioned the influence of donor interests within the budget process. However, given Uganda's high reliance on donor funding, it is unlikely that the role of donors in the budget system can be minimized at present" (Owomugasho/World Bank website). In December 2012, for example, donors announced

> deeper and longer aid cuts … in response to massive public corruption. The European Union ambassador to the country announced … that the EU, the United Kingdom, the World Bank, Austria and other countries had suspended up to $300 million promised in budgetary support each year, up to 2013 … Sweden and Ireland had earlier suspended their project support and thus the new agreement suspends all their funds to Uganda while Norway withdrew all of its support in 2011. (Jeanne and Njoroge 2012)

It is the third category, "off-budget funding", "where donors and other development partners implement projects without the involvement of Government, either directly or through NGOs and CSOs" (Republic of Uganda 2011: 2), that tells the enormity of the tale. Funding is given directly to local organisations to carry out the programming of international donors, without having to be accountable to the GOU and without the GOU's knowledge or consent. To some extent, donors act as patrons, not partners, in the sector (Nesiah 2016). Many NGOs themselves admit to allowing international donors to call the tune and to set the agenda for their programmatic decision-making. It is true that large, well-established NGOs have a higher degree of autonomy, relative to other NGOs, but even they admit to being frustrated by identifying real needs in Ugandan society and then struggling to find funding to allow them to work on those particular issues. The executive director of the Refugee Law Project expressed his frustration at donors' inability to deal with ongoing issues like those related to transitional justice, which do not fit neatly into budget cycles, or necessarily translate to the programmatic priorities that donors have set (Dolan interview 2015). This was echoed by another Refugee Law Project staffer, who noted that "[government expects that] donors have their priorities set by the government. Government has said transitional justice is not a priority so funding has been pulled. Post-Juba, donors had different agendas" (Oola interview 2015). The same holds true for INGOs: "The kind of funding we have is driven by what the donors decide. You might have a very good proposal, but you will fail to find funding for it" (Businge interview 2016).

In an ideal world, "planning [must] come first, then development … Before raising a single dollar, an institution should have a clear sense of its mission, aspirations, and priorities—and take the lead … Too much donor control is hazardous to a nonprofit organization's integrity" (Donor Direction 2000). This is because "all aid, at all times, creates incentives and disincentives" (Uvin 1999: 4). Some donors seek "to (maximally and directly) control the use of funds, either by keeping the funds and their use in the hands of the donor, or by delegating them to third parties (NGOs or multi-bi-arrangements)" (Uvin 1999: 10). "What is at issue is how [donors'] financial power is translated into a set of operational relationships in a contentious sphere, particularly given contested legitimacy and weak capacity of governments in recipient countries" (Macrae et al. 2002: 68). And so donors become "pushers and prodders" (Macrae et al. 2002: 70).

This is important in trying to understand how and why thinking about and programming in support of customary justice and reconciliation have all but disappeared from the landscape. Because the majority of NGOs in Uganda simply do not have the luxury of having continued budget support that allows them to pick and choose the kinds of work they pursue, they are beholden to the donors, which drive particular agendas. The deputy director of programmes at a national NGO told me that "most NGOs have only project support, so it is difficult to divert support to other priorities" (Muwanga interview 2012). Another described it this way: "Local organisations might not have their own resources to tackle these, so there is a tendency to look at where is the donor focus to tap into that" (Apunyo interview 2012). As a result, another said, "organisations will shift and people break off and go to where the money is" (Ocan interview 2012). Several people also reported that the number of NGOs has dropped off considerably since their peak in 2004, citing "donor fatigue" (Ocan interview 2012; Omona interview 2012).

Many NGOs do try to act in ways they think the donors want, so as to attract funding. Interviewees reiterated to me that the problem of attracting and keeping donor funding was common across Ugandan NGOs and INGOs, many of whom rely on donor funding. "There is a popular thought of making the *mzungu* [white person] like you, so you do what they want" (Ocan interview 2012). A faith-based organisation staffer told me that "NGOs have to follow the donor lead regarding our priorities" (Nalwoga interview 2012), and so, as her co-worker said, "we tend to look at the international donors' focus in determining our priorities" (Apunyo interview 2012). Another interviewee confirmed that "donors have always called the shots" (Otobi interview 2012). The trouble, as one INGO manager told me, is that "when you're dancing to the tune of the donor, you're not looking after the people you want to help. Those other NGOs are trying to go to Karamoja because that's where the donor wants them to go, but without understanding why, and what situation they will find there" (Byamukama interview 2012). Indeed, "more than 70% of our NGOs began after the early 2000s. They distorted the way that our people live, and offered a better alternative to their life. It affected the people negatively and positively" (Opobo interview 2012).

Being too eager to please can be a problem, particularly when donors seek to advance a particular agenda. As one interviewee put it, "donors are the blue-eyed girl for Uganda. Now NGOs are becoming cautious" (Nalwoga interview 2012). "It is a problem for NGOs to know their role", though, reported one research organization's executive director (Okello interview 2012). "Many times", an INGO representative told me, "donors drive the agenda because they have the envelope. But many NGOs don't locate the debate in the international instruments that are available, so they don't help themselves" (Barigye interview 2012).

Donors themselves may not always know what the important issues are on the ground. "Even donors may not know precisely what they wish to advance", one faith-based organisation representative told me (Otobi interview 2012). I frequently heard from NGOs and INGOs that "donors often make decisions based on a lack of knowledge, where there is a lack of information given to them, and on what they know from back in Europe. Sometimes, there is a lack of cultural sensitivity" (Barigye interview 2012). "Sometimes donors do come to ask for inputs" about what NGOs think is best (Othieno interview 2012), but NGO and INGO interviewees indicated that this was rare. But there was no question among the people I spoke to that "donors help a lot to determine the agenda" (Ejoyi interview 2012). A great number of donors have shifted away from funding transitional justice issues, per se, while others persist in the sector.

In part, this comes from donors' own carefully defined stand on a variety of issues. "We can't just support an institution that doesn't recognise basic human rights", said the senior programme officer for the Democratic Governance Facility (Barigye interview 2012). For World Vision, a Christian INGO, for example, the spirit worship that is often part of customary justice in Uganda is problematic. Their approach was "not to stop [their initiatives in northern Uganda] from doing traditional practices, but we made it clear that donor money will not be used for these activities—although the children were free to do their own spiritual things" (Odong interview 2008). In another example related to me by a staffer at an international donor agency, the agency was approached for funding by *Rwot Acana*, the traditional cultural leader of the Acholi, but it had reservations regarding gender and deferred a review of the request until they could be sure that gender concerns would be properly mitigated (Confidential interview 2013).

Further confusion stems from lack of coordination, especially for those organisations funded outside of the GOU's budget process. Ugandan NGO interviewees expressed frustration about the confusion this can create. One, for example, told me that "NGOs don't know what each other is working on, and there's sometimes 80–90% of duplication of work. It can send contradictory messages to the community if two NGOs are working there from different angles" (Okello interview 2012). A now more than decade-old report recommended that to clear this confusion up, "a more systematic approach would improve efforts … which are often duplicated, or remaining gaps are often not addressed efficiently. There is a need for these institutions and policies to work together in better coordination on [these] issues" (NUPI 2006: iii).

Conclusions

NGOs and INGOs in Uganda that formerly worked in the "peace and justice" sector on issues related to the use of customary practices of justice and acknowledgement have gone madly off in all directions. No formal transitional justice policy has been enacted. The GOU has shifted its attention to the International Criminal Division of the High Court. NGOs are no longer working on "peace and justice", broadly speaking. They have been pushed by the GOU into working in the Karamoja region, where issues of acute conflict are not in evidence, and where there is not a need for transitional justice. NGO workers themselves have also moved on. As a result, programmes supporting customary justice—the only form of transitional justice that was much in evidence from 1986 to the time of writing—have all but disappeared. The official transitional justice mechanisms appointed by the GOU, meanwhile, have never come close to fulfilling their mandates, nor to effecting any kind of proper transition.

More important, the disconnect between actors has led to serious confusion. The GOU's failure to articulate any one particular position is problematic, as always. But the failure of JLOS to articulate a convincing strategy for policymakers to pursue is particularly worrying, because the "peace and justice" agenda has been left to them. Internationally funded NGOs have stepped in where they can, circumventing the funding and regulatory problems faced by nationally funded NGOs. But they face increasing pressure from both the GOU and from international donors to influence and support the official transitional justice policy process, which remains in draft form after years of negotiation. Even foreign NGOs are not immune from the vagaries of the GOU, as they, too, are regulated by the GOU's NGO Board.

The critical role of international donors, and of the influence they continue to exert, has been largely overlooked in analyses of how and why customary practices of justice and acknowledgement are or are not being pursued in Uganda. It is essential to understand that NGOs are caught between the GOU and international donors, without any real understanding of how to steer the process according to their own principles and unable to be informed by their own experiences in communities.

National NGOs have significant experience within communities across the country. In many cases, they are from the very communities that need assistance. Local staffers understand the ethnocultural specificities, as well as the practical limitations of any programmatic goal, although this is lessened when NGOs are staffed by Ugandans who come from other areas of the country and are less familiar with local practices. But NGOs are either unwilling or unable to articulate these ideas to international donors who simply need a group, any group, to carry out the programmes they seek to fund. This has not been helped by the rotating staff contingents that have passed through these NGOs, taking with them any institutional memory that once existed.

At the same time, with all available hands assisting programming that is either conceived of and funded by the ever-opaque GOU or by international donors that are not always, themselves, clear about what their on-the-ground programming should encompass, few are listening to communities' wants and needs. And so even though community members continue to ask for support for customary practices of justice and acknowledgement, and for more community-based approaches to resolving long-standing conflicts, none is forthcoming for now. People continue to use customary justice on a small scale to address transitional justice issues, at the community level, but any formalisation or codification of its use, or any justice across ethnocultural groups—as has been advocated by some—has not been carried out.

Civil society in Uganda is fundamentally constrained by the strict control of the GOU. The GOU is not interested in any real pursuit of transitional justice, which it fears would see its members held to account for their own past actions. For this reason, it is easier for the GOU to avoid committing to transitional justice and instead to use the guise of transitional justice as a tool for acquiring some semblance of legitimacy. NGOs, INGOs and other civil society actors have been pushed into other sectors, and those that continue to work in the "peace and justice" sector do so without much support.

References

Allen, T. (2006). *Trial justice: The International Criminal Court and the Lord's Resistance Army*. London: Zed Books.

Avocats Sans Frontières, & African Youth Initiative Network. (2013). *Victim and civil society actors' views on the draft transitional justice policy for Uganda: Lango sub-region: Victim and CSO consultation on June 6–7, 2013*.

Branch, A. (2014). The violence of peace: Ethnojustice in Northern Uganda. *Development and Change, 45*(3), 608–630.

Briggs, P. (1998). *Uganda*. Old Saybrook, CT: Globe Pequot Press.

Carver, R. (1990). Called to account: How African governments investigate human rights violations. *African Affairs, 89*(356), 391–415.

Donor Direction: How Much is Too Much?. (2000). *Association of Fundraising Professionals. [Website]. Excerpted from Advancing Philanthropy* (Nov./Dec.). Retrieved March 12, 2013, from www.afpnet.org/Ethics/EmergingIssuesDetail.cfm?itemnumber=4221.

Finnström, S. (2003). *Living with bad surroundings: War and existential uncertainty in Acholiland in Northern Uganda*. Uppsala: Acta Universitatis Upsaliensis.

Government of Canada. (n.d.). *Canada calls on Ugandan parties to maintain commitment to Juba peace talks and announces $2.5 million toward peace efforts*. Retrieved February 20, 2007, from http://www.reliefweb.int/rw/RWB.NSF/db900SID/RMOI-6Y22R5?OpenDocument.

Government of Uganda and Lord's Resistance Army/Movement. (2008, February 19). *Annexure to the agreement on accountability and reconciliation*. Juba.

Harlacher, T., Okot, F. X., Obonyo, C. A., Balthazard, M., & Atkinson, R. (2006). *Traditional ways of coping in Acholi: Cultural provisions for reconciliation and healing from war*. Kampala: Thomas Harlacher and Caritas Gulu Archdiocese.

Hovil, L., & Lomo, Z. (2004). *Behind the violence: Causes, consequences and the search for solutions to the war in Northern Uganda*. Kampala: Refugee Law Project.

Hovil, L., & Lomo, Z. (2005). *Whose justice? Perceptions of Uganda's amnesty act 2000: The potential for conflict resolution and long-term reconciliation*. Kampala: Refugee Law Project.

Jeanne, D., & Njorodge, J. (2012, December 4). Donors cut all budget support in Uganda until 2015. *Africa Review*.

Kanyana, G. (2012, April 3). Janet Museveni has truly silenced skeptics on Karamoja. *The New Vision*.

Macrae, J., Collinson, S., Buchanan-Smith, M., Reindorp, N., Schmidt, A., Mowjee, T., & Harmer, A. (2002, December). *The changing role of official donors in humanitarian action*. HPG Report 12, Humanitarian Policy Group, Overseas Development Institute.

Mamdani, M. (1996). *Citizen and subject*. Kampala: Fountain Publishers.

Ministry of Finance, Planning and Economic Development, Government of Uganda. (2004a). *Poverty Eradication Action Plan (2004/5–2007/8)*.

Ministry of Finance, Planning, and Economic Development, Government of Uganda. (2004b, August). *Post-conflict reconstruction: The case of Northern Uganda.* Discussion Paper 8.
Monitor Team. (2012, December 5). Uganda government plans budget cut after aid freeze. *The Daily Monitor.*
Museveni, Y. K. (1997). *Sowing the mustard seed.* London: Macmillan.
Nalugo, M. (2012, May 21). Karamoja leaders accuse First Family of land-grabbing. *The Daily Monitor.*
Ndrua, J. (1988). *A Christian study of the African concept of authority and the administration of justice among the Lugbari of north western Uganda.* M.A. Dissertation, Catholic Higher Institute of Eastern Africa.
Nesiah, V. (2016). *Public keynote lecture: Commissioning civil society.* Writers' Workshop: Transitional Justice and Civil Society in Asia and the Pacific. Australian National University, Canberra, Australia, September 29–30.
Northern Uganda Peace Initiative. (2006, February). *Issues paper on the development of a conflict resolution and peace building policy for the Government of Uganda.*
Novelli, B. (1999). *Karimojong traditional religion.* Kampala: Comboni Missionaries.
Ofcansky, T. P. (1996). *Uganda: Tarnished pearl of Africa.* Boulder, CO: Westview.
Office of the Prime Minister. (n.d.). *Northern Uganda.* [Website.] Retrieved March 11, 2013., from http://www.opm.go.ug/departments/management-of-special-programmes/northern-uganda.html.
Otim, M., & Kihika, K. S. (2015, June). *On the path to vindicate victims' rights in Uganda: Reflections on the transitional justice process since Juba.* International Centre for Transitional Justice Briefing.
Owomugasho, D., on behalf of the Uganda Debt Network. (n.d.). "Uganda." *World Bank Site Resources.* [Website.] Retrieved March 12, 2012, from http://siteresources.worldbank.org/EXTFINANCIALMGMT/Resources/313217-1196229169083/4441154-1196229856871/4441195/1196266506713/UGANDA.pdf.
Quinn, J. R. (2005). *Tried and true: The role of informal mechanisms in transitional justice.* A paper presented at the International Society of Political Psychology Annual Meeting, Toronto, July 6.
Quinn, J. R. (2008, April). *Accountability and reconciliation: Traditional mechanisms of acknowledgement and the implications of the Juba Peace Process.* A paper presented at the conference, "Reconstructing Northern Uganda," Nationalism and Ethnic Conflict Research Group, University of Western Ontario, Canada.
Quinn, J. R. (2009a). What of reconciliation? Traditional mechanisms of acknowledgement in Uganda. In J. R. Quinn (Ed.), *Reconciliation(s).* Montreal: McGill-Queen's University Press.
Quinn, J. R. (2009b). Chicken and egg? Sequencing in transitional justice: The case of Uganda. *International Journal of Peace Studies, 14*(2), 35–53.
Quinn, J. R. (2010). *The politics of acknowledgement: Truth commissions in Uganda and Haiti.* Vancouver: University of British Columbia Press.
Quinn, J. R. (2015a). Comparing formal and informal mechanisms in Uganda. In H. Carey & S. Mitchell (Eds.), *Trials and tribulations of international prosecution.* Lanham, MD: Rowman and Littlefield.
Quinn, J. R. (2015b). The impact of internal conflict on customary institutions and law: The case of Uganda. *Journal of African Law, 58*(1), 220–236.
Republic of Uganda. (1995). *Constitution.*
Republic of Uganda. (1996). *The Children's Statute, 1996.*
Republic of Uganda. (2006). *Non-Governmental Organisations Registration Act, 2006*, Cap. 113.
Republic of Uganda. (2007, September). *Peace, Recovery and Development Plan for Northern Uganda (PRDP) 2007–2010.*
Republic of Uganda. (2010, April). *National Development Plan (2010/11–2014/15).*
Republic of Uganda. (2011, November). *Peace, Recovery and Development Plan for Northern Uganda (PRDP): Phase 2 (July 2012–June 2015).*

Republic of Uganda. (2014). *The Anti-Homosexuality Act, 2014*.
Republic of Uganda. (2016). *The Non-Governmental Organisations Act, 2016*.
Republic of Uganda and Lord's Resistance Army/Movement. (2007, June 29). *Agreement on accountability and reconciliation*. Juba.
Republic of Uganda and Lord's Resistance Army/Movement. (2008, February 19). *Annexure to the agreement on accountability and reconciliation*. Juba.
Smith, D. (2012, June). Uganda bans 38 organisations accused of 'promoting homosexuality': Country's ethics and integrity minister claims banned NGOs exist to 'destroy the traditions and culture of this country'. *The Guardian*.
The British Colonial Office. (1961). *Report of the Uganda Relationship Committee*.
Uganda. (1998). Brooklyn: Interlink Books.
Uganda Law Reform Commission. (n.d.). *JLOS*. [Website.] Retrieved March 11, 2013. http://www.ulrc.go.ug/?p=159.
Uganda National Nongovernmental (NGO) Forum. (2003). *Constitution*.
Uganda: Constitution, Government & Legislation. (n.d.). [Article on-line]. Retrieved April 30, 2005, from http://jurist.law.pitt.edu/world/uganda.htm.
Uvin, P. (1999, September). *The influence of aid in situations of violent conflict*. Paris: Development Assistance Committee Informal Task Force on Conflict, Peace and Development Co-Operation.
Waddell, N., & Clark, P. (Eds.). (2008, March). *Courting conflict? Justice, peace and the ICC in Africa*. London: Royal African Society.
Wakabi, M. (2009, February). First Lady must tread carefully on Karamoja Development Agency. *The East African*. Retrieved March 11, 2013, from http://www.theeastafrican.co.ke/news/-/2558/533028/-/rka64cz/-/index.html.
Waldorf, L. (2006). Mass justice for mass atrocity: Rethinking local justice as transitional justice. *Temple Law Review, 79*(1), 1–88.
Waligo, J. M.. (2003). *The human right to peace for every person and every society*. A paper presented at Public Dialogue organised by Faculty of Arts, Makerere University in conjunction with Uganda Human Rights Commission and NORAD, Kampala, Uganda, Dec. 4. Author's collection.
Waligo, J. M. (2005). *On Kitewuliza in Buganda, 3 May 2005*. Author's collection.

Interviews

Adongo, J. F. (2012, May 29). *Senior Sociologist, Uganda Law Reform Commission. Interview by author*. Kampala, Uganda.
Apunyo, R. A. (2012, May 8). *Acting Program Officer Peace and Human Rights, Church of Uganda. Interview by author*. Namirembe, Uganda.
Barigye, S. (2012, May 16). *Senior Programme Officer, Rights, Justice and Peace, Democratic Governance Facility. Interview by author*. Kampala, Uganda.
Businge, R. (2016, August 1). *Country Manager, International Alert. Interview by author*. Kampala, Uganda.
Byamukama, M. (2012, May 10). *Uganda Country Representative, REPSSI. Interview by author*. Kampala, Uganda.
Confidential. Itseso woman who consults for international NGOs. (2012, May 17). *Interview by author*. Kampala, Uganda.
Confidential. Male Ugandan national international donor employee. (2013, May 2017). Kampala, Uganda.
Confidential. Muganda woman working in faith-based organization. (2012, May 8). Kampala, Uganda.
Confidential. Sabiny man studying at Makerere University. (2004, November 7). *Interview by author*. Kampala, Uganda.

Dolan, C. (2015, May 19) *Executive Director, Refugee Law Project. Interview by author*. Kampala, Uganda.
Draku, M. (2008, July 7). *Principal Public Relations Officer, Amnesty Commission. Interview by author*. Kampala, Uganda.
Ejoyi, X. (2012, May 17). *Interview by author*. Kampala, Uganda. All comments are made in Mr. Ejoyi's personal capacity.
Gashirabake, C. (2008, July). *Ministry of Justice and Constitutional Affairs. Interview by author*. Kampala, Uganda.
Gashirabake, C. (2012). *Director, Legal Advocacy, Ministry of Justice*. Interview by author. Kampala, Uganda.
Katatumba, G. W. (2008, June 28). *Enganzi (Prime Minister), Ankole Kingdom, and Chairman, Nkore Cultural Trust. Interview by author*. Kampala, Uganda.
Kizza-Aliba, E. (2012, May 28). *Executive Secretary, Catholic Commission for Justice and Peace. Interview by author*. Nsambya, Uganda.
Lokeris, P. (2004, November 18). *Minister of State for Karamoja. Interview by author*. Kampala, Uganda.
Muculezi, D. (2012, May 24). *Save the Children in Uganda. Interview by author*. Kampala, Uganda.
Mugumya, A. (2012, May 14). *Project Co-ordinator, Center for Conflict Resolution. Interview by author*. Kampala, Uganda.
Muwanga, S. (2012, March 18). *Deputy Director-Programs, Foundation for Human Rights Initiative. Interview by author*. Kampala, Uganda.
Nadduli, A. (2004, November 17). *LC5 District Chairman. Interview by author*. Luweero Town, Uganda.
Nalwoga, J. (2012, May 8). *Manager, planning, development and rehabilitation, Church of Uganda. Interview by author*. Kampala, Uganda.
Ocan, Rev. Ali. (2012, May 4). *Acting Director, JYAK. Interview by author*. Kampala, Uganda.
Odong, J. (2008, September 25). *Associate Director for Peace and Reconciliation, World Vision International. Interview by author*.
Odong, S. (2012, May 9). *Programs Manager, Human Rights Network-Uganda. Interview by author*. Ntinda, Uganda.
Ogoola, Hon. Jus. James. (2008, September 25). *Principal Justice, High Court and Chairman, Transitional Justice Working Group. Interview by author*. Kampala, Uganda.
Okello, J. (2012, May 10). *Executive Director, African Institute for Strategic Research Governance and Development. Interview by author*. Nankulabye, Uganda.
Okello, S. (2015, May 25). *Acting Secretary, National NGO Board. Interview by author*. Kampala, Uganda.
Okille, A. (2012, May 17). *Socio-Development Consultant and Executive Coach, Akijul: Enabling Change. Interview by author*.
Omona, J. (2012, May 9). *CSOPNU National Coordinator, Civil Society Organizations for Peace in Uganda. Interview by author*. Kampala, Uganda.
Oola, S. (2015, May 19). *Refugee Law Project. Interview by author*.
Opiyo, N. (2012, May 19). *International criminal lawyer. Interview by author*. Kampala, Uganda.
Opobo, W. (2012, May 15). *Director of Programmes, ACORD. Interview by author*.
Othieno, R. (2012, May 14). *Executive Director, Center for Conflict Resolution. Interview by author*. Kampala, Uganda.
Otobi, G. O. (2012, May 14). *Program Manager, Northern Uganda Women's Empowerment Program, CARE. Interview by author*. Kampala, Uganda.
Tabaro, Hon. Jus. Patrick. (2008, July 14). *High Court Justice. Interview by author*. Kampala, Uganda.

Tumuwesigye, S. (2012, May 9). *HURINET-U. Interview by author*. Kampala, Uganda.
Zarifis, I. N. (2012, May 21). *International Technical Advisor, Transitional Justice, JLOS. Interview by author*. Kampala, Uganda.
Zedriga, L. (2012, May 19) *Director, Women, Peace and Security, RACI. Interview by author*. Kampala, Uganda.

Focus Groups

Iteso focus group. (2006, August 31). *Conducted by author*. Kampala, Uganda.
Northern Uganda focus group. (2006, August 23). *Conducted by author*. Kampala, Uganda.

Chapter 8
Civil Society Engagement with Communities: Tradition, Authority and Transitional Justice in Rural African Communities

Andrew Iliff

Introduction

This chapter discusses engagement between civil society and communities in pursuit of transitional justice (TJ) in Africa, focusing on the role of civil society in leading and supporting community-based TJ processes. Civil society organisations (CSOs) and TJ practitioners have increasingly focused on community-based TJ processes in recent years, both as complements and alternatives to national TJ processes. While national TJ processes tend to garner more headlines, community initiatives, supported by civil society bodies, may better reflect the agency of survivors and more effectively unravel the complexities of local power dynamics that lie at the root of conflict (Arriaza and Roht-Arriaza 2008). However, CSO engagement with communities is shaped by local culture power dynamics. The impact of these local power dynamics on TJ processes and outcomes depends on the ability of CSOs to engage constructively and thoughtfully with communities and their leadership.

A single chapter cannot hope to cover more than a sampling of the most important issues, especially when, as here, the frame of reference is an entire continent. Questions of authority, inclusion and ownership are at the heart of civil society engagement with communities in the TJ field (Androff 2012). This chapter calls

I would like to thank the participants in the Centre for the Study of Violence and Reconciliation February 2015 workshop on civil society and transitional justice in Africa for their insightful presentations and thoughtful feedback. I would also like to thank Hugo van de Merwe and Jasmina Brankovic for their feedback and assistance in shaping and revising this chapter.

A. Iliff (✉)
Harvard Global Health Institute, Cambridge, MA, USA
e-mail: ailiff@gmail.com

J. Brankovic, H. van der Merwe (eds.), *Advocating Transitional Justice in Africa*, Springer Series in Transitional Justice,
https://doi.org/10.1007/978-3-319-70417-3_8

attention to two complementary dynamics that shape civil society engagement in rural African communities: the density of local authorities and the turn to "tradition".[1]

Local authorities—traditional, religious, elected and unelected—exist everywhere, but they proliferate in many rural communities. Non-governmental organisations (NGOs) are usually based in cities and typically depend on the mediation and approval of local authorities to gain effective access to communities. This mediation has ambivalent effects on civil society engagement with communities, constraining and supporting engagement depending on the partnership between NGOs and local authorities (Hovil and Okello 2011).

Just as the density of local authorities mandates a set of partnerships for NGOs undertaking TJ work in communities, ideas of "tradition" can shape such work. The framework of "tradition" has similarly ambivalent effects on community engagement: it can be the basis for successful community engagement with TJ processes, but may also exclude segments of the communities with which NGOs seek to engage. Religion has played a similar structuring role in many TJ processes, raising questions about authority and exclusion.[2]

This chapter explores these questions. It begins with a brief examination of the turn to community-based TJ processes and a discussion of the terminology of "community" and "civil society" in order to effectively analyse the role of NGOs in community-based processes in Africa. The chapter then moves to a detailed analysis of the role of "tradition" and local authorities in community-based processes, identifying features that both support and inhibit NGO engagement with communities. These features are then illustrated through three brief case studies, including the Fambul Tok process in Sierra Leone, the work of the Acholi Religious Leaders Peace Initiative in Uganda and the Peace Building Network of Zimbabwe. Finally, the chapter draws a few preliminary lessons and conclusions, principally regarding the necessity of adequate "due diligence" by NGOs in choosing their local authority interlocutors, and the necessity of interrogating ideas of "tradition" that may shape community-based TJ processes. These lessons are drawn both from literature and from my experience as a transitional justice practitioner and researcher in Zimbabwe, South Africa and Rwanda.

[1] Throughout this chapter, I have placed the word "tradition" in quotation marks to emphasise that, as discussed in this chapter, the canon of customary practice and philosophy designated "traditional" is neither static nor uncontested.

[2] In one of the most prominent examples, Archbishop Desmond Tutu's faith illuminated his articulation of the philosophy of *ubuntu*, which in turn was a guiding principle in the work of the South African Truth and Reconciliation Commission.

The Turn Towards Community-Based Transitional Justice Processes

The field of transitional justice first took shape around highly state-centric approaches in the 1980s and 1990s, with examples ranging from trials and national commissions in post-dictatorship Latin America to vetting and lustration programmes in post-communist Europe and the broad scope of the South African Truth and Reconciliation Commission. Since then, the scope of TJ has expanded to include supranational and subnational forums and processes. Supranational fora include the International Criminal Court (ICC), hybrid courts like the Special Court for Sierra Leone[3] and influential transnational human rights organisations like the International Center for Transitional Justice.[4]

Many national and supranational TJ processes have been criticised for their geographic and conceptual distance from those with the most at stake: victims, perpetrators and families and communities in which they live. Critics have noted that these processes are extremely expensive and have usually fallen short of their ambitious range of objectives (Annan 2004). Partly in response to these criticisms, subnational and specifically community-based TJ processes have become increasingly prominent in TJ discourse and practice (Shaw et al. 2010). Community-based TJ processes take a wide variety of forms, from local, elected commissions to "traditional" processes of reconciliation and social healing (Androff 2012; Huyse and Salter 2008).

The goals and methods of these processes are shaped by the engagement between NGOs and the communities in which the TJ initiatives take place. NGOs are an integral element of many TJ processes, but play a particularly important role in community-based TJ processes, which are the focus of this chapter. In community-based TJ processes, whether independent stand-alone processes or complements to state-driven processes, TJ NGOs serve a range of functions, including helping to identify, articulate and synthesise the diverse priorities of communities and acting as proxies and advocates for their constituent community members.[5]

In community-based TJ processes that take place without a formal mandate from the state, NGOs draw on their expertise and institutional experience to help formulate and manage effective interventions. The role of civil society becomes still more critical where the state constrains civic space, or deploys the rhetoric and form of TJ

---

[3] The Special Court for Sierra Leone sought an accommodation between demands for broad accountability and truth telling with recognition that many perpetrators could not be considered fully culpable due to threats and compulsion. While some may disagree with the categorisation of the ICC as a TJ body, the Court's policy of "positive complementarity", encouraging investigation by states parties wherever possible, has contributed to innovative accountability processes in, for example, Colombia.

[4] For a discussion of the ICTJ as norm entrepreneur, see Naftali (2010).

[5] In Sierra Leone, for example, the *Fambul Tok* community-based intervention (discussed below) operated alongside national level mechanisms including the Truth and Reconciliation Commission and the Special Court for Sierra Leone.

to pre-empt independent processes. In such scenarios, the low operational profile of national or subnational NGOs may be the only means of pursuing TJ objectives. In these circumstances NGOs must often present themselves as not only non-partisan, but also non-confrontational and non-punitive, targeting community healing objectives that are essentially "developmental" in nature, with benefits for communities as a whole rather than specifically for victims (De Greiff 2010). As a result, community-based processes typically roll out in a piecemeal, opportunistic fashion, as NGOs identify opportunities to engage with communities and windows of opportunity open or close.

In one sense, the objectives of community-based processes are relatively modest compared to the ambitious range of goals often ascribed to national TJ bodies, but for many communities riven by past conflicts, reconciliation is urgent and essential. Many rural communities fail or thrive in proportion to the ability and willingness of community members to support (or at least tolerate) each other. Without an adequately restored social fabric, community members (both perpetrators and survivors) may be profoundly isolated in the wake of conflict, unable to muster the resources for subsistence and unwilling to risk drawing on community resources.[6]

The shift towards subnational and community-based processes has thus been motivated by both principle and pragmatism. In principle, community-level TJ processes can be more victim/survivor centred, facilitating the participation of TJ's primary beneficiaries.[7] Community healing and reconciliation processes may contribute to broader TJ goals of national healing, both as constituent element and, where particularly successful, as model. Pragmatically, community initiatives may be the only way of accomplishing some TJ goals where national authorities are unwilling or unable to do so, including where there has been no substantive political transition, where perpetrators hold an effective political veto, or where resources for a state TJ initiative are not available.

Defining "Community" and "Civil Society"

A word about terminology. The rubric of "civil society engagement with communities" is in a sense a tautology, because communities *are* civil society—indeed, one of the most fundamental and important forms of civil society. Drawing a distinction between the two requires careful attention to the specific forms of "community" and "civil society" under consideration, so as not to reflexively reproduce the discursive dichotomy of rural village communities and urban-based, donor-funded NGOs.

It is essential to highlight and avoid the stereotypes and oversimplifications that are often packed into the rhetorical notion of the African "village", the poster-child

[6] Demobilised former child soldiers in Uganda, discussed briefly below, are an example of a particularly vulnerable group in rural communities that, in the absence of TJ and reintegration processes such as *mato oput*, often struggle to participate in community life (Baines 2007).

[7] For a discussion of the central role of victims as a constituency in TJ, see Findlay (2009).

for essentialist notions of community. Unproblematised, the notion of a village brings with it a set of implications concerning urbanity (not), modernity and mobility (not, or barely), diversity (homogenous) and authority (traditional, consolidated). In reality, many African villages defy these assumptions: rural "villagers" commute to the city, use WhatsApp, watch Al Jazeera and Nollywood films and vigorously debate the issues of the day. Most importantly, for purposes of TJ processes, these "villagers" are not a homogenous set: they have distinct priorities and divergent opinions, including on their "traditions" and the standing of their community leadership.

Acknowledging these features of rural African communities helps to foreground other forms of diversity that are often neglected: communities comprise a diversity of age, gender, politics and experience. They are also frequently ethnically diverse, sometimes in ways that are apparent only to members of the community.[8] For these reasons, community members are therefore seldom if ever univocal, on any issue, let alone those as complex and emotional as questions of TJ.

A community is a group of people with some important feature in common. The common feature may be abstract: a belief or an idea, as in a religious community, or a more visible identity, such as youth, veterans or the disabled. The simplest meaning of "a community", and one that is the focus in this chapter, is a set of people who share a common geography, on a scale such that members of the group share some sense of common identity based on mutual recognition: a small town, a neighbourhood, a village or even a scattered set of homesteads on a hill. (While residents of a city share a common geography, the anonymity of urban living is antithetical to the notion of a community as it is being used here.) When such communities organise themselves to pursue concrete objectives such as collecting refuse or indirect action, through lobbying, petitions, protests or other strategies, they participate in civil society.

Civil society is made up of organised non-state, non-commercial bodies of all kinds, operating at the interface between citizens and the state, and is referred to as "the realm of private voluntary association" (Foley and Edwards 1996: 38). Almost any assemblage of citizens outside of state structures may be deemed an instance of civil society.[9] A community meeting convened to discuss management of the grounds and environs of a state-funded public school is (arguably) not an instance of civil society, while the same community gathering to collect refuse outside the school is an instance of civil society. As discussed in this chapter, state-sanctioned community forums can shade into more spontaneous civic action and back again fluidly.

---

[8] In some resettlement communities in Midlands province in Zimbabwe, for example, communities are fractured between Shona dialect groups such as Karanga, Zezuru and Rozvi.

[9] The challenge of defining "civil society" is taken up with varying success by a range of political theorists seeking to answer difficult questions about the role of revenue generation, partisan politics, kinship, advocacy and power relations between members, coercion of different kinds and many other definitional challenges. See, e.g., Young (1994). For a discussion of the origins of the idea, see Seligman (1992).

Perhaps the most local type of organised civil society is a community-based organisation (CBO), in which a community organises itself to take civic action. However, the more familiar (and more visible) type of civil society is the formally constituted NGO, complete with a bank account, government certification, a charter laying out its mission and offices, typically in the capital city. It is these formal, professional NGOs, both national and international, that typically drive non-state TJ processes, including most of those that take place in local communities. This chapter is focused on the role of national and subnational NGOs and their engagement with communities in community-based TJ processes.

The Role of Civil Society in Community-Based Transitional Justice Processes

Civil society typically plays a crucial role in promoting and pursuing TJ at all levels, including through advocacy, provision of technical and legal expertise, facilitating communication between different stakeholders and building institutional capacity.[10] The role of civil society in community-based processes is at least as essential as in national level processes. In community-based TJ processes, NGOs can act as educators, champions, facilitators and convenors. Indeed, it can be argued that without support and engagement by civil society in some or all of these roles, community-based TJ processes will usually fail (Hovil and Okello 2011).

It is possible to conceive of an emergent grassroots TJ process in which community members go about the profoundly challenging and often dangerous task of pursuing healing and reconciliation in their community without the support of any formal organisation or superstructure. Indeed, examples can occasionally be found of heroic individuals whose skill and charisma have been sufficient to advance effective TJ initiatives within their communities.[11] But the demands of TJ work—the challenges and risks faced, the range of skills required and the resources necessary (monetary, structural and psychosocial)—usually require a more structured base of operations for successful and durable implementation. Advocating for and marshalling the necessary resources to enable communities to achieve objectives overlooked or neglected by the state is quintessentially the role of NGOs.[12]

---

[10] For a typology of the different roles of civil society in TJ processes, with particular reference to international norms of law and human rights, see Boesenecker and Vinjamuri (2011).

[11] In northern Nigeria, for example, two religious leaders—Pastor James Movel Wuye and Imam Muhammad Nurayan Ashafa, popularly known as "the Pastor and the Imam"—have sought to reconcile Christian and Muslim militias by drawing on their own personal histories and relationship, creating a grassroots organisation.

[12] Other fundamental functions of TJ NGOs—lobbying national governments and commissions, and making representations to supranational bodies—are addressed in other chapters in this book. Civil society does *oppose* certain TJ initiatives in some cases, but here we are concerned with civil society that seeks to support and promote TJ objectives broadly conceived. See, for example, Stan (2013). In Africa, Victor Igreja and Elin Skaar have described Mozambican urban civil society as rejecting a truth commission and remaining on the sidelines of the TJ debate (Igreja and Skaar 2013).

Civil society engagement is predicated on the ability of non-state actors to convene citizens outside of official state processes.[13] In the liberal paradigm that underpins much civil society action, this sub-state civic space is open, at least in principle. There are two distinct senses in which civic space is perceived as open: citizens are legally entitled to meet and organise comparatively unhindered by official repression; and there are relatively few sub-state authorities crowding the field and pre-empting civic action.

In contrast to this paradigm, many African societies feature a dense array of different local authority structures, the legacy of both authoritarian colonial states and their successor nationalist states, as well as the persistence of "traditional" leadership structures (Miller 1968). Crawford Young has remarked that the colonial state "left only furtive, marginal space for a 'civil' society" (1994: 38). Many early post-colonial states, having inherited colonial governance structures, pursued a consolidated "integral state", in which nationalist movements remade the colonial state in their own unified image (Young 1994: 40). A more recent drive to decentralise power for reasons of efficiency and/or democracy has resulted in local councils operating in parallel with chiefs and representatives of the central state (Crawford and Hartmann 2008). Church and other religious structures may form additional authority structures. The divergent sources of legitimacy and power of these different local authority structures frequently result in divergent interests and agendas, particularly with respect to the sensitive work of TJ.

Local authorities fall on a spectrum from formal/official to informal/ad hoc.[14] In many African countries, the ability of traditional leaders to mediate modern and customary values gives them great influence in their communities regardless of their legal standing, which has waxed and waned considerably. Colonialism's practice of "indirect rule" through petty officials such as district commissioners populated much of rural Africa with a powerful hierarchy of sub-state authorities, many of which have persisted with relatively little modification in the postcolonial era. Although many Africans view different local authority structures as integral elements of a unitary system of government, local authorities often have divergent interests as a result of their distinct power bases and sources of authority (Logan 2009; Ray 2003).

African NGOs are typically viewed as interlopers in the communities in which they work. With the exception of locally based CBOs, NGOs can claim to represent the interests of the communities in which they operate only imperfectly at best, for a number of reasons. NGO staff do not live in the communities. Generally, NGO staff enjoy secure salaries, often at a level of income well out of reach of the rural

[13] Alexis de Tocqueville, one of the great observers and theorists of civil society, observed, "If men living in democratic countries had no right and no inclination to associate for political purposes, their independence would be in great jeopardy. … If they never acquired the habit of forming associations in ordinary life, civilization itself would be endangered" (quoted in Young 1994: 35).

[14] Donald Ray (2003) distinguishes between "government" and "governance" to differentiate between formal state mechanisms and the wider circle including unofficial political activities and culture.

community members with whom they work. Community members are also vulnerable to persecution by local officials in ways that NGO staff typically are not. After NGO staff have returned to the city, community members may have food aid withheld, or their use of communal land revoked, or be shunned (or worse) by their communities in retaliation for collaboration or mere participation with NGOs whose interventions are viewed as politically or otherwise controversial. NGOs, meanwhile, must report to their donors using metrics that are often unintelligible to community members, and subject to the variable fashions of the donor community.

As a result, NGO objectives seldom align perfectly with community objectives. TJ NGOs often prize long-term, abstract objectives such as "truth" and "justice" more than community members, whose primary concern may simply be to feed their families and avoid violence. Even where community members endorse TJ objectives, they may prioritise tangible returns: compensation over truth telling, for example.[15] In Zimbabwe, this sentiment—conditioned by more than a decade of disillusionment with the fruits of human rights discourse in the context of an ever-deepening political and economic crisis—is expressed in a phrase often flung at human rights NGO staffers: "You can't eat human rights". Reconciling this divergence in priorities requires skilled and thoughtful engagement and 'sensitisation' by NGOs. Indeed, the use of 'sensitisation' to mean an effort to inform and secure the approval of communities and authorities—"community awareness raising but also … social marketing"—appears to be limited to the work of civil society across Africa (Krech 2003: 125).[16]

These divergences between community and NGO, as well as within communities themselves, mean that this representational problem cannot be overcome, only managed and minimised. Consensus is almost always fictional to some degree, and results from the silencing of segments of the community. Furthermore, the NGO–community power differential should alert practitioners to power differentials within communities, particularly when, as is typical, NGOs partner with community leadership in order to convene TJ interventions. While, as discussed below, custom and "tradition" can be powerful structuring frameworks for TJ processes, customary processes also typically privilege older men of the dominant ethnicity. NGOs promoting "traditional" processes, such as *mato oput* in Uganda, must seek to broaden participation in such processes to honour their commitments to social and gender equity.

At their best, NGOs can assist communities to identify and articulate their priorities, furnish relevant technical expertise for implementation and help to convene

[15] For example, Khulumani Support Group, a membership-based organisation for survivors of human rights violations in South Africa, launched the Asikaqedi campaign in 2014, insisting on the need to address the "unfinished business" of the country's Truth and Reconciliation Commission, chiefly reparations and rehabilitation (Khulumani 2014).

[16] The (mis)use of the term "sensitisation" to refer to almost any sort of NGO intervention in Sierra Leone is described in Shepler (2005). The term assumes a more hegemonic aspect in Catherine Bolten's (2012) description of the reintegration of ex-combatants in Sierra Leone, in which "sensitisation" refers to the uneasy relationship of these ex-combatants to the official discourse of peace and amnesty.

effective and inclusive TJ processes. Where the state is indifferent or resistant to the TJ agenda articulated by communities, civil society can act as champion, pressing the case domestically and internationally. Where the state continues to resist national level processes, civil society can help convene community TJ processes, drawing on global networks of experience, technical expertise and institutional capacity to support the needs of local communities.

"Tradition" and the Legitimation of Transitional Justice

Many community-based TJ initiatives in Africa have drawn on "traditional" processes to structure their interventions, including the *gacaca* courts in Rwanda, Fambul Tok in Sierra Leone, *mato oput* and other community processes in Uganda and the *magamba* spirit rituals in Mozambique (Huyse and Salter 2008). Community TJ processes typically entail significant personal costs for all participants, whether survivors, perpetrators or witnesses, including confronting neighbours and revisiting traumatic experiences with no immediate or guaranteed benefit. TJ processes framed in ways that are more readily understood and appreciated by would-be participants, and that can secure their cooperation, will fare better than unfamiliar processes. In the fragmented arena of postcolonial, postconflict Africa, community-based TJ processes have often turned to the authority of "tradition", usually adapting the form of precolonial accountability processes.

However, the embedded claim of "tradition" to familiarity and relevance cannot be taken for granted. "Traditions" are constantly in the process of being (re-) invented, especially in (post-)conflict scenarios. In Rwanda—the most prominent example of "traditional" TJ processes to date—the revived "tradition" of *gacaca* had a distinctively statist, authoritarian cast; NGOs were notably absent from both formulation and implementation. Yet the discourse of "tradition" and its implication of grassroots endorsement helped to legitimate the *gacaca* process with respect to civil society, and to render the immense challenge of post-genocide accountability in terms that are familiar to most Rwandans (Waldorf 2010; Ingelaere 2009).

"Traditions" do not lie static, stable and legible, ready for deployment, especially in the cultural upheaval caused by transition; they must be revived and retooled to be applied to the complex needs of postconflict communities.[17] It is therefore important to critically examine the motivations of those responsible for reinventing these "traditions" (Arriaza and Roht-Arriaza 2010). "Traditional" processes are also most relevant in communities with a single ethnic and customary identity, particularly where victims and perpetrators adhere to the same canon of "traditional" practice.

"Traditional" processes may present an important opening for NGOs to support TJ in local communities, but NGOs must be mindful of who is privileged and who

[17] Abdullahi Ahmed An-Na'im has discussed the need to foreground "indigenous formations of justice" in transitional justice processes, and the need to reimagine traditional justice processes in order to address contemporary conflicts (2013: 199).

silenced. Those subordinated by "traditional" discourses (and their reinvention) can shift abruptly according to an evolving political calculus. Only through rigorous and careful attention to questions of justice and equity can NGOs fairly and accurately represent the communities with which they work.

"Traditional" processes are typically restorative rather than retributive, seeking to repair social fabric with a view to the future rather than an emphasis on the crimes of the past. This restorative emphasis is a good fit with non-punitive community-based TJ processes, but where community members feel they have little choice but to participate in such processes, it can risk enforcing a public attitude of forgiveness on victims who do not wish to forgive their perpetrators (Ingelaere 2009). Where communities are ethnically diverse, "traditional" processes may perpetuate or exacerbate ethnic and cultural cleavages (Ingelaere 2008). Finally, the successful deployment of "traditional" processes will usually depend to a significant extent on the standing of "traditional" leaders in a given community. Where "traditional" leaders are viewed as partisan, corrupt or irrelevant, it may be difficult to convene "traditional" processes without reproducing community cleavages (Latigo 2008).

The Impact of the Density of Local Authorities on Transitional Justice

Civil society engagement with communities is shaped by the local authorities operating in those communities. "Tradition" specifies one important local leadership structure, but many communities boast a dense array of local authorities, with ambivalent effects on NGO engagement. NGOs that cannot effectively and strategically navigate the local gatekeepers will see their interventions obstructed or opposed, with risks for both NGO staff and community members.

Often, multiple local authority structures function as gatekeepers over communities in their purview, exercising veto power over NGO initiatives. In these circumstances, NGOs and their community partners face a daunting challenge navigating the whims of petty local authorities requiring pain-staking, time-consuming preliminary "sensitisations", consultations and coaxing before actual work can begin. Within the liberal paradigm, the process of "sensitisation" of local authorities, and the signing of a "memorandum of understanding" that may follow, is not strictly necessary. Provided that NGOs are not breaking the law, it can be argued that local authorities have no business vetting their work. Yet in many African communities, established practice gives local authorities veto power over all community-based activity, on the grounds that these authorities are gatekeepers of community integrity, values and culture.[18]

NGOs seeking to engage these communities in TJ work must bridge the divergent philosophies of such authorities to arrive at a viable partnership, assuaging the

[18]The difficulty of these multiple vetoes in the context of traditional leadership in South Africa is discussed in Mashele (2004).

multiplying anxieties, concerns and equivocations of the full array of local authorities.[19] On the other hand, as in the discussion of tradition above, these same local authorities can provide effective partners for NGOs seeking to engage communities in TJ processes. Partnership with local authorities has significant advantages for NGOs, including increased legitimacy and protection from interference by other local authorities. The potential for local leaders to help convene community TJ processes is particularly important given the tendentiousness of these processes. Where community leaders have genuine support and standing in their communities, they can help to reassure community members that the potential gains of a TJ intervention justify the very real hazards of confronting a troubled past. In a sense, local leaders can act as proxies for TJ NGOs, providing a point of entry to the community, assisting with identifying and navigating key community concerns, and lending their endorsement to a divisive, unfamiliar and risky process.

Partnership between NGOs and community leaders also has its risks for both parties, as well as for the success and integrity of the TJ process itself. NGOs risk inadvertently promulgating the local authorities' bias in gender, ethnicity and other areas, and thus silencing segments of the population through, for example, favouritism in the selection of participants in community-based TJ processes. A TJ process convened by an ineffective or illegitimate leader may be abortive, and will struggle to secure the support of other local leaders.

Community leaders also take a considerable risk by supporting TJ initiatives, which typically represent a calculated gamble that confronting past conflicts will yield real rewards, by reducing future conflict or fostering community solidarity, without inflaming dormant conflicts. Should this gamble not pay off—if for example perpetrators derail the process, or take revenge on witnesses or even simply refuse to participate—leaders who convened such a process will at least have their standing undermined, and may stand to lose their positions entirely.

Such partnerships therefore require on both sides a fine, context-sensitive balancing of the potential benefits of TJ intervention and the risk of reigniting, perpetuating or exacerbating conflicts. Only a scrupulous and frank self-assessment of NGO work can appropriately guide this crucial decision, ideally guided by rigorous and candid monitoring and evaluation. Patience and modesty are crucial virtues. All too often, the imperative of growth and the internal logic of NGO missions trump concern for the well-being of community members whose welfare is at the nominal heart of the mission.

[19] Alexander Laban Hinton, following Anna Tsing, describes this interaction between global and local priorities in the context of transitional justice "transitional frictions" (Hinton 2010: 9).

Case Studies

Sierra Leone and Fambul Tok

The Fambul Tok community-based process launched in Sierra Leone in 2007 illustrates many of the points raised in the discussion above, including the complex power dynamics between NGOs and communities and the advantages and potential drawbacks of deploying the discourse of "tradition" and of collaborating with local authorities. Like *gacaca*, Fambul Tok claims to revive a "traditional" form of community mediation and conflict resolution (Fambul Tok 2011). A 2010 report by the Fambul Tok organisation places "consultation" at the heart of its work, describing its engagement with communities in a process of "emergent design" over several months and sometimes longer. Fambul Tok works with a community for 3–4 months to prepare for its signature reconciliation bonfire (Caulker 2010). This preparation involves the selection of a District Executive Committee composed of existing community leaders (Park 2010).

Fambul Tok seeks "total community participation", insisting on the inclusion of leadership from women, youth and other historically marginalised groups (Fambul Tok 2011). However, local chiefs play a pivotal role. One Fambul Tok report devotes a two-page spread to "a portrait in leadership" of Chief Ndolleh, who is quoted as saying, "I realized no one would be brave enough to talk unless we involved the chiefs". The report asserts, "The chiefs represent an older, more traditional leadership system that, in spite of the ways it was misused leading up to and during the war, villagers know and trust" (Fambul Tok 2011: 28). The Fambul Tok organisation therefore collaborates with chiefs to structure and legitimate its TJ intervention.

However, as Fambul Tok acknowledges, the central role of chiefs can be a cause for concern. Before the civil war, chiefs oversaw a system of patrimonial exclusion that contributed to the revolt of young men who formed the Revolutionary United Front (Jackson 2006). Fambul Tok notes that Chief Ndolleh was accused of wartime theft but chose to "reconcile" with his accuser, rather than prosecute her as the law permitted. Further concerns over the involvement of chiefs in community accountability processes are raised by the historical role of chiefs in "a local judicial system regularly handing down fines that were grossly incommensurate with the offences committed", though Fambul Tok does not permit money to change hands as part of its process (Fanthorpe 2006: 30). Finally, the communal work entailed by "peace gardens" may recall the practice of chiefs calling upon youth for unpaid community labour, another deeply resented "traditional" practice (Fanthorpe 2001).

If, as is the case in Sierra Leone, "chiefs remain closely involved in almost every aspect of everyday governance in rural areas", they may be indispensable partners for NGOs seeking to engage communities in TJ processes (Fanthorpe 2006: 28). In such circumstances, as Fambul Tok seems to acknowledge, it may be necessary to transform troubled but persistent local authorities that cannot be effectively circumvented (Graybill 2010). Fambul Tok's strategy has been to balance chiefly authority with other local authorities, so that chiefs are only one component of the Fambul

Tok committees, alongside religious leaders, "Mommy Queen" women leaders and youth. As word of Fambul Tok's work has spread, interest has grown, enabling the organisation's heads to sideline recalcitrant chiefs in favour of other local leaders (Libby Hoffman, telephone interview with author, September 2011).

Northern Uganda and the Acholi Religious Leaders Peace Initiative

The Acholi Religious Leaders Peace Initiative (ARLPI) works in the communities of northern Uganda. ARLPI substantially shaped national TJ processes in Uganda, including pushing through a blanket amnesty for ex-combatants from the rebel Lord's Resistance Army (LRA), having traditional community reconciliation and reintegration mechanisms included in the terms of peace settlements, and widespread deployment of these traditional mechanisms (Baines 2007; "Agreement on Accountability," 2017; Khadiagala 2001).

ARLPI combines elements of a CBO and a more prototypical NGO.[20] Initially called Joint Justice and Peace, it was formed in 1997 by a multi-faith group of northern Ugandan religious leaders. In 1998, ARLPI met with Ugandan President Yoweri Museveni to present its memorandum, "A Call for Peace and an End to Bloodshed in Acholiland", securing its legitimacy with local government officials in northern Uganda (Khadiagala 2001: 4). It subsequently received funding from the United Nations Development Programme and worked with a wide range of government and local authorities. In September 1998, ARLPI was formally requested to lead a campaign of peace education and sensitisation at a meeting of local government authorities. ARLPI's advocacy was crucial to the passage of the Amnesty Act in 2000 (Khadiagala 2001).

As a counterpart to its endorsement of legal amnesty, ARLPI promoted "traditional" Acholi reconciliation processes as a practical means of reintegrating former combatants into their communities (Khadiagala 2001). ARLPI had a close relationship with the Acholi traditional leaders' associations, sharing funding partners and public statements. Tim Allen argues that "the current consensus about customary Acholi conceptions of justice has largely emerged from the aid-funded collaboration between these groups" (Allen 2006: 132). The prominence of these "traditional" processes has been such that they were formally incorporated into the agenda of the Juba peace talks, and have since been formally adopted in the Ugandan Government's draft Transitional Justice Policy and promoted by international donors.[21]

ARLPI and its allies were successful in promulgating "traditional" community-based TJ processes such as the *mato oput* reconciliation ceremony for a number of reasons. "Traditional", community-based processes generally have greater traction

---

[20] Boesenecker and Vinjamuri (2011) identify ARLPI as a "norm reflector" in their typology.

[21] The Republic of Uganda, "National Transitional Justice Policy", prepared by the National Transitional Justice Working Group (3rd draft, May 2013).

in communities in which, as in northern Uganda, the majority of those affected by the conflict, both as victims and as perpetrators, belong to a single ethnic group. The Acholi have a relatively coherent and uniform set of "traditions" that exerts considerable influence on both sides of the conflict.[22] The notion of "indigenous" and local (as opposed to national) solutions may also be attractive in light of the widespread sense that northern Uganda was deliberately marginalised, abandoned and even betrayed by the central Ugandan Government (Latigo 2008).

The conciliatory approach of Acholi "traditional" mechanisms, in comparison to criminal justice, both national and international, suits the terrible complexities of the conflict in northern Uganda, in which there are few "simple" perpetrators. The vast majority of LRA combatants were abducted and conscripted, compelled to fight and commit atrocities under mortal threat, and often abused themselves by senior commanders or combatant "husbands".

ARLPI's engagement with Acholi communities embraces "tradition" as a structuring framework for TJ interventions and cedes authority to local authorities, rather than attempting to exert centralised authority over community TJ processes (Otim 2009). *Mato oput* and similar "traditional" ceremonies depend on the convening authority of traditional leaders. Yet "cultural practices are limited by the context of the conflict, where resources are scarce and social and family structures have been shattered" (Baines 2007: 111). Where communities have been disrupted by conflict, the standing of traditional leadership is typically weakened, particularly with respect to youth, who form the majority of the Acholi population as well as the main victims and perpetrators of violence.

Furthermore, *mato oput* and other Acholi ceremonies have not been used to seek accountability on the part of perpetrators (Baines 2007). The emphasis on forgiveness can enforce an attitude of forgiveness on victims and survivors, with little opportunity for them to share their experiences, or to decline to participate. This enforced narrative of forgiveness may become even stronger as the Ugandan Government puts into operation its draft Transitional Justice Policy, which suggests that it will draft legislation concerning "traditional" processes, raising concerns of a *gacaca*-like statist TJ process claiming grassroots legitimacy.

In light of these concerns, it is the responsibility of civil society to continue to engage with northern Ugandan communities to improve the accessibility, inclusivity, flexibility and relevance of community-based processes. This engagement should proceed from the recognition that, as discussed above, "traditional" TJ processes are "invented". Although historical antecedents are a crucial component of their authority and success, such processes inevitably evolve in response to changing circumstances (Latigo 2008). Civil society must engage with community leaders to ensure that "traditional" processes are adapted so as to serve, as much as possible, the needs of all survivors of the conflict.

[22] *Mato oput* and other Acholi rituals have been criticised for failing to encompass the other ethnic groups affected by the northern Ugandan conflict (Baines 2007).

Zimbabwe and the Peace Building Network

The halting progress of national TJ processes in Zimbabwe, where the government has to date obstructed and pre-empted effective initiatives, has left community-based processes as one of the only viable means for communities to repair the damage to the social fabric caused by 15 years of often violent political crisis.

In the early stages of the post-2000 Zimbabwean crisis, NGOs seized the TJ initiative, setting out an ambitious agenda for a wide-ranging national commission in a 2003 symposium. Since that symposium, however, the government has strategically appropriated and deployed the form and rhetoric of TJ without any substantive action, through state initiatives such as the Organ for National Healing, Reconciliation and Integration and the National Peace and Reconciliation Commission, which at the time of writing had recently appointed commissioners but not had implementing legislation passed or a secretariat appointed more than 3 years into its 10-year tenure. As a result, the most effective TJ engagement to date is by smaller NGOs undertaking bespoke peace building work, including the member organisations of the Peace Building Network of Zimbabwe (PBNZ).[23] These NGOs typically gain access to communities through careful sensitisation and engagement with a dense array of local authorities.

Somewhat surprisingly, very few Zimbabwean NGOs have turned to "tradition" to structure peace building work. One exception is the work of Heal Zimbabwe Trust, which has collaborated with traditional leaders to organise a limited number of "traditional" rituals (Benyera 2014). However, the extent of such "traditional" interventions appears to be quite limited, for a number of reasons. There does not appear to be broad consensus on an appropriate set of "traditional" Shona or Ndebele processes or ceremonies that could form the basis for community-based TJ interventions. It is possible that TJ NGOs reject some traditional practices as "pagan" (Benyera 2015). Furthermore, "traditional" processes are typically led by chiefs or other traditional leaders, yet these leaders are widely viewed as politically partisan. Chiefs, including the Zimbabwe Council of Chiefs, have publicly declared their loyalty to President Robert Mugabe and the ruling party ZANU-PF (Makumbe 2010). Chiefs have also been implicated in political violence, undermining their standing as potential peace builders (NGO Forum 2013). Zimbabwean NGOs are compelled therefore to generate and legitimise their own community processes, typically outside of the structuring framework of "tradition".

Rather than working as a complement to national level TJ initiatives, community TJ processes in Zimbabwe must operate in a political environment that is indifferent and unsupportive at best, and often hostile. Without state support, NGOs can only scale up slowly, approaching and securing entrance to each community one at a time. Piecemeal processes lack the benefit of a broader, national conversation about

---

[23] While peace building and TJ are helpfully conceived of as distinct fields, in the absence of a transition from a violent political regime, the ongoing threat of violence requires that primarily retrospective approach of TJ be complemented by the prospective orientation of peace building work to try and reduce the continuing vulnerability of communities.

past injuries and the way forward. In combination with the density of the local authorities that govern rural Zimbabwean communities, their politicisation and the acute sense of vulnerability produced by the experience of violence and persecution of civic activists, the operations of TJ NGOs in Zimbabwe have been severely constrained, including their engagement with communities (National TJ Working Group 2014).

Nonetheless, community TJ processes have taken place. For better or worse, NGOs can only engage communities with the approval and, ideally, collaboration of the local leadership. In Zimbabwe, the formal authority structure of rural communities includes District Administrators (appointed by the central government), locally elected councillors and three levels of traditional leadership. These authorities each have broad, ill-defined powers and responsibilities that are construed so as to give them a gatekeeping role in almost any civic process. They also come together in a range of assemblies and committees that meet at irregular intervals, charged with considering and approving development plans for their areas. Typically, any one of these authorities is able to effectively veto an NGO's engagement in their community, either by simply withholding their approval, calling on their constituents to boycott the engagement or reporting the NGO to local law enforcement.

How do Zimbabwean NGOs navigate this "triple veto"?[24] Some local authorities, having witnessed the damage done to their community by political conflict, are prepared to take the considerable risk of convening TJ processes in their communities. Local authorities may be persuaded to "de-role" and engage with initiatives as equal members of their communities rather than as leaders or representatives of political interests. Other local authorities may be brought on board by framing TJ initiatives as unthreateningly as possible—as not only non-partisan but also non-confrontational and non-punitive. Some initiatives serving broad TJ objectives such as collective memory and institutional reform may be presented as supporting community development broadly defined by, for example, facilitating collaboration on communal initiatives such as the renovation of a local school, or else pursuing a general idea of "peace".

Given the history of political violence in Zimbabwe, a key feature of local authorities is their perceived political affiliation. Councillors are typically elected on the basis of their membership in a political party, making it difficult for them to convene inclusive processes in politically divided communities. District Administrators, who are appointed by and serve at the pleasure of the Minister for Local Government, are (justifiably) understood to be affiliated with the ruling party, despite their nominal role as senior civil servants.

Traditional leaders have had a tortuous political history in Zimbabwe. The Mugabe government, feeling betrayed by chiefs for their collaboration with the Rhodesian state during the liberation struggle, sidelined traditional leaders until the late 1990s (Makumbe 2010). But in 1997, seeking to bolster its support in rural areas, the government passed the Traditional Leaders Act, granting expanded legal

[24] For analysis and discussion of rural local governance and the resultant "triple veto", see Centre for Conflict Management and Transformation (2014).

powers and responsibilities to traditional leaders, and thereby securing the allegiance of many (Makumbe 2010).

In this context, PBNZ was formed in 2007 to facilitate the sharing of ideas and expertise between member NGOs, and to support community dialogue through a "bottom-up" approach. Although no longer active, at its height PBNZ had 19 members covering a range of methodologies, philosophies and organisational sizes.[25] Typically, PBNZ member organisations worked in a small number of communities, drawing on the reputational benefits of long-standing relationships with local leadership. PBNZ members typically solicited invitations from local authorities, or from CBOs with sufficient standing in the community to prevail upon local authorities, before beginning work in a community. Invitations were generated by sensitisation, outreach and a snowballing reputation, in which an effective intervention in one community may come to the attention of local authorities facing similar challenges in their own communities.[26]

Following an invitation from or successful outreach to community leaders, PBNZ members would collaborate with the leadership to identify a community intervention, drawing on the NGO's methodology and expertise but also suited to the community's circumstances and needs. This process required a series of consultations with other local authorities and community members until the member had sufficient confidence that the intervention would not be opposed by a significant segment of the community, and that there would be sufficiently broad participation. Once the community had been canvassed, the member NGO usually asked the local authority partner to convene the intervention, which was often some variation on the NGO workshop process. By convening the process, the local authority gave it his imprimatur, shielding it to a limited extent from meddling by parallel authorities, and offering some assurances to participants (Iliff 2012).

The selection of participants for community TJ processes is an especially fraught question in the partnership between NGOs and local leadership. Participation in NGO interventions is viewed as a privilege and a limited good. The convening local authority typically retains final approval over the group of participants, both as a prerogative of his role as convener, and because PBNZ members—all of whom are urban based—are unable to freely select community participants themselves.

Unsurprisingly, the resulting selection of participants is often skewed. During the 2009–2013 Government of National Unity one PBNZ member holding its first community healing intervention in a rural community realised on the third day of the intervention that the participants were all members of the local ZANU-PF chapter, including some who had been perpetrators of violence in the previous elections. More recently, another PBNZ member holding a preliminary workshop in a community found that the participants all belonged to a single faction in the ongoing leadership struggle within the ruling party. In both cases, the intervention risked

[25] Much of the following analysis draws on the author's experience working directly with three PBNZ member NGOs, and indirect insight into the work of other members.

[26] For further discussion of grassroots transitional justice work in Zimbabwe, see the discussion of PBNZ member organisation Tree of Life in Iliff (2012).

being viewed by community members as merely a gambit in a political conflict, undermining any TJ objectives. Directly addressing the question of participation may cost NGOs their access to communities, creating a dilemma. In some cases, the NGO may decide that the value of the intervention outweighs the appearance of partiality. In other cases, the NGO may decide to withdraw from the community rather than becoming an instrument of community schisms. The work of Zimbabwean TJ NGOs has thus been profoundly shaped by the density of local authorities in the communities in which they work, for both better and worse.

Consideration of the role of "tradition" and local authorities in civil society's transitional justice engagement with communities in three different scenarios leads to some broad conclusions, outlined below.

Conclusions

This chapter has discussed a few key features of civil society engagement with African communities in transitional justice processes. While recognising that both "civil society" and "community" are extremely broad terms encompassing a wide range of groups, and including some functional overlap, the chapter has focused on the engagement of urban-based NGOs with rural African geographic communities. The chapter has elaborated two broad features that shape many of these engagements between NGOs and communities: the use of "tradition" as a structuring framework for community healing and reconciliation processes, and the role of local authorities that govern many rural African communities.

Both of these features are ambivalent in their effect on NGO–community engagements. "Tradition" can furnish a familiar structure for otherwise novel TJ processes, increasing participation and legitimising the process. However, notions of "tradition" can also be deployed to exclude segments of the community. The dense array of local authorities in many African communities makes them indispensable partners for NGOs supporting community-based TJ processes. Yet, local authorities may hinder NGO–community engagement by interposing multiple gatekeepers who must each be appeased before permitting it to go forward. Failure to secure this consent can jeopardise not only the initiative itself, but may put NGO staff and community members at risk. Nonetheless, the diversity of local authorities, and their intimate understanding of their communities, challenges NGOs to identify effective and insightful partners.

TJ NGOs seeking to engage with communities must consider the particular features of the social, political and cultural landscape in which they operate to consider how this analysis applies, never losing sight of the fact that communities and their constituent members are not merely the substrate for TJ interventions, they are the stakeholders and direct beneficiaries.

This chapter has identified the role of NGOs in promoting gender, ethnic and age equity in the communities with which they engage as a central challenge. While responding to the needs of communities and accommodating their political and customary landscape, NGOs must refuse to become complicit in the privileging and silencing that divides many communities.

For TJ-oriented NGOs seeking to engage with African communities, "traditional" processes may offer an important conceptual framework promoting participation by community members in an otherwise unfamiliar and fraught initiative. NGOs can play an important role in identifying and "reinventing" such traditional processes, as ARLPI has done in northern Uganda. While NGOs cannot typically prescribe a particular "traditional" ceremony without the participation of traditional leaders, they can foster debate around the role of "tradition", particularly where indigenous customs have been overlooked or undervalued as a source of potential TJ norms and processes, as Fambul Tok has done in Sierra Leone. NGOs can seek the reinvention and revitalisation of such processes so as to promote accessibility and inclusivity, including taking account of contemporary values such as gender equality.

To do so, it is essential that NGOs foster broad grassroots engagement, across lines of gender, politics, ethnicity and other cleavages, which are particularly acute during and after conflict. Community cleavages are not always evident, even to experienced field staff. Before embarking on an intervention, NGOs must meet and consult not only with official community leaders but also with representatives of women, youth and minorities. The demands of such engagement may hinder the rapid rollout of NGO interventions, as in the case of the work of PBNZ, but supports long-term outcomes.

The density and strength of local authorities make them necessary community partners for NGOs, who must develop a nuanced understanding of their range, influence and motivations. In Zimbabwe, community micro-dynamics often trump the meta-narratives familiar from national headlines, and the political leanings of local authorities cannot be taken for granted. NGOs must remain alert to the potential distortions generated by local authority partners, such as the role of chiefs in the Fambul Tok process, and seek to address these wherever possible. Doing so requires considerable time investment, as demonstrated by the work of all the NGOs considered in this chapter. The rollout of community-based TJ processes does not proceed in a straight line, but piecemeal, in fits and starts as opportunities open and close. It is the responsibility of TJ NGOs to help communities best take advantage of the opportunities that arise.

References

Agreement on Accountability and Reconciliation between the Government of the Republic of Uganda and the Lord's Resistance Army/Movement. (2017). UN Security Council S/2007/435. Retrieved from https://peacemaker.un.org/sites/peacemaker.un.org/files/UG_070629_AgreementonAccountabilityReconcilition.pdf.

Allen, T. (2006). *Trial justice: The International Criminal Court and the Lord's Resistance Army.* London: Zed Books.

Androff, D. K., Jr. (2012). Can civil society reclaim truth? Results from a community-based truth and reconciliation commission. *International Journal of Transitional Justice, 6*(2), 296–317.

An-Na'im, A. A. (2013). Editorial note: From the neocolonial 'transitional' to indigenous formations of justice. *International Journal of Transitional Justice, 7*(2), 197–204.
Annan, K. (2004). *The rule of law and transitional justice in conflict and post-conflict societies*. United Nations, Report of the Secretary-General to the Security Council.
Arriaza, L., & Roht-Arriaza, N. (2008). Social reconstruction as a local process. *International Journal of Transitional Justice, 2*(2), 152–172.
Arriaza, L., & Roht-Arriaza, N. (2010). Weaving a braid of histories: Local post-armed conflict initiatives in Guatemala. In R. Shaw, L. Waldorf, & P. Hazan (Eds.), *Localizing transitional justice*. Stanford, CA: Stanford University Press.
Baines, E. (2007). The haunting of Alice: Local approaches to justice and reconciliation in Northern Uganda. *International Journal of Transitional Justice, 1*(1), 91–114.
Benyera, E. (2014). Exploring Zimbabwe's traditional transitional justice mechanisms. *Journal of Social Sciences, 41*(3), 335–344.
Benyera, E. (2015). Presenting ngozi as an important consideration in pursuing transitional justice for victims: The case of Moses Chokuda. *Gender and Behavior, 13*(2), 6760–6773.
Boesenecker, A. P., & Vinjamuri, L. (2011). Lost in translation? Civil society, faith-based organizations and the negotiation of international norms. *International Journal of Transitional Justice, 5*(3), 345–365.
Bolten, C. (2012). 'We have been sensitized': Ex-combatants, marginalization, and youth in post-war Sierra Leone. *American Anthropologist, 114*(3), 496–508.
Caulker, J. (2010). *Sierra Leone: A long and difficult journey to reconciliation—The role of civil society*. Paper presented at African Transitional Justice Research Network workshop, 'Advocating Justice: Civil Society and Transitional Justice in Africa,' Johannesburg, South Africa, August 30–31.
Centre for Conflict Management and Transformation. (2014). *Roles and responsibilities in rural local governance in Zimbabwe*.
Crawford, G., & Hartmann, C. (2008). *Decentralisation in Africa: A pathway out of poverty and conflict?* Amsterdam: Amsterdam University Press.
De Greiff, P. (2010). *Transitional justice, security, and development: Security and justice thematic paper* World Development Report 2011.
Fanthorpe, R. (2001). Neither citizen nor subject? "Lumpen" agency and the legacy of native administration in Sierra Leone. *African Affairs, 100*(400), 363–386.
Fanthorpe, R. (2006). On the limits of liberal peace: Chiefs and democratic decentralization in post-war Sierra Leone. *African Affairs, 105*(418), 27–49.
Findlay, M. (2009). Activating a victim constituency in international criminal justice. *International Journal of Transitional Justice, 3*(2), 183–206.
Foley, M. W., & Edwards, B. (1996). The paradox of civil society. *Journal of Democracy, 7*, 38–52.
Graybill, L. S. (2010). Traditional practices and reconciliation in Sierra Leone: The effectiveness of Fambul Tok. *Conflict Trends, 3*, 44–50.
Hinton, A. L. (2010). Introduction: Toward an anthropology of transitional justice. In A. L. Hinton (Ed.), *Transitional justice: Global mechanisms and local realities after genocide and mass violence*. New Brunswick, NJ: Rutgers University Press.
Hovil, L., & Okello, M. C. (2011). Editorial note. *International Journal of Transitional Justice, 6*, 333–344.
Huyse, L., & Salter, M. (2008). *Traditional justice and reconciliation after violent conflict: Learning from African experiences*. Stockholm: International IDEA.
Igreja, V., & Skaar, E. (2013). A conflict does not rot: State and civil society responses to civil war offences in Mozambique. *Nordic Journal of Human Rights, 31*(2), 149–175.
Iliff, A. (2012). Root and branch: Discourses of 'tradition' in grassroots transitional justice. *International Journal of Transitional Justice, 6*(2), 253–273.
Ingelaere, B. (2008). The gacaca courts in Rwanda. In L. Huyse & M. Salter (Eds.), *Traditional justice and reconciliation after violent conflict: Learning from African experiences* (pp. 23–58). Stockholm: International IDEA.
Ingelaere, B. (2009). 'Does the truth pass across the fire without burning?' Locating the short circuit in Rwanda's gacaca courts. *Journal of Modern African Studies, 47*(4), 507–528.

Jackson, P. (2006). Reshuffling an old deck of cards? The politics of local government reform in Sierra Leone. *African Affairs, 106*(422), 95–111.

Khuluman Support Group. (2014). *Khulumani launches the ASIKAQEDI CAMPAIGN, 29 October 2014*. Retrieved from http://www.khulumani.net/reparations/item/1029-khulumani-launches-the-asikaqedi-campaign-29-october-2014.html.

Khadiagala, G. M. (2001). The role of the Acholi Religious Leaders Peace Initiative (ARLPI) in peace building in Northern Uganda. Appendix from the report. *The Effectiveness of Civil Society Initiatives in Controlling Violent Conflicts and Building Peace A Study of Three Approaches in the Greater Horn of Africa.*

Krech, R. (2003). *The reintegration of former child combatants: A case study of NGO programming in Sierra Leone.* M.A. thesis, University of Toronto.

Latigo, J. O. (2008). Northern Uganda: Tradition-based practices in the Acholi region. In L. Huyse & M. Salter (Eds.), *Traditional justice and reconciliation after violent conflict: Learning from African experiences*. Stockholm: International IDEA.

Logan, C. (2009). Selected chiefs, elected councillors and hybrid democrats: Popular perspectives on the co-existence of democracy and traditional authority. *Journal of Modern African Studies, 47*(1), 101–128.

Makumbe, J. (2010). Local authorities and traditional leadership. In J. de Visser, N. Steytler, & N. Machingauta (Eds.), *Local government reform in Zimbabwe: A policy dialogue*. Bellville: University of the Western Cape Community Law Centre.

Mashele, P. (2004). Traditional leadership in South Africa's new democracy. *Review of African Political Economy, 31*(100), 349–354.

Miller, N. N. (1968). The political survival of traditional leadership. *Journal of Modern African Studies, 6*(2), 183–201.

Naftali, P. (2010). The subtext of new human rights claims: A socio-legal journey into the 'right to truth'. In *Diverse engagement: Drawing in the margins.* Cambridge: University of Cambridge Graduate Development Program.

National Transitional Justice Working Group. (2014). *Introducing the National Transitional Justice Working Group in Zimbabwe*. Retrieved from http://www.hrforumzim.org/wp-content/uploads/2014/09/National-Transitional-Justice-Working-Group-in-Zimbabwe1.pdf.

Otim, P. W. (2009, March). *The role of the Acholi Religious Leaders Peace Initiative in Uganda's peacebuilding*. Retrieved from http://www.beyondintractability.org/casestudy/otim-role.

Park, A. S. J. (2010). Community-based restorative transitional justice in Sierra Leone. *Contemporary Justice Review, 13*(1), 95–119.

Ray, D. I. (2003). Rural local governance and traditional leadership in Africa and the Afro-Caribbean: Policy and research implications from Africa to the Americas and Australasia. In D. I. Ray & P. S. Reddy (Eds.), *Grassroots governance: Chiefs in Africa and the Afro-Caribbean.* Calgary: University of Calgary Press.

Republic of Uganda. (2013). *National Transitional Justice Policy.* Prepared by the National Transitional Justice Working Group (3rd Draft, May).

Seligman, A. (1992). *The idea of civil society.* New York: Simon and Schuster.

Shaw, R., Waldorf, L., & Hazan, P. (Eds.). (2010). *Localizing transitional justice: Justice interventions and local priorities after mass violence*. Stanford, CA: Stanford University Press.

Shepler, S. (2005). The rites of the child: Global discourses of youth and reintegrating child soldiers in Sierra Leone. *Journal of Human Rights, 4*, 197–211.

Stan, L. (2013). Civil society and post-community transitional justice in Romania. In O. Simić & Z. Volčič (Eds.), *Transitional justice and civil society in the Balkans*. New York: Springer.

Tok, F. (2011). *Fambul Tok.* New York: Umbrage.

Waldorf, L. (2010). Like Jews waiting for Jesus: Posthumous justice in post-genocide Rwanda. In R. Shaw, L. Waldorf, & P. Hazan (Eds.), *Localizing transitional justice*. Stanford, CA: Stanford University Press.

Young, C. (1994). In search of civil society. In J. W. Harbeson, D. Rothchild, & N. Chazan (Eds.), *Civil society and the state in Africa.* Boulder, CO: Lynne Rienner Publisher.

Chapter 9
Navigating the Storm: Civil Society and Ambiguous Transitions in Egypt, Libya and Tunisia

Noha Aboueldahab

Introduction

Since the mass anti-government uprisings in the Arab Spring countries in 2010 and 2011, transitional justice has emerged as a key component driving the transition processes. In particular, prosecutions of former political leaders, including former ministers, took centre stage in Egypt, Libya and Tunisia. Far from the paradigmatic shift from authoritarian rule to liberal democratic rule, the transitions that emerged in these three countries were ambiguous and resulted in a military-backed authoritarian government in Egypt, the return of influential *anciens nouveaux* politicians in Tunisia, and violence, insecurity and weak governance in Libya. These varied transitional contexts pose complex challenges for transitional justice actors, particularly for civil society. In spite of the contrasting contexts, some commonalities in civil society strategy can be observed. These commonalities and variations provide a useful basis for making sense of the so-called universal versus the particular transitional justice approaches adopted by civil society.

The North African cases present an important contribution to scholarly discussions regarding the "proliferation" of transitional justice actors (Obel Hansen 2014). Egypt, Libya and Tunisia demonstrate that various actors and factors drive transitional justice processes and that civil society was and continues to be a crucial driving force. Given the restrictive environment that has dominated both the pre- and post-transition period in all three, civil society has had to devise imaginative strategies to advance criminal accountability.

I argue that civil society pursued three primary strategies designed to grapple with turbulent transitions that have morphed into renewed forms of repression. First, non-governmental organisations (NGOs) that were established both before

N. Aboueldahab (✉)
Brookings Doha Center, Doha, Qatar
e-mail: noha.dahab@gmail.com

J. Brankovic, H. van der Merwe (eds.), *Advocating Transitional Justice in Africa*, Springer Series in Transitional Justice,
https://doi.org/10.1007/978-3-319-70417-3_9

and after the uprisings have persistently documented human rights abuses. Second, individual lawyers and lawyers working on behalf of civil society organisations representing victims have been persistent in their litigation attempts, despite politicised and weak judiciaries. Third, the emphasis on economic crimes and corruption in the investigations and trials has been driven in part by civil society strategies that aimed to generate some form of accountability, even while many other human rights violations would remain unaccounted for.

The findings in this chapter are drawn from interviews conducted between 2012 and 2013 with human rights lawyers, activists, civil society organisations and international organisations in Egypt, Libya and Tunisia.[1] I use the term "civil society" to encompass a broad range of non-state actors that advocate for a common cause, including NGOs and individual lawyers and activists. The common cause relevant to this discussion is criminal accountability for crimes committed by high-level government officials, including heads of state and ministers.

The chapter proceeds as follows. First, I will briefly discuss the case selection, the importance of examining the role of civil society and the merits of examining pre- and post-transition strategies. I will discuss the centrality of prosecutions in the Arab Spring, thereby justifying the focus of this chapter on prosecutions as opposed to other transitional justice mechanisms. I will then explain the role of civil society in driving and shaping prosecutions in pre- and post-transition Egypt, Libya and Tunisia through a discussion of their documentation and litigation strategies, as well as their focus on corruption and socio-economic crimes. Finally, I will reflect on the implications of the findings for civil society and transitional justice scholarship and practice.

Varied Transitions and the Importance of Civil Society

North Africa is important for the development of transitional justice research and practice not least because of the varied types of transitions that have emerged since 2011 and the divergent transitional justice paths pursued. The cases around which the transitional justice field was formed are largely drawn from Eastern Europe and Latin America, which shaped the "normative assumptions" of the field and represented transitions that resemble "Western liberal market democracy" (Sharp 2013: 149). This contrasts with the transitions that unfolded in Egypt, Libya and Tunisia. In Egypt, the transition has been marked by a shift to a renewed form of authoritarianism, under the leadership of President Abdel Fattah El Sisi and his military-backed government. Libya constitutes a transition that continues to reel from ongoing violence involving militias and non-state-armed groups, and from political tensions between two competing governments. While Tunisia has often been described as the most successful transition to democratic rule in the region, deep

[1] This chapter does not address the post-transition developments that have occurred in Egypt since 2013, namely, the military coup that ousted President Mohamed Morsi and its aftermath. While the role of transitional justice in these developments is important, it is beyond the scope of this chapter. Eleven interviews were conducted in Egypt, 7 in Libya and 14 in Tunisia.

state problems remain and they directly impact on decisions regarding prosecution in particular and transitional justice more generally. Its current president, for example, held several ministerial positions both under former President Habib Bourguiba and under the ousted Ben Ali regime.

Egypt, Libya and Tunisia share crucial attributes. In all three countries, massive uprisings within the same time period took place, the leaders were toppled and a drastic political transition ensued. Almost simultaneously, a flurry of activity surrounding the prosecution of political leaders unfolded. The three cases, however, are also sufficiently different so as to enable a meaningful comparative study. Egypt and Tunisia prosecuted their political leaders and issued verdicts. Both continue to pursue prosecutions against former regime leaders. However, Egypt experienced a strong military presence and influence in its transitional process, which sets it apart from the civilian government elected in Tunisia. Libya's transition emerged from a violent civil war between Gaddafi loyalists and anti-Gaddafi militias and with the aid of the North Atlantic Treaty Organisation (NATO) military intervention to oust Muammar Gaddafi and his regime. Libya has also been engrossed in a jurisdictional tug of war with the International Criminal Court (ICC), which issued arrest warrants targeting the former leader, his son and the former intelligence chief. These are important differences between the case studies that have impacted on both transitional politics and transitional justice, particularly decisions regarding prosecutions.

While a significant number of new civil society organisations and actors emerged immediately following the uprisings in Egypt, Libya and Tunisia, many that had been active for decades persisted and even intensified their work post-transition. These long-standing individuals, organisations and their networks constitute one of the most resilient actors that suffered repression in the pre-transition period and, in many cases, continue to face significant challenges in the post-transition period. A close look at their activism and strategies with regard to criminal accountability in the pre-transition period is thus important as it provides insight into how civil society has adapted its strategies from one authoritarian context to another (Egypt), from an authoritarian context to one plagued with violence and insecurity (Libya) and from an authoritarian context to one where the *anciens nouveaux* have been resistant to a comprehensive transitional justice process (Tunisia). The term *anciens nouveaux* refers to the re-emergence of certain key figures from the previous regime that have morphed into the post-transition regime (Yousfi et al. 2014). This chapter, then, attaches great importance to the study of how civil society worked towards criminal accountability over time, thus allowing for some critical comparisons between the pre- and post-transition period.

The Centrality of Prosecutions in the Arab Spring

Immediately following the ouster of Egyptian President Hosni Mubarak, Tunisian President Zine El Abidine Ben Ali and Libyan leader Muammar Gaddafi, prosecutions became central to the local transitional justice discourses and practices. In Egypt, mass street protests calling for a trial of Mubarak took place in the 2 months following his ouster, resulting in his arrest in April 2011 followed by the start of his trial in August 2011. Mubarak's two sons, Gamal and Alaa, were also arrested and put on trial, along with former Interior Minister Habib El Adly.[2] All faced multiple charges of corruption and human rights violations. The human rights charges were limited to the time period of the 18-day uprising in January and February 2011—specifically, the killing of protesters—whereas the corruption charges included the pre-uprising period. This constituted the highest level prosecution in Egypt. Several other high-level figures from the former Egyptian regime were also put on trial, and many still face prosecution more than 5 years later (Ahmed 2015).[3]

The Libyan uprising was in part triggered by the arrest of a prominent lawyer, Fathi Terbil, whose efforts were aimed at achieving justice for the victims of the Abu Salim prison massacre. Thousands of political opposition activists were imprisoned at Abu Salim and more than a thousand were executed following orders by Gaddafi and his regime in 1996 (Human Rights Watch 2012). Terbil's arrest on February 15, 2011, sparked protests in Libya's eastern town of Benghazi, which grew into a full-fledged massive uprising on February 17, 2011. In the midst of the subsequent NATO military intervention and a civil war between Gaddafi loyalists and anti-Gaddafi revolutionaries, the issue of justice and criminal accountability did not wane. Following arrest warrants issued by the ICC, Libya decided to prosecute its leaders domestically and refused to hand over suspects to The Hague.[4] It also won an admissibility appeal for former Intelligence Chief Abdallah El Senussi, resulting in the annulment of his ICC arrest warrant in July 2014. The ICC arrest warrants and the success of Libya's admissibility appeal for El Senussi were major developments in the transitional justice process in the country, not least because they revealed from a very early stage the tensions between domestic and international criminal accountability.

The ICC rejected Libya's admissibility challenge for Gaddafi's son, Saif al-Islam. Nonetheless, he, along with 36 other defendants, were? tried domestically in Libya on charges that include war crimes, the killing of protesters and corruption mainly related to embezzlement of state funds. Given that he was held by Zintan militias at the time, the trial of Saif al-Islam Gaddafi was conducted in absentia by a Tripoli court. Other defendants include former Prime Minister al-Baghdadi Ali al-Mahmoudi, former Foreign Minister Abdul Ati al-Obeidi and former Intelligence Chief Bouzid Dorda.

The trial of the 37 former Gaddafi regime members started in April 2014 and verdicts were issued in July 2015. Saif al-Islam Gaddafi, El Senussi, al-Mahmoudi and six other defendants were sentenced to death by firing squad for committing

[2] Gamal Mubarak, who was deputy secretary general of Mubarak's National Democratic Party, was active in Egyptian politics and was thought by many to be pushing his way to the presidency, following in the footsteps of his father.

[3] Details of some of the trials and charges are outlined in Ahmed (2015).

[4] The ICC arrest warrants were issued for Muammar Gaddafi, Saif al-Islam Gaddafi and Abdullah El Senussi in June 2011. Following the death of Muammar Gaddafi on October 20, 2011, the ICC terminated its case against him.

war crimes during the 2011 conflict (Jawad 2015). Seven others were each given a 12-year jail sentence, and four defendants were acquitted. The Supreme Court is currently reviewing the appeal for Gaddafi and the other former government officials' cases.

Tunisia saw numerous prosecutions immediately following the ouster of Ben Ali. Ben Ali was president of Tunisia for 23 years. He fled to Saudi Arabia, where he has lived in exile since January 2011. Calls for his extradition to Tunisia have been ignored. As a result, his trials were all conducted in absentia by a military court in Tunisia. The charges in the prosecutions of 22 former political leaders, including former Interior Minister Abdallah Qallel, are a mélange of corruption, economic crimes and human rights violations, with the majority of the latter pertaining to crimes committed during the uprising. Some verdicts have been issued, most of which have been light sentences and acquittals, and about 40 corruption cases filed since March 2011 are still being investigated. In addition, 420 businessmen were banned from travelling outside Tunisia pending investigation into their alleged involvement in corruption.

Other high-level Tunisian Government officials who were tried and issued with prison sentences include former Minister of Interior Rafiq Haj Kacem, former Director General of National Security Adel Tiouiri, former Director of the Anti-Riot Police Jalel Boudrigua, former Director General of Public Security Lotfi Ben Zouaoui and the powerful former Director of the Presidential Guard Ali Seriati. However, almost 20 Ben Ali-era senior government officials were set free, following decisions by appeals courts to significantly reduce their sentences to time served (Gall 2014). Human Rights Watch (2015) estimates that a total of 53 former government officials, including police and security officers, were tried in military tribunals in Tunisia in late 2011.

While the examples above represent a snapshot of the prosecutions in each country, there is no question that prosecutions of former high-level government officials were—and continue to be—central to the transitional justice processes in Egypt, Libya and Tunisia. Other transitional justice mechanisms have also begun to take shape. The Truth and Dignity Commission in Tunisia was established in 2014 for the purposes of public truth telling, national healing, compensation for victims and gathering of evidence for prosecutions. Certain financial reconciliation efforts in Egypt and Tunisia have also moved forward. However, those efforts have been led by government officials aiming to limit the extent of prosecutions. Tunisia, for example, passed a controversial financial and economic reconciliation law that shields corrupt public officials and business people linked to the Ben Ali regime from prosecutions once they return their ill-gotten gains. The law provoked mass street protests led by veteran civil society figures. It also led to the formation of the Manich Msemah (I will not forgive) campaign, whose principal message through social media, political lobbying and street protests was to say no to prosecutions. Egypt began to pursue a similar practice of economic reconciliation that has already benefited the Mubaraks, some former ministers and business tycoons, such as Hussein Salem, following their return of a large percentage of their illicit gains.

National reconciliation efforts aimed more at truth telling and national healing are still far from becoming reality. While other transitional justice mechanisms have not been ruled out, criminal accountability in the form of trials continues to occupy an important space in the transitional justice psyche of Egyptian, Libyan and Tunisian civil society. Of the three cases examined here, Tunisia is the only one that has passed a transitional justice law, in December 2013, and it specifically includes prosecutions. The reconciliation law, then, effectively creates a "two-tier transitional justice process," which contradicts the transitional justice law through the elimination of prosecutions (Yerkes & Muasher 2017).

The powerful symbolism of prosecutions and the retributive justice it foregrounds thus hold a central place in the Egyptian, Libyan and Tunisian transitions. Judy Barsalou and Barry Knight's survey of Egyptian justice expectations in post-Mubarak Egypt highlights strong popular support for trials, all the while recognising that a politicised and weak judiciary and police force have prevented the trials from satisfying the "public's desire for justice" (Barsalou and Knight 2013). In Tunisia, survey results by al-Kawakibi Foundation and No Peace Without Justice reflect strong popular support for both institutional reform and accountability (Al Kawakibi 2014). In Libya, support for prosecutions was also evident among high-level government authorities, such as Justice Minister Salah al-Marghani, who stated that it was the ministry's priority at the time to ensure prosecutions and accountability to address serious human rights violations. While it is never the case that such justice expectations reflect a national consensus on prosecutions, the above-mentioned examples illustrate that despite differences in opinion, strong popular support for prosecutions was still evident in the 5 years following the ouster of Mubarak, Gaddafi and Ben Ali.

Resilient Actors and New Forces: Civil Society as Drivers and Shapers of Criminal Accountability

The interview responses across the three case studies indicate that civil society actors who supported the anti-government uprisings advocated for fair and effective prosecutions of former senior political figures. However, given the repressive environment within which civil society actors had to work in the pre-transition period, they prioritized the documentation of human rights violations by each regime and its associated state agencies. The objective was to raise awareness and pressure governments to change their human rights practices. Second, litigation, instigated primarily by individual lawyers, figured heavily in the pre- and post-transition period. Third, an emphasis on corruption and its socioeconomic impact was a major feature of civil society's accountability agenda, particularly in Egypt and Tunisia. This section presents findings from research and interviews conducted in Egypt, Libya and Tunisia on the strategies used by civil society actors to advance criminal accountability for former high-level government officials.

Egypt

Documentation

Documentation of human rights violations was repeatedly cited as central to the work of civil society organisations in Egypt. It was used to raise awareness and put pressure on the government to change its human rights practices. Gamal Eid and Mohamed El-Shewy explained that despite working with a politicised judiciary, the aim of civil society documentation was to have enough evidence so that "one day", when an independent judiciary is in place, "we will be able to prosecute" (G. Eid, personal interview, December 8, 2013; M. El Shewy, telephone interview, November 24, 2013). Eid cited the lack of an independent judiciary as one of the strong motivators for documentation (G. Eid, personal interview, December 8, 2013). El-Shewy described documentation as one of the powerful tools of a civil society struggling with authoritarian rule. "Since there has been no real transition", he explained, "our approach is to go from the bottom up. Through victims' families, we are archiving and documenting things ourselves to try and have a strong series of cases so that we can then—when there is political will—really have a serious transitional justice programme" (M. El-Shewy, telephone interview, November 24, 2013). Ahmed Abdallah of the 6 April movement said that while civil society documentation does not count as evidence in a court of law, it has been a powerful means to mobilise and pressure the government to respond to grievances (A. Abdallah, personal interview, December 4, 2013).[5]

Most civil society documentation in Egypt addressed torture, police abuses and other civil and political rights violations. Some organisations, such as the Egyptian Center for Economic and Social Rights (ECESR), campaigned against both civil and political rights abuses and socioeconomic violations. Following the 2011 uprising, an increasing number of NGOs broadened their campaigning strategy, as El-Shewy explained:

> There was never really a focus on how to document abuses of economic and social justice violations. We at [the Egyptian Initiative for Personal Rights] began that much more strongly after the revolution because we realised [that both sets of rights] were linked—they are not mutually exclusive. They sustained one another. There was a realisation that if you simply went around prosecuting civil and political rights abuses then you wouldn't be getting into the structural reasons for why the revolution happened—and how Mubarak and his aides were able to maintain their power through their system of abuse. (M. El Shewy, telephone interview, November 24, 2013)

This link between civil and political rights and socioeconomic rights characterises the transitional justice discourse in Egypt. Unlike its predecessors in other parts of the world, the transitional justice that lawyers and activists sought in Egypt engages with these two sets of rights as closely intertwined. One of the reasons for

[5]The 6 April movement, an influential workers' rights and human rights mobilising force, was formed in 2008. Khaled Ali also mentioned that the courts and the prosecution do not accept civil society documentation as evidence (personal interview, December 9, 2013).

the emphasis on socioeconomic justice in the trials is the particular role played by civil society in Egypt.

Litigation

Civil society efforts, however, did not stop at documentation and public shaming. Litigation activism, whereby activists persistently in approached courts to file cases, was common in Mubarak's Egypt, and not just for corruption. Tamir Moustafa provides an insightful explanation of the complex role of courts in authoritarian Egypt and highlights their function both as "active sites of resistance" and as institutions of repression (Moustafa 2014). Specifically, he argues that "courts enabled activists to challenge state policy without having to initiate a broad social movement" (Moustafa 2014: 282). This proved crucial in a context where civil society had little room to form strong and effective social movements without violent repercussions. The ability of individual lawyers and organisations to access the courts for such litigation, then, became central to civil society's success—however partial—in advancing criminal accountability, or at least some awareness about it and its challenges. Moustafa further outlines how civil society's litigation strategy constituted a form of protest, despite its inability to bring about drastic change in state policy. "The purpose of litigation was", he explains, "not to win, but rather to expose the chasm between the regime's rule-of-law rhetoric and the realities on the ground" (Moustafa 2014: 288). Such legal mobilisation was used not only for cases pertaining to political repression and violence, but also for corruption crimes prior to the 2011 transition. The high-level corruption cases of *Madinaty* and *Palm Hills* in 2010, for example, were filed against the president, prime minister and minister of investment (K. Ali, personal interview, December 9, 2013).[6]

Corruption and Socioeconomic Accountability

Many high-level figures from the former Egyptian regime were tried for corruption (Ahmed 2015). The corruption cases included charges related to the embezzlement of state funds by politicians, in particular Mubarak and his family, illegal receipt of expensive gifts from state-owned media institutions, squandering of public funds, insider stock trading and violation of laws related to monopolistic practices, and graft and money laundering. The illegal sale of land also figured prominently in the charges. The *Madinaty* case is an example of how the corrupt execution of contracts related to the sale of land and companies reinforces socioeconomic inequality in Egypt. Land is sold below market value in deals between housing ministers and real estate tycoons and developers. Madinaty, a vast area east of Cairo, was sold to developer and real estate tycoon Hisham Talaat Mustafa without a public auction and significantly below market value, both of which are in violation of Egyptian

[6] For more on the Madinaty and Palm Hills cases, see Kassem and Fattah (2011).

law. Built to accommodate tens of thousands of luxury villas and a $3 billion commercial complex, the Madinaty contract also exempted Mustafa from construction taxes and fees. This blatant government corruption and waste in the context of millions of Cairenes without access to proper housing and public services intensified the visibility of corruption and socioeconomic inequality in Egypt.

Workers' movements and labour unions played a significant role before, during and after the uprisings. The general strike led by textile workers in the town of Mahalla in 2008, for instance, led to the formation of the 6 April movement, which became an influential workers' rights and human rights mobilising force. This movement, along with other similar independent workers' rights movements, led mass protests during and after the Egyptian uprising. Before the general strike in Egypt, the 6 April movement and a number of opposition groups and parties signed a statement that clearly lays out the socioeconomic and other human rights demands of the Egyptian opposition and workers' movements in 2008—a year that served as a key turning point in the lead-up to the uprising of 2011. What is striking about this statement is that the demands for social justice and for civil and political rights are on par with each other (Radsch 2008). There is no prioritisation of one set of rights over the other—the 6 April movement and its supporters clearly viewed social and economic rights as inseparable from civil and political rights.

Even before the formation of the 6 April movement in 2008, workers' protests and strikes constituted one of the strongest opposition forces in Egypt. Such labour mobilisation eventually led to the formation of the Egyptian Federation of Independent Trade Unions (EFITU) soon after the uprising began. EFITU was established in response to the overtly state-controlled Egyptian Trade Union Federation (ETUF), which was created in 1957 and whose leaders have always been appointed by the government rather than elected by workers. As Joel Beinin notes, the emergence of the independent labour movement—or "militant labour dissidence"—in Egypt saw an escalation of protests in the late 1990s as a result of ETUF's failure to adequately represent workers. Beinin argues, "Workers were by far the largest component of the burgeoning culture of protest in the 2000s that undermined the legitimacy of the Mubarak regime" (Beinin 2012: 1).

Labour mobilisation through street protests and strikes intensified in post-uprising Egypt, with calls for an increase in the minimum wage, the replacement of temporary contracts with permanent ones and the right to strike, among other demands. While some prominent figures from the independent labour movement accepted ministerial positions and parliamentary seats in the interim transitional governments and during Mohamed Morsi's short tenure as president, thousands of workers continued to be jailed for staging demonstrations, sit-ins and strikes. Beinin argues that the repression of these mostly local strikes has worsened in post-transition Egypt (Beinin 2013). Moreover, tensions between ETUF and EFITU persist and have led to a court case in which ETUF is charging EFITU with violating Trade Union Law No. 35 of 1976, which prohibits the establishment of independent labour unions (Mada Masr 2016).

The labour movement in Egypt did not operate alone. The Kifaya movement, for example, was persistent in its calls for transparent governance and democracy.

Kifaya, a coalition consisting of various opposition activists, was established in the run-up to the parliamentary and presidential elections in 2005. It called for free elections, civil and political rights and an end to authoritarian rule (Onodera 2009). These calls occurred mainly in the form of street protests and media campaigns. Those calling for civil and political rights, such as the right to freedom of expression, the right to assemble, and freedom from torture and arbitrary detention, were severely repressed through massive crackdowns led by the police and other state security forces, resulting in a significantly weakened human rights movement in Egypt. A heavily politicised judiciary, part of which was allied with the Mubarak regime, further worsened prospects of criminal accountability for human rights.

The relative success, then, of the Egyptian independent labour movement in bringing to the fore demands for social justice and an end to corruption shaped the content of the prosecutions. This is despite continued crackdowns on workers participating in sit-ins, strikes and demonstrations. The build-up of their influence over the years, however, played a big role in the consequent emphasis on corruption charges in the prosecutions. This largely occurred through legal complaints filed by lawyers working in organisations such as the ECESR and the Hisham Mubarak Law Center. Such organisations were also active in conducting research and disseminating data online and through campaigns. The ascension of certain independent labour movement figures to parliamentary and ministerial posts, however temporary, also ensured that certain demands, such as the minimum wage and a new trade union law, were placed on the political agenda. On the other hand, the harsh crackdowns on civil and political rights activists left a seriously weakened human rights lobby. As a result, the human rights movement was, with certain important exceptions, largely unsuccessful in ensuring criminal accountability for human rights abuses committed before, during and after the uprisings.

Taking Stock: Egyptian Civil Society and Transitional Justice Strategies

There are some notable developments in civil society strategies in pre- and post-transition Egypt. Documentation of human rights violations and of corrupt practices, particularly with regard to the embezzlement of state funds and corrupt real estate contracts, has continued. However, the use of social media to make this documentation accessible has increased significantly since the 2011 uprising. Moreover, the content of documentation has broadened to underline the links between civil and political rights violations and socioeconomic rights.[7] Second, litigation has been persistent despite the continued politicisation of the judiciary. Litigation activists have, however, become bolder in targeting an increasing number of high-level officials. They have also enhanced their methods of disseminating updates about their litigation attempts and trials, mainly through civil society organisations' websites and through local and regional media. Since the 2011 uprising, the increase in the

[7] The Egyptian Initiative for Personal Rights (EIPR) and the Egyptian Centre for Economic and Social Rights (ECESR) are examples of NGOs that have increasingly adopted this strategy.

number of independent media outlets, such as Mada Masr, has significantly strengthened public awareness of such cases, making the information more readily available. Accountability for corruption crimes and their socioeconomic impact has been stronger in the post-transition period. Whereas resistance was primarily through strikes and protests prior to the uprising, it is now increasingly conducted through the courts as well. The ECESR, for example, has been quite successful in its litigation through the Administrative Court, as it has won several rulings against corrupt public contracts.

That said, significant challenges remain for Egyptian civil society's work on transitional justice. A repressive protest law and the post-transitional government's systematic crackdown on NGOs and individual activists, journalists and bloggers all point to a renewed form of oppression that is all too familiar to such actors.[8] As a result, the momentum behind new initiatives in the immediate aftermath of Mubarak's ouster, namely the formation of political parties with the participation of youth activists, waned. It was instead quickly replaced with resorting to the "old" methods of documenting, using litigation as a resistance technique and a way of raising awareness about the flawed justice system and its inability to ensure social and political justice.

Libya

The authoritarian and repressive policies of the Gaddafi regime made it extremely difficult for domestic civil society organisations to have any real impact on criminal accountability for Libyan high-level government officials. Legal restrictions on the formation and independence of NGOs were significant. Law 19 of 2001 constituted an Associations Act that imposed further restrictions on the original Associations Act of 1970 (Law No. 111/1970) by securing oversight by the executive and placing government representatives in high positions within the organisations (Mikail 2013; Al Jurshi 2010). Foreign funding was severely restricted by the same law and stipulated that the government's General People's Committee must approve receipt of foreign financial donations. Moreover, Libyan civil society feared potential repercussions for collaborating with foreign funders and often avoided doing so. There were an estimated 22 NGOs operating in Libya before Gaddafi's fall in 2011, none of which were able to work independently (Mercy Corps 2011). This made for a very small and weak civil society in pre-transition Libya.

Gaddafi's regime also had to contend with the country's various tribes. In her discussion on Libyan tribes as "an alternative" to civil society, Amal Obeidi explains the nuanced and changing role of Libyan tribes during the Gaddafi era (Obeidi 2001). She notes that while Gaddafi was keen to do away with tribalism at the start of his reign, he eventually began to realise tribes' importance within Libyan society

[8] Law 107 (2013) on the Right to Public Meetings, Processions and Peaceful Demonstrations, in addition to Law 84 (2002) on Non-Governmental Organisations.

as they helped ensure internal stability. This was particularly important as Libya faced difficult external pressures, including sanctions. Tribes, then, served as an alternative to civil society in the sense that they were given space to provide certain social services, but they held no formal political role. This lent the regime a degree of legitimacy without allowing room for a real political threat to its existence.

As Libya increasingly began to suffer the consequences of international isolation during Gaddafi's rule, particularly following the United States bombing campaign against Libya in 1986 and the economic sanctions that followed, a slight release of the tight grip on the very few civil society organisations also began to emerge. More associations, particularly in the form of unions under the General Federation of Producers and Trade Unions, were allowed to form. This federation was tightly controlled by the government (Al Jurshi 2010). The only relatively influential charity organisations were run by Gaddafi's relatives.

Documentation

Organisations such as Human Rights Watch and Amnesty International were, however, active in documenting human rights violations in Libya to raise public awareness and put pressure on the Libyan Government to address violations. This continues to hold true in the post-transition period. Their position as international NGOs located outside of Libya no doubt facilitated the publication of their damning reports during Gaddafi's rule. Advocacy networks linking Libyan and international civil society organisations during Gaddafi's rule between 1969 and 2011 were, however, extremely weak, undermining the potential impact of the public awareness campaigns on government policy.

With the fall of the Gaddafi regime, this started to change. Lawyers for Justice in Libya, a group formed in 2011 by Libyan lawyers in the diaspora that now includes a network of lawyers in Libya, has been actively monitoring legal developments and making recommendations to the Libyan Government. Civil society organisations within Libya have been growing, but the level of engagement with international actors has remained low (Lawyers for Justice in Libya 2016). However, international NGOs such as No Peace Without Justice actively worked to train Libyan legal professionals and the judiciary to improve accountability for human rights violations in Libya. The United Nations Support Mission in Libya (UNSMIL) also trained and encouraged the Libyan Government to devise a prosecutorial strategy (UNSMIL 2012). Given the serious legal and security challenges to those involved in efforts to prosecute political leaders, most civil society organisations called for reconciliation as opposed to prosecutions (S. Moschini, personal interview, September 18, 2013). Stefano Moschini noted the initial growth of civil society soon after Gaddafi's ouster, which was quickly followed by their decline because of restrictions imposed by the government: "[Civil society] started off as 20,000 and now only twenty-five per cent of them operate" (S. Moschini, personal interview, September 18, 2013).

Litigation

Civil society's priorities in Libya reflect a prioritisation of constitution building and conflict resolution. As demonstrated in Carmen Geha's study of Libyan civil society post-transition, for example, NGOs such as the Forum for Democratic Libya focused their efforts on constitution building (Geha 2016). Indeed, most of her respondents indicated that the constitution is the highest priority area for civil society. It should be noted, however, that when asked what the priorities of the new constitution should be, more than half of respondents said "justice and reconciliation" (Geha 2016: 147). This may explain the fact that while international support for criminal accountability in Libya has waned significantly since 2011, the domestic trial of 37 former regime members still pressed ahead. Victor Peskin and Mieczyslaw Boduszynski explain the weakening of the United Nations Security Council's preoccupation with criminal accountability in their article on the rise and fall of the ICC in Libya, pointing to the "high degree of consensus for an ICC referral in February 2011 and the subsequent sharp fall in support" for the Court (Peskin and Boduszynski 2016: 527). They conclude that the Security Council used the ICC as a tool to help marginalise the Gaddafi regime. With the demise of Gaddafi, this aim was achieved and the ICC was perceived to be nonessential in the post-transition period.[9]

That said, the 1996 Abu Salim prison massacre served as a lynchpin for growing and persistent local public pressure, mostly by victims and their families who sought justice in national courts. This pressure proved crucial to keeping the issue of impunity for human rights on the radar of both ordinary Libyans and the government. In an Amnesty International report published before the Libyan uprising, the lack of prosecutions for Abu Salim was highlighted: "No member of the [Internal Security Agency] is known to have ever been charged or tried for committing human rights violations, including torture" (Amnesty International 2010: 31). As a result, public pressure for the truth about the Abu Salim massacre had been mounting for years. Protests led by lawyers, victims' families and supporters took place every Saturday for years. In response, Gaddafi appointed an investigative judge, Mohamed Bashir Al Khaddar, in 2008 (A. Maghur, personal interview, September 17, 2013; D. Al Mansouri, personal interview, September 18, 2013).

Nothing came of this judge's work. However, human rights lawyers and activists continued to push for accountability. Fathi Terbil was among them and represented the families of the Abu Salim victims. Terbil's arrest in February 2011 and the protests that ensued signify that the Libyan uprising was triggered both by the government's aggressive campaign against criminal accountability and by the victims' families' desire to bring the Abu Salim perpetrators to justice. As Amel Jerary noted,

[9]At the time of writing, the ICC issued two additional arrest warrants in Libya. One was issued under seal on April 18, 2013, for Al-Tuhamy Mohamed Khaled, former head of the Libyan Internal Security Agency. This arrest warrant was unsealed on April 24, 2017. The second arrest warrant was issued onthe 15th August 2017 against Mahmoud Mustafa Busayf Al-Werfalli, commander of the Al Saiqa Brigade.

"The aim of the revolution was to establish a state of law and to achieve justice for the Abu Salim victims" (A. Jerary, personal interview, November 8, 2012). It is revealing, then, that one of the very few pre-transition crimes with which Abdallah El Senussi is charged is the execution of the Abu Salim prisoners under his orders.

Given the severely restrictive environment within which lawyers and other civil society actors had to work, none of the interviewees was able to cite examples of criminal complaints filed against Gaddafi or his aides in the pre-transition period. Litigation activism in Libya was weak, and largely dependent on individual lawyers such as Dao al-Mansouri and Fathi Terbil. Litigation attempts were mainly limited to cases relating to the Abu Salim prison massacre, which remains deeply engraved in the societal memory of the Gaddafi regime's abuses in Libya.

Corruption and Socioeconomic Accountability

Some former regime officials faced corruption charges. Given the lack of public access to information about the trials, the list of charges remains unclear (Saudi, as cited in Aboueldahab 2014).[10] However, known charges include the squandering of public funds amounting to $2.5 billion by former Foreign Minister Abdul Ati al-Obaidi and former head of the General People's Conference Mohamed El Zway. These were the first verdicts issued against high-level officials since Gaddafi's ouster (BBC News 2013). These funds were used to compensate families of those killed in the 1988 Lockerbie plane bombing, as a way to get them to drop legal claims against Libya (Shennib 2013). However, this corruption charge, which notably relates to an offense committed before the 2011 uprising, was dropped and al-Obaidi and El Zway were acquitted in June 2013. No explanation was given by the judge for their acquittal, raising suspicions of the ongoing politicisation of the judiciary in Libya.[11]

Al-Mahmoudi, who was Libya's Prime Minister from 2006 to 2011, was charged with funnelling $25 million of public money to Tunisia to help Gaddafi forces fighting in the 2011 conflict. Saif al-Islam Gaddafi and his brother Saadi were also accused of "plundering state coffers to fund extravagant playboy lifestyles abroad" (Stephen 2014). The number of corruption trials, however, does not match that of the trials in Egypt and Tunisia.

Taking Stock: Libyan Civil Society and Transitional Justice Strategies

Given the great difficulty for NGOs and other civil society actors in Libya to work independently and without constant interference by the government, documentation of human rights violations in the pre-transition period was primarily conducted with

[10] Elham Saudi, for example, explained that her organisation, Lawyers for Justice in Libya, faced difficulty in obtaining information on the charges.

[11] Al-Obaidi and El Zway remained in detention, however, on other human rights charges.

the help of international NGOs such as Human Rights Watch and Amnesty International. While this continues to be the case in the post-transition period, organisations such as Lawyers for Justice in Libya work both in the Libyan diaspora and with Libyan lawyers on the ground to monitor legal developments and to advise the Libyan authorities on how best to move forward on issues related to constitution building and transitional justice.

Still, prosecutions remain a prominent and sensitive issue. They have solely targeted former Gaddafi regime officials without any serious investigation of crimes that may have been committed by the anti-Gaddafi revolutionary militias. A controversial amnesty law providing blanket protection for Libyan rebels from prosecution was issued, closing the door to a more comprehensive criminal accountability process. Civil society organisations such as Lawyers for Justice in Libya strongly opposed this law and issued statements condemning it (Lawyers for Justice in Libya 2012). Moreover, judges, lawyers and prosecutors have faced assassinations and death threats for being involved in any kind of legal defence of former Gaddafi regime officials. The security situation and weak governance in the country have thus had an adverse impact on litigation efforts.

While this does not mean that societal preference for accountability has waned, civil society has had to reorient itself towards conflict resolution, constitution building and justice and reconciliation. Finally, while the socioeconomic impact of corrupt practices by Libyan Government officials was less pronounced when compared to Egypt and Tunisia, major corruption charges related to embezzlement and squandering of public funds were still a central feature of prosecutions.

Tunisia

Documentation

The documentation of human rights abuses guided the work of Tunisia's civil society in the decades before the uprising. Working within a repressive environment, civil society organisations such as the Tunisian Human Rights League (*Ligue Tunisienne pour la Défense des Droits de l'Homme*, or LTDH), established in 1976, began to document and disseminate information, particularly following a 1978 general strike by labour unions, after which union members were tortured and faced other repressive measures. This, Messaoud Rhomdani argued, is what motivated the LTDH to document and disseminate information on human rights violations. Documentation of abuses signified anticipation of a time when prosecutions would be possible (M. Rhomdani, personal interview, April 25, 2012).

The proliferation of media outlets, increase in the number of civil society organisations, cooperation with international organisations such as *Avocats Sans Frontières* and establishment of Tunisia's Truth and Dignity Commission have all bolstered the documentation and dissemination of information regarding human rights violations in Tunisia post-2011. As of July 2017, the Truth and Dignity Commission had received 62,000 complaints (Belhassine 2017).

Litigation

While there were very few explicit attempts by civil society to trigger domestic prosecutions of political leaders before the 2010–2011 uprising, notable litigation efforts were made at the international level. Through universal jurisdiction laws, two cases targeted former Interior Ministers Abdallah Qallel and General Habib Ammar in Switzerland in 2001 and 2003, respectively. A third case in 2001 targeted Khaled Ben Said, a police superintendent in Jendouba who later became vice consul for Tunisia in the French city of Strasbourg.[12] These cases illustrate that, given the highly repressive context within which Tunisian civil society worked during the Ben Ali regime, a creative use of French and Swiss universal jurisdiction laws made a significant crack in the criminal accountability shell. They were successfully brought forward in part because of cooperation with international organisations, which helped file the universal jurisdiction cases, but also because of awareness of the applicability of universal jurisdiction among some of the victims.

Following the ouster of Ben Ali, civil society in Tunisia became emboldened in its pursuit of criminal accountability domestically. The majority of the complaints filed against former leaders were instigated by individual plaintiffs and by a group of lawyers called the *Groupe de 25*. The *Groupe de 25* was formed on January 14, 2011—the day Ben Ali was ousted. Amor Safraoui, the head of the *Groupe de 25*, explained that initial efforts aimed at prosecution came after it was evident that the public prosecutor would not take action to initiate prosecutions (A. Safraoui, personal interview, April 25, 2012). When I asked why they were more active in filing for corruption rather than human rights crimes, Charfeddine Kallel, a human rights lawyer for several victims of the uprising and a prominent member of the *Groupe de 25*, explained that most of the lawyers in the group did not have extensive experience nor expertise in how to prepare human rights cases (C. Kallel, personal interview, April 25, 2012).

Furthermore, while Tunisia's transition was not as repressed by interim authorities as in Egypt, many figures from the Ben Ali era, or the *anciens nouveaux*, retain power. Beji Caïd Essebsi, for instance, held senior government positions in both Bourguiba's and Ben Ali's governments and is now Tunisia's President.[13] Since winning the presidency in December 2014, Essebsi nominated three Ben Ali regime officials to senior political positions, including Habib Essid as Prime Minister (Petre 2015). As several of the incoming elites had ties to the former Ben Ali regime, the political will for a more comprehensive set of human rights cases was weak. This is because, as one diplomat argued, such *anciens nouveaux* feared that they "might not be spared" from prosecution for their involvement in human rights violations in the past (anonymous, personal interview, May 22, 2012). A politicised public prosecutor, allied with the ruling political party, has meant that many human rights cases continue to be blocked (M. Rhomdani, personal interview, April 25, 2012;

---

[12] Jendouba is a city in northwestern Tunisia. Habib Nassar brought my attention to this case (FIDH and Human Rights League 2010).

[13] Habib Bourguiba was Tunisia's first post-independence president from 1957 to 1987.

A. Safraoui, personal interview, April 25, 2012). Essebsi' strong push for the reconciliation bill is the latest and boldest statement against criminal accountability in Tunisia.

Corruption and Socioeconomic Accountability

Nevertheless, some success was had with socioeconomic accountability. The social and political processes that unfolded in Tunisia point to the significant role workers' movements and labour unions played before, during and after the uprising. Moreover, Tunisian civil society was predominantly made up of labour union activists, particularly as they faced repressive measures from the Bourguiba and Ben Ali regimes from early on.

A series of mass revolts and strikes against unemployment and economic inequality in the Tunisian town of Gafsa in 2008, which resulted in several deaths and many serious injuries, are widely seen as a turning point in the lead-up to the uprising two and a half years later (M. Rhomdani, personal interview, April 25, 2012; A. Boubakri, personal interview, April 26, 2012; anonymous, personal interview, April 24, 2012). Gafsa and its aftermath helped chip away at the fear barrier that prevented many Tunisians from challenging the regime's repressive policies. It also demonstrated the strength of mobilisation in the face of an often brutal police force.

Prior to the Tunisian uprising, the General Union for Tunisian Workers (UGTT) played a leading role in challenging government policies from its establishment in 1946. It was the country's strongest opposition, despite its complex relationship with the Ben Ali regime, which often meant that the union's executive office was staffed with individuals loyal to the regime (A. Morai, telephone interview, May 2, 2013). Nonetheless, the UGTT led a general strike during the uprising and oversaw sit-ins at the Casbah thereafter, all of which strengthened its influence as the government's most serious opposition. Moreover, even with the formation of at least three other trade union federations in Tunisia since the uprising, the UGTT has maintained its powerful position of influence in Tunisia's labour movement.

As in Egypt, the Tunisian labour movement did not operate alone—human rights activists such as Moncef Marzouki, Sihem Bensedrine, Hama Hammami and others were persistent in their calls for democracy and respect for human rights. Those calling for civil and political rights, such as the right to freedom of expression, the right to assemble, and freedom from torture and arbitrary detention, were severely repressed through massive crackdowns led by the police and other state security forces, resulting in a significantly weakened human rights movement in Tunisia. In contrast, the labour movement, at the head of which sits the UGTT, was slightly more tolerated. This is in part due to the fact that the UGTT's leadership has functioned as both ally and rival to Tunisia's Government since its establishment during colonial rule.

The relative success of the Tunisian labour movement in bringing to the fore demands for social justice and in fighting corruption impacted on the content of the prosecutions and the emphasis on corruption. As in Egypt, workers' movements and labour unions served as one of the drivers of a certain degree of criminal accountability for socioeconomic rights violations. On the other hand, the harsh crackdowns on civil and political rights activists left a seriously weakened human rights lobby that has been largely unsuccessful in ensuring criminal accountability for abuses committed both before and during the uprisings. A politicised judiciary, part of which is allied with the Ben Ali regime, is one reason efforts to bring about human rights prosecutions have been hampered.[14]

It should be noted, however, that, as in Libya, other priority areas have consumed civil society's work in Tunisia. In particular, efforts geared towards political reconciliation, primarily between the Islamist Ennahda party and the secular Nidaa Tounes party, became central to the work of civil society. The Nobel Prize awarded to the so-called Tunisian "quartet" in 2015 served as a strong recognition for the work of four civil society organisations in helping to resolve a political crisis, but not criminal justice.[15] Still, the significance of the prize lies in its recognition of the influence civil society has had in post-transition Tunisia and it does not negate the centrality of prosecutions in the country's pursuit of transitional justice.

Taking Stock: Tunisian Civil Society and Transitional Justice Strategies

Documentation has persisted in post-transition Tunisia, although in a much more organised manner and with a clearer mandate. Organisations such as *Avocats Sans Frontières* have worked with Tunisian civil society organisations to ensure more effective documentation (S. Rougeaux, personal interview, April 25, 2012). The proliferation of media outlets and of civil society organisations post-transition has also bolstered documentation and dissemination of information regarding human rights violations. While journalists, bloggers and human rights activists in Tunisia continue to face repercussions, such as arbitrary arrest and restrictions on freedom of expression, political dialogue and resistance in the form of protests are still much more tolerated in the post-transition period than they were under Ben Ali.

Universal jurisdiction played an important role in pre-transition Tunisia as it drew attention to abuses allegedly committed by high-level government and police chiefs. Some of these cases, particularly the Abdallah Qallel torture case, were revived post-2011 and were addressed via domestic trials. Prosecutions at the domestic level, then, have emboldened individual lawyers and victims to file complaints against an increasing number of high-level government officials. This is further illustrated by the large protests that took place following the government's

[14] The establishment of Tunisia's Truth and Dignity Commission in 2014 may, however, provide a potential avenue for pre-transition human rights prosecutions. Mandated with investigating crimes committed by state and organised groups from Tunisian independence in 1955 to December 2013, the Commission has acquired a "quasi-judicial" nature to investigate both corruption and civil and political rights crimes (Robinson 2014).

[15] The four organisations that constituted the quartet are the *Union Générale Tunisienne du Travail*, the *Ligue Tunisienne des Droits de l'Homme*, the Confederation of Industry, Trade and Handicrafts and the Tunisian Order of Lawyers.

consideration of the financial and economic reconciliation law, which grants corrupt officials immunity from prosecution in exchange for the return of their ill-gotten assets.

As in Egypt, corruption and its socioeconomic impact were foregrounded prior to the uprising in Tunisia and mostly led by the UGTT and related workers' movements. Protests, strikes and negotiations with the government for policy reform were common pre-transition and continue to figure heavily in the post-transition period. Accountability for corruption through the courts is the most distinctive shift in strategy in post-transition Tunisia, and continues to hold a central place in the transitional justice process.

Conclusion

Transitions are highly contentious processes and the North African cases are no exception to this. The prosecution of political leaders in Egypt, Libya and Tunisia has unfolded within a muddled transitional justice context, marked by ambiguous transitions that do not neatly follow a shift from authoritarian rule to peaceful, liberal democratic rule. Civil society, then, has had to devise strategies to advance criminal accountability while also fighting for a transition that is conducive to a meaningful transitional justice process. These strategies primarily constitute the documentation of abuses and persistent litigation attempts, despite an opaque judiciary and very weak prospects for fair prosecutions. Moreover, the emphasis on accountability for corruption in all three cases was in part driven by civil society strategies that aimed to generate some form of accountability, even if it meant that decades of human rights violations would remain unaccounted for. However, as the case of Egypt demonstrates, the link between civil and political rights and socioeconomic justice has become stronger in the work of civil society actors post-transition.

The challenges faced by civil society in Egypt, Libya and Tunisia are quite similar. Repressive government policies stifled the formation of civil society organisations and their actions both pre- and post-transition. A politicised judiciary meant human rights prosecutions were repeatedly blocked. Fear of violent repercussions for pursuing cases against high-level government officials meant that human rights litigation, particularly in Libya, was muted. It comes as no surprise, then, that the efforts of individual plaintiffs and of lawyers working on behalf of civil society organisations representing victims in Egypt, Libya and Tunisia were and continue to be the primary ways in which criminal cases against high-level government officials are brought forward. The absence of Egyptian and Libyan efforts to pursue universal jurisdiction, in contrast to Tunisia, may point to a lack of awareness among civil society and lawyers of the possibility of holding officials accountable in another country. This, however, is a question that requires further research.[16]

[16] The Arab Network for Human Rights Information has worked with foreign legal organisations to bring torture charges against former Intelligence Chief Omar Suleiman (G. Eid, personal interview, May 2, 2012).

Following the uprisings, documentation and litigation have continued, but with a significantly heightened level of awareness of the transitional justice context within which civil society actors work.

Domestic civil society activism is, of course, insufficient on its own to drive decisions regarding prosecution (Aboueldahab 2017). Analyses of previous transitions are telling. In Argentina, for example, the post-transition presidential leaderships of Raúl Alfonsin (1983–1989), Carlos Menem (1989–1999) and Nestor Kirchner (2003–2007) each shaped decisions regarding prosecution differently (Engstrom and Pereira 2012). This succession of governments in Argentina and its impact on the ebbs and flows of amnesties and prosecutions over decades point to the significance of the political leadership's influence on decisions regarding prosecution. This, however, does not diminish the significance of non-state actors, using tactics such as mass protests and civil society pressure, in pushing for such decisions.

International actors have had mixed success in impacting decisions regarding prosecution in Egypt, Libya and Tunisia. While international NGOs played a significant role in documenting and raising awareness about human rights violations in the three countries, they have also faced challenges related to accusations of "foreign interference" in the domestic affairs of the state—a charge usually levelled by the governments. Moreover, as many domestic civil society organisations rely heavily on foreign funding for their work, they have also been accused of "collaboration" with foreign donors and harming the sovereignty of the state. These repercussions have ranged from arbitrary arrests to serious legal restrictions, such as Law 84 (2002) on Non-Governmental Organisations—a Mubarak-era law that continues to restrict civil society's ability to work and that imposes arbitrary restrictions on NGO receipt of foreign funding.

In the face of continued repression against civil society and in particular against efforts aimed at criminal accountability, Egypt, Libya and Tunisia demonstrate that not all transitions are created equal. The ouster of a head of state has not necessarily meant the end of authoritarianism. Even in Tunisia, often described as a beacon of hope for other Arab Spring countries undergoing tumultuous transitions, the *anciens nouveaux* have proven fairly resistant to a comprehensive transitional justice process and to prosecutions in particular. This has been particularly apparent in Tunisia's recent enactment of the financial and economic reconciliation bill (Jamaoui 2015). Such conditions in the North African cases have resulted in civil society advocating for criminal justice while also battling counter-revolutionary forces that would rather do away with transitional justice altogether.

Civil society actors have had to grapple continuously with repressive regimes, violence, insecurity and human rights violations in pre- and post-transition Egypt, Libya and Tunisia. Their resilient documentation, litigation, foregrounding of corruption and its link to human rights violations, and activism "against all odds" over decades make them one of the most important actors to pursue criminal justice in such uncertain times.

References

Aboueldahab, N. (2017). *Transitional justice and the prosecution of political leaders in the Arab region: A comparative study of Egypt, Libya, Tunisia and Yemen*. Oxford: Hart.

Ahmed, N. (2015, January). Show me the money: The many trials of Mubarak's men. *Mada Masr*. Retrieved from www.madamasr.com/sections/politics/show-me-money-many-trials-mubaraks-men.

Al Jurshi, S. (2010). The Arab civil society: Hindrances and prospects. In *Towards a better life: How to improve the state of democracy in the Middle East and North Africa*. Istanbul: Global Political Trends Center.

Al Kawakibi Democracy Transition Center, No Peace without Justice, and the Transitional Justice Academy. (2014, June). Accounting for the past in Tunisia: An assessment of accountability and transitional justice expectations and perceptions across the country. Retrieved from www.npwj.org/sites/default/files/documents/AccountingforthePastinTunisia_BaselineReport_June2013.pdf.

Amnesty International. (2010). *Libya of tomorrow: What hope for human rights*?

Barsalou, J., & Knight, B. (2013, January). Delayed or denied: Egyptian expectations about justice in post-Mubarak Egypt. International Human Rights Funders Group. Retrieved from https://www.ihrfg.org/sites/default/files/Barsalou%20and%20Knight%20-%20Justice%20in%20Post-Mubarak%20Egypt.pdf.

BBC News. (2013, June). Lockerbie compensation: Libyan officials acquitted. Retrieved from www.bbc.com/news/world-africa-22936678.

Beinin, J. (2012, June). *The rise of Egypt's workers*. Washington, DC: Carnegie Endowment for International Peace.

Beinin, J. (2013, August). Egyptian workers after June 30. Middle East Research and Information Project. Retrieved from http://www.merip.org/mero/mero082313?ip_login_no_cache=2a7cc00364b6b9b26a78462ac934c309

Belhassine, O. (2017, July). Guilt and denial at Tunisia's truth commission hearings. Justinceinfo.net. Retrieved from www.justiceinfo.net/en/justice-reconciliation/34145-guilt-and-denial-and-at-tunisia-s-truth-commission-hearings.html.

Engstrom, P., & Pereira, G. (2012). From amnesty to accountability: The ebbs and flows in the search for justice in Argentina. In F. Lessa & L. Payne (Eds.), *Amnesty in the age of human rights accountability: Comparative and international perspectives*. Cambridge: Cambridge University Press.

FIDH. (2010). *Appeal trial of Khaled Ben Said, a Tunisian national: French justice system faced with the challenge of judging the most serious international crimes*. Retrieved from https://www.fidh.org/IMG/article_PDF/article_a8456.pdf.

Gall, C. (2014, July). Questions of justice in Tunisia as ousted leaders are freed. *The New York Times*.

Geha, C. (2016). *Civil society and political reform in Lebanon and Libya: Transition and constraint*. London: Routledge.

Human Rights Watch. (2012, June). Libya: Abu Salim prison massacre remembered. Retrieved from www.hrw.org/news/2012/06/27/libya-abu-salim-prison-massacre-remembered.

Human Rights Watch. (2015, January). Flawed accountability: Shortcomings of Tunisia's trials for killings during the uprising. Retrieved from www.hrw.org/report/2015/01/12/flawed-accountability/shortcomings-tunisias-trials-killings-during-uprising.

Jamaoui, A. (2015, November). Tunisia: The dispute over the economic reconciliation bill. Nawaat. Retrieved from https://nawaat.org/portail/2015/11/01/tunisia-the-dispute-over-the-economic-reconciliation-bill.

Jawad, R. (2015, August). Libya death sentences cast long shadow over rule of law. BBC News. Retrieved from www.bbc.com/news/world-africa-33855860.

Kassem, M., & Fattah, Z. (2011, May). The man behind Egypt's real estate rebellion. *Bloomberg News*. Retrieved from https://www.bloomberg.com/news/articles/2011-05-26/the-man-behind-egypts-real-estate-rebellion.

Law No. 107 for 2013. (2013). *For organizing the right to peaceful public meetings, processions and protests*. Retrieved from http://www.constitutionnet.org/vl/item/egypt-law-no107-2013-organizing-right-peaceful-public-meetings-processions-and-protests.

Law No. 84 for 2002. (2002). *Law on non-governmental organizations*. Retrieved from http://www.bu.edu/bucflp/files/2012/01/Law-on-Nongovernmental-Organizations-Law-No.-84-of-2002.pdf.

Lawyers for Justice in Libya. (2016). *Transitional justice programme*. Retrieved from http:// www.libyanjustice.org.

Lawyers for Justice in Libya. (2012). *LFJL strongly condemns new laws breaching human rights and undermining the rule of law*. Retrieved from http://www.libyanjustice.org/news/news/post/23-lfjl-strongly-condemns-new-laws-breaching-human-rights-and-undermining-the-rule-of-law.

Mada Masr. (2016, June). Trial to outlaw independent labor unions referred to Egypt's highest court. Retrieved from http://www.madamasr.com/news/trial-outlaw-independent-labor-unions-referred-egypts-highest-court.

Mercy Corps and the Governance Network. (2011). *Beyond Gaddafi: Libya's governance context*. Retrieved from www.mercycorps.org/sites/default/files/capacity_to_govern-libya_26_aug_2011.pdf.

Mikail, B. (2013). Civil society and foreign donors in Libya. Retrieved from http://fride.org/download/WP_Lybia.pdf.

Moustafa, T. (2014). Law and courts in authoritarian regimes. *Annual Review of Law and Social Science, 10*, 281–299.

Obeidi, A. (2001). *Political culture in Libya*. Surrey: RoutledgeCurzon.

Obel Hansen, T. (2014). The vertical and horizontal expansion of transitional justice: Explanations and implications for a contested field. In S. Buckley-Zistel, T. Beck, C. Braun, & F. Mieth (Eds.), *Transitional justice theories*. London: Routledge.

Onodera, H. (2009). The *Kifaya* generation: Politics of change among youth in Egypt. *Journal of the Finnish Anthropological Society, 34*(4), 44–64.

Peskin, V., & Boduszynski, M. (2016). The rise and fall of the ICC in Libya and the politics of international surrogate enforcership. *International Journal of Transitional Justice, 10*(2), 272–291.

Petre, C. (2015, January). Tunisia, let's not forget about revolution already. *Middle East Monitor*. Retrieved from www.middleeastmonitor.com/articles/africa/16310-tunisia-lets-not-forget-about-the-revolution-already.

Radsch, C. (2008, April). April 6th general strike in Egypt draws together diverse groups using newest technologies. Retrieved from www.radsch.info/2008/04/using-facebook-blogs-sms-independent.html.

Robinson, I. (2014). Truth commissions and anti-corruption: Towards a complementary framework? *International Journal of Transitional Justice, 9*(1), 33–50.

Sharp, D. (2013). Interrogating the peripheries: The preoccupations of fourth generation transitional justice. *Harvard Human Rights Journal, 26*, 149–178.

Shennib, G. (2013, June). Gaddafi officials acquitted but stay behind bars. Reuters. Retrieved from www.reuters.com/article/2013/06/17/us-libya-trial-idUSBRE95G0S120130617.

Stephen, C. (2014, April). Gaddafi sons war crimes trial begins in Libya amid security fears. *The Guardian*. Retrieved from http://www.theguardian.com/world/2014/apr/13/gaddafi-sons-war-crimes-trial-libya.

United Nations Support Mission in Libya. (2012, September). *Transitional justice: Foundation for a new Libya*.

Yerkes, S., & Muasher, M. (2017, October). *Tunisia's corruption contagion: A transition at risk*. Carnegie Endowment for International Peace Briefing.

Yousfi, H., Majeri, W., Hmed, C., Djelidi, S., & Ben Abderrazak, S. (2014, November). En Tunisie, le retour de l'ancien regime n'est pas une rumeur. Liberation. Retrieved from www.liberation.fr/debats/2014/11/21/en-tunisie-le-retour-de-l-ancien-regime-n-est-pas-une-rumeur_1147107.

Chapter 10
Conclusion: The Role of Local Civil Society in Shaping Transitional Justice in Africa

Hugo van der Merwe

The Global Trajectory of Transitional Justice

In order to place local civil society innovations in the context of the broader transitional justice field and understand how they may contribute to its development, it is useful to take a step back and look at the historical trajectory of the field.

Transitional justice emerged from practice and is continually reshaped by the shifting forms of policy and practice. Its key ideas, boundaries and mechanisms have been shaped through global developments where academics, practitioners and national and international policymakers built a set of tools and a body of knowledge. This set of assumptions, relating to the underlying causes of conflict, the goals that transitional societies should pursue and the value of different processes in achieving these goals, has evolved over time. Civil society is generally an enthusiastic participant in the promotion of this knowledge, and at times also contributes to its development.

The term "transitional justice" was initially coined in response to debates about dealing with transitions from authoritarian rule to democracy in Latin America in the 1980s (Arthur 2009). The main tension that these policy deliberations sought to address was how to balance the fragile nature of democratic consolidation with the need to affirm norms of accountability that could serve to build a human rights culture. While the dilemma of how to deal with legacies of mass abuses committed by a past regime has been a question that has confronted many policymakers over the ages (from ancient Greece to the transitions to independence from colonial rule), the global politics at the end of the Cold War created an opportunity to frame these challenges and opportunities through a human rights lens. Rather than defining a completely new

H. van der Merwe (✉)
Centre for the Study of Violence and Reconciliation, Cape Town, South Africa
e-mail: hvdmerwe@csvr.org.za

J. Brankovic, H. van der Merwe (eds.), *Advocating Transitional Justice in Africa*, Springer Series in Transitional Justice,
https://doi.org/10.1007/978-3-319-70417-3_10

form of social policy, these deliberations sought to present political transitions as a critical juncture for promoting or compromising a human rights agenda.

The transitions from communism in Eastern Europe, which were framed through a democratisation and human rights lens, provided further impetus to these debates and added new challenges in relation to the need to reform deeply entrenched authoritarian cultures in key state institutions. These challenges generated a range of innovative solutions that provided alternative forms of accountability (such as public truth telling), alternative forms of justice for victims (with a greater emphasis on reparations) and more vigorous approaches to institutional transformation (particularly in the form of vetting). Justice, in the context of transitions, incrementally took on a much broader meaning than its conventional retributive focus, and was infused with human rights discourses (particularly those relating to civil and political rights). These transitional justice innovations not only provided new mechanisms of state engagement with legacies of past abuses, but also redefined the playing field in other significant ways. New actors were identified as key stakeholders, new goals were introduced and a broader integrative or holistic approach to transitional processes was adopted.

The South African Truth and Reconciliation Commission (TRC) further pushed the field's boundaries. South African policymakers, emboldened by the idealism of the historic turning point of a new democracy, added reconciliation into the mix of goals to be pursued through transitional justice. The proposed model for the TRC, based on conditional amnesty, sought to combine accountability with reconciliation while making some accommodation for erstwhile perpetrators who feared prosecution. This new model further elevated the hype about transitional justice as an intervention that could also embody deeper transformative aspirations. Rather than a deal with the devil, the amnesty agreement was praised as an enlightened achievement that transcended the short-term quest for retribution. With the added status leant by figures such as Nelson Mandela and Desmond Tutu, and a clearly articulated theology of forgiveness, this model for transitional justice found new traction in shaping expectations for other contexts across the globe. It was particularly welcomed as a signpost for other African countries facing transitional dilemmas.

Transitional justice ambitions would expand again in subsequent manifestations, particularly in countries that sought to apply it in contexts of transition from war to peace. While most previous practical applications had occurred in transitions from autocratic repression, transitional justice was now called on to address the vast legacies of civil wars. It was thus expected to heal rifts not just between the state and society, but also between deeply divided groups, ethnicities and regions within a state. In many cases this involved countries where the idea of nationhood or the legitimacy of the state was deeply contested.

The field thus became a vehicle for social transformation. In contrast to the more humble and narrowly focused ambitions (framed as painful compromises) of its early proponents, transitional justice developed into a vast social engineering exercise that sought to embody all the ambitions for a society's long-term peace and justice. Inevitably, such ambitious goals were questioned, not just in terms of their viability but also in terms of their ideological underpinnings.

While transitional justice gradually developed as an international normative mantle, establishing a set of expectations for each new peace agreement or downfall of a dictatorial regime, the underlying agenda of this globalised toolkit was increasingly questioned by critical scholars and activists (Madlingozi 2010). The narrowly focused human rights agenda (prioritising civil and political rights) and the obsession with western legal procedures raised suspicions of a barely concealed neoliberal agenda that assumes the ultimate goal of transition to be the establishment of a liberal democracy integrated into a global capitalist economy.

At the same time, actual transitional justice processes were often very selective in how they applied (or avoided applying) these international norms. National policymakers proved adept at using the form and symbolism of transitional justice while discarding the human rights content. Much of the international academic discussion about transitional justice presented the field as one that automatically promotes human rights, peace, justice and reconciliation, sometimes simply by reference to its defined purpose. Empirical reality showed a much more complex terrain, with mixed outcomes in relation to benefits and shortfalls. Truth commissions, trials and vetting, and terms such as reconciliation, peace, victimhood and truth also proved to be useful tools in the hands of autocrats and self-serving elites (Mihr 2017).

In the face of this feared co-optation and hijacking of transitional justice, progressive activists and scholars did not abandon the field. It instead provoked two types of responses: first, an *expansive* approach, with an attempt to redefine or reclaim the field as an expression of a more radical socio-economic agenda, and second, a *targeted* approach, which seeks to pursue more limited benefits for specific critical shorter term or incremental gains.[1]

Civil society has been at the forefront of trying to articulate what these two approaches should look like in practical terms in specific contexts. In claiming that transitional justice can serve more radical causes, they have argued how transitional justice can respond to demands for social justice and deeper social transformation that addresses the causes and not just the consequences of violence (Gready and Robins 2014). In practice, this has meant a more proactive attempt to frame and build collective momentum around transitional justice agendas that outline a bigger vision underpinning specific transitional justice interventions (particularly well illustrated by the Kenya Transitional Justice Network, discussed by Andrew Songa in this volume).

In its attempt to claim targeted and concrete gains, civil society has used its knowledge of local contexts and engagement with local constituencies to develop programmes that speak to the priorities of communities and victim groups. Cautioning about an ever-expanding set of goals that loses sight of more attainable objectives, these scholars and activists have pushed for a more sustained strategy to ensure that particular gains are prioritised and consistently pursued. African civil society organisations (CSOs) have, for example, managed to articulate victims' needs relating to reparations and have helped develop strategies to have this right

[1] Lorna McGregor (2013) argues, for example, that torture was one of the key initial focuses of transitional justice, but that the field has had little direct impact on its prevalence due to the failure to develop a clear strategy that engages with its causes and context.

recognised and enforced through courts and transitional justice mechanisms (as discussed by Zukiswa Puwana and Rita Kesselring in this volume).

For local civil society, these debates are about concrete advocacy strategies and policy choices that they confront in their national and community contexts. Local policy processes of transitional justice have always been an arena of fierce contestation. Both the goals that seek to frame a transformative vision for transitional societies and the specific mechanisms that are developed can be approached from very different perspectives and serve competing goals. The end of open warfare or the fall of a dictatorship does not spell the end of conflict. It opens up new battle lines between those seeking to shape the future. While shifting international norms may inject new intellectual capital, strengthen certain bargaining positions and introduce new role players into these debates, agreement on the policy choices in pursuing competing agendas has remained elusive.

Transitional justice has proven itself amenable to serving different goals and surprisingly pliable to manipulation by powerful actors in some contexts. The field can more usefully be conceived in a non-normative sense, as a range of processes used by societies to address the legacies of past offenses both in pursuing democratisation and in consolidating authoritarian rule. There are various agendas that drive transitional justice, ranging from human rights and peacebuilding to regime legitimation and elimination of political opponents. The devil is often in the detail of how these processes are framed and how their mandates and operations are determined.

This chapter situates local civil society within this political milieu. Civil society is a political actor that pursues particular agendas in transitional contexts. Its role and effectiveness can be better understood by reflecting on its location in terms of international, national and local politics. While much attention in the literature is given to international norms and their diffusion through civil society, the chapter seeks to balance this by giving more attention to the local politics of transitional justice on the African continent.

In this chapter I will unpack why transitional justice is a particularly vexed question in the African context, due to the continent's multilayered experience of local and international conflict. Building on the contrasting approaches to transitional justice outlined above (expansive versus targeted), I seek to explain some of the tensions between global and local conceptions of transitional justice, before locating civil society in these debates. The chapter concludes with a review of the various CSO strategies examined in this volume and what they tell us regarding the meaning and trajectory of transitional justice.

Transitional Justice in the African Context

When a society adopts transitional justice processes, the stakes can be very high. Transitional justice discourses and mechanisms frame a moral narrative of victimhood and abuse, present diagnoses of what ails a society, prescribe institutional restructuring to heal it and authorise concrete actions that can remove individuals or whole sets of actors from office or political influence. Where a peace deal has been concluded, this is often the terrain where the battle for power continues.

Transitional justice has by no means been reduced to a neutral set of mechanisms with accepted outcomes. While there have been significant developments in framing tools that are more commonly used, conventions regarding key principles and increased international scrutiny by donors and international bodies, national level transitional justice debates remain highly fluid and contested. The increased legalisation, bureaucratisation and standardisation of the field have not served to depoliticise the policy choices of key local actors.

In part, this contentiousness is an inevitable product of local politics. The norms and values for addressing conflict, as well as the narratives of conflict, are embedded in a political contestation relating to competing ideologies, ethnic identities, notions of the nation and attempts to frame and consolidate the role of the state. Transitional justice does not exist above the fray. It provides a powerful new vocabulary, toolkits and analytical frameworks for making sense of these challenges and legitimising certain agendas.

The state has been the master of this terrain for many years. Local civil society is a relatively newcomer. Yet by building bases of legitimacy among local stakeholders, forging ties with international actors and drawing on formidable technical expertise, civil society has emerged as a very vocal player within African transitional justice debates.

Civil society faces particular challenges in Africa, both because of the nature and history of conflict on the continent and because of the specific obstacles confronting state legitimacy and capacity. Transitions have been a common feature of African states over the last 60 years. Dealing with transitions from colonial rule to independence provided a significant primer for some governments in managing transitions. Many lessons were learnt: how to maintain continuity while managing change, how old or emerging elites can manipulate shifting political institutions and narratives to their own ends, how postcolonial dependencies and imposed economic structures continue to oppress societies and how new visionary narratives can inspire and build unity but also marginalise and delegitimise dissent.

Transitional justice norms in African countries have their own historical precedents that were established through colonial institutional cultures, and by their respective attempts to reframe the nature of the state and build national identity through reinvented political narratives. The fluidity of politics on the continent provides rich soil for attempts to formulate new social contracts that transform and build on the colonial legacy of institutionalised violence and mass violations. Postcolonial African states have responded in contrasting ways to these legacies of abuses and institutionalised forms of repression.

Many states have also managed transitions from authoritarian rule to democracy, and from war to peace, since independence. In most cases these transitions were controlled by a narrow set of elites, military rulers and powerful regional and international actors. Civil society is now interfering in a process that was previously the preserve of a more exclusive set of actors.

African state practices in dealing with transitions (even without civil society intervention) have been highly diverse. As the contributors to this volume show, examples of amnesty and amnesia, vengeance and victor's justice, national unity and reconciliation commitments, and even investigative and truth processes occurred across the continent in the decades preceding the end of the Cold War. These processes served a range of goals, from consolidating national independence and nation building to elite entrenchment, state legitimation and ethnic reconciliation. And today, transitional justice is a concept viewed by various states through quite different lenses—useful for purposes that seem contradictory. While "transformative justice" has become a popular term among critical transitional justice scholars (Gready and Robins 2014), the transformative goals of African transitional justice agendas have always been apparent. Transformation of the state and society in the African context has been pursued in dramatic and diverse ways.

Ever since removing the shackles of colonial rule, African states have struggled with the challenge of redefining their identity and destiny. Transitional justice, at least in its broader definition, clearly speaks to this journey. The meaning of transition, the need to deal with a legacy of abuses and build a sense of nationhood united by a common identity and unifying values, has been at the centre of African politics since independence.

Transitional justice in Africa, in this sense, still struggles with the unfinished business of its colonial legacy. In addition, there is the burden of conflicts that have ravaged countries since independence, alongside continuing global political and economic inequalities (Muvingi 2009; Abou-El-Fadl 2012). An attempt at a decisive break with the past using "revolutionary justice" to deal with the colonial legacy in Mozambique (Igreja 2010) elicited fierce responses from the West (and local resistance), resulting in a brutal drawn-out civil war that necessitated further transitional arrangements to revisit the colonial legacy and address subsequent abuses.

The African colonial context provides a toxic mix of unresolved historical agendas that provide fuel for ongoing conflict. Conventional international transitional justice approaches are generally biased towards shorter, more manageable time frames and narrowly defined sets of abuses (Balint et al. 2014). Apply this to a context where horrendous colonial abuses happened just over the (conveniently placed) horizon, and internationally prioritised abuses are civil and political violations by postcolonial states themselves rather than inherited local and ongoing international social inequalities, and the reasons for scepticism about an imposed agenda driven by former colonial powers become all too obvious. Transitional justice agendas that present colonial inheritances, or the moment of independence, as the unquestioned foundation—the point of reference to which present governments need to return—come across as an international agenda that seems to reaffirm African dependency and inferiority. It presents the end of colonialism as the point where things started going wrong rather than as the foundation for subsequent conflicts.

A common theme shaping state agendas in many transitions has understandably been nation building and state consolidation. In countries with fairly recent ideas of nationhood, riven by ethnic divisions that were encouraged by colonial rulers, the need to build a national identity, frame a vision of a common destiny and consolidate national boundaries as meaningful to identity has been a key challenge that each transition has had to revisit in some manner. Similarly, the legitimacy of the state and a constitution, and the value of centralised authority, has been incremental achievements that require repeated assertion in each transitional arrangement.

African civil society presents an additional layer of transitional justice demands and methodologies that it hopes will replace or be integrated in these state-led policy processes. One would thus be remiss to view the role of civil society as simply (or even mainly) being proponents of transitional justice in the face of state resistance to such measures. Both the state and civil society seek to pursue transitional justice, but on their own terms.

Local Engagement with Global Transitional Justice

Earlier in this chapter I argued that civil society transitional justice advocates operate at two levels: an *expansive* versus a *targeted* approach to social change. Seeking to frame the goals of transition or to shape the strategies used during transition in order to secure certain gains positions civil society in relation to both international and state agendas. Civil society has been presented as a conduit for global norm diffusion, but it often also interacts with these norms in a more creative and critical manner.

CSOs have been strident consumers of transitional justice knowledge, gained through their networks with other regional and international CSOs and their donors, and through their exposure to globalised education, training and literature. Many have themselves become voices in the international debates which contribute to shape the development of the field. This engagement involves exposure to a matrix of power and knowledge that can be quite seductive and co-optive. The institutionalisation of transitional justice through the adoption of standardised "pillars" of knowledge and best practice (namely truth seeking, accountability, institutional reform and memorialisation) and through funding commitments to expert-led processes has framed difficult dilemmas for local practitioners and advocates.

International norms regarding transitional justice have been concretised significantly in the last 20 years, but are, in large part, not clearly articulated or justiciable as yet. Where they have been more clearly spelled out, and slightly more enforceable, as in the Rome Statute, they remain highly contested. They are embedded in the exercise of global politics and the imbalance in global governance structures. This growth of the field has produced a messy collection of enforceable imperatives, best practices, "common-sense" knowledge, standardised strategies and cutting-edge developments.

Nonetheless, as transitional justice gained traction as a specialised area of intervention adopted by international agencies, international policy proponents have focused on the technical process whereby the state employs a range of mechanisms to resolve complex legal, political and social challenges that threaten the new social order after transition. Aimed at pursuing short-term conflict termination and a stable political order, this form of transitional justice comprises a set of issues that need to be settled by the parties to the conflict. In this constricted sense, transitional justice seeks to create a formalised framework for managing some of the most contentious issues that could lead to renewed conflict if not managed carefully. It is concerned with establishing a carefully regulated environment for managing obstacles to transition, without raising too many questions about what the goals of transition might entail.

The more constricted technical framing of transitional justice identifies the objectives as seemingly unbiased, commonly accepted norms such as rule of law, human rights protection and legal accountability. This approach suggests the need for strong (legal) expertise, neutrality and institutionalised procedures. Such processes have lent themselves to generic toolkits and transferable expertise that can be applied to local contexts as if they are experiencing analogous forms of conflict and seek to pursue similar longer term outcomes (Zunino 2011).

This technical approach has contributed to a myth of transitional justice being an apolitical field, where neutral experts can be called upon to implement policies that serve common goals amid a broad international consensus about the ultimate destination. Critical scholars have pointed out that this approach can be used to obfuscate structural injustices and legitimise new forms of inequality (Mamdani 2002), and are in fact tied to a particular end goal, namely a liberal democracy that is integrated into a global capitalist economy (Sharp 2015).

While some civil society actors have enthusiastically taken on the role of technical experts operating in a neutral space, or global proponents of models such as the South African TRC, many have raised questions about this approach. CSOs have often sought to reclaim a political agenda for transitional justice—bringing issues such as gender justice, land distribution and colonial abuses within its mandate. They have argued against the imposed agendas of international actors, reframing transitional justice as part of a national social justice agenda and questioning the motives of international actors, particularly when they are themselves implicated in historical or ongoing abuses or unjust trade relations. Sometimes this stance provides common ground with national state actors who also wish to advance radical change and challenge global inequalities or colonial dependencies. Just as often, it puts civil society in conflict with state actors who simply want to consolidate the status quo.

While remaining critical, civil society has seized on the utility of some international norms and templates when they serve particular targeted goals. The procedural fairness, accountability and inclusiveness principles that have been promoted as part of the standard transitional justice template have been used by advocates for marginalised groups such as victims, vulnerable communities or others seeking a voice in the political arena.

In addition, while transitional justice mechanisms provide a narrowly framed space for participation, local CSOs have found them to be useful tools for political or legal leverage. For example, the key principle of victim participation in transitional justice, which is now widely promoted (or at least acknowledged) by the United Nations and the African Union, opens opportunities that were not previously recognised as a consensus norm. Similarly, increased recognition of the right to reparations provides a gradual shift in the power dynamics that shape the transitional justice playing field. African CSOs have thus embraced the advances in the global transitional justice norms that empower them and their constituencies as stakeholders in promoting the needs of previously marginalised groups.

Where international norms have bolstered efforts to reform authoritarian state institutions, they have also been welcomed by some local civil society actors. While not necessarily linked to a radical transformative agenda, these shifts do speak to important incremental shifts that strengthen civil society capacity as critical stakeholders in relation to the state. CSOs have however been careful to position themselves as independent agents, rather than as promoters of foreign agendas, pushing for social transformation rather than "regime change".

African states have generally been less welcoming of these global transitional justice advances. Rather than bolstering the powers of the state to take decisive action to address the causes of civil war, the massive economic inequalities that drive conflict or the international disparities that emerged under colonial domination, transitional justice is viewed generally as a western normative intervention that has imposed further obligations on states and restricted their scope for discretion. Even where there are convergences that respond to national agendas, the field of transitional justice has moved fairly slowly to build institutional or normative capacity to make it more attractive to African reform agendas. For example, increased attention has been given to the need for accountability of international corporate actors and corrupt international financial transactions, as well as reparations for colonial-era abuses, but normative and institutionalised processes to address these have not been forthcoming.

The narrow technical agenda presented by international transitional justice templates also does not speak directly to more ambitious or immediate national political agendas relating to peace and security. The fragility of the postcolonial state, its limited reach in certain regions or sectors of a country, its tenuous link to a unified and hegemonic sense of nationhood, and its elusive regional and international status set transitional justice debates within a much more contentious playing field.

African states have however found value in some of the ideas and formulas presented by transitional justice. Rather than just rejecting it as a foreign imposed agenda, the African Union has been increasingly enthusiastic about promoting African transitional justice norms that are more responsive to African values and local conflict dynamics. African CSOs have played a key role in these processes of indigenising transitional justice to make sure that its values are rooted within African human rights norms and that its discourse resonates with African experiences of conflict and peacebuilding.

While the language of transitional justice has become more locally resonant, the politics of the policy choices remain highly contentious. The histories of most African countries provide a vast menu of abuses and victim experiences stretching over many decades. Different political agendas and transformative ideals would select and prioritise these in contrasting ways within a transitional justice agenda. The technical side of the transitional justice field generally seeks clear time frames to work with: cut-off points for legal claims, turning points in history that mark an era of abuses, or start and end dates for regimes whose rule was particularly heinous. This search for neat manageable solutions also frames the selection of types of cases that can be incorporated into the mandate of the mechanisms, such as deaths, torture and legally categorised crimes such as international crimes, or acts established as illegal under national law. Each time frame or abuse category choice comes with costs and opportunities for different role players in the political conflict. Each policy choice carries implications for bolstering or undermining a particular narrative of historical and present conflicts.

The most recent outbreak of war or phase of authoritarian rule is just one historical layer that requires contextualisation within a longer history of conflict. Each phase of a conflict, from precolonial to various subnational episodes and cross-national tensions since independence, provides additional challenges to framing an inclusive and consensus-based agenda for transitional justice. These tensions pit national against international actors, and also local political stakeholders against each other, in framing what are the technical parameters, and who controls the narrative for guiding the mechanisms and interpreting past events. The battle over transitional justice is thus fought on a number of fronts: whether to embark on it, what forms it should take, how broad its mandate should be, how quickly to wrap it up and which historical narrative should frame its goals.

These are all questions that create different divisions and alliances locally and internationally. For civil society, they contain big questions relating to an expansive agenda for social change, as well as shorter term strategic questions about the priority gains that need to be secured during a particular window of opportunity. These strategy choices require a situational analysis and carefully negotiated relationship with the state.

Locating African Civil Society in Relation to the State

Using the broader definition of transitional justice I discussed above, which incorporates its manipulation for various agendas (rather than just serving as a human rights or peacebuilding tool), allows us to analyse the relationship between CSOs and the state in Africa in a more nuanced manner. Rather than viewing the state's position as simply being a promoter or an obstacle to CSO transitional justice agendas (or as for or against human rights or democratisation), I argue that its interests in particular framings of this agenda need to be better understood.

In some cases, it does appear that the state is a somewhat reluctant passenger on the international transitional justice bandwagon, and simply tries to limit the damage to particular political party interests. Whether states want it or not, international expectations are now that an end to war or transition to democracy would be accompanied by some form of transitional justice. In some instances, the state appears to have little stake in transitional justice—not viewing it as a terrain where it can bolster its legitimacy or consolidate its power, but rather as a series of hoops it needs to jump through to placate powerful actors. State engagement with transitional justice is then largely disingenuous or superficial, lacking substantive commitment and consequently failing to deliver on promises the state was pushed into making. Its main goal may simply be to undermine or marginalise the impact of these measures.

As Joanna Quinn argues in this volume, in Uganda the government tends to "use the guise of transitional justice as a tool for acquiring some semblance of legitimacy"

(Chap. 7). Knowing that the international community has prioritised transitional justice, governments are under pressure to show some commitment, but often appear to have little real intention to deliver. Local civil society thus has a critical role in keeping these unresolved issues in the spotlight, both at a national and international level. These strategies involve both engagement with the expansive agenda that seeks to highlight national transformative goals and various attempts to bolster specific interventions when the state allows space for local initiatives.

Just as often the state seeks to reframe the purpose and shape of transitional justice to direct its activities towards its own goals. The question for local civil society then becomes one of negotiating collaborative spaces and opportunities within this framework, or of challenging and limiting the state's activities where they oppose its goals or actions. In these contexts, civil society needs to be strategically aware of the opportunities to shape spaces for public participation and for promoting particular values or specific groups' interests.

The case of Rwanda is perhaps most instructive as a state that actively took control of its transitional justice agenda, framed explicit goals and devised a strategy with a well-thought-out theory of change. Civil society in Rwanda was supportive of these efforts (albeit in part because of the repressive environment) and international civil society was left divided and confused about what aspects of the programme to support and what to challenge (Comlan 2010).

This more ambitious proactive intervention, where the state enthusiastically adopts a controversial transitional justice agenda, is a worrying scenario when we recognise how transitional justice language and mechanisms are open to manipulation by the most repressive actors, who have become sophisticated in influencing public sentiment regarding ideas of victimhood and are able to manipulate the media to play on people's insecurities. This battle over the public narrative between the state and CSOs is clearly illustrated in Kenya's engagement with the International Criminal Court, where the discourse of victimhood was dominated by the state's presentation of the president as a victim of international intervention rather than as the perpetrator of mass abuses (Lugano 2017). Justice and truth agendas can be defined in ways that focus on accountability and exposure for carefully selected abuses, with particular time frames and geographical jurisdictions that centre narratives of blame and victimhood around certain group interests.[2]

The Zimbabwean case, as discussed by Shastry Njeru in this volume, is particularly illuminating in this regard. Zimbabwe has had, broadly speaking, three instances of national transitional justice processes, and ongoing narrative contestation over allocating blame for past abuses. The state carefully controlled the 1980 post-independence "reconciliation" process, the 1985 response to the Gukurahundi Massacre and the 2009 Inclusive Government agreement, where the need for state accountability was consistently discounted. The state's overriding narrative of abuse remains focused on colonialism and its legacies, particularly in terms of land

[2] Richard Wilson (2001) provides a critique of the South African TRC which presents its mandate and operations as an exercise in legitimating the new political order and thus serving to justify the ongoing legacy of apartheid inequalities.

ownership. In contrast, the Zimbabwe Human Rights NGO Forum, a national coalition of CSOs concerned about transitional justice, has focused its call for accountability on the abuses of the present government, framing the transitional justice agenda to the exclusion of more historical grievances, both by the colonial power and by the Rhodesian pre-independence government.

Transitional justice mechanisms have thus been used (or abused) by authoritarian states to rewrite history, marginalise opponents and consolidate centralised control over various institutions.[3] This is particularly the case where transitions have led to compromised state institutions and unresolved social divisions. Where some elite groups who are complicit in abuses survive the transition unscathed and continue to subvert accountability and reform processes, civil society has played a particularly critical role. Pre-transition elites often prove very resilient and manage to form alliances with those in the new regime—as illustrated in this volume by Puwana and Kesselring in the case of South Africa and by Noha Aboueldahab in the case of Tunisia—CSOs are critical in ensuring that transitional justice mechanisms do not shield certain perpetrators who seek to reinvent themselves in the new dispensation. They challenge new elite compromises built on deals that seek to sweep the past under the carpet.

The nature of civil society in transitional contexts is also often unclear and does not always fit conventional Western conceptions regarding its composition and role. The notion of civil society is one derived from Western democracies where they have a more clearly defined historical role. In African societies there are no generally understood conventions for how they should be regulated or what form of politics they can or should be engaged in. In transitional contexts, these rules of the game are revisited and debated.

An opening up of political space happens under continued resource and political constraints that create an uneven playing field. In some instances this space can become dominated by international non-governmental organisations (INGOs), professional bodies or state-linked NGOs. The constraints on more locally rooted representative forms or organising can remain quite limiting. Even for more agile professional local NGOs, it may take a long time to (re)build effective capacity after lengthy periods of repression or conflict. The legitimacy of civil society in these contexts may also be highly contested in terms of their allegiance to foreign donors or to a state that both controls the flow of resources and often continues to provide limited scope for independent thinking. Neat categories such as state, civil society, family and business are either alien to local socio-political environments or they have been distorted by years of conflict and international intervention, as examined by Jasmina Brankovic in this volume.

Civil society enters this fray with its own baggage and limitations. The context of civil war and repression creates a hostile environment for civil society. As illustrated by the authors in this volume, local civil society has taken many forms during

[3] This is also illustrated through case studies in Europe by Anja Mihr (2017).

periods of repression and war that do not necessarily conform to conventional ideas of civil society. The lack of formal political space has pushed organisations that have broad legitimacy in a particular society, such as trade unions, religious structures and traditional authorities, to take on roles of representing certain interests or engaging the state to advocate for policy changes.

The inverse may also be true. In some contexts, such as Liberia, where long-term conflict devastated state and customary institutions, local civil society and faith-based structures stepped in to provide essential services for large parts of the population and became key role players in the peace process. This has often provided them with broad legitimacy and positioned them as trusted public servants. As pointed out by James Dhizaala in his chapter, in Liberia their subsequent participation in governance structures during the transition however led to a critique that they had been co-opted and lost their legitimacy due to their association with corrupt structures. They ultimately failed to provide an effective counter to the warlords-turned-politicians who were still in charge. Their ability to advocate for effective accountability mechanisms and follow through on the Liberian truth commission's recommendations was consequently even more limited.

Particularly where transitional justice processes are being pursued in the context of an untransformed state, the capacity of more conventional CSOs remains highly restricted. In addition to the ongoing vulnerability of victims and the risks involved for them in engaging in litigation, local civil society actors face regular state harassment, even when simply gathering views from communities about transitional justice options, as pointed out by Njeru and Andrew Iliff in the case of Zimbabwe in this volume.

The social divisions that drive political conflict can also cause ongoing divisions within civil society. As Wendy Lambourne explains in this volume, difficulties persist in promoting collaborative approaches among CSOs in Burundi due to perceived linkages between them and particular ethnic groups.

In addition, CSOs need to be understood as comprising an elite in their own right. As has been observed by scholars in other transitional justice contexts, CSOs are part of an educated elite with ties to the formal economy and international networks (Millar 2010). There are thus serious challenges in terms of their ability to relate to and represent the interests of marginalised and vulnerable groups. A key focus of Iliff's chapter in this volume is to unpack the relationship between largely urban-based, modern CSOs and the more rural and traditional communities whose needs they seek to address. Unless carefully managed, this divide is a serious stumbling block that undermines the legitimacy and effectiveness of CSOs.

Local civil society is however a key stakeholder without which the whole endeavour of transitional justice would be substantially diminished. CSOs contribute new ideas, advocate for key principles, facilitate participation of new or marginalised voices and ensure broader participation in policy processes. The chapters in this book provide a rich overview of the numerous ways that civil society has expanded, challenged and reimagined official political frames of transitional justice and also pushed these ideas beyond the conventional international thinking.

Local Civil Society as Shaper of Transitional Justice in Africa

Local CSOs have generally embraced transitional justice as an idea, a set of practices or a discourse that empowers them to pursue their goals in challenging contexts. Yet, transitional justice can serve as a state-sanctioned policy framework that legitimatises and regulates civil society activities—and directs their resources to particular problems and particular regions prioritised by the state. CSOs can be tempted to simply follow these international prescriptions or national policy frameworks as a way to secure funds for their own survival. Sometimes this is done quite uncritically or with a narrow self-interested agenda. For example, Lambourne in this volume suggests that some pro-state and donor-dependent NGOs in Burundi adopt specific transitional justice agendas that match these political/ideological allegiances.

Some CSOs have also opportunistically framed their foundation and mission in relation to transitional justice agendas in the hope of riding the international wave of interest in this field. Quinn, also in this volume, notes the dual restrictions placed on CSOs in Uganda: on the one hand, the restrictive state regulatory environment and, on the other, donor agendas that are not generally sensitive to local political and cultural dynamics. The space for innovation and independent critical thinking is often quite limited for smaller CSOs.

At other times, African CSOs have engaged quite critically with these international instruments, and instead fashioned local processes and transitional justice policy proposals that are responsive to their analysis of local priorities, capacities and opportunities. The chapters in this book provide a number of illustrations of this adoption, adaption and critical reframing of transitional justice ideals and concepts.

The local CSOs discussed in greater detail in this book (e.g. Kenya Transitional Justice Network, Zimbabwe Human Rights NGO Forum, Quaker Peace Network Burundi and Khulumani Support Group) are however more well established, with legitimacy in certain communities, professional staff or international reputations. They have clear commitments to serving the concerns of victim groups and marginalised communities, or promoting particular values and social change agendas. Transitional justice, for them, is essentially a new lens through which to explain their work, a new avenue that they can use to further their objectives. While for some it is quite a stretch to make their work legible in this new language, for others it is an exciting conceptual field that allows them to provide a more comprehensive and comprehensible explanation of their work and their long-term goals and strategies for social change.

In an attempt to make sense of the range of local civil society engagements with the international transitional justice framework, we previously proposed a typology (Van der Merwe and Brankovic 2016) that categorises CSO strategies as falling into ideal types that highlight some of the underlying tensions that characterise transitional justice politics. This typology, which identifies how CSOs position themselves in relation to the conventional transitional justice regime (e.g. implementers, opponents, reframers), proves difficult to apply directly to the case studies in this volume. The complex strategies described by the contributors span different categories, and these shift over time. A precise or consistent labelling is therefore not possible.

As illustrated by Njeru, the Human Rights NGO Forum in Zimbabwe initially adopted a conventional international framework, along with its legal formalities and template of four pillars (truth seeking, accountability, memorialisation and institutional reform), but re-evaluated its approach after receiving feedback from local participants that information on alternative strategies was needed. A broad internationally framed template may provide an easier basis for initially building an inclusive coalition of different CSO interests around a common campaign, but, as Njeru notes, these templates are challenged once the campaign is faced with quite diverse geographic and generational agendas around human rights abuses.

In Burundi the shifting national political environment created new constraints for CSO engagement with transitional justice issues. As Lambourne notes, local CSOs sought to encourage and generate the development of community-based and customary approaches to transitional justice, particularly in the face of a stalled national process and a constricting political landscape. Those CSO representatives who persevered with key demands of legal accountability have had to flee the country.

Established CSOs have managed to transcend these boundaries by engaging in more fluid interactions with different actors, adjusting their language and strategies to respond to particular forums, relationships or shifting political landscapes. As political space opens, CSOs expand their activities, and as new state mechanisms get established, CSOs reframe their discourse to be more effectively heard. With shifting funding agendas, CSOs also relabel their transitional justice activities to fit with new funding categories, for example shifting from "reconciliation" to "social cohesion" or revising its language to fit with the United Nations' Sustainable Development Goals.

Against this local backdrop, CSOs constantly have to assess the value of the transitional justice lens. Does it provide recognition for their analysis of the problem and framing of solutions? Does it allow them to present their work in a way that gives them access to funding? Does it allow them to present a vision of their work that has traction with local constituencies? And does it frame their work as potentially collaborative or as oppositional to the state? Transitional justice may not serve these shifting demands and could quite reasonably be rejected in favour of other frameworks or social change theories as CSO needs and contexts evolve.

While relatively malleable as a conceptual framing of transitional challenges, transitional justice discourse has been used as a strong epistemic instrument to define problems and solutions in a way that seems to translate all too readily into toolkits, templates, lessons, policy prescriptions and a set of expertise to be wielded by international consultants. Makau Mutua cautions against

> the dominant transitional justice programs based in the West, which have become a cottage industry. This approach has spawned a college of professionals with prescriptive country antidotes at the ready. This is a paternalistic and imperialistic approach that should be rejected out of hand. (2015: 5)

The very direct intervention role of the international community described in Lambourne's chapter on Burundi illustrates the way that such prescriptive approaches are presented as solutions to local contexts with little sensitivity to local priorities.

While these concerns are flagged in several of the case studies in this volume, the contributors focus more on the local innovations and pragmatic approaches adopted to use transitional justice in ways that are often beyond conventional international thinking. Local solutions need to be pragmatic in the sense that they can offer direct short-term benefits to local stakeholders rather than simply forming part of an international campaign that promises long-term global benefits. They need to be innovative in the sense that they are reinvented to fit specific local needs, opportunities, resources and constraints.

The pragmatic approach of practitioners thus helps us shift from the broad idealised understanding of transitional justice to one that unpacks specific interventions in terms of strategies and tactics that can be judged on their utility in particular contexts for particular problems, and address the needs of particular constituencies.

Local civil society in Africa has been pushed (sometimes through trial and error) to play a critical role in shifting the focus from the big political deals involving institutional change and high-level prosecutions to addressing the needs of marginalised communities and victims. A number of the chapters provide rich detail on the way that CSOs have sought to address the needs of victims. With some organisations, this engagement started with a focus on legal representation, which then expanded into the provision of other services such as psychological support and humanitarian assistance. A more victim-focused approach also led to a broader advocacy approach that sought to respond to concrete security and survival needs of victims.

At the same time, local CSOs may struggle to develop effective processes of including or responding to victims' priorities. Songa's reflections on the case of the Kenya Transitional Justice Network show that this linkage can easily be taken for granted until victims find their own voice and point out the tensions between their goals and those of other human rights organisations. On the whole, the linkage between professional NGOs and victim constituencies is something that challenges CSO conceptions of who they are and whose interests they serve. The assumption that promoting certain values, mechanisms and processes is automatically in the interest of victims is regularly challenged when victims are in a position to articulate their own needs and priorities.[4]

Some CSOs have emerged to present victims' interests directly, such as Khulumani Support Group, a South African membership-based victim organisation. Their power dynamics, legitimacy claims and capacity to generate ideas and engage

---

[4] Efforts to conduct research that empirically documents victims' demands, such as that conducted by Simon Robins (2011) in Kenya and other contexts, provide challenging findings to NGOs that take their own knowledge of victim needs for granted. See also Brankovic (2010) for CSO practitioners' reflections on this challenge.

with policy and conceptual debates put them into quite a different category from the other CSOs covered in this volume. Yet there are important parallels, and strategic collaboration, between them and more conventional CSOs, which make them key role players in these debates.

In their chapter, Puwana and Kesselring outline the complex process of a victim group's balance or shift between strategies of collaboration and opposition when dealing with a truth commission and the new state. They discuss the challenges of a movement that seeks to address the immediate livelihood needs of a group with a political agenda that challenges the elite compromise that has marginalised the unfinished business of the TRC, and the continuation of apartheid injustices and inequalities. While struggling to make headway using conventional strategies such as litigation, Khulumani has bolstered its sustainability and political legitimacy through its accountability to a membership base.

Many CSO-run transitional justice initiatives relate to attempts to build community capacity to engage with and respond to national processes. In response to the limitations in official capacity to educate the public and build more spaces for political participation, civil society groups such as the Transitional Justice Working Group in Liberia worked alongside the truth commission to help with its outreach to communities across the country. As explained by Dhizaala, where the truth commission's hearings were not seen as effective forums or safe spaces, CSOs organised alternative spaces for community dialogue. Such processes of community engagement and helping to bridge the gap between local communities and national policies or mechanisms present tough challenges that require CSOs to learn quickly and reflect critically on their assumptions and theories of change.

Similarly, Iliff points to the role of local authorities, both state and traditional, as stakeholders and gatekeepers in local community engagement processes. He illuminates the way that these role players mediate entry and limit opportunity, but also points to their potential interest in facilitating the resolution of transitional justice challenges. CSOs need to carefully analyse these local authority networks to be able to gain entry to these spaces and engage with complex local conflict dynamics.

While sometimes seeking to represent certain interest groups directly, local civil society has gone further by using transitional justice debates and mechanisms as tools for broadening democratic participation. While transitional justice is conventionally seen as contributing to democratisation, civil society has seized the opportunity to turn public dialogue spaces about conflict and transitional processes into forums for increased active citizenship and deliberation.

While relying on international transitional justice concepts, the Zimbabwe Human Rights NGO Forum nevertheless sought to educate communities across the country and discuss their transitional justice needs. This shift towards broad public engagement and ownership of a transitional justice agenda resonates with the other case studies. It is not just the substance of transitional justice that speaks to a democratic agenda, but also the opportunities that are created to engage publicly on issues that previously were censored or considered taboo.

In addition to promoting more modern liberal or participatory democratic models of engagement, local civil society has sought to resuscitate local capacity that was repressed or marginalised. Civil society has in some cases drawn on and affirmed traditional resources to be used for pursuing transitional justice goals, such as local mechanisms for dialogue and healing. Lambourne describes how local CSOs in Burundi worked with communities to develop more locally rooted transitional justice alternatives. Quinn points out that in Uganda traditional processes were a key focus for CSOs, which recognised them as more accessible, sustainable and legitimate than conventional mechanisms. They provided an avenue to concretely address community needs in a context where the state provided recognition for these processes but failed to provide substantive support, and where the national policy process did not include much space for civil society input. The Uganda experience raises deeper concerns about the transitory nature of some CSOs' engagement with transitional justice, where these remain dependent on international interest and national political agendas. Where the funding or the political space shifts to new concerns, many CSOs are tempted or forced to refocus their interventions.

Iliff, in his analysis of community-based processes in Zimbabwe, Sierra Leone and Uganda, unpacks the way that CSOs have engaged with tradition and traditional authorities, pointing out the fluidity of this category and the dangers of re-affirming or consolidating certain power structures that were undermined during conflict. He demonstrates opportunities to revitalise and reinvent these structures as more inclusive and accessible spaces, if done in a context-sensitive and carefully negotiated manner. Rather than being simply a recovery of past capacity, this process can and should involve innovation and broad participation in its development.

Alongside this broadening and deepening of participatory processes, the Centre for the Study of Violence and Reconciliation in South Africa has engaged with transitional justice as an avenue to build social consensus regarding a more radical transformative agenda that speaks to structural injustices that continue from one regime to the next. Local civil society has used the politics of transitional justice as a focal point for broader mobilisation regarding institutional reform and debates about inequality and underlying causes of violence. Songa, in his chapter on the Kenya Transitional Justice Network, argues that civil society managed to mobilise a broad network of organisations in a coordinated fashion to push for a more comprehensive transitional justice agenda. While facing various challenges, this broad collaborative venture sought to use transitional justice debates to pursue transformative agendas that went beyond just the narrow mandate of the truth commission. Aboueldahab in her analysis of North African criminal accountability processes describes the way CSOs have linked with labour movements to pursue accountability for economic crimes as part of a broader social justice agenda that addresses the legacies of structural inequality.

This diversity of strategies demonstrates most of all the adaptability of the various CSOs examined in this volume. While there are clear common reference points and conceptual frameworks that show a deeper common agenda, it appears that African civil society has primarily learnt to develop its own toolkit to fit each context.

Conclusions

Where do the case studies in this book position African CSOs in adopting, resisting and reinventing this complex agenda? What do they say about the meaning of transitional justice in Africa, where they need to locate themselves at the intersection of intense national politics and an evolving international transitional justice framework of norms and institutions?

All the cases presented here show some level of local adoption and adaption of international concepts and mechanisms. While drawing on the form and substance of transitional justice as internationally defined, local CSOs have very clearly localised the concept to make it relevant to their contexts and speak to specific local needs and aspirations. These reframed transitional justice strategies speak to expanded national transformative agendas as well as the practical measures needed to address the immediate needs of marginalised communities. Some particular tactical lessons that these case studies illustrate include the following:

- Transitional justice politics need to be addressed through engaging with public imagination. The human rights discourse does not have automatic traction with the broader public and CSOs need to actively campaign to engage the public in developing a narrative about the past. This requires, among others, outreach programmes that can engage communities at a local level and link transitional justice to more immediate safety and survival concerns.
- Spaces for engaging with transitional justice interventions are unevenly spread in different regions and sectors of a society. Civil society needs to be adaptable and responsive to shifting opportunities to engage the state at national and local levels, and take the gap when political windows open, as these are often short lived.
- Transitional justice needs to have traction with local cultural practices. Building legitimacy for a process, particularly in the face of state resistance or reluctance, is key to ensuring sustainability.
- Local cultural practices are a resource that provide tools, ideas and sources of power for innovation. While drawing on this resource requires engagement with complex local power dynamics, creative and negotiated avenues can be opened up for interventions.
- State agendas on transitional justice are constantly shifting and CSOs need to have a clear reading on what drives these agendas and what opportunities they create for complementary activities.
- The reach of the state is often very limited, both in terms of its geographic scope and its capacity to provide transitional justice interventions. Civil society often has important resources to contribute and great legitimacy to lend, which it can use to shape transitional justice processes in a manner that is more directed at the needs of local communities and victims.
- In the early stages of transition, state transitional justice agendas are not clearly developed or articulated, and civil society can play a more influential role in framing the discourse in a more inclusive and wholistic manner.

- Transitional justice is a process that requires long-term interventions and intergenerational engagements. Civil society needs to expand ownership of this agenda beyond the state to ensure buy-in to broader social, cultural and economic transformations.
- Transitional justice can be reframed by local advocacy agendas that do not fit the conventional civil and political rights framework of mainstream international transitional justice approach.

On the other hand, the case studies also point to certain shortcomings and limits to what CSOs can accomplish, even when they appear to have the right expertise, contacts and local knowledge:

- Local community and victim engagement is something that CSOs need to learn to do through engagement that opens them to local voices and accountability. The entry point is too often a problematic position of assumed knowledge and assumed legitimacy.
- The state's ability to control public transitional justice debates often keeps civil society on the back foot and positions it to respond to state initiatives and narratives rather than shaping them.
- CSOs sometimes have windows of opportunity to influence key policy choices, but these windows are transitory and their ability to sustain engagement to ensure impact is dependent on more secure funding streams or a strong local constituency.

The selection of case studies does not provide sufficient basis for making any claims about the trends among CSOs across the continent, or to speculate about how much influence this might have on the way the field develops in the future. What is clear is that local civil society provides a dynamic experimental theatre for testing the utility of transitional justice to address a range of local and national problems. While drawing on this evolving international discourse, civil society responses have varied tremendously in their form and shape. This reflects the different local contexts and priorities that they bring to these processes. It also reflects the constantly changing field itself. CSOs are continuously exposed to new lessons, policies and knowledge and have proven resourceful in drawing inspiration from these examples and abstract ideas. Rather than applying international norms in a cookie cutter manner, they have drawn on these norms as inspirations for framing the discourse, and for building campaigns and alliances.

Local civil society initiatives provide a counterweight to narrow state interests, challenge certain elite bargains, contribute to opening public spaces for democratic participation and campaign vigorously on behalf of marginalised and vulnerable groups. These stories provide inspiration, but very seldom lend themselves to simple transferable lessons or directly question international conceptual frames. At their best, they show that global ideas can be remoulded to address local problems in a way that does justice to these local needs. Breaking the transitional justice mould when working locally seems inevitable, either through intentional design or through the practice of working with concrete situations and real people.

Transitional justice in Africa is a battlefield of ideas that often pits civil society against the state. It is also a landscape of challenges and opportunities that present options for collaboration between apparent enemies. The international transitional justice policy debates are often presented in overly simplistic terms: international transitional justice proponents versus national political resistance to this agenda. The reality is that certain types of changes and certain strategies are promoted and resisted by both sides. There has been a very conscious shift towards African ownership of transitional justice discourse, both by the states and by African civil society. As local solutions are increasingly generated by state and civil society initiatives, the terms of the debate in Africa are increasingly on its own terms. International transitional justice norms and institutions are still a key point of reference, but they no longer present a filter that limits the options and opportunities that local policy advocates can see.

Civil society has a responsibility to constantly question and examine the motives of the big policy players. Civil society can enter this space most effectively when it is creative in finding common ground to build sustainable peace, and ensuring that the process is ultimately accountable to local communities and vulnerable groups.

Civil society needs to engage transitional justice as a broad social reconstruction process, providing a vision of a new just social order. There is a need for leadership in shaping the grand transitional justice agenda. At the same time, civil society needs to engage in the details of how a society can be healed and reconstructed, using local resources and addressing local needs and local priorities. The global field of transitional justice can constrain and limit CSO thinking in this regard, but it can also provide inspiration for new ideas and new hope.

References

Abou-El-Fadl, R. (2012). Beyond conventional transitional justice: Egypt's 2011 revolution and the absence of political will. *International Journal of Transitional Justice, 6*(2), 318–330.

Arthur, P. (2009). How 'transitions' reshaped human rights: A conceptual history of transitional justice. *Human Rights Quarterly, 31*(2), 321–367.

Balint, J., Evansy, J., & McMillan, N. (2014). Rethinking transitional justice, redressing indigenous harm: A new conceptual approach. *International Journal of Transitional Justice, 8*(2), 194–216.

Brankovic, J. (2010). *Advocating justice: Civil society and transitional justice in Africa.* Cape Town: African Transitional Justice Research Network and Centre for the Study of Violence and Reconciliation.

Comlan, E. (2010). *Justice and reconciliation in Rwanda: What role for civil society?* Paper presented to African Transitional Justice Research Network Workshop, Advocating Justice: Civil Society and Transitional Justice in Africa, convened by CSVR, Johannesburg, South Africa.

Gready, P., & Robins, S. (2014). From transitional to transformative justice: A new agenda for practice. *International Journal of Transitional Justice, 8*(3), 339–361.

Igreja, V. (2010). Frelimo's political ruling through violence and memory in postcolonial mozambique. *Journal of Southern African Studies, 36*(4), 781–799.

Lugano, G. (2017). Counter-shaming the International Criminal Court's intervention as neocolonial: Lessons from Kenya. *International Journal of Transitional Justice, 11*(1), 9–29.

Madlingozi, T. (2010). On transitional justice entrepreneurs and the production of victims. *Journal of Human Rights Practice, 2*(2), 208–228.
Mamdani, M. (2002). Amnesty or impunity? A preliminary critique of the report of the Truth and Reconciliation Commission of South Africa (TRC). *Diacritics, 32*(3–4), 33–59.
McGregor, L. (2013). Transitional justice and the prevention of torture. *International Journal of Transitional Justice, 7*(1), 29–51.
Mihr, A. (2017). Regime consolidation through transitional justice in Europe: The cases of Germany, Spain and Turkey. *International Journal of Transitional Justice, 11*(1), 113–131.
Millar, G. (2010). Assessing local experiences of truth-telling in Sierra Leone: Getting to 'why' through a qualitative case study analysis. *International Journal of Transitional Justice, 4*(3), 477–496.
Muvingi, I. (2009). Sitting on powder kegs: Socioeconomic rights in transitional societies. *International Journal of Transitional Justice, 3*(2), 163–182.
Mutua, M. (2015). What is the future of transitional justice? *International Journal of Transitional Justice, 9*(1), 1–9.
Robins, S. (2011). *"To live as other Kenyans do": A study of the reparative demands of Kenyan victims of human rights violations*. New York: International Centre for Transitional Justice.
Sharp, D. N. (2015). Emancipating transitional justice from the bonds of the paradigmatic transition. *International Journal of Transitional Justice, 9*(1), 150–169.
Van der Merwe, H., & Brankovic, J. (2016). The role of African civil society in shaping national transitional justice agendas and policies. In S. Williams & H. Woolaver (Eds.), *Civil society and international criminal justice in Africa: Challenges and opportunities*. Cape Town: Juta.
Wilson, R. (2001). *The politics of truth and reconciliation in South Africa: Legitimizing the post-apartheid state*. Cambridge: Cambridge University Press.
Zunino, M. (2011). Releasing transitional justice from the technical asylum: Judicial reform in Guatemala seen through Technē and Phronēsis. *International Journal of Transitional Justice, 5*(1), 99–118.

Index

J. Brankovic, H. van der Merwe (eds.), *Advocating Transitional Justice in Africa*, Springer Series in Transitional Justice,
https://doi.org/10.1007/978-3-319-70417-3

Kolibri 360 GmbH
Ferdinand-Jühlke-Straße 7
99095 Erfurt, Deutschland
produktsicherheit@kolibri360.de